*The Role of Judicial Decisions and Doctrine
in Civil Law and in Mixed Jurisdictions*

UNDER THE AUSPICES OF
THE LOUISIANA STATE UNIVERSITY LAW SCHOOL
INSTITUTE OF CIVIL LAW STUDIES AND
THE BAILEY LECTURE SERIES

The Role of
JUDICIAL DECISIONS AND DOCTRINE IN CIVIL LAW
and in
MIXED JURISDICTIONS

Edited by Joseph Dainow

EMERITUS PROFESSOR OF LAW
DIRECTOR, INSTITUTE OF
CIVIL LAW STUDIES,
LOUISIANA STATE
UNIVERSITY

LOUISIANA STATE UNIVERSITY PRESS

Baton Rouge

ISBN 0-8071-0080-3
Library of Congress Catalog Card Number 73-90871
Copyright © 1974 by Louisiana State University Press
All rights reserved
Manufactured in the United States of America

Designed by Dwight Agner and set in Linotype Electra, designed by W. A. Dwiggins. Composed and printed by Heritage Printers, Inc., Charlotte, N.C.

"A Renaissance of the Civilian Tradition in Louisiana," by Mack E. Barham, originally appeared in the *Louisiana Law Review*, XXXIII (1973). "Authorities in Civil Law: France," by Jean Carbonnier, originally appeared in *Droit Civil*, I (8th ed., 1969), and is translated and published here with the permission of the author and of the publisher, Presses Universitaires de France. "The Open Legal Development: Germany," by Karl Larenz, was originally published as Larenz, K.: Methodenlehre der Rechtswissenschaft, 2. neubearbeitete Auflage 1969 © by Springer-Verlag Berlin Heidelberg-New York, 1969, and is translated and published here by permission of the author and of the publisher, Springer-Verlag. "The Italian Legal Style III: Interpretation," by John Henry Merryman, originally appeared in the *Stanford Law Review*, XVIII (1966), copyright 1966 by the Board of Trustees of the Leland Stanford Junior University, and is reprinted here with the kind permission of that journal.

TO THE MEMORY OF F. F. D.,
A CONTINUING INSPIRATION

Contents

	Foreword, *by Joe W. Sanders*	ix
	Prefatory Note, *by Paul M. Hebert*	xi
	Preface, *by Joseph Dainow*	xv
I	The Impact of the Common Law on the Civilian Systems of Louisiana and Quebec, *by Jean-Louis Baudouin*	1
II	The Role of the Judge in Mixed Jurisdictions: The Louisiana Experience, *by Albert Tate, Jr.*	23
III	A Renaissance of the Civilian Tradition in Louisiana, *by Mack E. Barham*	38
IV	Jurisprudence and Doctrine as Sources of Law in Louisiana and in France, *by A. N. Yiannopoulos*	69
V	Authorities in Civil Law: France, *by Jean Carbonnier*	91
VI	Supereminent Principles in French Law, *by René David*	119
VII	The Open Legal Development: Germany, *by Karl Larenz*	133
VIII	The Italian Legal Style III: Interpretation, *by John Henry Merryman*	163
IX	Judicial Decisions and Doctrine in Scots Law, *by David M. Walker*	202
X	The Role of Doctrine and Judicial Decisions in South African Law, *by Ellison Kahn*	224
XI	Codification and Case Law in Israel, *by G. Tedeschi and Y. S. Zemach*	272

XII	Judicial Lawmaking in Israel, by *U. Yadin*	296
XIII	Stare Decisis, Doctrine, and Jurisprudence in Mexico and Elsewhere, by *Woodfin L. Butte*	311
XIV	A Selective Bibliography, by *Charles Szladits*	331
	Index by Vera Bolgár	345

Foreword

This book is the product of a number of contributors to the annual civil-law seminars conducted at the Louisiana State University Law School by the Institute of Civil Law Studies. In it are grouped a series of scholarly essays, treating generally of the role of judicial decisions and doctrine in civil-law jurisdictions. Special attention is given to the legal systems of Quebec, France, Scotland, South Africa, Israel, Mexico, and Louisiana, as well as Germany and Italy.

The development of this publication is due in no small measure to the leadership of Joseph Dainow, director of the Institute of Civil Law Studies. An outstanding legal scholar, he has long been an exponent of the civil law. He has taught and written in virtually all major areas of the Louisiana Civil Code. He is probably best known, however, for his work in producing the 1972 *Compiled Edition of the Civil Codes of Louisiana*. Through his teaching and writing, he has made a major contribution to the law.

The distinguishing features of the civil law are often difficult to trace, especially in jurisdictions that have seen the admixture of elements from other systems. The techniques of both analysis and synthesis are required. This anthology of legal essays uses both techniques. By the use of the comparative method, the writers illuminate the role of jurisprudence and doctrine in the civil law. In so doing, they produce a clear picture of the civil law as a major legal system.

The book reflects scholarship, experience, and careful preparation. It will be of assistance to judges, lawyers, teachers, and students who labor daily in the field of the law.

Joe W. Sanders
Chief Justice
Supreme Court of Louisiana

New Orleans, Louisiana

Prefatory Note

In the spring of 1972, Jean-Louis Baudouin of the University of Montreal delivered the Bailey Lectures on the subject of "The Future of Civil Law in a Mixed Jurisdiction." At the same time, this subject constituted the culmination of a series of seminars for Louisiana appellate judges under the auspices of the Institute of Civil Law Studies. A combination of these two programs, with the objective of providing a permanent scholarly contribution to the legal literature, stimulated the compilation of this volume of essays.

The James J. Bailey lectureships were established at the Law School from gifts made by Mrs. Fairfax Foster Sutter as a memorial to her late husband, James J. Bailey, a distinguished leader of the Baton Rouge bar. Mr. Bailey was a graduate of the class of 1934. He had a remarkable mind which was put to good use in a dedicated career as lawyer and public servant. For a time he represented the parish of East Baton Rouge as state senator. He enjoyed the confidence and respect of a large clientele and was highly regarded by his colleagues in the legal profession and by his fellow citizens. Throughout his career he maintained a deep interest in the Law School and was especially active in the alumni gatherings of his class. Mr. Bailey's association with the Law School made it particularly appropriate that a special lecture program should be founded in his honor. Publication of the lectures was contemplated as a means of assuring valuable contributions to legal literature.

The 1965 Bailey Lectures were devoted to the Uniform Commercial Code and were delivered by Soia Mentchikoff of the University of Chicago, Robert Braucher of Harvard, William Hawkland of the University of Buffalo, Grant Gilmore then of Yale and now of Chicago, and Norman Penny of Cornell. The 1965 Bailey Lectures were published in volume twenty-six of the *Louisiana Law Review*, 189–316 (1966).

In 1967, Hardy C. Dillard, dean of the University of Virginia School of Law, delivered the Bailey Lectures on the subject of international law. There were also two lectures by Arthur L. Goodhart of Oxford University on the relationships between English and American law, and on the subject of torts.

The 1968 Bailey Lectures formed the basic core of the Symposium on the Civil Law of Obligations and they were supplemented by additional articles for the volume, *Essays on the Civil Law of Obligations*, published by Louisiana State University Press in 1969.

In 1969, the Bailey Lectures were delivered by Jaro Mayda of the University of Puerto Rico, on the subject of "François Gény and Modern Jurisprudence." At the same time, under the auspices of the Institute of Civil Law Studies, Professor Mayda conducted a seminar on the same subject for a group of Louisiana judges, lawyers, and law teachers.

The 1970 Bailey Lectures were delivered by Arvid Pardo, ambassador from Malta to the United States, on the subject of "Development of Ocean Space—An International Dilemma." This was published in volume thirty-one of the *Louisiana Law Review*, 45–72 (1970).

The Institute of Civil Law Studies was established under the academic sponsorship of the Louisiana State University Law School as a means of promoting the study of civil law in all its aspects and relationships, with particular emphasis on the Louisiana civil law. One of the primary purposes of the institute is to encourage and facilitate research and publication in the civil law, and considerable progress has already been achieved. The first two volumes of Professor Yiannopoulos' treatise on Property have been in use for some time, the third is in preparation, and the fourth has been planned. Professor Litvinoff's first volume of a treatise on Obligations has recently come off the press, and the second volume is under way.

In collaboration with the Louisiana State Law Institute, there have been published Professor Lazarus' English translation (with Louisiana annotations) of the Aubry and Rau treatise on Testamentary Successions and Gratuitous Dispositions, and the English translation by Jaro Mayda of the works on Prescription by Baudry-Lacantinerie, Aubry and Rau, and Carbonnier. Similarly, the 1972 *Compiled Edition of the Civil Codes of Louisiana*, edited by Joseph Dainow, has appeared as volumes sixteen and seventeen of West's Louisiana Statutes Annotated–Civil Code

Annotated series. The Institute of Civil Law Studies also published René David's *French Law* in the English translation by Michael Kindred (Louisiana State University Press, 1972).

Louisiana may have lost some portion of its civilian heritage, but the substantive private law is still basically the Civil Code. Certainly it calls for interpretation, understanding, and reformation; for law is essentially the order prescribed in human affairs and it must be responsive to the needs of its age. It is the role of legal scholars in the universities to have predominant influence upon the direction and the improvement of the Louisiana civil law. There are some heartening signs on the horizon. We witness this in some differences in judicial attitudes toward the civil law, in the greater availability of a literature in this field, and in the work of the law schools and of such organizations as the Louisiana State Law Institute and this school's Institute of Civil Law Studies. All of these developments, and there are more to come, must be expanded and intensified. The present volume of essays, *The Role of Judicial Decisions and Doctrine in Civil Law and in Mixed Jurisdictions*, constitutes another step in that direction, and will undoubtedly contribute to a wider understanding of this important aspect of the civil law.

PAUL M. HEBERT, Dean
Louisiana State University Law School

Preface

One of the programs developed by the Institute of Civil Law Studies of the Louisiana State University Law School has been an annual seminar for a group of Louisiana appellate judges.[1] There are seven justices of the Louisiana Supreme Court and about twenty-five judges of the Louisiana Courts of Appeal so that, with an attendance of fifteen to twenty each time, most of these judges have participated in one or all of the seminars. Each seminar consisted of two round-table sessions with an original presentation by an outside speaker who then became moderator and leader for the discussions which followed. In 1970 the topics were "The Place of Judicial Decisions in a Codified System" and "The Use of Decided Cases in Opinion Writing." The 1971 topics were "The Writing of Opinions under Civil Law Principles" and "The Use of Doctrine in Opinion Writing." The 1972 topics were "Difficulties of Preserving Civil Law in a Mixed Jurisdiction" and "The Future of Civil Law in a Mixed Jurisdiction."

The speaker and discussion leader for the three seminars was Jean-Louis Baudouin of the University of Montreal. His consolidation of these programs constitutes the first essay in this volume which has been compiled around the core topics in order to bring together in the English language some comments and observations to reflect the developments in different countries and different legal systems, with one focus on civil law and a special interest in so-called "mixed jurisdictions."

[1] In the years preceding these seminars for the judges by themselves, there had been a 1969 seminar for a group of thirty judges, lawyers, and professors on "François Gény and Modern Jurisprudence," and a 1968 Symposium (including also a student audience) on "The Civil Law of Obligations." The latter was expanded and published as Joseph Dainow, ed., *Essays on the Civil Law of Obligations* (Baton Rouge: Louisiana State University Press, 1969), and a special monograph is planned for the Gény topic.

Professor Baudouin's article focuses particularly on Quebec and, with the special interest of Louisiana as the other island of civil law surrounded by the common law, there are contributions from Albert Tate, Jr., and Mack E. Barham of the Louisiana Supreme Court, and A. N. Yiannopoulous of Louisiana State University.

Since a good deal on these topics has already been written in France and Germany, two excerpts from outstanding French scholars have been included in English translation. One is from Jean Carbonnier of the University of Paris, and the other is from René David, formerly of the University of Paris and now at Aix-en-Provence. Similarly, there is included the English translation of excerpts from the prominent German scholar Karl Larenz. A discussion of the situation in Italy is presented by John H. Merryman of Stanford University in an article reprinted from the *Stanford Law Review*.

From Scotland, there is an essay by David Walker of the University of Glasgow, and from South Africa, one by Ellison Kahn of the University of the Witwatersrand in Johannesburg. From Israel, there is one essay by Guido Tedeschi and Y. Zemach of the Hebrew University in Jerusalem and another by Dr. Uri Yadin of the Israel Ministry of Justice.

Woodfin L. Butte of the University of Texas has prepared an article which includes the special developments in Mexico.

In a multi-author project like this, some delays and disappointments were inevitable and certain individuals have had to renounce their commitments. Regrettably, essays describing the situation in Switzerland and the developments in Puerto Rico could not be obtained in time for publication.

To make the volume a more useful work for reference and research, there is a selected bibliography with a special section of works in English, prepared by the outstanding comparative law bibliographer Charles Szladits of Columbia University. The index was prepared by Vera Bolgár of the University of Michigan.

This volume of essays does not purport to constitute a complete or comprehensive coverage of the whole subject, but rather a compilation of the relevant contributions that the editor was able to obtain within the time available. Each author presents his own views and ideas, and as a result there may be differences as well as repetitions. No attempt was made to fix on a single focus, and no general conclusions are implied from the volume as a whole. Each article is an individual study. Since there does not appear to be any similar publication in English, these essays should help achieve a clearer comprehension of the subject matter by jurists in their own civil-law or mixed jurisdictions as well as by people in other places who are trying to understand these systems.

JOSEPH DAINOW

I

The Impact of the Common Law on the Civilian Systems of Louisiana and Quebec*

Jean-Louis Baudouin
PROFESSOR OF LAW, UNIVERSITY OF MONTREAL

In both Louisiana and Quebec, there seems to have been for a certain time a fear of the loss of legal identity, a fear that these two jurisdictions would eventually lose their "civilian heritage" and melt slowly into the neighboring common-law system. This is by no means a recent phenomenon. In 1937, an article published by Gordon Ireland in the *Tulane Law Review* under the title "Louisiana's Legal System Reappraised" stirred up quite a controversy [1] and brought a strong rebuttal from other Louisiana scholars.[2] It seems quite evident for today's reader that in trying to evaluate whether or not Louisiana's system was civilian, Professor Ireland made the mistake of comparing what he saw in Louisiana with what existed in traditional civilian jurisdictions like France. In much the same fashion, Quebec scholars have often objected to the introduction of common-law concepts and interpretative techniques, arguing that the Quebec private-law system would slowly lose its identity and become common law by adopting common-law techniques, common-law terminology, or common-law ideas.[3]

---

* The present paper is a synthesis of presentations made by the author at the Louisiana Appellate Judges Seminar held under the auspices of the Institute of Civil Law Studies of the Louisiana State University Law School, 1970–1972.
1 Ireland, "Louisiana's Legal System Reappraised," 11 TULANE LAW REVIEW 585 (1937). See also Crabites, "Louisiana Not a Civil Law State," 9 LOYOLA LAW REVIEW 51 (1928); and Greenburg, "Must Louisiana Resign to the Common Law?" 11 TUL. L. REV. 598 (1937). A list of the abbreviations used in this chapter appears on page 22.
2 Daggett, Dainow, Hebert, and McMahon, "A Reappraisal Appraised: A Brief for the Civil Law of Louisiana," 12 TUL. L. REV. 12 (1937).
3 See, inter alia: Mignault, "L'Avenir de notre civil," 1 REVUE DU DROIT 56 (1923); Mignault, "Les Rapports entre le droit civil et la common law au

It is the author's belief that the problem of the future of civil law in mixed jurisdictions like Louisiana and Quebec should today be considered in a somewhat different light and subjected to a different approach. The first and basic premise that Quebec and Louisiana jurists should admit is that, although both systems are French inspired and codified, one should not necessarily refer to the overall picture of civil law in France in 1972 as a model to determine whether or not Quebec and Louisiana are still civil-law jurisdictions. In other words, it is not because the Quebec doctrine differs from the French, or because the Louisiana Supreme Court techniques are not those of the Cour de Cassation, or because the Quebec interpretation of Civil Code Article 1054 is different from the French interpretation of Article 1384 of the Napoleonic Code, that Louisiana and Quebec are not civil-law jurisdictions. No one would really dispute the fact that Germany, Italy, Spain, etc., are civil-law jurisdictions; yet in these countries the codification experiences, the case law, the doctrine and methods of reasoning are different from their French counterparts. In many instances, hasty and unscientific evaluation of mixed-jurisdiction systems has been based on a superficial comparison with the mother-system. If the mother-system had not been meticulously followed the conclusion was often drawn that the affiliate system had been "corrupted" by the common law and thus was really nothing more than a bastardized civil-law system.[4]

Canada, spécialement dans la Province de Québec," 11 REVUE DU DROIT 201 (1932); Mignault, "Conservons notre droit civil," 15 REVUE DU DROIT 28 (1936); L. Baudouin, "Les Aspects généraux du droit privé dans la Province de Québec," 81 (1967), L Baudouin, "La Réception du droit étranger en droit privé québécois," in "Quelques aspects du droit de la Province de Québec," 3 McGILL LAW JOURNAL 51 (1956); L. Baudouin, "Originalité de droit du Québec," 10 REVUE DU BARREAU 121 (1956); L. Baudouin, "Méthode d'interprétation judiciaire du Code civil du Québec," 10 REVUE DU BARREAU 397 (1950); L. Baudouin, "Les Apports du code civil de Québec," in CANADIAN JURISPRUDENCE 71 (1958); Johnson, "The Codfication of the Common Law," REVUE DU BARREAU 165 (1957); Morin, "L'Anglicisation de notre droit civil," 40 REVUE DU NOTARIAT 145 (1937); WALTON, SCOPE AND INTERPRETATION OF THE CIVIL CODE OF LOWER CANADA (1907).

4 It is interesting to note that many Quebec authors have often judged the Louisiana civil-law tradition to be no longer existent and have sometimes cited Louisiana to Quebecers as an example of what not to do. See, for instance, Mignault, "L'Avenir de notre droit civil," 1 REVUE DU DROIT 56 (1923); L. Baudouin, "Méthode d'interprétation judiciaire du Code civil du Québec," 10 REVUE DU BARREAU, 387, n. 2 (1950). The first of these authors relied on the commentaries of SAUNDERS, LECTURES ON THE CIVIL CODE OF LOUISIANA (1920).

On the other hand, mixed jurisdictions is a very privileged and fertile field of observation for the sociology of law. This is particularly true of Quebec and Louisiana where the world's two greatest legal traditions meet. Louisiana and Quebec scholars are unfortunately not usually aware of the tremendous possibilities of such investigation because, most of the time, the approach remains at the level of basic comparative law only. In other words, we are often much more preoccupied with determining whether or not the solution given to a problem is one of common law or of civil law, rather than asking ourselves whether or not the style laid down is sociologically sound and fits into the general pattern of the legal system as a whole. A Quebec scholar once called the Quebec civil-law system a "modèle vivant de droit comparé"[5] (a living model of comparative law), thereby implying that Quebec jurists were born comparatists. Quebecers and Louisianians are knowledgeable both in civil and common law, being governed by a legal structure which draws from both systems. Although Louisiana and Quebec remain basically civil-law jurisdictions, exposure to the common law has given their jurists the ability to move in both systems with ease. This does not, however, necessarily imply that they are true comparatists, for being a comparatist implies the ability to judge one's own system through another; and in these two jurisdictions the system of reference is, to a certain degree, already integrated in the object of the comparison.

The purpose of this essay is not to restate what has already been written or said much better than the writer could ever hope to do[6] I will try to give an idea of how the interpenetration of common law and civil law operates with particular reference to the Quebec situation, on two different levels: that of legislation and that of judicial decisions.

---

5 L. BAUDOUIN, LE DROIT CIVIL DE LA PROVINCE DE QUÉBEC, MODÈLE VIVANT DE DROIT COMPARÉ (1953).

6 It would take too much space here to list the considerable literature that has been devoted to the analysis of this question both in Louisiana and Quebec. However, since almost all of it is in the French language it may be useful for English-speaking readers to have a brief list of references written in the English language concerning Quebec law. See, inter alia, Anglin, "Some Differences between the Law of Quebec and the Law as Administered in the Other Provinces of Canada," 1 CANADIAN BAR REVIEW 33 (1923); Friedmann, "Stare Decisis at Common Law and under the Civil Code of Quebec," 31 CAN. B. REV. 723 (1953); L. Baudouin, "The Influence of the Code Napoléon," 33 TUL. L. REV. 21 (1958); Fabre-Surveyer, "The Civil Law in Quebec and Louisiana," 1 LOUISIANA LAW REVIEW 649 (1939); Fabre-Surveyer, "The Civil and Common Law in Canada," 5 REVUE LÉGALE nouvelle série 329 (1899).

I. LEGISLATION

The functioning of the legal systems of Louisiana and Quebec implies constant reference to a dual system of legislation: that of the civil code, where the law is expressed in terms of general principles; and that of the statutory legislation, where, on the contrary, the legislative will is greatly detailed and minutely laid out. Jurists in both countries have to deal with these forms of legislation and implicitly with the set of values of which they are the incarnation, for behind formulas and words rests the legal philosophy of which these are but the express manifestation or phenomenon. It is thus extremely interesting to observe the reactions and attitudes of the judiciary,[7] of jurists, as well as of the doctrine itself to these different forms of legislative activity, for it is possible through this analysis to ascertain the basic creeds and legal attitudes toward civil and common law. One should, however, be careful in this respect not to overgeneralize, and some distinctions must be made between the Louisiana and Quebec situations.

The Quebec Civil Code enacted in 1866 is extremely close to the French Napoleonic Code of 1804 and a good many of its articles were copied from the French code and expressed in a style and terminology that are almost identical. One of the main features of French and Quebec codifications is that, far from being didactic, they only express broad general principles laid down in simple terms with an economy of words. On the contrary, the 1870 version of the Louisiana Civil Code is of a different format. First, it is much more detailed in its expression than its French or Quebec counterparts. One should not forget that the Louisiana codifiers of 1870 benefited from past experience and had the opportunity to include in the 1870 version of their code the rules that had been laid down by the courts in France and Louisiana. Thus, it is not uncommon in the Louisiana code and more particularly in the Title IV on "Obligations," to find articles that go much further than simply expressing an abstract general rule or principle. One can find many instances where the Louisiana legislator deemed it advisable to incorporate in the article itself a practical illustration or an example showing how the rule was meant to operate. It is interesting to note, in that respect, that a certain number of

---

7 See below the observations concerning the ways in which the Quebec or federal courts interpret the Quebec Civil Code.

these articles are taken out of the works of Pothier or Toullier and that the illustrations stated in the law are almost identical to those given by these authors in their works.[8] A good example of this legislative technique can be found in the civil code articles dealing with error as to the nature and object of the contract. There, the classical illustrations of the ingot of ordinary metal sold for an ingot of silver, of the gold-plated vase sold for a solid gold vase, form part of Articles 1843 and 1844 of the Louisiana Civil Code. The comparison of legal draftsmanship between the Louisiana and the Quebec codes is interesting. It remains to be explained why the Quebec codifiers did not see fit to express rules that had already been subject to French judicial interpretation in a more detailed form.[9] It may be submitted as a simple hypothesis which would need to be verified, that in detailing their code, the Louisiana codifiers went a long way to prevent a more substantial impact of common-law rules in areas like offer and acceptance which, for instance,[10] would have been stronger yet, had it not been for the detailed rules laid out in Articles 1797 to 1818 of the Louisiana Civil Code. It would indeed be of substantial interest to try to verify that hypothesis through a systematic study of the Louisiana Civil Code and evaluate whether or not the parts of the civil law that were more influenced by common law are not those which are only dealt with under the form of broad general principles. The area that immediately comes to mind is that of the offenses and quasi offenses dealt with by only ten articles (La. C. C. arts. 2315–2324) and which is said to have been almost totally eclipsed by the common law of torts.[11]

The Quebec Civil Code, on the contrary, has followed a somewhat different path. Although it is now in the process of being completely revised and one can expect a new codification within the next four years, it was left to age during the first hundred years of its history. Up to 1966, a rough calculation indicates that the Quebec legislature only

---

8 See the references given under these articles by LITVINOFF, OBLIGATIONS: BOOK 1 (1969).
9 One should note, however, that they did in certain instances, but it is the writer's belief that they could have benefited more from the French experience.
10 LITVINOFF, OBLIGATIONS: BOOK 1 (1969), 209–351.
11 Stone, "Tort Doctrine in Louisiana: From What Sources Does It Derive?" 16 TUL. L. REV. 489 (1942); Stone, "Tort Doctrine in Louisiana: The Aggressor Doctrine," 21 TUL. L. REV. 362 (1947): Stone, "Tort Doctrine in Louisiana: The Concept of Fault," 27 TUL. L. REV. 1 (1952). See also the authorities cited in Note 22 below.

amended the civil code 281 times, repealing in whole or in part 180 of the original articles and adopting 228 new ones,[12] whereas Louisiana promulgated its first code in 1808 and enacted a new one in 1825 and again in 1870. As was recently pointed out,[13] the passive attitude of the legislator in regard to the civil code of Quebec was due to both philosophical and political factors. In the first place, the Quebec Civil Code, like its French counterpart, was considered to be the perfect incarnation of "reason and natural justice," and thus it was thought to be immune from changes brought about by time. This had a somewhat disastrous influence on the role of the civil code itself, for every time a change was needed the legislator, instead of amending the code, preferred to deal with it by special statutory legislation, thus creating a bulk of "civil law"[14] outside the code, drafted in the statutory form and thus subject to statutory rather than codal canons of interpretation. A good example of this state of affairs is the law on adoption[15] which would naturally have found its place in the section of the civil code on filiation,[16] but which was passed as a separate entity and drafted in the typical English statutory fashion. In the second place, the civil code, being part of the cultural heritage of France, was believed to constitute the best available defense against the "pernicious menace of common law." The Civil Code as such was thus deified and, as is the case with idols, it almost ended up in a museum of antiquities. As Paul-André Crépeau well remarked,[17] this state of affairs

12 J.-L. Baudouin, "Le Code civil québécois: Crise de croissance ou crise de vieillesse," 44 CAN. B. REV. 391: 393, n. 6 (1966).
13 Crépeau, "La Révision du Code civil au Québec," in PROCEEDINGS OF THE NINTH INTERNATIONAL SYMPOSIUM ON COMPARATIVE LAW (Ottawa, 1972). See also Crépeau, "La Renaissance du droit civil canadien," in "Le Droit dans la vie familiale," I LIVRE DU CENTENAIRE DU CODE CIVIL (1970).
14 Unfortunately, despite the existence of the Quebec Civil Code Revision Office, the legislator seems to continue following the same pattern. This past year the legislature enacted as a separate statute legislation concerning consumer's protection (1971 Statutes of Quebec, Chap. 74) and has not seen fit to incorporate it in whole or in part in the civil code. One must point out also that the draftmanship of this piece of legislation is simply atrocious. On the other hand, one should congratulate the Quebec government for having incorporated into the civil code provisions concerning the disposal of one's body as well as provisions affecting transplant operations (see Quebec Civil Code, arts. 18–23, as amended by 1971 S. of Q., Chap. 84).
15 "Quebec Adoption Act," 1969 S. of Q., Chap. 64.
16 Quebec Civil Code, arts. 218 ff.
17 Crépeau, "La Révision du Code civil au Québec," in PROCEEDINGS OF THE NINTH INTERNATIONAL SYMPOSIUM OF COMPARATIVE LAW (Ottawa, 1972), 7.

explains to a great extent the absence, for a long time, of doctrine and the timidity of judicial decisions as a whole in Quebec. It also went a long way in letting the Quebec civil law be penetrated and permeated by common-law principles. Through judicial decisions a certain number of common-law rules, common-law source materials, and common-law institutions were brought in to allow the civil law to adapt to economic and sociological changes.

In the traditional civilian approach, legislation is considered the one and only authoritative source of law to which all others, including case law, are subordinated.[18] It is probable that the idea of the supremacy of legislation over other sources of law finds its origin mostly in political and sociological reasons. In prerevolutionary France, the absolutism of monarchy had bred a very heavily politicized justice. The royal judges, appointed directly by the king, were not as distant and independent from politics as their English brothers. One of the main concerns of the French Revolution was precisely to separate sharply the judicial and legislative functions. The expression "Que Dieu nous garde de l'équité des Parlements," reflects the distrust in which the judicial function was then held. The doctrine of the separation of powers as introduced in France by Montesquieu—who believed it existed in England—was the very basis of the segregation between legislative and judicial powers. It was not for the courts to say what the law should be or even what the law was; their only role and function were to apply the legislation and to interpret it where it was not clear. A good illustration of the very restrictive role that the revolutionary French wanted the courts to play, is the original structure of the Tribunal de Cassation and the system of the *référé législatif* under which, if the legislation was not certain, interpretation was to be obtained from the legislature itself.[19]

18 See, generally, DAVID & BRIERLEY, MAJOR LEGAL SYSTEMS IN THE WORLD TODAY (1968), 81 ff.; 307 ff.; 360 ff. See also Dainow, "The Civil Law and the Common Law: Some Points of Comparison," 15 AMERICAN JOURNAL OF COMPARATIVE LAW 419 (1967); MERRYMAN, THE CIVIL LAW TRADITION (1969); Loussouarn, "The Relative Importance of Legislation, Custom, Doctrine, and Precedent in French Law," 18 LA. L. REV. 235 (1958); Pound, "Hierarchy of Sources and Forms in Different Systems of Law," 7 TUL. L. REV. 475 (1933); Von Mehren, "The Judicial Process in the United States and in France—A Comparative Study," 22 REVISTA JURIDICA DE LA UNIVERSIDAD DE PUERTO RICO 235 (1953) and, of course, GÉNY, METHOD OF INTERPRETATION AND SOURCES OF PRIVATE POSITIVE LAW (J. Mayda transl. 1963).
19 Loi du 27 novembre 1790; loi du 1er décembre 1790.

In the second place, the secondary role attributed to judicial decisions brought about a particular view of the judicial function. Unlike his British or American brother, the French judge was not considered the keeper or guardian of individual civil liberties vis-à-vis the legislative power. Although esteemed, he did not command the same respect, for he was considered only an interpreter and not a creator of law. Moreover, the form under which he was required to express his judicial opinion did not particularly foster the creation of case law.

In Quebec and in Louisiana, the principle of the supremacy of legislation over other sources of law seems to be accepted as a premise. However, it would be futile to argue that this principle carries the same impact as it does in France, unless one forgets that both Quebec and Louisiana adopted the common-law procedure, most of the common-law rules of evidence, the common-law trial techniques, and, most important of all, the common-law respect and attitude towards the judiciary and the judicial function as a whole.

One must also take into account the fact that both Louisiana and Quebec judges have to administer a mixed system. Not only do they have to rule upon the interpretation of civil code articles, but they also apply Canadian or American federal statutes as well as provincial or state legislation drafted in the common-law fashion. The duality of role and of mental attitude, the duality of the canons of interpretation, cannot really be carried out by the judiciary without some kind of interpenetration from one system to the other. It was foreseeable that in certain cases the judge sitting in a civil-law case would treat the subject as he would have if it had been common law, thus bringing into the civil law, common-law judicial attitudes, legal processes, and rules of interpretation.[20]

This goes a long way toward explaining why legislation both in Quebec and Louisiana is not, technically and practically speaking, looked upon by the judiciary in the same perspective as in the French tradition. The creative role that the Louisiana and Quebec courts believed they had in subjects not directly connected with the civil code interpretation encouraged them, in many instances, to assume the same authority and role

20 For the warnings given against that attitude by Mignault while he was a judge at the Supreme Court of Canada, see: Colonial Real Estate Co. v. Soeurs de la Charité, 57 Supreme Court Reports 585, 603 (1919); Desrosiers v. The King, 60 S.C.R. 105, 126 (1920); Curley v. Latreille, 60 S.C.R. 131, 177 (1920).

when dealing with strict codal interpretation, perhaps much more so in Louisiana than in Quebec.

As a Louisiana scholar once pointed out,[21] it seems that in its dealings with the civil code the Louisiana judiciary has had over the years a much stronger propensity than the Quebec courts to a "mere application of common law solutions." There seem to have been some instances where the Louisiana courts have more or less completely disregarded the express or implied rule of the civil code and adopted what they believed was a better rule than that expressed by the legislator, thus creating law in contradiction to legislation. One example of this seems to be the retention by the Louisiana courts of the common-law doctrine of contributory negligence instead of the civil-law comparative-fault approach.[22] This tendency is not, however, so strong in Quebec, where one cannot really cite a clear example of blatant disregard by the judiciary of a codal legislative enactment. Nevertheless, this is not to say that Quebec judges have not in certain instances interpreted the code so broadly as to really create a rule of law that the legislator certainly did not have in mind, under the pretext or disguise of "interpretation"; they may have used the same pretext to adopt a common-law solution. There are, indeed, certain areas of the Quebec Civil Code that have been given a different interpretation than that given by the French to similar provisions, due to the influence of common-law sources or precedents. I submit that a great deal of the confusion often created by conflicts of sources and of techniques or interpretation would have been avoided in Quebec had the legislator thought it fit to intervene more often so as to maintain the Quebec Civil Code as the primary source of law in private-law matters. Amendments to the code when necessary to end a controversy, or when required by sociological changes or by bad case law, would no doubt have made of

---

21 DAINOW & AZARD, TWO AMERICAN CIVIL LAW SYSTEMS: QUEBEC CIVIL LAW AND LOUISIANA CIVIL LAW (1964), 12. See also SAUNDERS, LECTURES ON THE CIVIL CODE OF LOUISIANA 1920), and the analysis by Pascal, "A Report on the French Civil Code Revision Project," 25 TUL. L. REV. 205 (1951).

22 Comment, "Comparative Negligence in Louisiana," 11 TUL. L. REV. 112 (1936); Smith, "A Proposed Code Provision on Tort Liability," 10 LA. L. REV. 253 (1950); Malone, "Comparative Negligence, Louisiana's Forgotten Heritage," 6 LA. L. REV. 125 (1945); Cotton, "Comparative Negligence Is Not in the Public Interest," 17 LOUISIANA BAR JOURNAL 205 (1969); Stone, "Comparative Negligence," 17 LA. B. J. 13 (1969); Gainsburgh, "A Brief for Comparative Negligence," 17 LA. B. J. 121 (1969).

the civil code a stronger instrument in the hierarchy of legal sources. The problem of the relative importance of legislation and case-law, which is probably the most significant difference between civil- and common-law systems, could have easily been solved in Quebec by a more active role of the legislator. By ignoring codal reforms when they were initially necessary, the Quebec legislator let the courts fulfill part of his role and, in fact, delegated to a great extent his legislative power. As we will see, this delegation was very often used by the courts in a way incompatible with either the general civil-law philosophy or civil-law legal concepts. Looking for quick and easy solutions, courts would most naturally turn to the common law for an answer and thus incorporate whole Anglo-American doctrines into the civil law.

Although similar in legal theory, the role played by legislation in legal practice is different to a certain extent in Louisiana and Quebec from that of countries like France. That difference lies mostly in the attitude of the courts towards legislation as a source of law. One may feel that in Quebec, and perhaps even more in Louisiana, the degree of respect for legislation, and for the basic principles implied by it, is less than it is in France. Moreover, the "interpretation" of legislation will in certain instances be so broad as to allow under this disguise the introduction into the civil law of solutions devised by the imagination of the judiciary itself.

II. JURISPRUDENCE

Perhaps the most significant and critical point of disagreement between common- and civil-law lawyers, concerns the role and impact of "jurisprudence"[23] or judicial decisions upon the legal system as a whole. The comparative-law literature reflects this traditional opposition between "judge-made law" and "la jurisprudence servante du législateur." Under its best-known aspect, that of *stare decisis* or the authority of precedent, jurists in Canada, the United States, England, and France have tried to ascertain exactly how influential a source of law previously decided cases are, and how they determine the subsequent conduct of the courts.[24] No

---

23 The word "jurisprudence" will be used in the present article in the Continental (*i.e.* case law) rather than in the Anglo-American sense of the term.
24 Since it would be unrealistic to try to give an exhaustive list of what has been written in these countries on the subject, I thought it preferable to refer here only to the main contributions on the subject in Quebec and Louisiana law. For Quebec, see: L. Baudouin, "Les Aspects généraux du droit privé dans la

legal topic has, however, been treated with so much oversimplification or with so many half-truths. It is perhaps easier for jurists in mixed jurisdictions, because they are exposed to both systems, to see the real differences and to destroy the myths that some consciously or unconsciously hold about the other's system. On the other hand, mixed jurisdictions like Quebec and Louisiana are at the center of this controversy since case law has often been singled out as the vehicle par excellence for the introduction of common law into the civil law.[25] One may note that in recent

---

Province de Québec," 61 ff. (1967); Friedmann, "Stare Decisis at Common Law and under the Civil Code of Quebec," 31 CAN. B. REV. 723 (1953); Mignault, "The Authority of Decided Cases," 3 CAN B. REV. 1 (1925); Mignault, "Les Rapports entre le droit civil et la common law au Canada," in MÉLANGES LAMBERT 87 (1938); Anglin, "Some Differences between the Law of Quebec and the Law as Administered in the Other Provinces of Canada," 1 CAN. B. REV. 33 (1923); Laverty, "Some Differences between the Common Law and that of the Province of Quebec," 9 CAN. B. REV. 13 (1931); Joanes, "Stare Decisis in the Supreme Court of Canada," 36 CAN. B. REV. 175 (1958); Graveson, "De l'influence de la common law sur les systèmes de droit civil existant dans le Commonwealth britannique," 5 REVUE INTERNATIONALE DE DROIT COMPARÉ 658 (1953); Pouliot, "L'Autorité de la jurisprudence dans notre droit," in MÉLANGES BISSONNETTE (1963); Mayrand, "L'Autorité du précédent judiciaire en droit québécois," 10 THÉMIS 69 (1959–60); Azard, "Le Problème des sources du droit Civil dans la Province de Québec: Conception québécoise du rôle de la jurisprudence," 44 CAN. B. REV. 417 (1966); Mignault, "L'Autorité judiciaire," 6 REVUE LÉGALE 145 (1900); Mignault, "L'Autorité des arrêts," 24 REVUE DU NOTARIAT 118 (1921); MAURIN, RÔLE CRÉATEUR DU JUGE DANS LES JURISPRUDENCES CANADIENNES ET FRANÇAISES COMPARÉES, (1938). For Louisiana, see: Daggett, Dainow, Hebert, and McMahon, "A Reappraisal Appraised: A Brief for the Civil Law of Louisiana," 12 TUL. L. REV. 12 (1937); Dainow, "The Method of Legal Development through Judicial Interpretation in Louisiana and Puerto Rico," 22 REV. JUR. U.P.R. 108 (1952); Jolowicz, "The Civil Law in Louisiana," 29 TUL. L. REV. 491 (1955); Morrow, "Louisiana Blueprint: Civilian Codification and Legal Method for State and Nation," 17 TUL. L. REV. 537 (1943); Pound, "Hierarchy of Sources and Forms in Different Systems of Law," 7 TUL. L. REV. 475 (1933); Comment, "Stare Decisis in Louisiana," 7 TUL. L. REV. 100 (1932); Tate, "Techniques of Judicial Interpretation in Louisiana," 22 LA. L. REV. 727 (1962); Tucker, "The Code and the Common Law in Louisiana," 29 TUL. L. REV. 739 (1955); Robertson, "The Precedent Value of Conclusions of Fact in Civil Cases in England and Louisiana," 29 LA. L. REV. 78 (1968); Tate, "Civilian Methodology in Louisiana," 44 TUL. L. REV. 673 (1970); Sanders, "The 'Civil Law' in the Supreme Court of Louisiana," 15 LA. B. J. 15 (1967); Ireland, "Louisiana's Legal System Reappraised," 11 TUL L. REV. 585 (1937); Morrow, "Civilian Codification under Judicial Review: The Generality of Immortality in Louisiana," 21 TUL. L. REV. 545 (1947); Pascal and Tête, "Law in General: The Obligatory Force of Decisions," 31 LA. L. REV. 185 (1971).

25 For Quebec, see the authorities cited in Note 24 above, and J.-L. Baudouin, "Le Code civil québécois: Crise de croissance ou crise de vieillesse," 44 CAN. B. REV. 391 (1966).

years in Louisiana a considerable effort has been made by judges to get a clearer view of the role of previously decided cases on one hand, and of the attitude that courts should adopt in regard to them on the other hand. The Louisiana supreme court judges' awareness of civilian theory,[26] and the place and importance granted by law reviews to the discussion of civilian methodology[27] are factors that should contribute in a very substantive way to a new redefinition of the hierarchy of sources in mixed jurisdictions.

It has often been pointed out that the common-law system, for historical reasons, developed from case law and that the doctrine of strict *stare decisis* was then necessary to give stability to the system as a whole, since the courts, in the absence of legislation, were both creators and expositors of the law.[28] On the other hand, in civil-law jurisdictions like France, the role of case law for opposite historical reasons was restricted to the syllogistical application of legislation and to the filling in of gaps that may have been left by the legislator. These comments are historically substantially correct and would result from a comparison of seventeenth-century England with early nineteenth-century France. However, three centuries of legislation in England and more than a century and a half of code interpretation in France have very evidently somewhat changed the situation. French scholars do admit that "jurisprudence," although not technically an authoritative source of law, has a considerable moral impact and that it plays a dynamic role in the development of the law.[29] On the other hand, the strict principle of *stare decisis* has been abandoned by the House of Lords, and the English courts do have less and less

---

26 See, for instance, Sanders, "The 'Civil Law' in the Supreme Court of Louisiana," 15 La. B. J. 15 (1967); Tate, "Civilian Methodology in Louisiana," 44 Tul. L. Rev. 673 (1970); Tate, "Techniques of Judicial Interpretation in Louisiana," 22 La. L. Rev. 727 (1962).

27 For instance, the fourth issue of Volume 44 of the *Tulane Law Review* is published in honor of Clarence J. Morrow, devoted to civilian methodology.

28 For a very sharp criticism of the philosophy of *stare decisis* in England see Goodhart, "Precedent in English and Continental Law," 50 Law Quarterly Review 40 (1934).

29 See, *inter alia*, Boulanger, "Notations sur le pouvoir créateur de la jurisprudence civile," 59 Revue Trimestrielle de Droit Civil 417 (1961); Esmein, "La Jurisprudence et la loi," 50 Rev. Trim. Dr. Civ. 17 (1952); Maury, "Observations sur la jurisprudence en tant que source du droit," in 1 Mélanges Ripert 28 (1950); Malaurie, "La Jurisprudence combattue par la loi," in Mélanges Savatier 603 (1965).

de facto power to really "create" law, on account of the growing body of statutory law. More than often enough, however, the role of jurisprudence in common- and civil-law jurisdictions has been analysed only at a historical and theoretical level rather than at a functional one, thus overemphasizing distinctions that are not really differences. Today, no one would seriously dispute, for example, the fact that a lower court in France, England, the United States, Louisiana, or Quebec is morally bound to follow the dictum of the Cour de Cassation, the House of Lords, or the Supreme Court on a point of interpretation. However, it is also clear that common-law jurisdictions may feel bound by only one pronouncement of a higher court, whereas civil-law jurisdictions may require a continuous line of jurisprudence or what can be called "*jurisprudence constante*" or "*coutume jurisprudentielle.*"[30]

The differences between the two systems on that point may then be of two kinds: one of intensity, the other of approach. The first difference is in the intensity of the moral persuasion of the de facto value of previously decided cases upon lower courts. It is, however, by no means really a difference of which the courts themselves are fully aware but rather one that can be observed by looking at the continuity of jurisprudential opinions over a certain number of years on a particular subject. In traditional civil law, lower courts will respect precedent and feel bound by it if and only if the rule thus established does not contradict legislation and if it has the following qualities: it represents a *jurisprudence constante*, and it is still consistent with the contemporary juridical, economic, and sociological context. *Jurisprudence constante* means a continuous line of decisions creating a sort of judicial custom rather than a single case. In other words—and the difference of intensity lies really in the attitude of the judge—the lower court will feel the authority of precedent to be so intense as to impose it upon itself if and only if this rule has been decided and approved more than once by the highest court.

On the other hand, in strict traditional English law, the judge will feel bound by precedent even if a higher court has only once decided the

---

30 For the difference between *stare decisis* and *jurisprudence constante*, see: Henry, "Jurisprudence Constante and Stare Decisis Contrasted," 15 AMERICAN BAR ASSOCIATION JOURNAL 11 (1929); Deák, "The Place of the 'Case' in the Common and the Civil Law," 8 TUL. L. REV. 337 (1934), especially the authorities cited on p. 340, n. 6.

question.[31] An example can be found in the rejection by English common law of the physicians' privilege. The origin of that rule can be traced back to a 1776 decision of the House of Lords in the *Duchess of Kingston* case[32] at a period when doctors were apothecaries and there was no real possibility of adequate control over the profession.

The historical intensity of precedent will oblige the judge, when he feels that times have changed or that it is time for a change, to adopt one of the two following attitudes: he can distinguish or he can yield. The first technique consists of finding a distinction (sometimes extremely artificial), allowing him to disregard the precedent by pure and simple elimination. The second consists of obeying the rule while using language expressing his regrets at having to do so with the hope that an appeal by the losing party may change the situation.[33] A recent Louisiana case shows the difference of attitude in that respect with regard to a civil-law jurisdiction. In the *Pringle-Associated Mortgage Corp. v. Eanes* case,[34] an appellate judge found that a rule laid down by the supreme court concerning the interpretation of the civil code was bad and obsolete law. However, instead of adopting the passive-obedience technique, he clear-

31 On the difference of attitude concerning *stare decisis* in the United Kingdom see: Sweeney, "L'Exposition du droit par le juge, source d'un malentendu sur le droit des Etats-Unis et le droit français," 12 Rev. Int. Dr. C. 685 (1960).
32 Duchess of Kingston's Case, 20 State Trials 355 (1776); 168 English Reports 175.
33 *For example, see* McDougall J. (dissenting) in Brompton Pulp and Paper Co. Ltd. v. Grégoire [1950] King's Bench 329, p. 342: "If it were not for the decision of the Supreme Court in *Fortier v. Longchamps*, I would have no hesitation in reaching the conclusion that . . . and that decison I feel obliged to follow"; and Lacost C.J. in Vassal v. Salvas (1896) 5 K.B. 349, 358, "Cette décision de *Taplin v. Hunt* bouleverse notre jurisprudence. Si, cependant, la Cour Suprême persiste, il sera de notre devoir d'accepter sa propre jurisprudence."

However, in certain instances judges stated expressly that they did not feel bound by Supreme Court decisions which they believed were contrary to the code. See Tellier J. in Despatie v. Herbert (1932) 53 K.B. 81, 88: "Malgré le profond respect que je professe pour ce haut tribunal, je me croirais encore lié par notre loi. . . . Dans un pays où c'est la Législature qui fait la loi mais non les tribunaux, le devoir du juge tel que je le comprends, me paraît être de s'en tenir à la plutôt qu'aux précédents en cas de conflit entre la loi et les précédents"; and in Darling v. Bricault, 37 K.B. 388, 393 (1924): "Je sais bien que sur cette question de prescription je vais à l'encontre de l'opinion exprimée par la Cour Suprême dans Meloche v. Simpson; mais cette opinion ne doit pas être suivie si, comme je le crois, elle est en désaccord avec le Code." See also Bissonnette J. in Bellefleur v. Lavellés (1957) Revue Légale 193, 203.
34 Pringle-Associated Mortgage Corp. v. Eanes, 208 Southern Reporter, second series, 346 (La. App. 1st Cir. 1968); 254 La. 705, 226 So 2d 502 (1969). Comment, 44 Tul. L. Rev. 847 (1970).

ly disagreed with the supreme court decision, indicating that he could not feel bound by a decision that, in his opinion, was bad law. This eventually brought the supreme court to change its mind, although some of the supreme court justices expressed strong disagreement as to the technique used.

The second difference is one of psychological attitude which is only really a reflection of the conception of the sources of law. The civilian judge is trained to look first at legislation to find the answers to problems submitted to him. Only if he cannot find a clear-cut answer in the code itself will he then try to deduce one from the broad general principles underlying the basic code rules. Cases will only be used to reinforce his arguments or as illustrations of what other judges have done in analogous situations. In other words, precedent may enter only at the end of the second phase of his intellectual process and will to a certain degree, at least in theory, have no more weight than of doctrine. On the contrary, the common lawyer has been trained to find his law in cases; thus, his natural reflex when on the bench is to try to analogize by finding a similar case in fact and law. For him, law is really a series of *ad hoc* solutions to *ad hoc* problems between which relationships may be made through the process of analogy. For the civilian, law is an organized and structured abstract system, to which each jurisprudential solution must relate. In other words, it is my opinion that the functional versus the theoretical, as well as the sectional versus the global, psychological, and educational approach of common-law and civil-law lawyers is reflected in the way the judiciary approaches and considers jurisprudence as a source of law.

In that respect, both Louisiana and Quebec offer a very interesting field of comparative investigation. It is clear in Quebec, and probably even more so in Louisiana, that the courts do place a great deal of weight on previously decided cases. Suffice it to say that any lawyer when pleading in Quebec will invoke *"la jurisprudence"* and cite it abundantly in his brief. Suffice it to look at judgments rendered every day by the Quebec courts to see that, in many instances, the courts do cite previously decided cases to reinforce their opinion. The question then really is to determine how the Louisiana and Quebec courts operate and what their position is on previously decided cases as a source of law.

Two preliminary remarks must be made. The first is that the format of judgments both in Quebec and in Louisiana is the common-law format and not the French one, thus encouraging direct references to previous cases. It would be futile to think that, in this respect, the form has not had an influence on the substance. There can be little doubt that the adoption of the French style of judgment in Quebec would have considerably lessened the use of previously decided cases.

The second remark that should be made concerns the fact that Quebec and Louisiana judges do not in their daily task differentiate necessarily, as a preliminary step in their legal approach, between those cases that could be labeled "strict civil-law cases" from the "strict common-law or statutory cases" or from the "mixed cases." There is then a strong flexibility in the reasoning process, the choice of arguments, the consideration of potential sources to apply to the problem. This flexibility and adaptability to both systems will increase the likelihood of a judge's using (in whole or in part) common-law terminology, concepts, reasoning process, and attitudes in dealing with civil-law problems or, for that matter, the reverse. This comment should not, however, be taken necessarily as a criticism. It is my belief that mixed jurisdictions are privileged, in that a sound and good comparative law cross-fertilization will no doubt help to ensure and promote better solutions, provided that case-law does not substitute itself for legislation as the principal source of law. However, it is evident that in Quebec and perhaps much more so in Louisiana, there is a danger that the civil law may completely lose its identity and be replaced gradually by common law. As far as Quebec law is concerned, this danger springs from four techniques used by the courts.

The first and perhaps the most important danger comes from interpreting the civil code in the same way, with the same rules and canons of interpretation, as an ordinary statute.[35] Perhaps the most evident miscon-

35 See L. Baudouin, "Méthode d'interprétation judiciaire du Code civil au Québec," 10 REVUE DU BARREAU 397 (1950); L. Baudouin, "Les Aspects généraux du droit privé dans la Province de Québec," 81 (1967), 73 ff.; Comment, "Interpretation of Codes and Statutes by Civil and Common Law Courts: The Doctrine of Ejusdem Generis," 5 TUL. L. REV. 266 (1931); Elliott, "Techniques of Ejusdem Generis," 5 TUL. L. REV. 266 (1931); Elliott, "Techniques of Interpretation," in THE CODE NAPOLÉON AND THE COMMON LAW WORLD 80 (1956); Mignault, "Le Code civil de la Province de Québec et son interprétation," 14 REVUE DU DROIT 583 (1936); Mignault, "Rédaction et publication des lois," 1 REVUE DU BARREAU 175 (1941); Morin, "Interprétation des lois," 1 REVUE DU BARREAU 229 (1941); Pouliot, "Règles d'interprétation du droit," 2 REVUE DU BARREAU 42 (1942). For Louisiana, see, more particularly, Tate, "Techniques of Judicial Interpretation in Louisiana," 22 LA. L. REV. 727 (1962) and Tate, "Policy in Judicial Decisions," 20 LA. L. REV. 62 (1959).

ception of a certain number of judges was that of the "literal" interpretation of the articles of the code, which had the effect of putting the code in a straitjacket. A literal interpretation of the articles of the code prevented the interrelations between its different parts on one hand, and on the other hand always favored a conservative rather than a liberal interpretation. To this rule one must add also that set out by the Supreme Court of Canada, to the effect that no reference should be made in the code interpretation to the "*travaux préliminaires*" or to the codifiers' intention.[36] The consequence of this method of approach was to divorce the civil code from all general basic principles and to force the judge to look at the trees instead of the forest. It is only fair to say that this state of affairs was brought about almost exclusively by decisions of the Supreme Court of Canada and of the British Privy Council, and that it appears that this rule has no longer been retained. An illustration of that tendency can be found in the interpretation the Supreme Court of Canada gave to the word *descendant* in Quebec Civil Code Article 1056, interpreting it literally to mean legitimate children, thus excluding recovery by natural children or parents in case of wrongful death.[37] It took a recent legislative amendment to get rid of this unwarranted and obtrusive statutory interpretation.[38]

The second danger is the indiscriminate use of previously decided cases of common-law jurisdictions to interpret civil law. It is essential in this respect to remind the reader that the Canadian judicial system provides for a Supreme Court of Canada which is the court of last resort for all provincial as well as federal cases. The number of judges sitting on that court has varied from six to seven to nine justices. Presently there are nine judges, three of them appointed from among former members of the bar of the province of Quebec, and the other six from among members of the bars of the other Canadian provinces. Thus there are presently three judges trained in civil-law methodology. Since the court has sat as a bench of five justices in 85.35 percent of the cases, there is a good chance that civil-law cases coming from Quebec will now be heard by a

---

36 Gosselin v. The King, 33 S.C.R. 255 (1903). See also Stewart v. Molson Bank 4 K.B. 11, 17 (1895); City of Montreal v. Standard Light and Power, 20 Legal News 263 (1897).
37 Town of Montreal West v. Hough, S.C.R. 113 (1931).
38 Quebec Civil Code, article 1056 as amended by "An Act to amend the Civil Code respecting natural children," 1970 S. of Q. Chap. 62.

bench on which the three "civilian" judges, will be in the majority. This, however, was not the case before.

The Quebec judge has usually been exposed to some common law before sitting as a judge, whereas an Ontario judge, for instance, has most probably never been exposed to civilian techniques and methodology. Over the years, it becomes clear that in certain periods of its existence the Supreme Court of Canada did a somewhat poor job for the civil law. The common-law judges, being totally ignorant of civilian principles, would render judgments in civil-law problems using common-law techniques. In certain cases the end result of the judgment was good but the reasons given in support of making it were sadly lacking in terms of civil-law content.[39] The danger to the civil law was generally from the indiscriminate systematic use of English or Canadian precedents to explain civil law.

In a nutshell, the pattern adopted in that respect was usually the following: the common-law judge would first try to ascertain what solution he would give to the case presented to him. Being ignorant of the civil law, and most of the time even incapable of reading French materials or sources, he would naturally turn to his law (i.e., common-law precedents) to justify his solution. In doing this, he would analyze common-law precedents to find that the solution given in common law was not substantially different from that of civil law. Here again, the end solution may have been correct but the methodology was often common-law precedent rather than articles in the civil code or basic civilian principles. Through this process, the foreign source of law had a tendency to replace the local one, and the approach, language, and methodology of the common law was carried into the civil law.[40] It is only fair, however, to point out some exceptions to that pattern from certain common-law judges such as Anglin, who in some of his judgments seems at least to have been concerned with these problems.[41]

The third wrongful technique sometimes used by Quebec courts or

---

39 J.-L. BAUDOUIN, ETUDE DE SOCIOLOGIE JURIDIQUE SUR LE COMPORTEMENT DE LA COUR SUPRÊME DU CANADA DANS L'INTERPRÉTATION DU DROIT QUÉBÉCOIS 15 (1967).
40 Space does not permit an exhaustive list of these cases here. See, as *illustrations*, Drysdale v. Dugas, 26 S.C.R. 20 (1897), on abuse of right; Ross v. Dunstall, 62 S.C.R. 393 (1922), on responsibility for manufactured products; The King v. Lapérière, S.C.R. 415 (1946), on responsibility of children.
41 See Anglin J. in Curley v. Latreille, 60 S.C.R. 131, 133 ff. (1920).

by the Supreme Court of Canada in the interpretation of the civil code was the reference to foreign common-law interpretations of civil code articles. There are, for example, some provisions in the Quebec Civil Code that have been copied from English statutes. Article 1235 represents, for instance, an attempt to codify the principal rules of Lord Tenterden's Act,[42] best known as the Statute of Frauds. Similarly, Article 1056 appears to be a codification of the principle laid down by Lord Campbell's Act concerning the right of action of dependents in cases involving wrongful death.[43] In many cases, the courts recognizing the common-law origin of the legislation looked to the interpretation given to it by common law not only simply for guidance, but as a sort of imperative. For example, Quebec Civil Code Article 1235 being of English origin and there being no commencement of proof in writing in English law, no derogation could be brought to the rule laid down by that article even if Article 1233 clearly established the general proposition that testimony was admissible in all cases where there was such a commencement of proof in writing.[44] Another excellent illustration of this state of affairs is the interpretation given by the Supreme Court of Canada to the right to moral damages (*solatium doloris*) in cases of wrongful death. Civil Code Article 1056, governing the right of action of the dependents in the case of wrongful death, does not deal with what damages can be claimed. It only lists those persons who are allowed a recourse and the conditions under which the action can be brought. Yet in the celebrated case of *Canadian Pacific Railway Co. v. Robinson*,[45] the Supreme Court of Canada, basing itself on a highly criticizable interpretation of this article, held that *solatium doloris* could not be granted primarily because Article 1056 was of English origin and that English law did not recognize that kind of damages. It should be noted that the solution may not be

---

42 29 Car. II, Chap. 3 (1676); 9 Geo. IV, Chap. 14 (1828).
43 On the question of the origins of Quebec Civil Code, art. 1056, see: L. Baudouin, "Le Solatium doloris," 2 CAHIERS DE DROIT 55 (1955); FRENETTE, L'INCIDENCE DU DÉCÈS DE LA VICTIME SUR L'ACTION EN INDEMNITÉ (1961); Wasserman, "'Solatium Doloris' as an Element in the Awarding of Damages Arising from Delict and Quasi-Delict," 13 REVUE DU BARREAU 127 (1953); Schecter, "The Original Development of the Law Relating to Damage for Loss of Life in Quebec," 17 REVUE DU DROIT 7 (1938).
44 Charest v. Murphy, 3 K.B. 376 (1893); Malleur v. Mitchell, 14 K.B. 74 (1904); Baril v. Read Motors, 46 K.B. 174 (1928); Duchaine v. Bédard, S.C. 394 (1956); Banque Canadienne Nationale v. Tanguay, S.C.R. 379 (1962).
45 Canadian Pacific Railways Co. v. Robinson, 14 S.C.R. 105 (1888).

bad at all since it is extremely difficult to evaluate the tears and suffering of a wife, of a father, or of a child for the loss of a loved one. However, the reasoning process is entirely wrong. It is not because the common-law courts have chosen to bar recovery for purely moral damages that the common-law interpretation should have been given to Article 1056. In other words, when one borrows a rule from another jurisdiction it does not necessarily mean that one wants to borrow as well the foreign interpretation of that rule, especially as in the above example where, both under general principles of civil law and under Articles 1071 and following, moral damages are admissible. This may just be, of course, a reflection of intellectual laziness, for there is less effort required if one takes the position that what was good for the common law is also good for the civil law, than if one has to examine whether the solution is in conformity with the civil-law rules. Whatever the possible explanation, the result is that through this process a common-law rule and the common-law interpretation displace the civil law. However, one should point out that the *Robinson* case was decided in 1883, at a time when the Supreme Court of Canada felt that it had a mission to unify the law throughout Canada. This unification was, of course, always at the expense of the civil law.[46]

Finally, a fourth area of penetration of common law within the civilian judicial process is through the importation of common-law doctrinal structures in the civil law. This is perhaps the least successful in Quebec for it is the most obvious and thus allows for immediate criticism. A good example can be taken from the law of torts. A problem that faces all jurists the world over is determining the responsibility of the property-owner for damages suffered by a person while on his property. The common law appears to a civilian extremely complex when it comes to distinguishing between an invitee, a licensee, and a trespasser. No such distinction exists in French law, where the courts, irrespective of the quality

---

46 See Taschereau J., in Canadian Pacific Railways Co. v. Robinson, 14 S.C.R. 105, 125 (1888). See also Ritchie J., p. 110, "I think it would be much to be regretted if we were compelled to hold that damages should be assessed by different rules in the different provinces through which the same railroad may run." See also Taschereau J. in Magann v. Auger, 31 S.C.R. 186, 193 (1902): "By the conclusion we have reached upon the question, we declare the law to be in the Province of Quebec upon the same footing as it stands in the United Kingdom and in the rest of the Dominion . . . as of great importance especially in commercial matters."

of the person entering on someone's property, use the test of the "*bon père de famille.*" It is probable that in many instances, here again, a similar solution would be given to the same set of facts in common law as well as in civil law. Yet the way of arriving at a solution is different. In common law, the judge has to first ask himself whether the victim falls in the category of a licensee, a trespasser, or an invitee. Then, having ascertained this fact, he deduces immediately the intensity of the duty of care owed by the owner. In civil law, the judge will have to ascertain, taking into consideration all the circumstances of the case, whether or not the conduct of the defendant was faulty, as being contrary to that expected of a "*bon père de famille.*" As was pointed out by one commentator, the difference between common and civil law on that point may be more than one of method.[47] It is an interesting hypothesis that the apparent severity of the English common law towards the trespasser may come from the whole attitude of the English tradition towards private property.

In Quebec, some judgments[48] have purely and simply imported the licensee, invitee, and trespasser doctrine into the Quebec law of civil responsibility without really any necessity for it, since the problem was one that civil law had been faced with before and for which strict civil-law solutions had been found (one has even heard of that theory being applied in France where trespass also presumably exists). It is only with difficulty, however, that a majority of recent Quebec cases have rejected the trespasser, invitee, and licensee theory.

This very brief analysis of some of the difficulties experienced by the Quebec and Louisiana civilian traditions is by no means exhaustive. Although, in a general way, the penetration of common law has certainly been deeper in Louisiana than in Quebec, the writer does not share the view that civil law in Louisiana is nothing but an empty reality or a hollow concept. Quebec has not been isolated from French doctrinal and jurisprudential sources. There is no doubt that this played a very important role in the preservation of civil law. Louisiana on the contrary, be-

---

47 Mayrand, "A quand le trépas du trespasser?" 21 REVUE DU BARREAU 1 (1961).
48 Caza v. Clercs de St.-Viateur, 41 REVUE DE JURISPRUDENCE 70 (1935) criticized by Mignault J. in "Conservons notre droit civil," 15 REVUE DU DROIT 28 (1936); Lapointe v. Canadian Pacific Railway Co., S.C.R. 386 (1949), and cases cited in Mayrand, cited in Note 7 above.

cause of a language barrier, was until very recently completely isolated from other civil-law jurisdictions. This explains perhaps why the bench and the bar became more attracted by common-law sources which of course were more readily available. The genuine revived interest for civil law that the writer was able to observe in Louisiana, the translations that were made of major French doctrinal works and the publication of authentic Louisiana treatises are indications that after a long period of uneasiness, the Louisiana jurists have decided that the challenge was worth the fight. It is true that Louisiana, like Quebec, will probably never be a civilian jurisdiction in the same way that France is, but it will still offer an original system that draws from the civilian and the common-law families and one which can observe the cross-fertilization of these two legal systems. Much in the same way, however, the future of the civilian heritage in both these jurisdictions really lies in the hands of the courts. Only they can truly orient the legal methodology in the civilian tradition.

ABBREVIATIONS

Can. B. Rev.	Canadian Bar Review
K.B.	King's Bench
L.N.	Legal News
La.	Louisiana Reports
La. B. J.	Louisiana Bar Journal
La. L. Rev.	Louisiana Law Review
Rev. Int. Dr. C.	Revue Internationale de Droit Comparé
Rev. Jur. U.P.R.	Revista Juridica de la Universidad de Puerto Rico
Rev. Trim. Dr. Civ.	Revue Trimestrielle de Droit Civil
S. C. R.	Supreme Court Reports
S. of Q.	Statutes of Quebec
So. 2d	Southern Reporter, second series
Tul. L. Rev.	Tulane Law Review

II

The Role of the Judge in Mixed Jurisdictions: The Louisiana Experience

Albert Tate, Jr.
ASSOCIATE JUSTICE, SUPREME COURT OF LOUISIANA

Louisiana is a mixed jurisdiction: our basically civilian tradition has been partly overlaid and replaced by Anglo-American common law. As English is richer because of the fecund intermixture of Teutonic and Romantic modes of expression and word-derivations, so is a mixed jurisdiction the richer for the continual cross-pollination among legal concepts and institutions from the two great legal systems of Western civilization. Similarly, it is my belief that the judge of a mixed jurisdiction such as Louisiana has the best of both worlds; available to him for the performance of his judicial function are the techniques and perspectives of both legal systems.[1]

THE LOUISIANA JUDGE TODAY

The Louisiana judge does not regard his role as limited to that of the traditional civilian judge, at least as this role is viewed by our own academics. The *Louisiana Blueprint* articles[2] of the late Clarence Morrow are perhaps the most comprehensive statement of this view. Morrow's remarks include: "In the civilian system the Code is central: judges and case-law have a distinctly inferior position, in comparison with common law jurisdictions.[3] . . . The opinions contain no doctrinal writing, for

---

[1] The present paper is to some extent an elaboration and amplification of views previously expressed in Tate, "Techniques of Judicial Interpretation in Louisiana," 22 LA. L. REV. 727 (1962); Tate, "Civilian Methodology in Louisiana," 44 TUL. L. REV. 673 (1970); and Tate, "The Law-Making Function of the Judge," 28 LA. L. REV. 211 (1968). A list of the abbreviations used in this chapter appears on page 37.

[2] Morrow, "Louisiana Blueprint: Civilian Codification and Legal Method for State and Nation," 17 TUL. L. REV. 351, 537 (1943).

[3] *Id.* at 548.

this is not the province of the judge, but the law teacher, who wields a powerful influence in giving direction to the law."[4]

Despite this classic view of the limited role of the judge in a civilian jurisdiction, Morrow himself admitted that, in practice, Louisiana lawyers and judges primarily rely on decided cases, just as do common lawyers.[5] Joseph Dainow has similarly commented: "The attitude of the bar and the bench is more inclined to the search for cases in point or at least analogous ones, rather than toward the interpretation of basic principles with the aid of doctrinal analysis and elaboration."[6]

Most commentators ascribe this condition to several causes: the absence of civil law–trained lawyers and judges, especially in our formative years as an American jurisdiction; the dearth of doctrinal materials on the Louisiana civil law; the efficiency of our national law-publishers in classifying and reporting Louisiana cases along with the common-law decisions; the natural influence of the development of the law in sister American jurisdictions, influenced by similar social conditions and social institutions, enforced by the isolation of Louisiana's civil-law system from the legal resolution of contemporary social conflicts by other civilian jurisdictions.

To these reasons for the importance of case-law, I must add, without apology, the historical role of the Louisiana judge: how he views himself, and how the community and the legal profession view him.

In a pure civilian jurisdiction, the judge may resemble a career member of a bureaucracy. He enters its ranks soon after finishing his academic law training, and he spends his lifetime within it in anonymous and often specialized study.[7] On the other hand, the common-law judge enters the judiciary only after a (usually extended) period of practice. He becomes a judge as a generalist rather than a specialist, in that he is not specifically trained for judicial duties. His signed opinions, whether majority, con-

---

[4] Id. at 550.
[5] Id. at 394. See also other articles by Morrow: "The Future of Codification in Louisiana," 29 TUL. L. REV. 249, 250 (1955); "An Approach to the Revision of the Louisiana Civil Code," 23 TUL. L. REV. 478, 479 (1949).
[6] Dainow, The Louisiana Civil Law, in CIVIL CODE OF LOUISIANA xv at xvii (Dainow ed. 1961). See also, e.g., Pascal, "A Report on the French Civil Code Revision Project," 25 TUL. L. REV. 205, 212–13 (1951).
[7] Dainow, "The Constitutional and Judicial Organization of France and Germany and Some Comparisons of the Civil Law and Common Law Systems," 37 INDIANA LAW JOURNAL 1, 11, 27–28, 43–44 (1961).

curring, or dissenting, manifest his personal responsibility for his judicial needs. In the judicial tradition within which he practices, he serves a law-making as well as an interpretative function, since his decisions create binding precedents.[8]

ORIGIN AND DEVELOPMENT OF HIS ROLE

The institutional origin of the Louisiana judge has common-law rather than civil-law roots: rather than being a civil servant chosen for his technical skills, he is an officer of the government chosen through the political process to exercise his independent (but impartial and professionally correct) judgment in interpreting and applying the law. His opinions are not impersonal emanations from a judicial bureaucracy but, rather, are recognized as authored by him, although they are recognized as representing a collegiate view, and although they do attempt to define results in impersonal legal values rather than in personal predictions. He accepts doctrinal exposition as part of his duty in explaining his decision, since by historical necessity this became part of his function in the exposition of local Louisiana law, in the earlier absence of scholarly legal centers and extensive legal literature.

The attributes of the Louisiana judicial office were developed in "new" country, devoid of ancient traditions and settled on the frontier of the civilized world in comparatively recent times. The judge met "new" legal conditions and questions, and he was expected to settle them —to settle them on the basis of preexisting law when laws reasonably intended to apply could be found, but to settle them in a sound and practical way even in the absence of any "old" law reasonably intended to regulate the present "new" conflict of interest.[9] It was recognized that the skimpy legislation of the amateur part-time legislators left large interstices for judge-made law to regulate.

---

8 *Id.* at 40–47.
9 Compare Renthorp v. Bourg, 4 Mart. (O.S.) 97 (La. 1816), finding that, based on traditional civilian doctrine, title to the bed of a public highway after its construction belongs always to the sovereign or public and is a public thing, with Hatch v. Arnault, 3 LOUISIANA ANNUAL 482 (1848), finding that the conditions which gave rights to this ancient rule under Roman law could not apply to rural roads in frontier country (where the public interest not infrequently may require the roads to be changed or abandoned, etc.), so that the public enjoys merely a servitude and the title remains in the proprietor of the estate over which the road passes.

By the third decade of this century there was substantial support for the view that the judges of Louisiana used the techniques and performed the function of common-law judges rather than of civilian ones.[10] This view precipitated the celebrated academic debate whether Louisiana was still a civil-law jurisdiction.[11] The counterattack in defense of civil-law methodology gave perhaps the initial impetus to the counterrevolution, now triumphant, by which Louisiana is accounted among the civilian or mixed jurisdictions, rather than among the common-law ones.[12]

The Louisiana State Law Institute spearheaded this civilian renaissance. As part of its contribution, it has made available to the English-speaking Louisiana bench and bar translations of French doctrinal writing[13] and has sponsored the production of civilian-oriented treatises on Louisiana law.[14] In addition, the law reviews of our state law schools have added considerably to the available doctrinal studies which emphasize the civilian concepts and interpretations and functional reasons underlying the law-rules of our civil code. All of these sources reinforce the modern resort to the civilian portion of our heritage when our courts devise or revise substantive law-rules.

ADDED DIMENSIONS IN DEVELOPMENT OF SUBSTANTIVE LAW

My primary emphasis concerns the advantages in judicial techniques available to a mixed-law judge, who may draw from the civil- and common-law traditions. Nevertheless, I should note briefly the added dimensions of insight and resources possessed by a Louisiana mixed-law judge when he creates or modifies rules of substantive law.[15]

10 Ireland, "Louisiana's Legal System Reappraised," 11 TUL. L. REV 585 (1937); Comment, "Stare Decisis in Louisiana," 7 TUL. L. REV. 100 (1932).
11 The 1937 dispute and the leading articles involved are briefly summarized in Brosman, "A Controversy and a Challenge," 12 TUL. L. REV. 239 (1938).
12 Tucker, "The Code and the Common Law in Louisiana," 29 TUL. L. REV. 739, 757–59 (1955).
13 PLANIOL, CIVIL LAW TREATISE (La. St. L. Inst. transl. 1959, 6 vols.); GÉNY, METHOD OF INTERPRETATION AND SOURCES OF PRIVATE POSITIVE LAW (La. St. L. Inst. transl. 1963); CIVIL LAW TRANSLATIONS (La. St. L. Inst. transl. 1965–72, 5 vols.: Vols. 1–4, AUBRY & RAU, COURS DE DROIT CIVIL FRANÇAIS: OBLIGATIONS; PROPERTY; TESTAMENTARY SUCCESSIONS AND GRATUITOUS DISPOSITIONS; and INTESTATE SUCCESSIONS; Vol. 5, BAUDRY-LACANTINERIE & TISSIER, AUBRY & RAU, CARBONNIER, PRESCRIPTION).
14 YIANNOPOULOS, CIVIL LAW OF PROPERTY (1966); YIANNOPOULOS, PERSONAL SERVITUDES (1968); LITVINOFF, OBLIGATIONS: BOOK 1 (1969).
15 Some reference is made to this in Dainow, "Planiol Citations by Louisiana Courts: 1959–1966," 27 LA. L. REV. 231, 265–67 (1967). See, for instance,

For instance, in the field of products liability, the common law utilized a variety of substantive law theories to impose strict liability upon the manufacturer to an ultimate user or bystander injured by a defective product made by the defendant.[16] In Louisiana, the courts were able to employ simpler additional or alternative reasoning, based upon our own civil code article and the doctrinal interpretations of its French predecessor.[17]

Similarly, the difficulty of the common law in awarding damages for prenatal injuries[18] was avoided in Louisiana by reference to our civil code provision, drawn from the French, that children in the mother's womb are considered as already born.[19] Again, in determining the regulation of activities by an occupier of property which interferes with his neighbor's enjoyment of his own property, and the liability of the occupier therefor, the Louisiana judge could draw upon both civilian- and common-law sources in an attempt to work out appropriate law-rules.[20] Or, to take yet another example, the nineteenth-century Louisiana judge felt free to discard comparative negligence possibilities in our civil code and to draw upon the Anglo-American concept of contributory negli-

---

Standard Motor Car Company v. Standard Indemnity Company, 97 So. 2d 435 (La. App. 1st Cir. 1957), discussed in Tate, "Policy in Judicial Decisions," 20 LA. L. REV. 62, 72–74 (1959).

16 Prosser, "The Assault upon the Citadel (Strict Liability to the Consumer)," 69 YALE LAW REVIEW 1099 (1960). Cf. Prosser, "The Fall of the Citadel (Strict Liability to the Consumer)," 50 MINNESOTA LAW REVIEW 791 (1966).

17 La. Civ. Code art. 2545 (1870) provides that "the seller who knows the vices of the thing he sells . . . is answerable to the buyer in damages." Drawing upon this article and French interpretations of FRENCH CIV. CODE art. 1645 (of which the Louisiana article is almost a direct translation), our high court early in this century declared that the manufacturer-seller conclusively knows of the vices of his product and is therefor answerable in damages to a consumer injured by his product, irrespective of the absence of proof of negligence. Doyle v. Fuerst and Kraemer, 129 La. 838, 56 So. 2d 906 (1911). The fault principle thus enunciated likewise applies to impose liability under La. Civ. Code art. 2315 (1870) ("Every act whatever of man that causes damages to another obliges him by whose fault it happened to repair it.") for damage caused to a third person, whether he be a customer or not. Weber v. Fidelity & Casualty Insurance Co. of New York, 259 La. 599, 250 So. 2d 754 (1971).

18 White, "The Right of Recovery for Prenatal Injuries," 12 LA. L. REV. 383 (1952).

19 La. Civ. Code art. 29 (1870); Cooper v. Blanck, 39 So. 2d 352 (La. App. Orl. 1923); Note, "Tort—Prenatal Injuries—Louisiana Law," 12 LA. L. REV. 519 (1952).

20 See, e.g., majority and concurring opinions in Robichaux v. Huppenbauer, 258 La. 139, 245 So. 2d 385 (1971).

gence, in response to the felt needs of his time;[21] in response to the needs sensed in a later era, perhaps this judge-made importation may be judicially restricted, modified, or even repudiated by resort to the civilian interpretations of the provisions of other civil codes similar to our own.[22]

EFFECT OF CIVILIAN RENAISSANCE

The civilian renaissance, and the ferment of intellectual inquiry and reevaluations resulting from it, brought reminders from our latter-day academics of the theoretically more limited role of a traditional civilian judge and the derelictions of Louisiana judges as measured by that standard. By this time, however, we were in truth a mixed jurisdiction. We had absorbed many common-law concepts and techniques—not least of which was the role of the judge as law- and doctrine-developer rather than as merely controversy-decider. The judge so viewed himself, the lawyers who argued cases so viewed him, and Louisiana law schools, no less than those in common-law jurisdictions, so viewed him, for the basic course-teaching greatly utilizes judicial material. The course of history could not be turned back, nor (it is my thesis) should it be.

Today, despite the renewed importance of the civilian sources of our substantive law, there is little support in the Louisiana bench and bar for the civilian theory that the role of the judges is to decide cases only, leaving doctrinal development to the scholarly writers. Aside from our firmly settled tradition to the contrary, the needs of our society demand that judges continue to formulate law-rules and to develop their reasoned doctrinal bases. Our small body of academicians is required to devote its energies primarily to educating law students, not to doctrinal exposition in any large degree. The courts, meanwhile, must solve rapidly and rationally, in the absence of such doctrinal literature, the teeming new problems of a society ever more complex and more populated, as they emerge in litigation.[23]

21 Malone, "Comparative Negligence—Louisiana's Forgotten Heritage," 6 LA. L. REV. 125 (1945).
22 See, e.g., Stone, "Comparative Negligence," 17 LA. B. J. 13 (1969).
23 I should here note that at least some commentators suggest that the modern French civilian judge, no less than the Louisiana mixed-law judge, plays in fact a more important part in doctrinal exposition and in formulating law-rules than the limited role ascribed to him by ideal theory. Loussouarn, "The Relative Importance of Legislation, Custom, Doctrine, and Precedent in French Law," 18 LA. L. REV. 235 (1958); Deák, "The Place of the 'Case' in the Common and the Civil Law," 8 TUL. L. REV. 337 (1934).

Subject to revision or rejection by the legislature (a relatively rare event), these amplified or new rules of private law formulated by the courts provide guidance to the regulation of men's affairs, to the settlement without litigation of disputes, and to the decision of future disputes if they result in suit. Considering that the development and revision of law-rules requires a weighing of social values as well as scholarship and a consistency with doctrine if possible, it is perhaps more appropriate that the judges of Louisiana, chosen through the political process as an arm of democratic government, have the ultimate responsibility in articulating the doctrinal bases. Of course, in fulfilling this responsibility, the judges will rely greatly upon the writings and perceptions of the academics, whose long view of history and lifetime of study devoted to a particular area of law can enrich the understanding of the court. As each issue arises, the court must resolve it quickly, along with many others, in addition to the processing of the millrun of the court's week.

The Louisiana judge, like his common-law brother, is a law-announcer as well as a case-decider. Nevertheless, the civilian renaissance reinforced insights and techniques from his civilian heritage which help free him from the sterile concept extant in many American common-law jurisdictions that, save in the exceptional case, the judge is just a precedent-hunter and a rule-applier.

PRESENT-DAY LIMITATIONS UPON THE COMMON-LAW JUDGE

Unfortunately, by the time we in Louisiana started to worry self-consciously about what judges do, and also about what they *should do*, most American common-law jurisdictions paid at least lip service to a notion of the function of the common-law judge more restricted in scope than that originally conceived. Karl Llewellyn described the change of notion in his great work, *The Common Law Tradition*.[24]

The "Grand Style" of old, as he describes it, was "a way of thought and work, not . . . a way of writing," "a way of on-going renovation of doctrine."[25] It welcomed precedent, but it tested the value of precedent for the present dispute against three types of reason: (a) The "reputation of the opinion-writing judge"; (b) " 'principle' [which] means no mere

---

24 K. LLEWELLYN, THE COMMON LAW TRADITION: DECIDING APPEALS, *passim*, but especially at 36–45, 62–76 (1960).
25 *Id.* at 36.

verbal tool for bringing large-scale order into the rules, it means a broad generalization which must yield patent sense and order"; and (c) " 'policy,' in terms of prospective consequences of the rule under consideration, [which] comes in for explicit examination by reason in a further test of both the rule in question and its application." Llewellyn described the "tone and mark" of the grand style: "an of-courseness in the constant questing for better and best law to guide the future, but the better and best law is to be built on and out of what the past can offer; the quest consists in a constant re-examination and rewriting of a heritage."[26]

He compared this grand style of the early part of the nineteenth century, with the "Formal Style" of the latter part of that century and the first half or so of this—the latter, the judicial work of men with pygmy notions of their craft and function, as compared with the giant-like earlier approach. The formal style, "the orthodox ideology" of its period, comprised these notions: "the rules of law are to decide the cases; policy is for the legislature, not the courts, and so is change even in pure common law. 'Principle' is a generalization producing order which can and should be used to prune away those 'anomalous' cases or rules which do not fit . . . sense is no official concern of a formal-style court."[27]

With a few notable exceptions, the Louisiana judge of the last century and the first third of the twentieth century was a formal-style rather than a grand-style man, like his brethren from other American jurisdictions. Even today the type lingers on, although with the recognition of our civilian heritage there is less theoretical and historical foundation for his ideology. The prototype of the modern Louisiana jurist, however, is more the grand-style judge of the common law, not the technician judge of Europe whom some of our own academicians cite to us as exemplars.

MIXED-LAW PERSPECTIVES BEYOND THE GRAND STYLE

The form of appellate decision in Louisiana tends to exposition of the doctrinal, the jurisprudential, and, it is hoped, the legislative bases for the law-rule, which are then applied to the facts before the court. Both the grand-style and formal-style judges of the common law use this format, though with different emphases and values. This characteristic of

26 Ibid.
27 Id. at 38.

the Louisiana judicial function and judicial opinion results from the infusion of common-law techniques and approaches into our decisional process.

But from our civilian heritage our judicial function has drawn attributes in some ways similar to those of a grand-style common-law judge and in some ways different, sometimes only subtly so. These differences concern (a) the importance of legislation and its use as a generating principle of decision; (b) the respect paid to prior precedents; and (c) the use of a technique of interpreting legislation which permits expansion of judicial discretion whether to apply its principle to social conditions unforeseen at the time of enactment.

LEGISLATION AND PRECEDENT

By tradition, a fundamental difference in common- and civil-law theory concerns the role and importance of precedent as opposed to statute.[28] For the common lawyer, the precedent itself is law; a statute is often regarded as an intruder in the garden of judge-made law and, as we say in the watch-that-metaphor department, to be "narrowly construed." A judicial decision construing a statute is the law, though the construction is logically, historically, and actually erroneous—so that statute-cum-construction (erroneous) can only be changed by the legislature (which did not make the mistake), and not by the court (which did).

In this respect, the civilian judge differs fundamentally, be he grand-style or formal-style, from his common-law brother. His civil code tells him, "Law is a solemn expression of the *legislative will*,"[29] and he believes it. (Sometimes he believes it too well, as when he applies literally a legislative provision not intended to apply in a subsequent statutory context.)[30] Furthermore, statutory principles not directly applicable

---

28 B. SCHWARTZ, THE CODE NAPOLEON AND THE COMMON-LAW WORLD (1956); Dainow, "The Constitutional and Judicial Organization of France and Germany and Some Comparisons of the Civil Law and Common Law Systems," 37 IND. L. J. 1 (1961); Rheinstein, "Common Law and Civil Law: An Elementary Comparison," 22 REV. JUR. U.P.R. 90 (1953); Von Mehren, "The Judicial Process in the United States and in France," 22 REV. JUR. U.P.R. 235 (1953); A. YIANNOPOULOS, LOUISIANA CIVIL LAW SYSTEM, Part 1, pp. 99–109 (1971).
29 La. Civ. Code art. 1 (1870).
30 Hibbert v. Mudd, 187 So. 2d 503 (La. App. 3d Cir. 1966), critically discussed in Note, 14 LOYOLA L. REV. 189 (1967), and Note, 41 TUL. L. REV. 942 (1967).

may be freely drawn upon by analogy to create judicially a principle or law-rule for application in conflicts of interest arising in other fields of law.[31]

Since the overriding importance of legislation is recognized, prior errors in judicial interpretation, even those establishing a rule of property,[32] may be overruled as erroneously construing and applying civil code provisions or other legislation. Prior judicial precedents, being mere interpretations, may be freely overruled,[33] and even a lower court may refuse to follow a higher court precedent which is contrary to the statute it interprets.[34] An earlier construction of a statute may be judicially overruled, though the legislature has met many times since this construction and has not seen fit to amend the statute.[35]

An eminent authority has stated that the common-law judge employs

---

31 See, e.g., Langlois v. Allied Chemical Corporation, 258 La. 1067, 249 So. 2d 133 (1971), where the civil code property articles regulating a landowner's use of his property in relation to his neighbor's were drawn upon by analogy to furnish a rule of strict liability ("fault") to third persons off the premises injured by harmful use of the premises.

32 Miami Corporation v. State, 186 La. 784, 173 So. 315 (1936), overruling State v. Erwin, 173 La. 507, 138 So. 84 (1931).

33 Daggett, Dainow, Hebert, and McMahon, "A Reappraisal Appraised: A Brief for the Civil Law of Louisiana," 12. TUL. L. REV. 12, 22 (1937) notes that the Louisiana Supreme Court overruled its own prior decisions at least seventy-six times during the preceding twenty-five years. See also the writer's articles cited in Note 1 above for reference to other instances.

34 Coulon v. Anthony Hamlin, Inc., 93 So. 2d 557 (La. App. Orl. 1957), aff'd 233 La. 798, 98 So. 2d 193 (1957).

35 McDermott v. Funel, 258 La. 657, 247 So. 2d 567 (1971); see also Pringle, cited below.

The writer should admit, however, that strong views to the contrary of these broad statements can be found in even recent expressions of our high court. See, e.g., Pringle-Associated Mortgage Corp. v. Eanes, 254 La. 705, 226 So. 2d 502 (1969), with harsh words on original hearing for failure of intermediate court to follow the latest expression of high court interpreting statute, followed by opinion on rehearing adopting as correct the intermediate court's differing interpretation of the statute. See also Johnson v. St. Paul Mercury Insurance Company, 256 La. 289, 236 So. 2d 216 (1970), indicating a severely limited doctrine of overruling prior precedents; and Cartright v. Firemen's Insurance Company of Newark, New Jersey, 254 La. 330, 223 So. 2d 822 (1969), indicating that a judge-made rule on liability for latent brake defects could be changed only by the legislature.

However, he submits that the general practice of our courts over the last decades, either explicitly articulated (see Miami Corporation v. State, cited in Note 32 above, at 173 So. 320–22), or not, support the broad statements made in the text.

basically three types of reasoning.[36] The first type is reasoning by example, that is from case to case. The second type of reasoning is applied to statutory interpretation in the framework of the common law. In this type of reasoning, precedents in effect become part of the text of the statute. The third type of reasoning is applied to constitutional provisions. Here the judge is entirely free to go to the principles established by the constitution and to overrule or modify precedents. A Louisiana judge applies to the civil code and other legislation the type of reasoning that a common-law judge applies to a constitutional provision, and he may thus disregard interpretations of past generations in order to apply the principles underlying legislation to the resolution of contemporary problems.

In determining the principles underlying the words of legislation, often a controversy over law-rule is presented to the court simply because no clear intendment of legislation can be ascribed—either because no legislation relied upon is directly in point, or because the legislation claimed to be controlling is only ambiguously so, or because two or more enactments may possibly apply in whole or in part. In all such instances, by creative interpretation the judge must ascribe "legislative intent" or deny it, he must limit or extend competing statutes which arguably apply, he must synthesize from these competing or ambiguous statutory regulations a judge-made law-rule to apply in the penumbra. The role of the Louisiana judge may be different when he interprets contemporary statutes and when he interprets the civil code. Contemporary statutes may well be hastily drafted and the judge may perforce deal with them as described by the text. When, however, the judge interprets the civil code, he has to take into account the civilian tradition as a whole. Here the legislative intent is not merely a fiction. The enactment of the civil code shows a clear legislative intent to adopt the tradition except as expressly modified. After all, the code is like an iceberg in the ocean of the tradition. The 10 percent that has been legislated rests its weight on the hidden 90 percent. Of course, this does not mean that the legislative intent of 1808, 1825, or 1870 ought to control today in all respects. In the unprovided case the judge must act as if he were the legislator.[37]

The perspective we have gained from our civilian heritage is that,

---

36 LEVI, AN INTRODUCTION TO LEGAL REASONING (1949).
37 See La. Civ. Code art. 21, cited in text at Note 42 below.

when a judge so interprets and applies or does not apply legislation, our decisional theory can frankly acknowledge that it is the *judge* who formulates the law-rule actually applied, not the legislature. Unlike our common-law brother, who performs the identical function but under the guise of doing what (he thinks) the legislature would have intended to do had this issue been actually considered by it, our judges can recognize and admit that in most of these instances "legislative intent" is a fiction, since the many-membered and otherwise preoccupied legislature simply never considered or foresaw the problem or the changed conditions which created it.

JUDICIAL DISCRETION AND RESPONSIBILITY

We are indebted to Gény[38] and other civilian analysts for this perception and for the decisional function which results from it. As Gény points out, legislation is enacted to regulate the social and living environment of a living society. To apply it to the unforeseen or substantially changed conditions of other times, even though the original statutory purpose is no longer served, is to apply mechanically an abstract formula which does not represent the will of any legislator or of the legislature.[39] Thus, to apply the statute to unforeseen or changed conditions unknown to the legislature at the time of enactment is to do so by creation of a *judicial*, not a *legislative* rule—with the important consequence that, recognizing the formulation to be judicial rather than legislative, the judge need not apply (i.e., he is not legislatively commanded to apply) the rule deduced from the words of the statute if such rule be unsound or unwise as applied to present facts.[40]

The important consequence of this perception is that Louisiana judges can frankly accept responsibility for the law-rules thus formulated as in the instance of the unprovided-for case, and can formulate them

---

[38] GÉNY, METHOD OF INTERPRETATION AND SOURCES OF PRIVATE POSITIVE LAW (La. St. L. Inst. transl. 1963).

[39] *Id.*, §§ 51–59, 92–108.

[40] *Id.*, passim (e.g., §§ 101, 106, 107). For instance, the social conditions the legislation was enacted to regulate may have so changed as to make the literal application of the statute to the modern facts beyond any legislative intent, as in Mooney v. American Automobile Insurance Company, 81 So. 2d 625 (La. App. 1st Cir. 1955). There, a provision of the 1938 highway regulatory act, enacted at a time when there were only two-lane highways, was held inapplicable to the changed social context of the four-lane highways of the later day.

according to their soundness and social utility, as would a legislator.⁴¹ This is as our civil code commands us: "In all civil matters, where there is no express law [i.e., legislation], the judge is bound to proceed and decide according to equity. To decide equitably; an appeal is to be made to natural law and reason, or received usages, where positive law is silent." ⁴²

Of course, in devising the rule to apply, the judge will draw upon generative principles of legislation or doctrine applicable to comparable conflicts of interest, in an effort to regulate somewhat similar interests consistently, when the underlying reasons of fairness and social utility are so similar as to indicate analogous treatment should be afforded both. On the other hand, if the best rule for the present conflict of interest cannot thus be devised, the judge can draw upon not only purely legal materials, but also other data drawn from the living institutions of society which are relevant to the formulation of the best rule as a matter of legal and social policy.⁴³

In short, where legislation is sought to be applied beyond its originally intended scope or in such different social context as to be outmoded, the Louisiana judge is ideologically permitted to create and apply the different and sounder rule, and to base this new rule upon its actual reasons of social practicality and fairness (i.e., policy). He need not pretend he is deducing this rule by word-logic from prior precedent or legislation, nor is he limited by such word-logic, since he is free of the conceptual limitations of the judicial role under which the judge in many common-law jurisdictions must operate.

EXPANDED DIMENSIONS OF MIXED-LAW JUDGING

Because of the differences in judicial function founded upon our civilian heritage, the Louisiana mixed-law judge has doctrinally available to him

---

41 GÉNY, METHOD OF INTERPRETATION AND SOURCES OF PRIVATE POSITIVE LAW, passim (e.g., §§ 101, 106, 107). See, e.g., Hill v. Lundin & Associates, Inc., 260 La. 542, 256, So. 2d 620 (1972) and Pierre v. Allstate Insurance Company, 257 La. 471, 242 So. 2d 821 (1970) (opinion on rehearing).
42 La. Civ. Code art. 21 (1870).
43 GÉNY, METHOD OF INTERPRETATION AND SOURCES OF PRIVATE POSITIVE LAW, §§ 167, 168. See, e.g., Ross v. Board of Levee Comm'rs. of Nineteenth Louisiana Levee Dist., 182 La. 841, 162 So. 639 (1935). Naquin v. Callais, 191 So. 2d 885 (La. App. 1st Cir. 1966) (syllabus 9); and Anderson v. Rowan Drilling Co., 150 So. 2d 828 (La. App. 3rd Cir. 1963) (dissent). See also Santobello v. New York, 404 U.S. 257, 92 S. Ct. 495 (1971).

more advantageous techniques and perspectives, in my opinion, than those of his common-law comparable. On the other hand, because of the institutional origin of his office in the common-law tradition, the Louisiana judge can validly and explicitly perform as part of his function his important work in expounding and developing legal doctrine and law-rules for the better governing of society's relationships and the better decision of its controversies before or after they come to court.

As with the common-law judge, he views himself not merely as a technician but also as a scholar and law-maker and exponent of doctrine. However, as with a modern-day civilian judge, he is essentially more free than his common-law counterpart from the mechanical effects of "binding" precedent; more free to return, independent of intervening judicial precedents, to the initial legislative concepts and to use creative analogies and constructs based upon them; or, in the absence of legislation expressly intended to apply, more free to devise socially just and sound rules to regulate the unprovided-for case.

I am aware that some common-law judges and some common-law jurisdictions have devised techniques and approaches not greatly dissimilar to those of the civil law.[44] In civilian jurisdictions, too, the judge is often not in actuality the sterile technician depicted by theoretical literature. The judge of the mixed jurisdiction has, nevertheless, the advantage of both of them (who must break from history so to perform), in that the philosophical framework in which he performs his functions explicitly justifies them through the natural synthesis of civilian and common-law components of his heritage.

CONCLUSION

In modern-day America the checks in the legislative process so predominate that it is more difficult to achieve positive action than to negate it. This, I judge from the experience of the third and fourth French re-

---

44 I need only to refer to the work and influence of such great American common-law judges as Cardozo, Stone, Schaefer, and Traynor, and the writings in which they articulated their views of the relationship between statute and precedent and the judge's creative utilization of both in the ongoing revitalization of legal precept. See, e.g., CARDOZO, THE NATURE OF THE JUDICIAL PROCESS (1921); SCHAEFER, PRECEDENT AND POLICY (1956); Stone, "The Common Law in the United States," 50 HARVARD LAW REVIEW 4 (1936); Traynor, "Statutes Revolving in Common-Law Orbits," 17 CATHOLIC UNIVERSITY LAW REVIEW 4 (1936).

publics, is not a characteristic of the legislative process of the twentieth century peculiar to America. The great public issues of a complex, industrialized modern society—taxation, welfare, defense, major social and economic issues—occupy the time and interest of the legislatures far more than routine areas of private law. If only for this reason, the courts must, more and more, undertake a continuous revision and updating of the rules of private law—always subject to legislative revision and rejection, of course. Further, the courts must affirmatively recognize this to be their duty, rather than performing such function by subterfuge or else abdicating it.[45]

The judicial methodology and ideology required for the courts to meet these needs of today may well be furnished by the mixed jurisdictions, synthesized from the strongest values of judgecraft developed in the civil- and in the common-law traditions. Just as the common law constantly draws from the civil law for substantive and procedural concepts and techniques, and just as the civil law likewise may draw from the common law, so the mixed jurisdiction may contribute to as well as draw from both systems of legal thought and judicial method.

45 Leflar, "No Task for the Shortwinded," 54 JUDICATURE 366 (1971).

ABBREVIATIONS

Ind. L. J.	Indiana Law Journal
La.	Louisiana Reports (1900 to present)
La. Ann.	Louisiana Annual Reports (1846–1900)
La. App. Orl.	Louisiana Court of Appeal (Orleans)
La. B. J.	Louisiana Bar Journal
La. L. Rev.	Louisiana Law Review
Loyola L. Rev.	Loyola Law Review
Mart. (O.S.)	Martin's Reports (Old Series) [Louisiana reports, 1809–1823]
Rev. Jur. U.P.R.	Revista Juridica de la Universidad de Puerto Rico
So. 2d	Southern Reporter, second series
Tul. L. Rev.	Tulane Law Review

III

A Renaissance of the Civilian Tradition in Louisiana

Mack E. Barham
ASSOCIATE JUSTICE, SUPREME COURT OF LOUISIANA

A recently published coursebook[1] on Louisiana's civil-law system has prompted me to examine the resurgence of the civil-law tradition. I use the terms *civil-law tradition* and *civil-law system* advisedly with intent to convey two entirely different concepts.

John Henry Merryman[2] has defined a legal system as "an operating set of legal institutions, procedures and rules." He says that in this sense there is no such thing as a civil-law system, a common-law system, or a socialist-law system, for each sovereignty tends to deviate from its original or basic system. He defines a legal tradition as "a set of deeply rooted, historically conditioned attitudes about the role of law in the society and in the polity, about the proper organization and operation of a legal system, and about the way law is or should be made, applied, studied, perfected, and taught. . . . It puts the legal system into cultural perspective."

As used in this paper, *civil-law tradition* means that tradition of legal concepts and principles as generally applied today by a community of jurisdictions with a somewhat similar development and evolvement from the Twelve Tables of Rome and the work of Roman jurisconsults. It will refer to concepts of the nature and role of law, the methods of operation of a legal system, the manners of applying and perfecting the law which are most commonly accepted and practiced by the numerous civil-law systems. *Civil-law system* or *civilian system* as used here will be more nearly aligned with *civil-law jurisdiction*. It will mean the system of law

---

[1] YIANNOPOULOS, LOUISIANA CIVIL LAW SYSTEM (1971). A list of the abbreviations used in this chapter appears on page 68.
[2] MERRYMAN, THE CIVIL LAW TRADITION (1969).

employed in a particular jurisdiction that intentionally attempts to embody the civil-law tradition.

REAPPRAISAL OF "A REAPPRAISAL APPRAISED"

In 1937, in response to an article which contained the statement that "Louisiana is today a common law State,"[3] four eminent professors of law in a reappraisal of the civil-law system in Louisiana[4] concluded that Louisiana was then still "a civil law jurisdiction." We were then and are now a *civilian jurisdiction*, and had and have a *civilian system*. Again, however, a reappraisal will be made here to determine to what extent we did and do adhere to the *civil-law tradition* in Louisiana.

The law schools have played a dominant role in bringing lawyer, legislator, teacher, and judge back to the civilian tradition in Louisiana. Most lawyers, teachers, and jurists believe in retaining a strong civilian tradition. However, the necessity of earning a living by the practice of law, by teaching law students how to be winning advocates, and by making quick judicial decisions to keep up with an ever-increasing caseload has made it expedient for the lawyer, the teacher, and the judge to adopt methods and give answers which, if they do not detract from the civil-law tradition, at least do not support it.

In a consideration of only the role and function of the judiciary in the civil-law tradition, there are found in our jurisprudence deviations from that tradition which, if followed, would seem to require that lawyers, teachers, and judges not use a civilian approach. Under our code and through the historical civilian tradition, jurisprudence is not a major source of law, yet it has been and it remains such in reality. Perhaps to a greater degree than in nonmixed jurisdictions, the belief in jurisprudence as a primary source of law is embedded in the minds of many of the judiciary and the practicing bar of Louisiana. Though we may really believe that legislation is the primary source of law, we practice under the principle that jurisprudence is a major source of law. Lawyers may only perfunctorily examine legislative expression before they turn for final authority to the jurisprudence to resolve the legal question posed by their clients' cases. Often when the court asks the lawyer in argument to give

---

3 Ireland, "Louisiana's Legal System Reappraised," 11 TUL. L. REV. 585 (1937).
4 Daggett, Dainow, Hebert, and McMahon, "A Reappraisal Appraised: A Brief for the Civil Law of Louisiana," 12 TUL. L. REV. 12 (1937).

the authority for a point which he advocates, the court expects a case citation even where there is positive codal or statutory authority. As a result of the pressure under which we perform our various roles in our legal system, there has been a tendency to stray from strict civilian methods and concepts.

The teacher, the lawyer, and the judge vary in their understanding of their respective functions and roles in the civil-law system. Because of these differences a variety of deviations from the civil-law tradition in these spheres of influence caused the formation of a vicious circle of departure. The faculties of the law schools may feel compelled to emphasize cases as a means of fulfilling the students' immediate need to pass the bar examination (designed by the lawyer), and to become successful practitioners before the courts. Then these attorneys, practicing in our courts, cite the opinions of the courts as the primary authority of law in their legal arguments. It is immaterial whether the courts actually require or have merely learned to expect the citation of decisions as a primary source of law, for their opinions do in fact often hinge upon the holdings in particular cases. These decisions are then studied in the law schools in order to prepare their graduates to respond with what courts' opinions indicate is decisive of litigation. This circle can be broken at any one point, but if we are to begin a return to a true civilian concept, it must be obliterated. Fortunately, its destruction has already begun, and this beginning must be attributed to the law schools.

THE ACADEMICIANS: WELLSPRING OF THE RENAISSANCE

The renaissance of Louisiana as a civil-law jurisdiction practicing in the civilian tradition has come about through a number of factors. The increasing enrollment of students in our law schools required able administrators to assemble larger faculties. They have retained civilian scholars with national reputations, but also they have carefully enlarged the faculties to include professors with broad comparative and civil-law backgrounds. Faculty members new and old have produced a growing library on the Louisiana civil-law system. Our law reviews have been expanded and, under the supervision of able faculty members, revitalized. They furnish authoritative and learned writings in every field of civilian law and are a primary source of doctrine in Louisiana.

In France and in most European jurisdictions, doctrine is a tremendous force in shaping the legislative expression as well as the judicial application of the law. Until recently, Louisiana had little doctrine available in the English language, and the scarcity of French translations for lawyer, legislator, and judge deprived Louisiana of a most necessary tool in a legal system following the civilian tradition. For example, in France doctrinal criticism often was and is more impressive for future legislation and judicial interpretation than the brief statements in the decisions by the courts.[5] One of the most helpful continuing doctrinal sources in Louisiana is the annual symposium on the work of the appellate courts by the faculty of the Louisiana State University Law School through the *Louisiana Law Review*. Tulane University School of Law proposes, in addition to its law review, periodic publications of research papers limited to examination of specific areas of the civil law.

A powerful force which tends to keep Louisiana a civil-law system in the best of the civil-law tradition is the Louisiana State Law Institute. It was created by legislative act in 1938[6] and has in numerous ways contributed to our return to the civilian tradition. The Law Institute (under charge from the legislature) produced the *projet* for our Criminal Code in 1942, our Revised Statutes of 1950, and the Code of Civil Procedure in 1960 with the corresponding revisions in the civil code necessarily accompanying it. Under legislative mandate and authority, it is constantly revising and attempting to update all of the laws of the state. The Law Institute has also made available what now amounts to a considerable library of translations of a number of French authorities.[7]

[5] DAVID and DEVRIES, THE FRENCH LEGAL SYSTEM: AN INTRODUCTION TO CIVIL LAW SYSTEMS 122–26 (1958); MERRYMAN, THE CIVIL LAW TRADITION 59–64 (1969).

[6] La. Acts 1938, No. 166. The Louisiana State Law Institute was conceived in 1932 within the faculty of the Louisiana State University Law School. A prospectus was drafted in 1933, but it was not organized until 1938 when the board of supervisors of Louisiana State University and the legislature chartered it in accordance with that prospectus as an "official advisory law revision commission, law reform agency and legal research agency of the state of Louisiana." John H. Tucker, Jr., who was its first and longtime president, along with Paul M. Hebert, dean of the law school, prepared the legislation. J. Denson Smith was and continues to be its first director. See Smith, *Historical Sketch of the Louisiana State Law Institute*, 245 La. 124 (1963).

[7] PLANIOL, CIVIL LAW TREATISE (La. St. L. Inst. transl. 1959); GÉNY, METHOD OF INTERPRETATION AND SOURCES OF PRIVATE POSITIVE LAW (La. St. L. Inst. transl. 1963); CIVIL LAW TRANSLATIONS (La. St. L. Inst. transl. 1965–72, 5 vols: Vols. 1–4 AUBRY & RAU, COURS DE DROIT CIVIL FRANÇAIS: OBLIGATIONS; PROPERTY; TESTAMENTARY SUCCESSIONS AND GRATUITOUS DISPOSITIONS; INTE-

The Institute of Civil Law Studies [8] at Louisiana State University also made a considerable contribution. It has conducted annually an in-depth seminar concentrating on the function of a judge in a civil-law jurisdiction in the best of the civilian tradition. The Louisiana State Law Institute and the Institute of Civil Law Studies have sponsored a number of civil-law treatises from our own doctrinal writers,[9] and others are in preparation. The de la Vergne Manuscript,[10] Batiza's Sources of the 1808 Civil Code,[11] and the scholastic debate [12] which followed their publication stimulated historical research into the various systems as our doctrinal writers sought for the sources of our code. Since the civilian judiciary is influenced by academicians far more than are the jurists in common-law systems, the Louisiana courts have responded to these new doctrinal sources. It is the resurgence of the civilian tradition, as expressed by the courts through their opinions under provocation by academic influence, that brings new hope for a stronger civilian tradition in our legal system.

One part of the law schools' response which has contributed to the resurgence of the civilian tradition in Louisiana has been the inclusion in the first-year curriculum of a course on introduction to the civil law.[13]

THE JUDICIAL ROLE AS A MEASURE OF THE CIVILIAN TRADITION

Legal scholars, jurists, and philosophers over the centuries have tried to define the civilian tradition. Each jurisdiction which attempts to follow

---

STATE SUCCESSIONS; VOL. 5 BAUDRY-LACANTINERIE & TISSIER, AUBRY & RAU, CARBONNIER, PRESCRIPTION).

8 The Institute of Civil Law Studies was founded in 1967 by a separate charter issued by the board of supervisors of Louisiana State University to function within the framework of the School of Law with Joseph Dainow as director. Its purposes are to encourage and facilitate research and publication in the areas of civil law and comparative law. It also sponsors seminars, symposia, and lecture programs in these fields of study.

9 YIANNOPOULOS, CIVIL LAW OF PROPERTY (1967); YIANNOPOULOS, PERSONAL SERVITUDES (1968); LITVINOFF, OBLIGATIONS: BOOK 1 (1969).

10 L. MOREAU LISLET'S copy of A DIGEST OF THE CIVIL LAWS NOW IN FORCE IN THE TERRITORY OF ORLEANS 1808 (de la Vergue Vol. 1968). See Dainow, "Moreau-Lislet's Notes on Sources of Louisiana Civil Code of 1808," 19 LA. L. REV. 43 (1958).

11 Batiza, "The Louisiana Civil Code of 1808: Its Actual Sources and Present Relevance," 46 TUL. L. REV. 4 (1971).

12 Pascal, "Sources of the Digest of 1808: A Reply to Professor Batiza," 46 TUL. L. REV. 603 (1972); Sweeney, "Tournament of Scholars over the Sources of the Civil Code of 1808," 46 TUL. L. REV. 585 (1972).

13 YIANNOPOULOS, LOUISIANA CIVIL LAW SYSTEM (1971); LITVINOFF AND TÊTE, LOUISIANA LEGAL TRANSACTIONS: THE CIVIL LAW OF JURIDICAL ACTS (1969).

the civilian tradition will have its own civil-law system with varying deviations from the numerous other systems throughout the world. Civil-law tradition is one of the oldest of all legal traditions and encompasses more national jurisdictions than any other. It has been more influential in the development of modern legal systems, and it has had more impact upon the other traditions than they have had upon it. We often oversimplify in making a definitive statement of what constitutes the civil-law tradition. Civil law is not necessarily codified law, for France was a civil-law jurisdiction without code before 1804, as were Germany before 1900 and Greece as late as 1946. Neither can we dismiss the common law with an oversimplified definition that it is jurisprudential law under the doctrine of *stare decisis*.

Civil-law tradition can best be examined comparatively with other legal traditions when we look to the natures and roles of the judicial and legislative processes. Even though there is not a total uniformity in the respective roles assigned to these branches of government in countries which follow the civil law, all civil-law systems have much in common which holds them together in a single tradition. Common to all civil-law systems is the fundamental tenet that legislative expression is the primary source of law, and common to all civil-law systems now is the comprehensive written and integrated basic text of that legislative expression. While the role, the authority, the province, and the power of the judiciary may appear on the surface to be the same in the many systems, in practice there is considerable variation.[14] This variation in the role and function of the judiciary appears in the decision-making process in cases where the written law is ambiguous or obsolete or where there is no written law.

Common-law scholars often depict the role of the judiciary in a civilian jurisdiction as mechanical,[15] but that opinion is based largely on the folklore and the fiction [16] which mask the actual role of the judiciary as played

---

14 Dainow, "The Method of Legal Development through Judicial Interpretation in Louisiana and Puerto Rico," 22 REV. JUR. U.P.R. 108 (1952); Loussouarn, "The Relative Importance of Legislation, Custom, Doctrine, and Precedent in French Law," 18 LA. L. REV. 235 (1958); Tate, "Techniques of Judicial Interpretation in Louisiana," 22 LA. L. REV. 727 (1962); Tate, "The Law-Making Function of the Judge," 28 LA. L. REV. 211 (1968).
15 Von Mehren, "The Judicial Process in the United States and in France—A Comparative Study," 22 REV. JUR. U.P.R. 235 (1953).
16 MERRYMAN, THE CIVIL LAW TRADITION 86 (1969); GÉNY, METHOD OF INTERPRETATION AND SOURCES OF PRIVATE POSITIVE LAW (La. St. L. Inst. transl. 1963).

in the many civil-law systems. Here in Louisiana, for example, the judge, the lawyer, and the layman all like to believe that a judge makes a judicial determination simply by applying "the law" which the legislator has enacted to the case before him. Actually, there is no invariable single judicial process which assures that a judge will be led not only to "the law" but also to a logical and reasonable application of that legislative expression to the facts and circumstances of the case he must decide. While many may wish that the judicial process was merely mechanical and functional, such a process would often require the judge to reach unconscionably unjust results.

The concept of the judge's role as purely mechanical or functional is largely formed through both lawyers' and laymen's anxiety for certainty under the law. Certainty is a quality which all men of the law assign as a primary requirement of the law. However, that certainty in the law which would be exacted by some would deprive the courts of the power to temper the harshness of the rule of law in a particular case and would permit prior erroneous expressions to prevail over major legislative policy considerations. Moreover, such certainty would prevent the primary attainment desired under the law, justice through reason. A purely mechanistic role for the judiciary would, in fact obviate the need for a judiciary, so that the sovereignty could function with only a legislator to express the law and an enforcer to put the law into effect.

François Gény (1861–1959), "an unquestioned member of the club of legal classics," [17] has been one of the most influential writers in determining the function and role of the judge in modern civil-law systems. Gény's critics have given many labels to his legal philosophy; perhaps the most appropriate philosophical category of his proposed approach concerning methodology in the judicial function is *eclectic* as suggested by Jaro Mayda, one of his translators and admirers, although this term is meant by some critics to be denigrating and derogatory.[18] Eclecticism is defined as selecting or choosing from various sources, not following any one system but selecting and using the best elements of all systems. In order to describe and to propose the proper judicial role or function in the best civilian tradition, Gény brings to the civil-law tradition the best

17 GÉNY, METHOD OF INTERPRETATION AND SOURCES OF PRIVATE POSITIVE LAW, critical introduction by Jaro Mayda, at v.
18 Gény was apparently considered by many of his contemporaries to be conservative or at least positioned in the middle of the road.

approaches of all of the systems that have used the civil law. Gény offers the "free scientific approach" as a replacement for the often fictional functional approach.

All of us who act as judges do so with some preconceived idea of the judicial function, with some deeply ingrained ideas of the role of the judge. With these preconceptions we turn out a work-product which we hope fits within the framework of what we believe is our constitutional and legal directive in a government organized for strict separation of powers. However, scrutiny through objective research will reveal that what we do is not always what we say or think we do. François Gény's greatest contribution is that he forces the modern jurist to look beyond the *fiction*, the *facade*, of the role of the judge.

FUNCTIONS OF A CIVILIAN JUDGE

In many civilian jurisdictions the sources of law available to the judge are established through the historical development of custom. Few codes in other civil-law systems contain the numerous definitions which are to be found in the Louisiana Civil Code. But perhaps it was fortunate that our code was express in defining the role of the court and the sources of law; for the members of the judiciary who attempted to interpret and apply the code, especially in the early years, were often trained at common law and acted without a historical heritage of the civil-law customs. Perhaps we in Louisiana now have such a heritage that our code would be better without the definitions, for the express words of the code assigning the sources of law have often been cause for dispute in our jurisprudence.[19]

The first chapter of our civil code is "Of Law" and contains only three articles. Article 1 provides that "Law is a solemn expression of legislative will," and Article 3 provides: "Customs result from a long series of actions constantly repeated, which have by such repetition, and by uninterrupted acquiescence, acquired the force of a tacit and common consent." Under the chapter "Of the Application and Construction of Laws," we find Article 13, which provides: "When a law is clear and free from all am-

---

19 Ellis v. Prevost, 13 La. 230 (1839); Dainow, "The Method of Legal Development through Judicial Interpretation in Louisiana and Puerto Rico," 22 REV. JUR. U.P.R. 108 (1953); for discussion of the statement that codes should avoid definitions, see Morrison, "The Need for a Revision of the Louisiana Civil Code," 11 TUL. L. REV. 213 (1937).

biguity, the letter of it is not to be disregarded, under the pretext of pursuing its spirit." And Article 21, also in that chapter, reads: "In all civil matters, *where there is no express law*, the judge is bound to proceed and decide according to equity. To decide equitably, an appeal is to be made to natural law and reason, or received usages, where positive law is silent."[20] (Emphasis here and elsewhere has been supplied.) These articles have no counterparts in the Code Napoleon.

Our code, then, has established in express language the primary source of law—legislative expression; the secondary source of law—custom; and even the tertiary source of law—natural law and reason or received usages. It is important to note the code's recognition that law is not always the legislative expression.[21]

While the French did not define the sources of law, their mandate to the judges under Code Civil Article 4 recognizes the need for sources other than the legislative written expression. That article states: "Judges who refuse to give a decision under pretext of silence, obscurity or inadequacy of legislation may be proceeded against as guilty of denial of justice." Just as Gény found many years after the enactment of the French code, that the legislative will or even intent was not always ascertainable, Locré[22] reached that same conclusion at the very time of the code's adoption. As Locré comments,[23] before the adoption of the code the French courts acted under a strict interpretation of an order of the Constitutional Assembly and concluded that they were forbidden to act when the legislation was not clear and express. Accordingly, they went to the legislature when they believed there was need for interpretation or new legis-

20 YIANNOPOULOS, LOUISIANA CIVIL LAW SYSTEM § § 34, 38 (1971); see also Dainow, "The Method of Legal Development through Judicial Interpretation in Louisiana and Puerto Rico," 22 REV. JUR. U.P.R. 108 (1953).

21 The original French version of Article 1 reads: "La loi est une déclaration solennelle de la volonté législative, sur un objet général et de régime intérieur." The pertinent part of the article, retained in our present code, reads in English: "Law is a solemn expression of legislative will." Most translators attribute to the French word *loi* the meaning *legislation*, and translate *droit* to encompass the law in all its aspects. Following the French version in our earlier codes Professor Yiannopoulos says that Article 1 ought to be translated "*Legislation* is a formal expression of legislative will." If this be so, that expression alone leaves room for sources of law other than legislation. A. YIANNOPOULOS, LOUISIANA CIVIL LAW SYSTEM § 32 (1971).

22 LOCRÉ, ESPRIT DU CODE NAPOLÉON (1805).

23 Paraphrasing an unpublished translation of a portion of LOCRÉ, ESPRIT DU CODE NAPOLÉON (1805) by Dean Joseph M. Sweeney of the Tulane University School of Law.

lation. Article 4 of the French code was designed to reinforce the judiciary's obligation to decide the specific litigation before it. Locré says: "The power to decide cases, even when the law is silent, is essential to the function of the courts.... If the nature of things could be so ordered as to write in advance in the text of the legislation a formal resolution of all conceivable disputes, judges would no longer be needed; the decisions being ready-made, there would no longer be need of persons to apply the law, but only of persons to enforce it."[24]

Let us examine and compare our code provisions defining sources of law with the actualities and practicalities of the judicial application of the law in Louisiana. As we do so, perhaps we will tear away the folklore and fiction which surround the role of the judge in Louisiana, and we may find that these are the same fictions behind which Gény urges us to look in examining the actual role of the jurist in the civil-law tradition.

24 Further quoting from Dean Sweeney's translation of Locré:
Indeed, legislation deals with the totality of men; considers men in the mass, never as individuals; it must not meddle with particular facts or with lawsuits which divide citizens. Were it otherwise, it would be necessary to make new laws daily; their multitude would destroy their dignity and endanger their observance. The judge would be without function, and the legislator, enmeshed in details, would soon be no more than a judge. Private interests would besiege the legislative power; they would divert it, at every moment, from the general welfare of the society.

There is a science for legislators, as there is one for judges; and the one does not resemble the other. The science of the legislator consists in finding, for each matter, the rules most favorable to the common good; the science of the judge is to put these principles into operation, to ramify them, to extend them, through wise and reasoned application, to private issues; to study the spirit of the law when its letter would be deadly; and not to expose himself to the risk of being in turn slave and rebel, and disobeying through servility.

The legislator must watch the case law; he may be enlightened by it, and he may, on the other hand, correct it; but there must be a case law. With the immensity of diverse issues which make up civil litigaton, and of which the decision requires, in the majority of cases, less the applicaton of a specific provision than the combining of several provisions which lead to the decision instead of providing it, one can no more do without case law than without legislation. Now, it is to case law that the Civil Code leaves the rare and unusual situations which cannot be included in a scheme of rational legislation, the details, too varied and debatable, which must not preoccupy the legislator, and all subjects which it would be useless to try foreseeing or which hasty foreseeing could not define without danger. As time goes on it is for experience to supply the gaps which the Civil Code leaves. The codes of a people *make themselves with time;* but properly speaking, *one does not make them.*

In enacting laws for every unforeseen issue, we would soon overwhelm our legislation with a prodigious quantity of laws which would destroy its unity and serve to shackle the administration of justice.

Louisiana judges are expressly mandated by the code to decide the litigation before them, and are given three sources of law for use in the decisional processes. The civil-law tradition implements these sources through doctrine and *jurisprudence constante*. In removing some of the fiction which surrounds the judicial process we might begin by accepting the fact that there is no express *legislative will* in any legislation which will be dispositive of *every* case. Since there are sources of law other than legislative expression, let us also dispose of the fiction that judges do not make law.

Codes in the civilian tradition are general statements of the law, statements of broad policy, statements of direction, statements of law which are meant to have a long continuity of existence. In some respects more similar to constitutions than to statutory enactments, civil codes are meant to provide a basic system of law which can acquire new life when necessary in changing times and circumstances. Codes in civilian jurisdictions do not seek to solve particular legal problems or to speak upon precise legal issues.

Louisiana's first civil code began as an attempt to compile an existing system of law. The original mandate to the drafters of the 1808 Civil Code was for a compilation of the Spanish laws in effect in Louisiana. However, our code of 1808 in end result had as its principal source the Code Napoleon or its *Projet* and the French doctrinal writers, with the Spanish influence persisting only in some particular areas. The Civil Code of 1825 expressly provided in Article 3521 that all prior laws in existence in Louisiana were repealed, "and that they shall not be invoked as laws, even under the pretense that their provisions are not contrary or repugnant to those of this Code." Two years later the Louisiana Supreme Court in *Flower v. Griffin*[25] attempted to continue in effect the provisions of the old code. Louisiana Act No. 83 of 1828 (§ 25) immediately following that decision, provided for the abrogation of "all the civil laws which were in force before the promulgation of the civil code lately promulgated." Our code, then, is actually a general statement of an original body of civil law for Louisiana.[26]

Civil codes differ drastically from the modern codes in common-law

25 6 Mart. (N. S.) 89 (La. 1827).
26 YIANNOPOULOS, LOUISIANA CIVIL LAW SYSTEM Chap. 5, pp. 53–70 (1971); Tucker, "Source Books of Louisiana Law," 6 TUL. L. REV. 280 (1932); Tucker, "Source Books of Louisiana Law," 7 TUL. L. REV. 82 (1932).

jurisdictions. The codes of the common-law states are merely compilations of case law or statutes, similar to our collection of statutory laws in the Louisiana Revised Statutes of 1950. Although statutory law is specific as compared to the statement of law in the civilian codes, the former, though more explicit, is still not designed to give express answers to all future litigation, for when the legislature enacts a statute, it usually is seeking to cure a specific evil and therefore narrowly views the future consequences of the enactment. Its attention will not be directed at other aspects of the evil or the natural consequences which must flow from the corrective process. Therefore under both the code and the statutes there will be many *lacunae* in the law which our civil code directs the judge to fill from another source.

It is in the filling of the gaps in the law that the judge most frequently plays the role of lawmaker. The method for supplying the law in such a situation will vary according to the problem presented. Perhaps the gap can be filled by use of custom in its historical meaning, but custom under this narrow definition is not applicable in modern society as frequently as it was when our code was adopted. Natural law, reason, and received usages as extensions of custom are more easily resorted to. Jurisprudence which has become accepted through long use and which is not contrary to express law, along with doctrine, also offers assistance. Basically, when the law is silent, the judge is called upon to reason how a legislative body would express itself upon the issue. Induction, deduction, analogy, exegesis, empirical logic, historical research, functional examination, free scientific research, and reasoning processes of many nomenclatures may be called upon singly or in combination according to the problem-solving needs for filling the void.

Another fiction which must be dispelled is that when the expression of the legislature is ambiguous, imprecise, or unclear, the judiciary can easily find the meaning of that expression by determining the legislative intent. Here the judge must look to the intent of the lawmakers who, at a time in the past, enacted the expression of law decisive of the issue to be adjudicated. The legislative intent may be ascertained by considering the precise expression in the context of the whole cloth of the law. It may be ascertained by an examination of laws *in pari materia*. It may be ascertained by analogy with some other expression upon the subject of the law. But many legal issues presented for adjudication today arise out of situations which could not have been encompassed within the most extreme fantasies and dreams of the legislators who enacted the laws perhaps a century before. Here is presented the serious problem of ascertaining legislative intent when no intent could have existed regarding the issue before the court. The supplying of this intent results in lawmaking by the court.[27] Supplying legislative intent becomes more difficult in modern society, for changes in economic, technological, and social conditions come about rapidly now instead of slowly over the years as in the past.

Rapidity of change also makes more onerous the judge's role in exercising the judicial function where a law has become so obsolete that a literal application of the written expression would produce a ridiculous result. The changing of constitutional interpretation by the United States Supreme Court also lays new burdens upon our state judiciary when civil laws regarded as valid for many years are suddenly held to be unconstitutional. Because the legislature is not constantly in session and because it often abdicates its responsibility to revise and update the laws, our courts are sometimes required to change positive expressions from the state legislature and supplement them with judicial expressions so as to harmonize our law with the United States Supreme Court decisions.

One other aspect of the judicial function in Louisiana should be examined, to lay guidelines for determining whether the judiciary is acting in a civilian tradition. Louisiana, like Quebec, Puerto Rico, and a few other civil-law jurisdictions, is enmeshed in a national system which follows another legal tradition. This situation may make it difficult for our courts to adhere to the civilian tradition, but at the same time we should recognize the very enviable position we occupy for the development and evolving of the best possible system of civil law. Though adhering to the civil-law tradition, our courts have ready access without any language barrier to a voluminous source of comparative law, the study of which can enrich our own law when the courts are unable to find express legislative will.

In the best of the civilian tradition our courts are required to look to our sister jurisdictions for custom, natural law, reason, and received usages. While we in Louisiana remain civilian in legal concept and in system, because of national ties and common interests we are also a people of one nation who often share common customs, a common understanding of

27 Levi, An Introduction to Legal Reasoning 19–23 (1949).

what the natural law should be, even a common approach to legal solutions through logic and reason. Because in a civilian tradition the source of law, second only to legislative will, is custom, our courts will of necessity resort to appraisals of customs without our state boundaries and within our national borders because we are a part of a larger community of common customs in many areas of law. As adherents of the civilian tradition, we initially examine the sources in our own system and our own law for enlightenment, but we must also make our system live in the context of its national existence. We benefit from this approach, and our search for and use of the law and the jurisprudence of common-law states for these purposes need not detract from, taint, or limit our search for good civilian methods in the best of its tradition.

AN INDEX OF THE RENAISSANCE

Are there concrete examples that there is a resurgence of the civilian tradition in Louisiana? Since the academicians who appraised our civil-law system in 1937 said that the ability of our courts to discard and overrule jurisprudence was an index for determining whether we were in fact a civil-law jurisdiction, a comparison of the situation they found in existence then and the present situation should be helpful.

While the overruling of case law is not, in and of itself, determinative of a civil-law approach by the courts, the recognition by the courts that jurisprudential law is not a binding source of law is necessary in a true civilian system. These appraisers[28] in 1937 found that seventy-six cases had been overruled in the previous twenty-five years. A cursory examination of the jurisprudence of the last five years shows that more than twenty-five cases have been expressly overruled and an incalculable number have been impliedly overruled.[29] Perhaps more important than the

28 Daggett, Dainow, Hebert, and McMahon, "A Reappraisal Appraised: A Brief for the Civil Law of Louisiana," 12 TUL. L. REV. 12 (1937).
29 A few examples will suffice to show the trend. In Blanchard v. Ogima, 253 La. 34, 215 So. 2d 902 (1968), the reasoning and language of a number of cases were impliedly overruled assigning a master's liability for the delicts of his servants, and it would appear that the rationale of a number of cases assigning liability of a husband for the delicts of the wife on a community errand will have to be overruled. See Comment, 33 LA. L. REV. 110 (1972). Bowen v. Doyal, 259 La. 839, 253 So. 2d 200 (1971), overruled two very recent supreme court cases. State v. Morales, 256 La. 940, 240 So. 2d 714 (1970), overruled one case. American Creosote Company v. Springer, 257 La. 116, 241 So. 2d 510 (1970), overruled two cases in Louisiana jurisprudence on one

overruling of individual cases by name is the fact that much of the present jurisprudence, by the very enunciation of the principles upon which the results rest, has modified, extended, or discarded the reasoning of prior jurisprudence. For example, *Laird v. Travelers Insurance Company*[30] and *Pierre v. Allstate Insurance Company*,[31] which are expansions of *Dixie Drive It Yourself System v. American Beverage Company*,[32] strike down the former defense of passive negligence, necessarily overruling numerous decisions on this issue. Moreover, they constitute the evolution of a new causation approach using cause-in-fact and duty-risk rather than proximate cause. A similar development may be observed in *Hill v. Lundin & Associates, Inc.*[33]

Langlois v. Allied Chemical Corporation[34] sets forth a new basis for assigning liability for damages from ultrahazardous activities. The application of other concepts involved in delictual responsibility such as last

---

point and four cases on another point. In State v. Ray, 259 La. 105, 249 So. 2d 540 (1971), the Louisiana Supreme Court overruled five cases, the latest of which was a 1967 decision. Moreover, in that case we used a vehicle seldom if ever used in Louisiana—the prospective overruling of jurisprudence, or what is commonly called the "Sunburst" approach. In Rockholt v. Keaty, 256 La. 629, 237 So. 2d 663 (1970), this court effectively overruled a decision by eliminating all the language and rationale of that decision not absolutely required for the facts presented there. Langlois v. Allied Chemical Corporation, 258 La. 1067, 249 So. 2d 133 (1971), without specific mention overruled the rationale of a number of cases upon two points of law discussed there. For some effects of Langlois, see the concurrence by the writer and Justice Tate in the denial of writs in Theriot v. Transit Casualty Company, 263 La. 106, 267 So. 2d 211 (1972). In a number of areas the language and rationale of previous decisions have been effectively discarded without specific overruling. In various aspects of workmen's compensation law, the court has effectively overruled prior jurisprudence. Bertrand v. Coal Operators Casualty Company, 253 La. 1115, 221 So. 2d 816 (1969), by necessary implication, overruled one supreme court decision and pointedly overruled a court of appeal case and a line of jurisprudence which had narrowly defined the accidental aggravation of a preexisting disease. McDermott v. Funel, 258 La. 657, 247 So. 2d 567 (1971), overruled three cases. United States Fidelity and Guaranty Co. v. Green, 252 La. 227, 210 So. 2d 328 (1968), expressly overruled three supreme court cases and six appellate decisions. State v. Sandoz, 258 La. 297, 246 So. 2d 21 (1971), overruled four cases. See also Heyse v. Fidelity & Casualty Co. of New York, 255 La. 127, 229 So. 2d 724 (1969).
30 263 La. 199, 267 So. 2d 714 (1972).
31 257 La. 471, 242 So. 2d 821 (1971).
32 242 La. 471, 137 So. 2d 298 (1962).
33 260 La. 542, 256 So. 2d 620 (1972).
34 258 La. 1067, 249 So. 2d 133 (1971).

clear chance and *res ipsa loquitur*, the interpretation of the Workmen's Compensation Act, and the jurisprudence determining the validity of testaments are just a few of the areas in which the court has shown its willingness to find new language and new rationale in applying statutory and codal law. A fuller treatment of this point in a particular situation is set out in connection with the case of *Blanchard v. Ogima*,[35] discussed below.

Furthermore, the written opinion reflects only a small part of the conceptual aspect of a jurist's reasoning process and the result reached in a particular case. The work, the research, and the intellectual battle consume far more of the judge's time than the reduction of all this to a written opinion. Like an iceberg, perhaps only one ninth of the mass—the real technique, method, legal concepts, and rationale—will be visible. Therefore one's own writings can be examined with a better knowledge (although it be subjective) of the total thought process which went into the opinions. The examples used here propose only to show an evolution of the juristic approach of one man trying to employ the civilian tradition as a judge in a civilian system within a nation adhering to a different system of law.

EVOLUTION OF A JURIST SEEKING THE CIVILIAN TRADITION

A. *Discarding Obsolescence.* Shortly after coming to the supreme court in 1968, I was the author of the majority opinion in *Blanchard v. Ogima*.[36] Here, although there was express language to the contrary in a particular provision of the code, we allowed a long and undeviating line of jurisprudence to remain in effect which disregarded that specific codal provision. It is the reasoning (why the express language in the code was not followed) which must be examined to see whether the opinion is in the civilian tradition.

Civil Code Article 2320 makes masters liable for their servants' delicts only when the masters "might have prevented the act which caused the damage, and have not done it." Although this provision was originally followed strictly in Louisiana, a long line of cases developed which dis-

35 253 La. 34, 215 So. 2d 902 (1968).
36 *Id.*

regarded this provision and attached strict vicarious liability to masters for their servants' delicts. The historical comparative analysis of the common-law and civil-law approaches in this field showed a parallel development with almost simultaneous extensions and limitations of responsibility in each system. Considering the jurisprudential departure in light of the development of vicarious liability in our common-law states, we were impressed that both our system and the system in the other states simultaneously used the same concept in approaching the socioeconomic problem of liability of a master for a servant in commerce. Examining the problem in the light of present-day commercial economic needs, I wrote for the majority: "Louisiana jurisprudence has not interpreted this restriction literally, and the demands of modern commerce and the needs of society would not permit such a stringent and severe limitation of the liability of the master for his servant. However, by inquiring into the overall relationship of the parties and the element of control, our jurisprudence has established reasonable definitions and limitations of vicarious liability to replace the literal codal restriction which has fallen into desuetude." We noted that the literal pronouncement of the code was not strictly one of vicarious liability, for it imposed liability only upon the negligent master, that is, one who by omitting to act was at fault. However, we concluded, after appraisal of the jurisprudence as a source deviation, and with a proper reconsideration of legislative purpose under prevailing economic realities, that the jurisprudential declaration was a logical response to present-day exigencies for fixing vicarious liability upon the master without regard to his own fault. In modern commerce the master's business practices have built-in extra charges for his services and products sufficient to cover economic recompense to those who are harmed by his servants in the exercise of his business pursuits for his financial advantage. Therefore the vicarious responsibility of the master for the damage caused by his servants' delicts in the pursuit of the master's economic interests, is imposed to give an economic source for recompense to innocent third parties.

Important also in *Ogima* is the fact that the court reaffirmed that this vicarious responsibility arose from a master-servant relationship under Civil Code Article 2320, and not from a principal-agent relationship under Civil Code Article 3000 treating of mandate in Louisiana. In this particular area the court could very well have followed through with an express overruling of a number of cases which in their reasoning and language used mandate terms rather than master-servant terms to impose liability under Civil Code Article 2320.[37]

B. *Returning to the Primary Source.* For purposes of a comparison we must remember that in *Blanchard v. Ogima* the court did not overrule prior jurisprudence which had deviated from the strict language of the code. Yet in *Carter v. Moore*[38] I wrote a concurring opinion which stated that three cases involving a so-called rule of property should be overruled. At first glance this would seem to be inconsistent with the position taken in *Blanchard v. Ogima*, but a careful reading of the *Carter* concurrence and the *Blanchard* opinion will show that there is no real divergence in the views expressed, for the result obtained in one and the result sought in the other are both founded on civilian approaches which are fitted to the problem-solving required in the particular cases.

I believe the concurrence in *Carter* to be my best approach to good civilian methodology in opinion-writing. It also reflects my view of the jurist's role as well as the role of jurisprudence in a civilian system. First examining the code articles pertinent to the issue raised there, next surveying the history of the evolution of the statutory law and the jurisprudence which also concerned the problem, then examining Louisiana doctrinal writings upon the subject, the concurrence concluded that three Louisiana Supreme Court cases—*Realty Operators v. State Mineral Board*,[39] *Humble Oil & Refining Company v. State Mineral Board*,[40] and *California Company v. Price*[41]—had departed from the code law and from other jurisprudence correctly interpreting that law and should be overruled.

Having found these three cases to be inversely pyramided,[42] I wrote:

---

37 See Blanchard v. Ogima, 253 La. 34, 215 So. 2d 902 (1968); Daggett, Dainow, Hebert, and McMahon, "A Reappraisal Appraised: A Brief for the Civil Law of Louisiana," 12 TUL. L. REV. 12 (1937); Comment, 33 LA. L. REV. 110 (1972).
38 258 La. 921, 248 So. 2d 813 (1971).
39 202 La. 398, 12 So. 2d 198 (1943).
40 223 La. 47, 64 So. 2d 839 (1953).
41 225 La. 706, 74 So. 2d 1 (1954).
42 "That jurisprudence begins with dicta, continues without resort to law, and ends in what it calls an 'unbroken line of jurisprudence'."

Finally, in my view the concept of this so-called rule of property has little or no validity in this civilian jurisdiction. That concept stems from the theory of stare decisis, is founded entirely upon common law, and finds no basis in our Constitution, in our Civil Code, or in our statutory law. A study of the jurisprudence will show that the rule has been used in order to obtain a result in some cases but just as quickly discarded in other cases. I favor stability of law, of course, and constancy of jurisprudence. Here, however, the reversal of the *Price, Humble,* and *Realty Operators* cases would restore the constancy of the jurisprudence and reinstate the long-standing law and public policy of the state.[43]

That concurrence and Tate's concurrence on application for rehearing show our concern over the fact that the *Price, Humble,* and *Realty Operators* cases are contrary to a basic concept of public policy ingrained in our civil law as it was practiced in Louisiana even before the adoption of the code and particularly contrary to that public policy as expressly stated in the code.

The basic policy question is how and to what extent our state controls navigable waters. Our concept has always been that the bottoms of navigable waters are "public things" insusceptible of private ownership, that they belong to the state, and that the necessary control of navigable waters below the surface, at the surface, and above the surface was exercised by the state under that concept. My feeling was that mere statutory interpretation through a few cases could not destroy such a fundamental, necessary concept of our law; that those jurisprudential holdings were not only *contra legem* but also against public policy.

C. *Interpreting through Doctrine. Dickson v. Sandefur* [44] afforded the opportunity of making an in-depth study of the history of the source and evolution of our Louisiana Civil Code Article 518, beginning with an examination of the minutes of the Council of State which passed the *Projet* of the French Civil Code, the comments of the members of the Council who worked on the *Projet*, proceeding to such doctrinal writers as Demolombe, Toullier, Laurent, Daviel, Chardon, and Planiol, and to Louisiana doctrine. The opinion showed the error of the court of appeal in applying the common-law doctrine of avulsion, and resolved the issue under the express language of Civil Code Article 518. This case is an example of many appellate opinions which indicate the great impact

---

43 Carter v. Moore, 258 La. 921, 959, 248 So. 2d 813, 826 (1971).
44 259 La. 473, 250 So. 2d 708 (1971).

upon our courts of the new translations of doctrinal writings and our own doctrinal writings.[45] It is also one of many examples where common-law doctrine is discarded for the express law of our code.

D. *Overruling Jurisprudence Which Contravenes Express Law.* In *Pringle-Associated Mortgage Corp. v. Eanes*[46] the Louisiana Supreme Court reviewed an opinion of the court of appeal overruling an old supreme court case, *Tilly v. Bauman*.[47] I stated in dissent on original hearing:

> The majority opinion fails to give meaning to the unambiguous language in the Civil Code, is contrary to the civilian concept of subrogation by law, disregards a long line of jurisprudence and the Code which make privileges *stricti juris*, and particularly repudiates and contravenes the direct legislative expressions of R.S. 9:4801 and 4812. I am in total agreement with a statement quoted by the majority from Ziegler, supra: "After all, on this question, is not the Code itself enough?" . . .
> I find that the Civil Code, our jurisprudence (except for *Tilly v. Bauman*), and our statutory law are explicit—so explicit that *Tilly v. Bauman* should be overruled as being erroneous, eddying alone and apart out of the mainstream of our law.[48]

On rehearing, the supreme court overruled *Tilly v. Bauman* and reinstated the judgment of the court of appeal.[49]

E. *An Attempt at Eclecticism.* A dissent best discloses that this writer has felt the need not only to examine the role of a judge and the methodology to be used in a civilian system, but also to show the evolution of the writer's juridical approach to civil-law problem-solving. The case of *Tannehill v. Tannehill*[50] posed the question of whether sterility could form the basis of an action *en desaveu*. The dissent answered:

> Not only do I disagree with the result and with the historical interpretation given to Article 185 of our Civil Code, but I strongly take issue with the majority's method and technique of judicial interpretation. The use of exegetical approach in isolation does not discharge the judicial obligation when our court works to and through the Code. While exegesis is certainly helpful,

---

45 Dainow, "Planiol Citations by Louisiana Courts: 1959–1966," 27 LA. L. REV. 231 (1967); Dainow, "The Use of English Translation of Planiol by Louisiana Courts," 14 AM. J. COMP. L. 68 (1965).
46 254 La. 705, 226 So. 2d 502 (1969).
47 174 La. 71, 139 So. 762 (1932).
48 254 La. 705, 734, 226 So. 2d 502, 512–13 (1969).
49 254 La. 734, 226 So. 2d 513 (1969).
50 261 La. 933, 261 So. 2d 619 (1972).

often very enlightening, it can entomb the court and the law in the darkness of the past. The combination of the exegetical, the empirical, and the functional methods of interpretation is required in order that the law serve the people, that the law be a reflection of the people's understanding, desires, and needs. Moreover, the more comprehensive approach is required under the mandate of our Code itself. [Quoting Louisiana Civil Code Articles 18, 3, and 21, and Code Napoleon Article 4.][51]

After discussing Tate's "Techniques of Judicial Interpretation in Louisiana,"[52] the dissent concluded:

While we may not in Louisiana be permitted the free rein Gény calls for, we certainly can use the techniques of Gény and the French jurists to determine our law when it is doubtful in language and dubious in meaning. We are a civilian jurisdiction, and we should as a court follow that tradition. . . .

What change in policy is needed here to reach the result this dissent offers? What has been the policy of the state on disavowal for sterility? The courts have been silent. The Code is silent. A functional approach supports the policy I advocate. Comparative law analysis supports that policy. The issue before us must be decided, and it cannot be deferred to legislative counsel. Basing its determination not to fairly adjudicate the issue before it, solely upon an historical excursion into the past, the court has not complied with the spirit of the Code or the letter of the Code in discharging the judicial function.

As our Code says, the most important consideration is to determine the true meaning, reason, and spirit of a law. Surely the vast majority of the people—and this would be reflected in their legislative representatives—would find it almost unfathomable that the law would allow disavowal for impotence but not for sterility. Is this fine distinction valid? Does it serve any purpose? Is it the custom of the people as reflected in their mental processes? Is this distinction the public policy of this state? Does the public believe and understand that one condition justifies bastardy and the other does not?[53]

F. Evolution of a Broad Principle of Law. A recent series of cases which illustrate the evolution of legal interpretation in a single area of the law started with *Reymond v. State Department of Highways*.[54] This has been called a *cause célèbre* wherein the writer, as author of the majority opinion, stated that the basis for assigning responsibility for damage from hazardous or inherently dangerous activities was not to be found in the

---

51 Id. at 954, 261 So. 2d at 627.
52 22 LA. L. REV. 727 (1962).
53 261 La. 933, 956, 261 So. 2d 619, 628–29 (1972).
54 255 La. 425, 231 So. 2d 375 (1970).

property law of Civil Code Article 667.⁵⁵ That article creates a true predial servitude upon one estate in favor of an adjoining estate forbidding the "construction" or the "making of works" which damage the neighbor or deprive him of the enjoyment of his estate. The opinion specifically said we did not overrule the result obtained in the jurisprudence which had allowed recovery for damages from use of dangerous instrumentalities or man's engagement in inherently hazardous activities; we simply found Article 667 inapplicable.

Voluminous criticism of this opinion appeared in the *Louisiana Law Review*.⁵⁶ Some of the critics—justifiably, because they were unable to determine from the case except *in dictum* the future basis for hazardous activity recovery—were concerned for the holding and its consequential effects. It must be remembered that an opinion can resolve only the issue before the court and cannot expound upon all the situations that might arise as a consequence of the holding, as can be done in law-review commentaries. However, in cases after *Reymond* the writer has attempted to unfold more of the rationale for the holding there and to set forth the consequences of that holding. The principle of law which has finally evolved is now almost uniformly accepted by the academicians.

In *Robichaux v. Huppenbauer*⁵⁷ the majority partially enjoined as a nuisance certain methods of operating a stable. In a concurrence this

---

55 La. Civ. Code art. 667: Although a proprietor may do with his estate whatever he pleases, still he cannot make any work on it, which may deprive his neighbor of the liberty of enjoying his own, or which may be the cause of any damage to him.

  La. Civ. Code art. 668: Although one be not at liberty to make any work by which his neighbor's buildings may be damaged, yet every one has the liberty of doing on his own ground whatsoever he pleases, although it should occasion some inconvenience to his neighbor.

  Thus he who is not subject to any servitude originating from a particular agreement in that respect, may raise his house as high as he pleases, although by such elevation he should darken the lights of his neighbors's [sic] house, because this act occasions only an inconvenience, but not a real damage.

  La. Civ. Code art. 669: If the works or materials for any manufactory or other operation, cause an inconvenience to those in the same or in the neighboring houses, by diffusing smoke or nauseous smell, and there be no servitude established by which they are regulated, their sufferance must be determined by the rules of the police, or the customs of the place.

56 "The Work of the Louisiana Appellate Courts for the 1969–1970 Term—Property, Torts, Mineral Rights and Expropriation," 31 LA. L. REV. 196, 217, 231, 263, 282, 325, 239, 335 (1971).

57 258 La. 139, 245 So. 2d 385 (1971).

writer expounded upon a footnote in *Reymond* which stated that Article 669 was a vehicle for defining the limits of the *activities* of man in use of property as they affect his neighbors. I discussed the source, the omission in translation from French to English in our earlier texts, and the evolution of that article.[58] I found that under Article 669 we could, according to "the rules of the police, or the customs of the place," determine all of those activities of man which were insufferable inconveniences in vicinage requiring abatement or control.

Then in *Langlois v. Allied Chemical Corporation*,[59] the implication in *Reymond* and the concurring statement in *Robichaux v. Huppenbauer* came full circle to a final conclusion. Here, in a delictual action where all parties litigant agreed that the defendant was responsible for damage ensuing when a poisonous gas escaped from its plant, numerous theories and code articles were argued as a basis for responsibility in order to advance or to meet the special defense to liability. Writing for the majority, I stated: "Their [the parties'] dilemma is partially the result of inconsistence in jurisprudential assignment of a legal basis for allowing recovery for damages resulting from the dangerous and harmful activities and enterprises." [60] Our court then held that Article 2315 was the basis for assigning delictual damages when man is at fault. More important, however, we clearly and concisely held that "fault" in Article 2315 encompasses more than just negligence. We said: "Here we find that proof that the gas escaped is sufficient, and proof of lack of negligence and lack of imprudence will not exculpate the defendant. The defendant has injured this plaintiff by its fault as analogized from the conduct required under Civil Code Article 669 and others, and responsibility for the damage attaches to defendants under Article 2315." We held the plaintiff's cause of action delictual under Article 2315, and, "after a study of the law and customs, a balancing of claims and interests, a weighing of the risk and the gravity of harm, and a consideration of individual and societal rights and obligations," [61] we concluded that the defendant had carried on an activity for which it must respond in damages if the activity causes injury to another even though the defendant acts as prudently as possible

---

58 Art. 669, 1972 COMPILED EDITION OF THE CIVIL CODES OF LOUISIANA, in 16 LSA-C.C. 409 (1972).
59 258 La. 1067, 249 So. 2d 133 (1971).
60 Id. at 1073, 249 So. 2d at 136.
61 Id. at 1084, 249 So. 2d at 140.

in the conduct of the activity. We held that the fault concept of Article 2315 may be supplied by analogy from other code provisions or statutes which lay down rules of conduct under particular relationships.

In these cases Civil Code Article 667 was defined as a law of real property creating a predial servitude; and Article 669 was defined as a nonproperty rule [62] and as the source for determining the insufferable inconveniences and hazardous activities which the law would control for all in the neighborhood. However, apparently the value of a distinction between the two articles was not clearly set forth.

Finally in dissent in *Hilliard v. Shuff* [63] I tried to supply what I believed to be the cogent reasons for making the exacting distinction between Article 667 and Article 669 which had not previously been clearly stated in the jurisprudence. Hilliard posed the problem of whether to require abatement of a construction on property adjacent to the plaintiff's which the evidence established possessed high potential for causing serious damage. The majority relied on Article 669, treating the inadequate storage tank (which contained volatile fuels under high pressure) as a "nuisance." The majority found some evidence in the record that the plaintiff had not been able *in fact* to fully enjoy his estate. It gave only partial relief, remanding for the trial court to find what remedy could be afforded so the plaintiff could have full enjoyment of his estate. Undoubtedly there was high potential for damage from the fuel tank as constructed and used on the border of the plaintiff's property. I found nothing in the record to support a finding that the plaintiff had in fact been damaged, suffered an inconvenience, or been deprived of the use and enjoyment of his estate, but I reasoned that I did not need to. I would, even in the absence of such findings, have ordered the removal of the offending tank or at least the abatement of its present use. The authority for my conclusion was the property rule of Article 667: "Although a proprietor may do with his estate whatever he pleases, still he can not *make any work* on it, which *may* deprive his neighbor of the liberty of enjoying his own, or which *may* be the cause of any damage to him." I reasoned that under this predial servitude the owner of the dominant estate, *on an objective*

---

62 By the terms of Article 669, there are not two estates, a dominant and a servient estate; it applies to people on the same premises, to the entire neighborhood, to people who are not owners or holders under any title susceptible of acquiring a servitude.
63 260 La. 384, 256 So. 2d 127 (1972).

finding of probability that at some time he might be deprived of the enjoyment of his property or suffer damage because of the work or construction made upon the servient estate, had the right to cause its removal.

Civil Code Articles 667 and 669 state legal causes of action for injunction and abatement as well as for damages. By analogy each also states a delictual cause of action for damages. Since we have discarded the theory-of-the-case pleading, the need for classifying the specific cause of action for damages has largely disappeared. It is when one of the articles is applied alone and not through Article 2315 by analogy that it is most necessary to understand that one is a law of property creating a true predial servitude, and that the other creates a legal obligation between persons. The nature of the cause of action becomes important because different rules of prescription apply to the respective situations, including the prescription provision [64] for the loss of the servitude under Article 667.

Because few if any legal principles stand in isolation, the examination of one principle under a set of facts must be limited to an acceptance of all other legal principles which bear upon it. While the court may address itself to the correction of error in relation to one code article or one statute, it more often cannot address itself to the whole body of law which may affect or be affected by the specific law considered. For example, the development of Civil Code Article 2315 by analogy with Civil Code Article 669 as a source for assessing liability for damages from ultrahazardous activities or dangerous instrumentalities was dictated by the prior jurisprudence on other aspects of delictual responsibility. Earlier decisions had upon many occasions awarded damages in these instances directly under Article 669 without requiring proof of any negligence. Our Civil Code Article 2317, in the exact language of a provision in the French Code Civil Article 1384, makes us responsible for "the things which we have in our custody." The French have assigned the liability for damages from hazardous activities and dangerous instrumentalities in the absence of negligence under their Article 1384, but in numerous Louisiana cases, the last as recent as 1969, *Cartwright v. Firemen's Insurance Company of Newark, New Jersey*,[65] our courts have said that we are respon-

---

[64] La. Civ. Code art. 789.
[65] 254 La. 330, 223 So. 2d 822 (1969); see discussion in Comment, 44 TUL. L. REV. 119, 147–49 (1969).

sible for things under our control under Article 2317 only when we are negligent, because that article is modified by Civil Code Article 2315. Before *Langlois v. Allied Chemical Corporation*,[66] fault under Article 2315 was defined as negligence. Therefore we could not remove the jurisprudential stricture upon Article 2317 until we held in *Langlois* that fault, as expressed in Article 2315, encompassed acts which cause damage other than negligent acts. In *Theriot v. Transit Casualty Company*[67] Justice Tate and I joined in a concurrence in a writ denial, noting that the rationale of the *Cartwright* case and the jurisprudence which limited recovery under Article 2317 to negligence were no longer applicable. If the court follows the concepts of *Langlois* and this concurrence, Civil Code Article 2317 may with Article 669, by means of Article 2315, provide a broader base for liability for damages from ultrahazardous activities and dangerous instrumentalities. Here may also be found a vehicle for resolving product-liability cases. The future will be determined by the doctrine which develops around the cases and by the briefs and argument of the attorneys as they persuade the courts of this state of the correct position to be taken under our civil code.

The discussion of the cases involving Articles 667 and 669 indicates the limitations upon a court when it approaches a problem requiring new rules of law. A court cannot lay down broad, general principles in a single piece of litigation under a particular set of facts. The court must weave these rules of law case by case, and the whole cloth cannot be seen until many particular issues have been judicially determined on the basis of, and in relation to, civil code or statute provisions. Actually, a court may move in the wrong direction and have to retrench when new rules of law are sought. *Rowe v. Travelers Insurance Company*[68] and *Laird v. Travelers Insurance Company*[69] are good examples of a learning process experienced by this writer. The two cases were factually similar, presented the same legal question, and required the same judicial determination. Since both opinions reached the same result, neither need be said to be wrong in result. However, a different approach, different language, and a different rationale were used in each. The error of using the wrong process in the judicial determination in the *Rowe* case was

66 258 La. 1067, 249 So. 2d 133 (1971).
67 263 La. 106, 267 So. 2d 211 (1972).
68 253 La. 659, 219 So. 2d 486 (1969).
69 263 La. 199, 267 So. 2d 714 (1972).

recognized in the *Laird* case, admitted, and corrected. A comparison of these two cases, which were decided only about two years apart, illustrates jurisprudential error and correction, and affords another reason for the validity of the principle that jurisprudence should not be the primary source of law. It also validates the Louisiana practice of overruling jurisprudence.

Although courts are not well suited for developing general statements of the law and although courts err in applying, interpreting, and developing law, it is apparent that jurisprudence, while not a primary source, is a valid source of law in some instances. Sometimes a legislature fails to fill a gap or to supply a new principle in place of one which has so fallen into desuetude that its application would bring an absurd result. Then the judiciary, which cannot avoid deciding a case before it, will finally evolve a broad principle or rule of law through a series of cases. It is such jurisprudence, formed in the exercise of this judicial function, which constitutes a source of law.

THE FUTURE OF THE RENAISSANCE

Perhaps the analysis of these writings will persuade the reader that the Louisiana judiciary is following the lead of the academicians and attempting to fulfill its role in the civil-law tradition. If our courts are truly acting in the civil-law tradition, the practicing lawyers of this state will find new challenges and opportunities and will assume greater responsibility for developing our law. If we recognize that the courts' first obligation in evaluating any case is to examine and research for an answer in the primary source of law, the codes or some other legislative expression, then the lawyer cannot necessarily determine the rights of his clients by finding a "goose case." He must first seek the legislative will through the codes and the statutes instead of the case law. If the written law is silent, ambiguous, or obsolete, he must look for other sources of law in preparing his case. The advocate will teach the court the underlying philosophy and theory of the principle he professes so that the court may ascertain the spirit of the law. Since jurisprudence is not one of the primary sources of law, the lawyer will most often cite and argue cases not as a source but as the rationale for the method of applying the law, as a basis for analogy, as an example of reason and logic, and as a good sample of judicial interpretation of the law. The cases will be used for their doctrinal value after an evaluation of the sources stating the doctrine.

I am convinced that there has been a renaissance of the civilian tradition in Louisiana. I am convinced that the law schools are dedicated to a preservation of the civil-law tradition in Louisiana. I firmly believe the judiciary of this state has its part in this renaissance, and that it will be a stronger force in the future. To fully accomplish a rebirth of the civil-law tradition and to assure its survival in Louisiana in a mixed jurisdiction require a reeducation of some of the practitioners and a program of continuing legal education for all practitioners.

If our courts do follow the lead of the law schools, the minimal requirements for the library of practicing lawyers today may differ considerably from those in the years of my early practice. In addition to our codes and statutes and our reported opinions, such a library must include the translations of the doctrinal works commenting upon the sources of our law, and must include a collection of Louisiana doctrine—books, treatises, and law reviews. Members of our court often go to these doctrinal sources immediately after examining the legislative expression. Since our court is actually influenced by and responsive to these doctrinal writings, it would be enlightening and useful for the practicing attorney also to become familiar with these writings. If such works do influence the members of the judiciary in finding their role in a civil-law tradition and in finding new methods for judicial interpretation, then it would appear that the practitioner should also want to study them. An excellent tool for an advocate before any court is a knowledge of what are the considerations which cause the court to make its judicial determinations.

One reason for believing that civil-law tradition will continue to strengthen in Louisiana is the new doctrinal writing in process, some of which is even now in press. My work with the civil code has been greatly facilitated by the *Compiled Edition of the Civil Codes of Louisiana.*[70] There is now available the new 1972 *Compiled Edition of the Civil Codes of Louisiana*, which not only affords a quick examination of the sources and evolution of our code provisions but also includes con-

---

70 3 LOUISIANA LEGAL ARCHIVES, COMPILED EDITION OF THE CIVIL CODES OF LOUISIANA (La. St. L. Inst., Part I, 1940; Part II, 1942) published pursuant to La. Acts 1938, No. 165.

cordance tables and cross-references to all the existing translations, treatises,[71] and other works already published. Forthcoming are a work on predial servitudes, an additional volume on obligations, and a book on Gény's theory of jurisprudence in the law.[72]

The appellate judges of this state have been given the opportunity for continuing education in the civil-law tradition. This opportunity must be extended to the entire judiciary. All of the first-year law students at some of the law schools are given the opportunity to study the basics of the civil-law tradition, and I propose that this should be a curriculum requirement at all Louisiana law schools. Only a few upperclassmen have had the advantage of an in-depth study of the philosophy and theory of the civil-law tradition. I believe that all upperclassmen who intend to practice in Louisiana need an in-depth comparative study of present civil-law systems as well as a study of the use of the civilian tradition in Louisiana's civil-law system. Also, there should be a greater consideration of programs in continuing legal education in the civil-law tradition for the practicing lawyer. The program should not be developed around single aspects of the civil law alone, but should include an approach to a philosophical understanding and evaluation of the whole of the civilian tradition.

A discourse upon the renaissance of the civil-law tradition in Louisiana must not omit mention of the Louisiana State Law Institute's continuous revision of the civil code. In addition to revision in that code accomplished through the institute's redaction of our new Code of Civil Procedure, the revision of Book II of the civil code is already well under way, and revision of Book III has begun. If I am correct in believing that a civil code is not a single restatement of law or jurisprudence, but a statement of the best law within the whole context of the system of law, then in revision it is to be hoped the legislature will not simply adopt prior jurisprudential statements or restatements of legal principles already outmoded and antiquated. The institute should not fear to propose the very best law as it presents portions of the code if that law fits within the total scheme of our code. It is the obligation of the legislature to express through the civil code this state's public policy. If the legislature

---

[71] 1972 Compiled Edition of the Civil Codes of Louisiana, 16 & 17 LSA-C.C.
[72] Mayda, François Gény and Modern Jurisprudence.

will not state public policy because the principle involved is controversial, it invites the judiciary to usurp the legislative function, for when an issue (whether controversial or not) becomes a case before the court, a pronouncement of basic policy may necessarily follow from the decision of the issue. Under several articles of the Code of Criminal Procedure the redactors' comments actually state that because the law in that particular area was in a state of flux or that the resolution of the law was controversial, that code purposely omitted to make a statement upon the law. When the legislature does this in one of our codes, the lawmakers have relegated themselves to a secondary role in making law. They actually force the judiciary into a function for which it is not designed, which it does not wish to assume, and which would, except for the abdication of the legislative responsibility and the existing code authority, be an unconstitutional exercise of power by the judiciary. As Professor Yiannopoulos has stated: "Common law statutes have the force of law because judges permit it; in civil law, judges can legislate because statutes allow the practice!"[73] As stated earlier, our civil code originally was a new statement of the best law as understood by the drafters. The revision of it should be a new expression of the best law which the reason of the people reflects through the will of the legislature.[74]

If this paper appears to overstate the present position of Louisiana's legal system or the academicians' and the jurists' roles in this system, this probably results from enthusiasm for future possibilities in the development of our legal system. In the judicial process in any system, justice through reason must always be sought. Reason is generally better derived in a democracy through the consensus of the people who compose it as expressed by their representatives. But reason in particular cases has been assigned to the adversary arena of the courtroom, where the academically trained advocate tries to bring a court's mind and conscience to a decision of justice through reason. Reason cannot always be drawn directly from a consensus of the people's will as expressed through their representatives. When the law is silent, or when there is ambiguity, obsolescence, absurdity, or undue hardship, then the lawyer and the judge must work

---

73 YIANNNOPOULOS, LOUISIANA CIVIL LAW SYSTEM § 29, at 77 (1971).
74 Morrow, "An Approach to the Revision of the Louisiana Civil Code," 10 LA. L. REV. 59 (1949) and 23 TUL. L. REV. 478 (1949); Morrow, "Current Prospects for Revision of the Louisiana Civil Code," 33 TUL L. REV. 143 (1958); Smith, "Law Revision in Louisiana in Retrospect," 19 LA. L. REV. 34 (1958).

together to resolve the problem by supplying words or even changing words to reflect the content which the community would give to them. It is here that all the legal profession will apply von Jhering's much-paraphrased aphorism: "Through the Code but beyond it." As we go to the light to see not the light itself but what it illuminates, so we go to the code for the enlightenment it provides.

To acknowledge that there can be no complete agreement as to reason under our institution of justice until it has been confirmed in the adversary arena of the court, is to understand the purpose for which the institution was fashioned.[75] With that understanding, the academicians and the attorneys and the judges will together fashion and preserve a civilian tradition in Louisiana which will constantly seek for justice through reason—through law.

75 Levi, An Introduction to Legal Reasoning (1949).

ABBREVIATIONS

Am. J. Comp. L.	American Journal of Comparative Law
La.	Louisiana Reports (1900 to present)
La. L. Rev.	Louisiana Law Review
La. St. L. Inst. transl.	Louisiana State Law Institute translation
Rev. Jur. U.P.R.	Revista Juridica de la Universidad de Puerto Rico
So. 2d	Southern Reporter, second series
Tul. L. Rev.	Tulane Law Review

IV

Jurisprudence and Doctrine as Sources of Law in Louisiana and in France

A. N. Yiannopoulos
PROFESSOR OF LAW, LOUISIANA STATE UNIVERSITY

The term *sources of law* has a variety of meanings.[1] For example, in the field of legal philosophy the term refers to the very foundation of legal order, and in the field of legal history it refers to the documents which contain information about the past of a legal system. For purposes of analysis of civilian institutions *sources of law* refers to the processes from which legal rules derive their existence.

In civil-law systems a distinction is made among authoritative and persuasive sources of law. There are two authoritative (or primary) sources of law: legislation[2] and custom.[3] Thus, Article 1 of the Louisiana

---

1 See, in general, ALLEN, LAW IN THE MAKING 1–66 (7th ed. 1964); PATTON, JURISPRUDENCE 140–41 (1961); 3 POUND, JURISPRUDENCE 379 (1959); SALMOND, JURISPRUDENCE 109–12 (12th ed. Fitzgerald 1966). A list of the abbreviations used in this chapter appears on page 90.
2 See, in general, ALLEN, LAW IN THE MAKING 426–82 (7th ed. 1964); 1 PLANIOL, CIVIL LAW TREATISE NO. 12 (La. St. L. Inst. transl. 1959); 3 POUND, JURISPRUDENCE 380 (1959); SALMOND, JURISPRUDENCE 115–30 (12th ed. Fitzgerald 1966). In civil-law jurisdictions, legislation is superior to every other source of law. Thus, La. Civ. Code article 1 (1870), declaring that legislation is a formal expression of legislative will, may be taken to establish the supremacy of legislation. This does not mean that a civilian will find all solutions in enactments that embody the declared will of the legislative assembly, but it means that if he finds a solution there nothing in the nature of jurisprudence, usage, equity, or doctrine can prevail against it. It is only in cases not covered by legislation that the lawyer or judge is entitled to look elsewhere for solutions.
3 See, in general, 1 PLANIOL, CIVIL LAW TREATISE NOS. 11–15 (La. St. L. Inst. transl. 1959); 3 POUND, JURISPRUDENCE 389 (1959); Loussouarn, "The Relative Importance of Legislation, Custom, Doctrine, and Precedent in French Law," 18 LA. L. REV. 235, 247–54 (1958). According to La. Civ. Code article 3 (1870), customary law arises from "a long series of actions constantly repeated, which have by such repetition, and by uninterrupted acquiescence, acquired the force of a tacit and common consent." This notion of customary

Civil Code of 1870[4] mentions legislation, and Article 3 of the same code refers to customs. The French Civil Code has no corresponding provisions, because it was thought that the definition of the sources of law is a matter of legal science rather than legislation.[5] From among modern civil codes, Article 1 of the Greek Civil Code declares that "the rules of law are contained in legislation and customs."[6] Legislation and customs are authoritative in the sense that they are binding on courts and individuals.

In addition to the two authoritative sources, there are certain merely persuasive (or subsidiary) sources of law: jurisprudence, doctrine, conventional usages, and equity.[7] These sources, whether or not mentioned in civil codes, may influence the determination of particular issues. It is in this sense that they are persuasive rather than authoritative. The following discussion is devoted to an analysis of the function of persuasive sources in general, and to the role of jurisprudence and doctrine in the legal systems of Louisiana and France.

A legal system admitting only legislation and customs as sources of law would be insufficient in at least two respects. First, it would be a static system unadaptable to evolution and changes in the political, economic, and social conditions of life. If legislation were to keep pace with these developments, necessary reforms ought to be enacted daily. This would

---

law was first formulated in Roman law during the period of the Republic. It is accepted today in most civil-law jurisdictions. Civil codes, however, do not ordinarily include definitions of customary law because according to modern legislative techniques definitions have no place in a legal text. Thus, although customs are recognized as an authoritative source of law in France, Germany, and Greece, the civil codes of these countries contain no definitions of customs or customary law.

4 La. Civ. Code article 1 (1870) declares that "law is a solemn expression of legislative will." In the French text of the Louisiana Civil Code, Article 1 reads: "La loi est une déclaration solennelle de la volonté législative," which, perhaps, ought to be translated "legislation is a formal expression of legislative will." Thus it may be said that Article 1 defines *legislation* rather than *law*, and leaves room for sources other than legislation.

5 See GÉNY, METHOD OF INTERPRETATION AND SOURCES OF PRIVATE POSITIVE LAW 72 (La. St. L. Inst. transl. 1963).

6 Greek Civil Code art. 1 (1940); BALIS, GENERAL PRINCIPLES OF THE CIVIL LAW 7 (7th ed. 1955) (in Greek).

7 See, in general, Dainow, "The Method of Legal Development through Judicial Interpretation in Louisiana and Puerto Rico," 22 REV. JUR. U.P.R. 108, 109–20 (1952); Franklin, "Equity in Louisiana: The Role of Article 21," 9 TUL. L. REV. 485 (1935).

not be desirable, even if it were possible, because frequent reforms tend to deprive legislation of its cogency and of the respect of courts and individuals. Nor can customs supply the requisite frequent reforms, because the formation of customs is too slow to cope with the growing demands of a developing society. Second, a legal system that does not admit of sources of law other than legislation and custom would be likely to lead to denial of justice or to judicial capriciousness in certain cases. Legislation and customs alone may not furnish rules of decision for all conceivable fact situations. Thus, Articles 1 and 3 of the Louisiana Civil Code of 1870, if strictly applied, would work havoc with "unprovided for" situations which are likely to arise with increasing frequency as the code ages and reflects less accurately the conditions of everyday life. In the presence of an "unprovided for" case, the judge might find himself cut off from all other possible sources, and might face the dilemma of a denial of justice or of a decision according to his personal predilections. Under these conditions, in order to save the judge from the horns of the dilemma, civil-law systems have developed the notion of persuasive or subsidiary sources of law.

In Louisiana, Article 21 of the 1870 code declares that "in all civil matters, where there is no express law, the judge is bound to proceed and decide according to equity. To decide equitably, an appeal is made to natural law and reason, or received usages, where positive law is silent."[8] It thus contains an authorization for judges to decide "unprovided for" cases, and indicates certain subsidiary sources of law that must furnish the rule of decision. Denial of justice or judicial capriciousness are excluded; moreover, the law is rendered flexible for application to new situations.

The text of Article 21 of the Louisiana Civil Code of 1870 has been borrowed from the draft of the French *Projet du Gouvernement*. It is almost an exact version of Article 11 of the draft that reads as follows: "In civil matters, where there is no express law, the judge must act as a minister of equity. Equity is the return to natural law, or to received usages where the positive law is silent." This provision was not adopted in the final version of the French Civil Code, because it was thought that matters of this kind are suitable for scientific elaboration rather than

---

8 La. Civ. Code art. 21 (1870); *Projet du Gouvernement* art. 11 (1800); cf. Swiss Civil Code art. 1 (1912).

inclusion in a legislative text. The code, however, should leave no room for denial of justice. Accordingly, an article was adopted which declares that "the judge who will refuse to decide under the pretext of silence, obscurity or insufficiency of the law, will be prosecuted as guilty of denial of justice." Thus, Article 4 of the French Civil Code is directed to the same general purpose as Article 21 of the Louisiana Civil Code of 1870.

I. JURISPRUDENCE

The courts have the task of giving life to rules of law, and of adapting them to the needs of everyday life. This task is particularly demanding in jurisdictions where codification occurred many years ago, as in Louisiana and in France. The civil codes of the two jurisdictions have been interpreted by courts for over a century and a half, and they have been applied to innumerable fact situations. A gloss of jurisprudence has thus developed, and the question arises as to its authority as a course of law.[9]

This question has given rise to interminable discussions, because it relates to fundamental issues concerning the nature of law and of the judicial process. A definite answer to the question of the authority of jurisprudence depends on the resolution of such issues as the lawmaking function of courts, methods of adjudication, and techniques of legal reasoning. Analysis of these issues, however, belongs properly to the domain of legal philosophy. At this point, discussion will be limited to the much narrower question of the effect of judicial precedents on the determination of a new case. Reference will be made to general civilian theory, but attention will be focused on Louisiana developments.

Theoretical considerations. According to traditional civilian theory, judicial precedents do not constitute a source of law because the legislative function is entrusted to the legislature and the people exclusively. The function of the courts is to interpret the law, whether enacted or customary, and to apply it to concrete cases. Judicial precedents thus merely

---

9 See, in general, Dainow, "The Method of Legal Development through Judicial Interpretation in Louisiana and Puerto Rico," 22 Rev. Jur. U.P.R. 108, 116–32 (1952); Deák, "The Place of the 'Case' in the Common and in the Civil Law," 8 Tul. L. Rev. 337 (1934); Loussouarn, "The Relative Importance of Legislation, Custom, Doctrine, and Precedent in French Law," 18 La. L. Rev. 235, 254–62 (1958); Tate, "Techniques of Judicial Interpretation in Louisiana," 22 La. L. Rev. 727, 743–47 (1962); Comment, "Stare Decisis in Louisiana," 7 Tul. L. Rev. 100 (1932).

demonstrate past applications of a legal text. These applications do not become part of the text, and it cannot be said that the text, as interpreted, is the law. The text alone is the law, and prior decisions do not insulate the judge from going directly to the text for its true meaning. The judge is supposed to decide cases by reference to legislation and custom rather than on the authority of prior cases, within the limits of a judicial discretion conferred upon him by law. Theoretically then, prior decisions, being merely demonstrative of past applications, may be disregarded.

In France, Article 5 of the civil code prohibits expressly judicial decisions intended to control future litigation (*arrêts de règlement*). This provision was prompted by the desire of the people to deny to the courts all power to create rules of law. According to ideas prevailing at the time of the revolution, legislation was the best possible expression of law, embodying the collective wisdom of the people and its representatives. As a result of this Article 5, a judge is not bound in France to follow a previous judicial decision, whether rendered by himself or by another court. Even decisions of the Court of Cassation, the supreme court of France, may in theory be disregarded by a lower court. But, by virtue of directly applicable legislation [10] lower courts must follow decisions of all the chambers of the Court of Cassation sitting together, or of the plenary Civil Law Chamber, when a case is remanded for determination according to instructions.

The Louisiana Civil Code of 1870 does not contain a provision corresponding to Article 5 of the French Civil Code. Decisions intended to control future cases were unknown in Louisiana, and their prohibition would be unnecessary. However, the redactors of the Louisiana Civil Code of 1825, Livingston, Derbigny, and Moreau-Lislet, had some very definite ideas about the function of the judiciary and the role of precedents.[11] It was their conviction that the legislative and judicial functions should be kept scrupulously apart. The unprovided-for case should be decided by the judge as if he were an amicable compounder, according to the dictates of natural equity. The decision in such a case should not have authority as a statement of the law for the future, unless, of course, it was given legislative sanction. Insufficiencies of the enacted law

---

10 See Laws of April 1, 1837; July 23, 1947.
11 See Preliminary Report of the Code Commissioners, Projet of the Civil Code of 1825, 2 La. Legal Archives (1937).

should be brought by the courts to the attention of the legislature so that rules would be supplied or errors would be corrected. The absence or insufficiency of positive law was thus regarded as a legislative shortcoming that should be remedied by the legislature alone in the framework of its constitutional authority. The legislature could adopt or reject the interim solutions reached by courts; new laws could be incorporated in proper places, and the whole body of the law would thus be kept up-to-date in a constant movement of progress toward perfection. It ought to be noted, however, that the Louisiana Civil Code contains no provision for a report by the judges to the legislature on imperfections of the law. It seems that this plan was abandoned as impracticable, but the fact remains that Livingston and his colleagues looked with great disfavor on judicial precedents as sources of law. Article 1 of the civil code, declaring that "law is a solemn expression of legislative will," still furnishes the basis for a conclusion that judicial decisions were not intended to be an authoritative source of law in Louisiana.

The theory that judicial precedents are not a source of law admits an apparent exception. In Louisiana and in France, a long line of decisions on a certain subject may be taken to establish rules of customary law. This is the doctrine of "settled jurisprudence" (*jurisprudence constante*).[12] Courts must follow this jurisprudence as customary law rather than as merely precedents. In France, this exception rests on doctrinal considerations; in Louisiana, there is legislative foundation for it in Articles 3 and 21 of the civil code.

Practical considerations. The theory that precedents are not a source of law at all may hardly be maintained in the light of actualities. It is true that the judge may not avoid the application of an enacted or customary rule of law on the pretext that he must follow a contrary precedent. This would be usurpation of the legislative function by the judiciary. But the judge may and should follow prior decisions as an interpretation of legislation or customary law. Thus, in practice, judicial precedents do influence determination of future cases; and it would be accurate to adopt the

12 See Johnson v. St. Paul Mercury Insurance Co., 256 La. 289, 236 So. 2d 216 (1970); Tucker, "The Code and the Common Law in Louisiana," 29 TUL. L. REV. 739, 757 (1955); Daggett, Dainow, Hebert, and McMahon, "A Reappraisal Appraised: A Brief for the Civil Law of Louisiana," 12 TUL. L. REV. 12, 18 (1937); DAVID, FRENCH LAW 170 (Kindred transl. 1972).

view that jurisprudence, though not an authoritative source, is in fact a persuasive or subsidiary source of law.

Recognition of precedents as a persuasive source of law tends to enhance rather than compromise the authority of legislation. This is proved by experience in France. A judge at the district court of Château-Thierry rendered decisions for twenty-five years toward the end of the nineteenth century without taking into account legislation or jurisprudence. He believed he was endowed with a peculiar sense of fairness, and decided cases according to his personal predilections. The result was a chaotic variation in his decisions, revealing that security of legislation requires adherence to precedent.[13]

In reality, there is no need for opposition between jurisprudence and legislation or customary law. The jurisprudence is legislation and customary law as reflected in decided cases. The problem is whether the judge may completely disregard the work of interpretation made before him, or whether he should apply a rule of law to a new case with all the explanations, additions, and modifications arising from prior decisions. Adoption of the second alternative seems to be indispensable for a number of reasons.

In the first place, there must be continuity and stability of law. Judges may come and go, but the law must remain certain and predictable. This demand for certainty, of course, runs counter to a demand for some flexibility, that the law be accommodated to changed conditions. Thus, when applied to new situations, the law should produce fair results yet still serve its original social purpose. Judges, being sensitive to these apparently contradictory demands and owing fidelity to the institutions of a well-ordered legal system, do not likely disregard precedents, even though in theory they are free to do so. In the absence of a manifest unfairness, a judge tends to follow prior decisions on the same question of law, even when he believes that a better-reasoned interpretation would provide a different application, one that he himself would have recommended if the question presented to him were one of first impression.

Second, the logic of the law and the economy of effort tend to establish the authority of precedents. The basis of a judicial decision is legal reasoning founded upon certain legislative precepts, and it is quite probable

---

13 See GÉNY, METHOD OF INTERPRETATION AND SOURCES OF PRIVATE POSITIVE LAW 496.

that two different courts will reach the same conclusion on a question of law by independent action. When this happens, and the soundness of prior adjudications is confirmed, precedents emerge victorious. As a general rule, however, economy of effort in these days of crowded dockets and the ever-increasing volume of litigation tends to preclude reexamination of legal rules or standards adopted in prior decisions. The courts simply do not have the time to retest and reformulate settled applications of legal principles in every case, particularly when the settled rule appears to be fair and practical. The courts are likely, therefore, to determine whether the general rules have been correctly applied to the case before them without reexamination of the validity of these rules.

Third, the authority of precedents is enhanced by the collegiate organization of the judiciary. Most courts of appellate jurisdiction are composed of a panel of judges, and decisions are rendered by the court rather than an individual judge. The membership of the court may change, but the court remains as an entity. Judges tend to be loyal to their court, and this contributes to the stability of the jurisprudence.

And last, but not least, the authority of precedents is enhanced by the existence of a judicial hierarchy. There are trial courts, courts of appeal, and a supreme court. The psychological coercion exercised by the higher courts on the lower secures the stability of jurisprudence. Upon review of a decision in the exercise of supervisory or appellate jurisdiction, a higher court does not merely affirm or reject the reasoning of a lower court; it disposes of the case and almost always furnishes a rationale, namely a juridical opinion supporting the disposition. A lower court may be in theory free to reach its own conclusion on a case before it; but when a higher court has expressed an opinion on a question of law, the lower court is likely to adopt that opinion because it does not wish to risk a reversal. Moreover, lower courts do not wish to cause unnecessary expense and delay to litigants by rendering a judgment that is likely to be reversed. Implicit in this attitude of lower courts is loyalty to the rule of law, and a feeling that acceptance of the higher court's ruling secures both public respect for the courts and an efficient administration of justice. For these reasons, in Louisiana and in France, pronouncements of the supreme court are frequently repeated by lower courts, to the point that they are regarded as equivalent to legislative provisions.

There is no general agreement as to the theoretical foundation of the view that judicial precedents constitute a subsidiary source of law in Louisiana and in France. According to one approach, precedents are a subsidiary source of law because the legislature has tacitly delegated authority to the courts to establish rules for the interpretation and application of legislation. A rule established by jurisprudence is thus implicitly adopted by the legislature. If the legislature fails to act, the jurisprudential rule becomes law. This is a pure fiction that must be dismissed. According to the prevailing view in France, the judge has authority to "tell" the law (*dire le droit*), but this authority is not unlimited.[14] Judicial decisions, in order to acquire validity as precedents, must meet the approval of the common opinion of jurists, namely, the informed members of the legal profession. If judicial opinions encounter the resistance of jurists, experience shows that they are likely to be overruled.[15] In these circumstances, the authority of jurisprudence as a subsidiary source of law must be ascertained by an investigation of the position of lower courts, doctrinal treatises, and prevailing practices. Perhaps the best explanation of the persuasive force of judicial precedents must be sought in factual rather than legal considerations. Jurisprudence derives its authority from facts rather than rules of law. These facts acquire legal significance when they reflect a juridical sentiment. In the last analysis, therefore, persuasive or even binding precedents of a settled jurisprudence may be regarded as stages in the development of a legal system by means of widely accepted custom rather than legislation.

Louisiana practice. Three decades ago, the question whether Louisiana courts had adopted the common-law rule of *stare decisis* or followed traditional civilian notions concerning the authority of precedents, was controversial.[16] Today, however, the consensus of judges, lawyers, and law professors is that Louisiana courts have basically adopted civilian ap-

---

14 See Loussouarn, "The Relative Importance of Legislation, Custom, Doctrine, and Precedent in French Law," 18 LA. L. REV. 235, 261 (1958).
15 See, e.g., Chaney v. Travelers Insurance Co., 259 La. 1, 249 So. 2d 181 (1971); Yiannapoulos, "Property" in "The Work of the Louisiana Appellate Courts for the 1970–1971 Term," 32 LA. L. REV. 172, 183 (1972); DAVID, FRENCH LAW 194 (Kindred transl. 1972).
16 See Comment, "Stare Decisis," 7 TUL. L. REV. 100 (1932); Ireland, "Louisiana's Legal System Reappraised," 11 TUL. L. REV. 585, 591 (1937).

proaches—with certain modifications tending to enhance the authority of precedents. This is only natural, because Louisiana is a mixed jurisdiction sharing the civil-law and the common-law traditions; and whereas the bulk of its private law derives from Roman-Continental sources, its public and commercial laws derive mostly from Anglo-American sources. Under the circumstances, pure civilian theory of precedents would be unworkable in Louisiana.

The common-law doctrine of *stare decisis* does not apply in Louisiana. We have never adopted this doctrine, "and whatever chances it had of creeping into our system have been reduced to the vanishing point by the passage of time. Our courts have always followed, and show every disposition to continue to follow, the essential civilian judicial technique of never letting today become either the slave of yesterday or the tyrant of tomorrow."[17] In comparison with courts in common-law jurisdictions, Louisiana courts have exhibited a much less reverent attitude toward precedents. This is evidenced by the frequency with which the Louisiana Supreme Court has overruled prior jurisprudence during the twentieth century.[18] Moreover, on several occasions, lower courts have refused to follow supreme court decisions that they believed to be erroneous. For example, in *Coulon v. Anthony Hamlin, Inc.*,[19] the court of appeal chose to apply a statute directly rather than follow precedents establishing a contrary rule. On certiorari, the supreme court affirmed, acknowledging error in its prior jurisprudence.[20]

Judicial precedents, however, carry much weight in Louisiana as a persuasive source of law. Moreover, they may be binding according to the *doctrine of jurisprudence constante* that our courts do follow. The most important differences between this civilian doctrine and the common-law rule of *stare decisis* may be summarized as follows. A single case affords sufficient foundation for the latter, while a series of adjudicated cases, all in accord, forms the basis for the former. Further, in civil-law jurisdictions,

---

17 Tate, "Techniques of Judicial Interpretation in Louisiana," 22 LA. L. REV. 727, 745 (1962); Tucker, "The Code and the Common Law in Louisiana," 29 TUL. L. REV. 739, 759 (1955).
18 See Daggett, Dainow, Hebert, and McMahon, "A Reappraisal Appraised: A Brief for the Civil Law of Louisiana," 12 TUL. L. REV. 12, 22, 23 (1937); Barham, "A Renaissance of the Civilian Tradition in Louisiana," 33 LA. L. REV. 357, 373 (1973), and in this volume, p. 38.
19 93 So. 2d 557 (La. App. Orl. Cir. 1957).
20 233 La. 798, 98 So. 2d 193 (1957).

a long line of precedents may be taken to establish rules of customary law; in common-law jurisdictions, judicial precedents represent a judge-made law. This means, in turn, that whereas settled jurisprudence in civil-law jurisdictions fills in gaps or supplies the deficiencies of legislation, precedents in common-law jurisdictions constitute an authoritative source of law equivalent to legislation. These differences reflect fundamentally opposing views as to the nature of law. If law is what the courts will do (rather than some abstract principle independent of judicial interpretation and application), precedents are authoritative sources of law—and perhaps the only authoritative source. If, on the other hand, the authoritative sources of law are legislation and customs, precedents must be regarded as an interpretation of the law. Theoretical differences notwithstanding, the use of precedents in practice is often similar in civil-law and in common-law jurisdictions. The essential difference may merely relate to the degree of sanctity with which precedents are regarded.

In the actual working of the Louisiana system, the legal profession regards an interpretation supported by a line of judicial decisions as a settled rule that the courts will follow with reasonable certainty. In theory, reference should be made first to legislation; in practice, however, the interpretation reflected in judicial decisions is almost invariably relied upon on the justifiable assumption that the settled rule will not be disregarded. Thus, most Louisiana judges look for guidance first to prior decisions of their own or of other courts; and most members of the bar rely principally upon precedents as their guide to the meaning of the law. Resort to legal texts, doctrine, or processes of legal reasoning, is frequently made for the purposes of either bolstering the authority of precedents or diminishing their effect.

Decisions of courts of subordinate or coordinate jurisdiction, decisions of federal courts on questions of state law, and decisions of courts of sister states or of civil-law jurisdictions, are merely persuasive, and they may be easily disregarded if the court feels that its own interpretation is better. Courts of appeal do not feel bound to follow decisions of lower courts or of other courts of appeal;[21] and the Louisiana Supreme Court

---

21 See, e.g., Ellis v. Travelers Ins. Co., 123 So. 2d 780 (La. App. 4th Cir. 1960); Washington v. Washington, 116 So. 2d 125 (La. App. 1st Cir. 1959); Collett v. Otis, 80 So. 2d 117 (La. App. 1st Cir. 1955); cf. Shreveport v. Baylock, 236 La. 133, 107 So. 2d 419 (1958).

does not hesitate to set aside a line of jurisprudence established by the courts of appeal if another interpretation appears to be preferable.[22]

Prior decisions of the same court are likewise merely persuasive. For various reasons, the court may be inclined to follow its own precedents; but when the court is convinced that there are legal, equitable, or practical reasons for a different rule, the court will change course. As a general rule, "the law as construed in an overruled case is considered as though it had never existed, and the law as construed in the last case is considered as though it has always been the law."[23] The new precedent thus operates both prospectively and retrospectively, unless property rights have been acquired in reliance upon the prior jurisprudence. In these circumstances, a court may decide to apply the old rule to the case before it and, at the same time, announce that it intends to apply a new rule to subsequent cases. The new precedent is thus given prospective effect only; the overruled prior jurisprudence continues to apply to antedating causes of action. The United States Supreme Court has sanctioned this technique.[24] Louisiana courts have also resorted to it.[25] The technique has been questioned as demonstrating too bold a display of judicial lawmaking. It would certainly be in violation of Article 5 of the French Civil Code, discussed above, and incompatible with the ideas of the redactors of the Louisiana Civil Code.[26]

Decisions of higher courts are almost invariably followed by lower courts in Louisiana. This practice has been justified in the light of both practical considerations and legal grounds. The Louisiana Constitution has vested the supreme court with authority to control the action of all inferior courts, and the courts of appeal with supervisory jurisdiction over inferior courts in their circuit.[27] Moreover, Louisiana judges "feel morally bound to honor a higher court precedent containing a considered holding

---

22 See, e.g., Gaspard v. Le Maire, 245 La. 239, 158 So. 2d 149 (1963); Duree v. Maryland Casualty Co., 238 La. 166, 114 So. 2d 594 (1959).
23 Norton v. Crescent City Ice Mfg. Co., 178 La. 135, 150 So. 855, 858 (1933).
24 See Great Northern Railway Co. v. Sunburst Oil & Refining Co., 287 U.S. 358 (1932).
25 See Levy v. Nitsche, 40 La. Ann. 500, 4 So. 472 (1888); Sumrall v. J. C. Penny Co., 239 La. 762, 120 So. 2d 67 (1960); Comment, "Retrospective Effect of an Overruling Decision," 7 LA. L. REV. 133 (1946).
26 See Note 11 above.
27 See La. Const. art. VII, §§ 10, 29 (1921), as amended in 1958.

squarely and clearly applicable"[28] to a case before them. And it may be said that there is a Louisiana tradition compelling respect for the jurisprudence of higher courts. A lower court, however, is not required to apply mechanically precedents of a higher court. Upon consideration of the underlying reasons for the pronouncement of a higher court, the lower court may find that the seemingly applicable precedent was not intended to apply to the situation before it. This is the technique of distinguishing precedents, so well known in common-law jurisdictions.[29]

It might be argued that a lower court should feel free to render a judgment that it considers correct, without regard to prior decisions of a higher court that appear to be erroneous. By doing so, the lower court will at least compel the higher court, upon review of the case, to reconsider its prior position. Nevertheless, this happens only in exceptional circumstances. For all practical purposes, precedents of a higher court are considered as binding. Judges thus prefer to follow precedents that they consider to be erroneous and to indicate why a more sound interpretation of a legislative text justifies a different rule, thus inviting the higher court to reconsider its previous interpretation.[30]

In *Pringle-Associated Mortgage Corp. v. Eanes*,[31] the Louisiana Supreme Court reversed and rebuked a lower court for having disregarded a single precedent interpreting an article of the Louisiana Civil Code. On rehearing, however, the supreme court overruled its own precedent and reinstated the decisions of the lower court.[32] In *Johnson v. St. Paul Mercury Insurance Co.*,[33] the Louisiana Supreme Court again reversed and rebuked in dictum a lower court for having departed from "settled jurisprudence" in a matter not regulated by statute. The supreme court

---

28 Tate, "Techniques of Judicial Interpretation in Louisiana," 22 LA. L. REV. 727, 751 (1962).
29 See, e.g., Barry v. United States Fidelity & Guaranty Co., 236 So. 2d 229 (La. App. 3rd Cir. (1970); Yiannopoulos, "Property" in "The Work of the Louisiana Appellate Courts for the 1969–1970 Term," 31 LA. L. REV. 196, 214 (1971).
30 See, e.g., Chaney v. Travelers Insurance Co., 238 So. 2d 847 (La. App. 1st Cir. 1970); Romero v. Leger, 133 So. 2d 897 (La. App. 3rd Cir. 1961); Rycade Oil Corp. v. Board of Commissioners for Atchafalaya Basin Levee District, 129 So. 2d 302 (La. App. 3rd Cir. 1961).
31 254 La. 705, 226 So. 2d 502 (1969).
32 226 So. 22d at 513.
33 256 La. 289, 236 So. 2d 216 (1970).

regarded this action as a failure of the lower court "to recognize its obligation to follow the settled law of this State."[34] Further, the court declared that "since the question is not regulated by statute, the law is what this Court has announced it to be."[35] The language used by the justices admits the supremacy of legislation in matters regulated by statute; but in asserting that the law is what the supreme court has announced it to be in matters not regulated by statute, the justices have used language inconsistent with Louisiana legislation. Indeed, there should be no doubt that jurisprudence in Louisiana is merely a persuasive source of law. The above dictum apparently implies that the supreme court has abandoned its previous position that even a single decision construing legislation is obligatory on lower courts.[36]

II. DOCTRINE

The word doctrine signifies the body of opinions on legal matters expressed in books and articles.[37] The word is also used to designate, collectively, the persons learned in the law who are engaged in analysis, synthesis, and evaluation of legal materials. It thus refers both to legal scholarship and the persons who devote their time to scholarly elaboration on texts.

In civil-law jurisdictions, doctrine is regarded as a persuasive source of law. It gives orientation to the legal system as a whole and paves the way for the development of legislation and jurisprudence. It expounds scientific principles, develops theories, and assists in the interpretation of legal texts. Rather than confining itself to isolated cases, doctrine gives a broadness of view to the law, stresses its logic and policy, and forces the synthesis of legal rules into integrated institutions. The authority of doc-

---

34 236 So. 2d at 217.
35 Id. at 217–18.
36 See Pascal and Tête, "Law in General: The Work of the Louisiana Appellate Courts for the 1969–1970 Term," 31 LA. L. REV. 185–89 (1971).
37 See, in general, DAVID, FRENCH LAW 188–93 (Kindred transl. 1972); Dainow, "The Planiol Treatise on the Civil Law: French and Louisiana Law for Comparative Study," 10 AM. J. COMP. L. 175 (1961); Dainow, "Planiol Citations by Louisiana Courts: 1959–1966," 27 LA. L. REV. 231 (1967); DAVID and DEVRIES, THE FRENCH LEGAL SYSTEM: AN INTRODUCTION TO CIVIL LAW SYSTEMS 122–26 (1958); GÉNY, METHOD OF INTERPRETATION AND SOURCES OF PRIVATE POSITIVE LAW §§ 150–55 (La. St. L. Inst. transl. 1963); Morrow, "Louisiana Blueprint: Civilian Codification and Legal Method for State and Nation," 17 TUL. L. REV. 351, 537 (1943); Tate, "Techniques of Judicial Interpretation in Louisiana," 22 LA. L. REV. 727, 739–43 (1962).

trine as a persuasive source of law stems from a traditional regard for legal scholarship and rests on the need for a critical evaluation of legal institutions. Its effectiveness is measured by its capacity to persuade the legislators and the judges and, through them, the practitioners. Its persuasiveness depends, not only on the prestige of an individual legal scholar, but on the extent to which an individual legislator or judge is willing to be persuaded.

The role of doctrine as a guide to legal development reflects a traditional civilian emphasis upon the prestige of legal scholarship and upon professional specialization in the interpretation and systematization of law. During the period of the Principate in Roman legal history, the opinions of jurisconsults certainly had persuasive force; in certain circumstances, these opinions were even binding.[38] Further, in the formative era of modern civil-law systems, when Roman texts were shaped decisively into a rational system capable of satisfying contemporary needs, the universities were the center of legal development. It was an era of continuous political struggle and only impartial scholars, skilled in the crafts of textual elaboration, could serve the need for an authoritative statement of legal principles with a claim to universality and permanence. The authority of doctrine in civil-law jurisdictions is thus the heritage of a professional class charged with the task of impartial guidance.[39]

The importance of doctrine in civil-law jurisdictions may be fully understood in the light of the judicial process and organization. The members of the judiciary form a body of career officials who have limited or no practical experience as advocates. As a result, they remain attached to academic learning, and their opinions reflect, in style and content, admiration for doctrinal writing. Judicial opinions are anonymous and almost always unanimous.[40] This bars the emergence of doctrine within the judicial process. By contrast, the organized exposition of legal principles has been traditionally the domain of the judiciary in common-law jurisdictions. Common-law judges have developed the ability to elaborate in their opinions on the legal system as a whole, and thus case law performs the function of a minimum of systematization. Judges are usually elected or

---

38 See WOLFF, ROMAN LAW 108, 160 (1951).
39 See DAVID, FRENCH LAW 191 (Kindred transl. 1972); 1 PLANIOL, CIVIL LAW TREATISE 86 (La. St. L. Inst. transl. 1959); and, in general, BONNECASE, LA PENSÉE JURIDIQUE FRANÇAISE (2 vols. 1933).
40 See HERZOG, CIVIL PROCEDURE IN FRANCE 124–36 (1967).

appointed from among the most successful members of the legal profession. Judicial opinions frequently embody the predilections of the individual judge, and other judges do not hesitate to exercise their freedom to write a dissenting or a concurring opinion. Under the circumstances, common-law judges tend to assume a role corresponding to some extent with that of doctrinal writers in civil-law jurisdictions.

France. Soon after the promulgation of the Civil Code of 1804, French jurists began the scientific elaboration on its text. At first, scholars and judges interpreted the code by the exegetical method, following closely its language and working out its implications in the light of preparatory works and seventeenth- or eighteenth-century treatises, particularly those of Pothier [41] and Domat.[42] Early publications assumed the form of commentaries on individual articles of the code, in the sequence of the code. The first treatise dealing with legal institutions rather than individual articles of the code was published in Heidelberg in 1808 by a German law professor, Zachariae von Lingenthal.[43] The work was translated into French and formed the basis for the treatise of Aubry and Rau.[44]

Among the most influential nineteenth-century treatises were those of Proudhon, Toullier, Delvincourt, Duranton, Aubry and Rau, Troplong, Demolombe, Maracadé, and Laurent.[45] Several of these treatises were further expanded in subsequent editions. Their significance today is mostly historical, marking a stage in the development of French law. There are a few, however, that continue to be influential for the determination of fundamental principles and for their application to concrete cases. For example, the treatise of Demolombe is still used in its midnine-

---

41 See OEUVRES DE POTHIER (10 vols. Bugnet ed. 1845–48).
42 See OEUVRES COMPLÈTES DE J. DOMAT (4 vols. Remy ed. 1828–30).
43 See ZACHARIÄ VON LINGENTHAL, HANDBUCH DES FRANZÖSISCHEN CIVILRECHTS (4 vols. 1808).
44 See AUBRY & RAU, DROIT CIVIL FRANÇAIS (5 vols. 1838–47).
45 See PROUDHON, COURS DE DROIT FRANÇAIS (2 vols. 1810); TOULLIER, LE DROIT CIVIL FRANÇAIS, SUIVANT L'ORDRE DU CODE (16 vols. 1811); DELVINCOURT, COURS DE DROIT (2 vols. 1813); DURANTON, COURS DE DROIT FRANÇAIS SUIVANT LE CODE CIVIL (14 vols. 1825); AUBRY & RAU, COURS DE DROIT CIVIL FRANÇAIS (5 vols. 1838–47); TROPLONG, LE DROIT CIVIL EXPLIQUÉ SUIVANT L'ORDRE DES ARTICLES DU CODE (27 vols. 1833–72); DEMOLOMBE, COURS DE CODE NAPOLÉON (32 vols. 1844); MARCADÉ, EXPLICATION THÉORIQUE ET PRATIQUE DE CODE CIVIL (13 vols. 1873–84); LAURENT, PRINCIPES DE DROIT CIVIL FRANÇAIS (33 vols. 1876–78).

teenth-century edition, and the treatise of Aubry and Rau is currently in its seventh edition.

During the nineteenth century, doctrine was generally ahead of the courts in the process of interpretation of the civil code. Courts, however, did not show exaggerated respect for doctrine, and, for a period of time, there were two currents of opinion to be found in jurisprudence and in doctrine respectively. Toward the end of the century, most scholars realized that it was absurd to continue to expound opinions that the courts were determined to reject. Accordingly, they set to work on practical treatises, relating the precepts of the code to the solutions of the jurisprudence. Gény had already pointed out the deficiencies of the exegetical method and led the way to a new methodology.[46] Instead of looking to the past, the new interpreters of the law asked the question, what should a contemporary legislator have done? To find the answer, they undertook a scientific exploration of legislation enacted since the adoption of the civil code, of surviving customs, of jurisprudence, and of related social sciences.

A great number of monographs and several treatises that appeared in the last years of the nineteenth century or in the first part of the twentieth century became standard references for any practitioner. Among them were the treatises of Baudry-Lacantinerie, Planiol, Colin and Capitant, and Planiol and Ripert.[47] These works continue to be up-to-date by means of subsequent editions. Currently, particular significance is attached to the treatises of Carbonnier and of Marty and Raynaud.[48] Contemporary treatises, as well as doctrinal comments in legal periodicals elaborating on the test of published decisions, serve as a dissent from or concurrence with jurisprudential solutions. They refer to legislation, doctrine, and past jurisprudence, and indicate grounds for the validity of judicial determinations.

---

46 See GÉNY, MÉTHODE D'INTERPRÉTATION ET SOURCES EN DROIT PRIVÉ POSITIF (1st ed. 1899); cf. JHERING, DER ZWEEK IN RECHT (2 vols. 1877–83).
47 BAUDRY-LACANTINERIE, TRAITÉ THÉORIQUE ET PRACTIQUE DE DROIT CIVIL (25 vols. 1895); PLANIOL, TRAITÉ ÉLÉMENTAIRE DE DROIT CIVIL (3 vols. 1899); COLIN & CAPITANT, COURS ÉLÉMENTAIRE DE DROIT CIVIL FRANÇAIS (3 vols. 1913); and PLANIOL & RIPERT, TRAITÉ PRATIQUE DE DROIT CIVIL FRANÇAIS (14 vols. 1925–34).
48 CARBONNIER, DROIT CIVIL (2 vols. 8th ed., 1969); and MARTY & RAYNAUD, DROIT CIVIL (3 vols. 1956–68).

Contemporary French doctrine thus tends to place the work of the courts in perspective, and to relate it to controlling legislation and social policy. Scholars do not hesitate to express the view that a certain course of judicial action is erroneous, in the same way that dissenting judges in common-law jurisdictions point out that a majority opinion is erroneous. Doctrinal writers consider themselves equal to the judges. It is assumed that the courts—under the pressure of routine duties, the need for dispatch, and the subjection to the influence of the facts of a particular case—are not in a position to appreciate all the consequences of their decisions in relation to general policies and the legal system as a whole. Doctrine, free of routine judicial duties, performs at leisure the mission of a guide, and is charged with the responsibility of maintaining cohesiveness and certainty of law.

Louisiana. Doctrine has never reached in Louisiana the degree of development that it has achieved in France. In the early stages of Louisiana legal history, the bar and bench were well acquainted with the sources and literature of the civil law, and had access to valuable doctrinal materials in French and Spanish. The redactors of the Louisiana Civil Code of 1825 relied heavily upon French and Spanish publications for the formulation of a great number of articles that have no equivalent in the French Civil Code.[49] The *Projet* of the Louisiana Civil Code of 1825 frequently identifies these publications and cites them as authorities for proposed additions or amendments. For the purpose of a proper interpretation of the Louisiana Civil Codes of 1808 and 1825, courts used likewise to rely heavily on nineteenth-century French and Spanish treatises. Toullier, Marcadé, and Aubry and Rau[50] achieved in this respect a position of eminence.

By the time of the civil war, however, and especially during the era of Reconstruction, the use of English became almost universal in Louisiana. As a result, reliance on doctrinal materials deriving from French or Spanish sources was substantially diminished. The development of Louisiana law took a new turn, common-law influence was expanded, and the 1870 code came to be regarded as just another statute suitable for literal

49 See Projet of the Civil Code of 1825, 2 La. Legal Archives (1937).
50 See TOULLIER, LE DROIT CIVIL FRANÇAIS (14 vols. 1811); MARCADÉ, EXPLICATION THÉORIQUE ET PRATIQUE DU CODE CIVIL (13 vols. 1873–84); AUBRY & RAU, COURS DE DROIT CIVIL FRANÇAIS (1838–47).

application only. It is true that during this period and up to the present time Louisiana has been fortunate enough to have a number of great scholars, especially judges, well versed in both the civil law and the common law. The Louisiana law reports furnish indications of the continuity of the civilian tradition in the state, and of the scholarship of great judges, who, like Provosty, undertook to write scholarly dissertations in the form of judicial opinions.[51]

Civil-law doctrine, and indeed civil-law development, reached its lowest point in the first quarter of the twentieth century. By the mid-thirties the question was asked whether Louisiana had a civil law at all.[52] Gradually, however, the legal profession adjusted to the idea that Louisiana is a mixed jurisdiction, sharing the civil law as well as the common-law tradition; and efforts were undertaken by faculties and interested groups of judges and lawyers for the strengthening of civilian institutions as well as for the development of the branches of law that derived from the reservoir of the common law. The last three decades have witnessed a renaissance of civilian studies in Louisiana. The movement has been spearheaded by work in the law faculties of the state and by projects undertaken by the Louisiana State Law Institute.

The Law Faculties. Faculties in Louisiana law schools have strengthened civilian offerings, created institutes for civil law and comparative-law studies, and undertaken far-reaching research projects. Some of these projects resulted in published monographs and collections of essays;[53] others have resulted in the publication of leading articles in the Louisiana, Tulane, or Loyola law reviews. Excellent contributions by members of the Louisiana legal professions as well as by civilians from other juris-

---

51 See Louisiana & A. Ry. Co. v. Winn Parish Lumber Co., 131 La. 288, 59 So. 403 (1912) (separate opinion by Provosty, J.).

52 See Pope, "How Real Is the Difference Today between the Law of Louisiana and That of the Other Forty-Seven States?" 17 GEORGE WASHINGTON LAW REVIEW 186–98 (1949); Ireland, "Louisiana's Legal System Reappraised," 11 TUL. L. REV. 585 (1937); Greenburg, "Must Louisiana Resign to the Common Law?" 11 TUL. L. REV. 598 (1937); Dart, "The Place of the Civil Law in Louisiana," 4 TUL. L. REV. 163 (1930); Crabites, "Louisiana Not a Civil Law State," 9 LOYOLA L. REV. 15 (1928).

53 See, e.g., ESSAYS ON THE CIVIL LAW OF OBLIGATIONS (Dainow ed. 1969); CIVIL LAW IN THE MODERN WORLD (Yiannopoulos ed. 1965). For detailed information, see WALLACH, LOUISIANA LEGAL RESEARCH MANUAL 243–46 (1972).

dictions are contained in past volumes of these reviews. These publications provide a constant critique and evaluation of our civil-law institutions, and they furnish the basis for a synthesis of our legislative texts, old and new, and of judicial decisions in their relationship to established legal principles.

In addition, student notes and comments, written under the supervision of the faculties or of leading members of the bar, furnish invaluable assistance in evaluating the background and contexts of legislation and judicial decisions, and in supplying perspective as to their history and intended meaning. Laboring under the demands of a crowded docket or busy practice, neither judges nor practitioners have the requisite time to undertake an exhaustive study of related and incidental matters bearing on a question of law. This important and time-consuming species of research is normally carried out in connection with notes and comments published in the law reviews.

The Louisiana State Law Institute. The Louisiana legislature established in 1938 the Louisiana State Law Institute, an official law-reform agency, in order "to promote and encourage the clarification of the law of Louisiana and its better adaptation to present needs, to secure the better administration of justice and to carry out scholarly research and scientific work."[54] In accordance with this broadly conceived mission of the institute, the Louisiana legislature passed in 1948 Act 335 by which the institute was specifically directed to prepare a *projet* for the revision of the civil code.[55] The legislative mandate was implemented in 1960 with the organization of the civil-law section of the institute. The objectives which this newly organized section aspires to fulfill may be summarized in the two propositions: the development of civil-law studies in Louisiana and the accomplishment of a revision of the civil code.

Since its foundation in 1938, the Louisiana State Law Institute has accomplished a number of major codifications, and has encouraged the revival of civilian thinking and theory. A successful revision of the civil code, indeed, presupposes the development of civil-law studies. Obviously, the work of revision would be deficient in the absence of doctrinal

---

54 La. Acts No. 166 (1938); SMITH, EIGHTEENTH BIENNIAL REPORT OF THE LOUISIANA STATE LAW INSTITUTE TO THE LEGISLATURE OF LOUISIANA (1972).
55 See Yiannopoulos, "The Civil Law Program of the Louisiana State Law Institute," 12 LA. B. J. 89–99 (1964).

studies furnishing a scientifically sound foundation. A civil code cannot be drafted, nor can it be expected to function properly, without a well-developed civilian doctrine. Civil codes have been generally conceived as self-sufficient bodies of legislation, as the law par excellence, supplemented only by custom and put to work by jurisprudence and doctrine. If these codes were destined to be interpreted and applied by a legal profession looking for guidance to common-law sources, they could soon lose their glamor and significance. Lawyers, judges, and the general public would look for authority to precedents interpreting the code rather than to the code itself; and difficulties connected with the handling of the code would certainly give rise to pseudo problems and might result in solutions contrary to the letter and spirit of the code. These considerations, highlighting the interdependence of codification and doctrine, have led to the adoption of a long-range program for the development of civilian doctrine in Louisiana. Several coordinated projects in various areas of interest have been studied and approved in principle. This program contemplates the production of comprehensive treatises and commentaries on the Louisiana Civil Code, the publication of annotated translations of selected French textbooks, and the collection of materials scattered in numerous periodicals.

Under agreement with the Louisiana State Law Institute, the West Publishing Company inaugurated in 1965 the publication of a long overdue *Louisiana Civil Law Treatise*. Volume 1 of the series has been reserved for a comprehensive study of the Louisiana legal system as a whole. Volume 2 is Yiannopoulos' *Civil Law of Property*, and Volume 3 *Personal Servitudes* by the same author. Volume 6 is Litvinoff's *Obligations: Book I*. Additional volumes, under preparation, will deal with the law of contracts, torts, family, and successions. These works analyze the historical background of particular provisions and institutions; interpret the code in the light of these historical materials, and ascertain, whenever this is possible, the intention of the redactors of the code; collect Louisiana jurisprudence and evaluate it critically in the light of the code and by reference to the exigencies of contemporary needs; and compare the Louisiana Civil Code with the codes of France and Germany as well as the codes of other selected civil-law countries.

In addition to the *Louisiana Civil Law Treatise* series, the institute has sponsored translations of French texts into English. These translations include Planiol's *Civil Law Treatise* (1959); Gény's *Method of Interpretation and Sources of Private Positive Law* (1963); Aubry and Rau's *Obligations* (1965), *Property* (1966), *Testamentary Successions* (1969), and *Intestate Successions* (1971). Additional translations are under preparation. These works have already had an impact on Louisiana jurisprudence, assisting the courts in the interpretation of the civil code in the light of its intended meaning and with reference to French experience.[56]

Today, doctrine plays a much more important role in Louisiana than most members of the bench or bar are ready to admit. Original treatises and translations from the French have played an important part in the establishment of guiding principles in various fields. These works furnish a scholarly perspective, bring knowledge and research into the background and purpose of legal precepts, assist in the evaluation of legislation and jurisprudence, and suggest the course of future developments. The bloom of Louisiana doctrine in the last three decades foreshadows an even greater role in times to come. The growth of our population and the increasing complexity of our civilization have produced such a mass of legislative materials and judicial precedents that the practitioner and the judge will have to turn with ever-increasing frequency to general works which synthesize and evaluate legislation and jurisprudence in their relation to fundamental legal precepts.

---

56 See Dainow, "The Planiol Treatise on the Civil Law: French and Louisiana Law for Comparative Study," 10 AM J. COMP. L. 175 (1961); Dainow, "Planiol Citations by Louisiana Courts: 1959–1965," 27 LA. L. REV. 231 (1967).

ABBREVIATIONS

Am. J. Comp. L.	American Journal of Comparative Law
La.	Louisiana Reports (1900 to present)
La. Ann.	Louisiana Annual Reports (1846–1900)
La. B. J.	Louisiana Bar Journal
La. L. Rev.	Louisiana Law Review
Loyola L. Rev.	Loyola Law Review
Rev. Jur. U.P.R.	Revista Juridica de la Universidad de Puerto Rico
So. 2d	Southern Reporter, second series
Tul. L. Rev.	Tulane Law Review
U.S.	United States Supreme Court Reports

V

Authorities in Civil Law: France*

Jean Carbonnier
PROFESSOR OF LAW, UNIVERSITY OF PARIS

English translation by John Brierley,
Professor of Law, McGill University, Montreal

Authorities in the civil law are not sources of law in the proper sense of the term; no binding rules of law flow directly from them. They are, however, elements taken into consideration in the interpretation of legal rules and, when the latter are silent or insufficient, the solution to a legal problem must be found. For the practitioner they are "authorities" —given respect in fact, if not in law. These moral rather than legal authorities are of two types: greater weight is attached to the *jurisprudence* (Section One) than to the *doctrine* (Section Two), but both employ a number of *methods of interpretation* and construction (Section Three).

SECTION ONE. THE JURISPRUDENCE

In a loose—and today somewhat archaic—sense, *jurisprudence* is the science or philosophy of the law. In the current and more technical sense, it means the decisions of the courts: the solution generally provided by judicial decisions to some legal question. It is thus an aspect of the application of the general principle that without continuity and imitation the law itself would be inexplicable. In effect, when the courts are faced

---

* The main idea of the plan of this work lies in the distinction between the two kinds of exposition it contains. On each subject there is, first of all, a systematic but summary explanation of the positive law—free (if that is possible) of personal views and unencumbered by the citation of authorities. Following this, the reader will find a number of sections generally entitled "Related Questions." These are designed to serve not as supplementary materials for examination purposes, but rather as a series of complementary perspectives in theory and practice, in legislative critique, in sociology and history, and in modern law. The hope is that law students, as well as others who are curious about the law, may be tempted to pursue these suggested paths in order to penetrate further each of the aspects evoked. [Excerpt from the Carbonnier preface, p. 7.]

In the original French publication, this material constitutes a chapter of Carbonnier, *Droit Civil* (8th ed. 1969), I, 119–42.

with a similar recurring question, they acquire the habit, more or less quickly, of providing a similar answer; they thereby assure equal treatment to their justiciables. And so it may be anticipated that a court at some future time will decide the same issue in the same way: it is not bound to do so in law, but it will probably do so in fact.

The jurisprudence thus appears to be the practice of the courts. How this practice is established, and what its force really is, are the questions now to be examined.

I. Formation of the Jurisprudence. The jurisprudence is constituted by individual *judgments*, taking into account their *repetition* and rank within the judicial *hierarchy of courts* from which they issue.

A. The judgments [1] of the courts of first instance, the courts of appeal and the French supreme court, the Cour de cassation, are the raw material of the jurisprudence.

The part of the judgment serving as a formative element for the jurisprudence is that within it which is most abstract and thus of some general value for later cases; this is found not in the actual decision of any instant case but rather in the legal reasoning adopted which has resulted in a decision favourable to one of the parties. A distinction is therefore drawn between the actual order of the court (*le dispositif*) and the reasons (*les motifs*) which have logically dictated the decision.[2] The judgment taken as a whole does, of course, have its importance, but it is the judicial reasoning in the interpretation or construction of the legal rule (the adoption, therefore, of legal reasons, *motifs de droit*, as distinct from reasons based on fact, *motifs de fait*) that is of importance in the creation of jurisprudence.

B. The fact of repetition is generally taken to be an element in the definition of the jurisprudence (*rerum perpetuo similiter judicatarum auctoritas*).[3] While this is, of course, true most of the time, it may neverthe-

[1] The term judgment is employed, *lato sensu*, to designate the *judgments* (*stricto sensu*) of the *tribunaux d'instance* or courts of first instance, the *arrêts* of the Cours d'appel or courts of appeal, and the *arrêts* of the Cour de cassation. A list of the abbreviations used in this chapter appears on page 118.
[2] The French style of written judgments is highly formal; it is distinguished by its concise, almost terse, summary narration of the facts and its abstract reasoning formulated within a series of dependent clauses, set off within the body of the decision itself by the use of *whereas* (*attendu que, considérant que*), the whole of which forms but a single sentence.
[3] Digest I, iii (*de legibus*) 38.

less happen that the jurisprudence relied upon is in fact established in a single, but decisive, decision of the Cour de cassation; its quality, one might say, makes up for the lack of quantity. This is not, however, an absolute rule; in some circumstances a single decision of that court will be considered an "isolated" one, insufficient to "make" or "establish" jurisprudence. The reason is quite simple: jurisprudence is not a source of law; it is no more than an opinion which may, with time, tend to become the law. A single case, therefore, even from the highest court, has only more or less authority according to the circumstances.

C. The hierarchy of courts established within the judicial organization has an effect upon the formation of the jurisprudence. The appeal and the petition for review on a question of law (*pourvoi en cassation*) help to assure a uniformity in the jurisprudence by imposing the opinion of courts higher in the hierarchy upon those lower down. This is achieved either directly (when upon either an appeal or a *pourvoi* the higher court substitutes its view to that of the lower court) or indirectly (when the lower court adjudicates in the sense already known to it to represent the higher court's views).

1. *Appeal.* Judgments may only be appealed once, but a right of appeal always exists in principle. Appeals may be taken from the judgments of the courts of first instance having general jurisdiction (the *tribunaux d'instance* or petty courts (judge sitting alone) and the collegial *tribunaux de grande instance*) to the courts of appeal (*Cours d'appel*) excepting cases in which the amount of money involved is too small. The procedure in appeal, which must be lodged within one month from the date of the service of the judgment,[4] has two effects: it suspends the execution process of the judgment against which appeal is taken[5] and it transfers the entire suit before the higher court, both as to matters of law and of fact. While no new claims may be initiated at the stage of appeal, new arguments, grounds (*moyens*), or reasoning may be pleaded in support of those already formulated.[6]

2. *Pourvoi en cassation.* The *pourvoi*, or petition for review on a question of law, is available within two months following the service of the decisions of either a court of appeal or a court of first instance whose de-

---

4 Article 444, *Code de procédure civile.*
5 Article 458, *Code de procédure civile.*
6 Article 464, *Code de procédure civile.*

cision was final. Neither of the effects attached to the lodging of an appeal occurs: the pourvoi does not suspend execution (except in a few cases, such as divorce) nor does the whole suit (questions of fact as well as of law) devolve to the Cour de cassation. Only previously argued questions of law are submitted—or rather, more accurately, only the holding of the lower court is examined insofar as it had decided them. No new claims may be made at this stage, nor may any new grounds be raised. The parameters of the legal debate have definitely been drawn. At most, therefore, only new arguments may be offered. The role of the Cour de cassation, it is often said, is to judge judgments, not suits; it is a court of law, and only of law, in contrast to every other court which may judge on the facts (juridictions du fonds).

In order, moreover, for the Cour de cassation to have jurisdiction, the pourvoi must invoke some ground giving rise to the right of review.[7] Putting to one side procedural irregularities[8] as well as grounds for review of a constitutional dimension,[9] the proper substance of the pourvoi en cassation is error of law, taken in the largest sense. Inaccurate interpretations of the law, incorrect application of law, or refusal to apply it, are all included. Maxims of the law and supereminent principles,[10] even though they may not have been formulated within legislative enactment, are equally protected (save for local or contractual usage since, in their regard, uniformity of application and interpretation is not essential). The practice of the Cour de cassation itself has added a further ground giving rise to review, "inadequacy of written reasons" (insuffisance de motifs) and "absence of legal basis" (manque de base légale) as, for example, in cases where the reasons given by the lower-court judges are so summary, or so vague, that it is impossible to say whether the decision has any real justification in law and whether, therefore, the court itself can effectively exercise its control.

7 Cf. the Constitution of the Year VIII, art. 66: The Tribunal de cassation . . . annuls judgments rendered in instances where procedural forms have not been observed.
8 Inobservation des formes de la procédure, incompétence.
9 Excès de pouvoir (i.e. a court has in its judgment usurped a legislative or executive function); contrariété de jugements (i.e., conflicting judgments rendered as between the same parties, on the same grounds, in different courts).
10 As to these principes généraux, cf. DAVID & BRIERLEY, MAJOR LEGAL SYSTEMS (1968), 107 ff.

If the division (*chambre*) of the Cour de cassation before which the *pourvoi* is brought dismisses it, the lower court's decision retains its full effect. On the other hand, if the petition is maintained, then the division quashes (*casse*) the decision attacked; and, since it has no power either to examine the merits of the case or to substitute its own decision, the division remands the case for a new judgment to another court of the same category as the first (which, in practice, usually means to another court of appeal) geographically proximate to that whose decision is annulled. Before this court ("the court of renvoi") the trial will be held again; but such court is not bound in law to observe the opinion of the Cour de cassation. However, if the court decides in the same way as the first judges (those whose decision was annulled), and its decision, in turn, is also the object of a further *pourvoi* based on the same grounds, this latter petition is submitted to the full court of the Cour de cassation.[11] In this event, there is, in effect, an open difference of opinion between one division of the court and the lower courts; and in this eventuality the full court, as the highest judicial authority in France, is called upon to decide the matter. The holding (*arrêt solennel*) of the full court either dismisses the *pourvoi*, in which case the lower court's view overrides that of the division, or allows it (the full court, then, adheres to the view of its division). In this last hypothesis, the quashed judgment is again sent before a third lower court which is, however, not free to render its own decision; it can do nothing other than register the decision of the full court.[12] This power of the Cour de cassation to impose finally its own view of the law on all lower courts gives it an effective supervisory control over the jurisprudence.

II. Legal Force of the Jurisprudence. While the jurisprudence is not a true source of civil law, comparable to legislation or even custom, it is an authority, and a considerable one, in the civil law of France.

A. *Jurisprudence is not a source of civil law.* Consider, first of all, the judgment—the basic ingredient of the jurisprudence. It is enclosed with-

---

11 The full court has been designated as *l'Assemblée plénière* since the law of July 3, 1967, arts. 3, 7, & 15 (v. Dalloz 1967, L. 250); it was previously called *les chambres réunies*.
12 Law of 1967, art. 16; in effect, if the second judgment rendered is quashed for the same reasons as the first, the full court may decide without remanding.

in a constitutional framework which is intended to prevent it from ever becoming a rule of law. Such is the objective of Code Civil article 5,[13] which formally prohibits judges from rendering judgments having a binding legislative or regulatory effect (*arrêts de règlement*) similar to that attributed to the *arrêts* of the former *parlements* of the pre–1789 period. The rule is a corollary of the principle of the separation of powers.[14] Similarly, the principle of res judicata, the relative effect of a decided case (*l'autorité relative de la chose jugée*),[15] tends to the same effect: a judgment only has authority, legal force, between those who were parties to the suit; it may not be invoked against third persons. On that score alone, of course, it is quite the opposite of a rule of law, a general provision applicable to everyone. A line of uniformly decided cases will never, therefore, constitute anything more than a series of individual decisions to particular cases with no greater status than that. Even the *arrêts solennels* of the full Cour de cassation only enjoy this limited stature and do not possess, apart from the cases in which they occur, anything more than a purely moral superiority or authority in fact before either the lower courts or any single division of the supreme court.

Nor may the jurisprudence be treated as rules of law under the guise of *custom*. It has none of the elements that go to the making of a customary law: its origins are not popular (jurisprudence is a law made by technicians), it lacks the substratum of duration (a single decision can establish jurisprudence). Moreover, and this is essential, the jurisprudence is devoid of the obligatory character attaching to custom, since any given court is not bound by its own previous decisions. Changes in established jurisprudence (*revirements de jurisprudence*) are always possible, and they are not rare. When they occur, such changes have a very different effect from changes brought about by ordinary legislative amend-

13 Article 5, *Code civil*: In the decision of cases submitted to them, judges are forbidden to lay down general rules of conduct. (English editions of the French *Code civil* are those of George Spence [1827], London; Henry Cachard [1895], London; and E. B. Wright [1908], London).
14 Cf. art. 127, para. 1, *Code pénal* which imposes forfeiture of office as a sanction applicable to judges and judicial officers who "interfere in the exercise of the legislative power"; the principle has been a constant feature of the various constitutions of the French Republic.
15 Article 1351, *Code civil*: The authority of *res judicata* extends only to the subject matter of the judgment. The claim must be for the same thing; it must be based on the same cause of action; it must be between the same parties, and brought by and against them in the same qualities.

ment. The change or reversal of jurisprudence is, by nature, retroactive—the new jurisprudential solution will automatically apply to whatever private persons may have done, or counted upon, on the basis of the former jurisprudence.

B. *Jurisprudence is an authority in the civil law*. For the judge or lawyer, in the process of forming a legal opinion as to which among several positions to adopt, the jurisprudence is one among several factors taken into account, a psychological force. It may be said therefore that it is an *authority*: an influence, of varying intensity, but never legally imposed.

Since it is no more than an authority in fact and never a legally binding rule, the real authority of the jurisprudence may be gauged. It is well known that not all precedents have the same weight and that distinctions may be drawn according to a number of criteria. There is, of course, first of all, the rank of the decision, corresponding to the rank of the court which rendered it within the judicial hierarchy; greater weight will be given to decisions of the full Cour de cassation than to those of lower courts. There is, further, an internal criterion applicable to decisions of the same court: distinctions are traditionally drawn, especially regarding decisions of the Cour de cassation, between those rendered rather more by reason of the particular facts in the case than by the light of the law in general terms (the *arrêt d'espèce*) and those where the legal question is given detailed study and a solution is proposed in terms of some general legal application (*arrêts de principe*). The latter, evidently, will enjoy a greater prestige than the former. The geographical location of the court may also be a factor. The courts of appeal, for example, and sometimes as well the commercial courts (*tribunaux de commerce*), often have their own traditions and tend to attribute greater importance to their own decisions than to those of a neighbouring court. The date of the decision, finally, will also be considered: the older the decision (from the early nineteenth century, for example) the less, in all likelihood, the respect it will have; what the practitioner wants in support of his point is the *latest* jurisprudence. As between two conflicting decisions of the same court, the later in time will be preferred.

Thus while the jurisprudence is no more than an authority, it is a *privileged* authority because the thesis in support of which it may be cited in litigation has the greatest chance of becoming the law in fact. This is why, when speaking of the "law" (*droit*) of a country, one must include within that term not only its enacted law (*loi*) but also its jurisprudence; and why, further, those who are, by reason of their profession, bound to know the law, must be as familiar with the jurisprudence of their country as with its legislation and would, if they didn't take it into account, commit a fault for which they would be held liable to their clients.

RELATED QUESTIONS: CASE REPORTS [16]

The jurisprudence should be published, not so much in the interest of litigants as in that of practitioners and judges, and in order that it take stock of itself. The present publication policy is fairly free, but controls are on the increase. A first and general observation must be made: the jurisprudence that does find its way into the judicial reports is only a very small part of the whole body of decided cases. We are, for example, ignorant of almost all the cases heard by petty-court judges (*juges d'instance*) save for a few of the more curious among their decisions; and only selected decisions of the courts of first instance (*tribunaux de grande instance*) and even the courts of appeal are reported. All of the decisions of the Cour de cassation, however, are published. The selection is inevitable by reason of the great bulk of decisions. The operative criterion is the *legal* interest of any individual case (which means, as a consequence, that those based on equitable considerations remain largely unknown) and this legal interest is empirically appreciated by the reporters or correspondents in the courts with which the various reports maintain a connection.

A. *Official Reports.* The *Bulletin des arrêts de la Cour de cassation*, published in two series (one for the civil chambers and one for the criminal) was reorganized and made official by the legislation of 23 July 1947 (Article 62). It is published on the basis of a central index (*fichier central*), established by the same law (Articles 10 ff.), in which all decisions are recorded under a single system of subject headings. This index (called the *service de documentation et d'études de la Cour de cassation* since the legislation of 4 August 1956) is designed to ensure consistency and uniformity in the jurisprudence of the different divisions and

---

16 [*Translator's note*: Further details are provided by SZLADITS, GUIDE TO FOREIGN LEGAL MATERIALS: FRENCH, GERMAN, SWISS (1959), 61 ff.]

within the court as a whole. The court's memory is, so to speak, henceforth recorded on index cards. . . . but could it not be suggested that forgetfulness is sometimes more precious than total recall? Mightn't the index encourage a purely routine approach?

B. *Private Reports.* These periodical publications reproduce the texts of certain selected decisions and provide additional features: the summary or headnote of the decision; and an annotation which explains, and sometimes gives a critical appreciation of, the decision. Sometimes the "note" is developed into an important doctrinal study and will then usually be signed by its author (the *arrêtiste*); sometimes it is no more than a series of references to previously decided cases and doctrinal studies on the same subject. These series are designed to form annual volumes, and they are cited by the year, the part, and the page:

1. *Sirey* (S.), named after its first publisher, was founded in 1791; it is still invaluable for the first decades of the nineteenth century and very useful for later periods because of its annotations (especially, at the end of the century, those by J. E. Labbé who is generally regarded as the master of the *arrêtistes*).

2. *Dalloz* (D.), after the name of its founder. The current series began in 1845, but its publication format has varied: from 1924 to 1942, it was published in two parts as *Dalloz* [*périodique*] (monthly) and *Dalloz* [*hebdomadaire*] (weekly) and cited D.P. and D.H.; from 1941 to 1944 its monthly and weekly titles were *Dalloz critique* and *Dalloz analytique*, cited D.C. and D.A. At the present time the *Recueil Dalloz* is weekly and contains three parts, separately paged: (i) "chroniques doctrinales" or doctrinal articles, cited as D. 1955 chron. 5; (ii) jurisprudence, cited as D. 1955, J. 229 (or, most often and more concisely, as D. 55.229); and (iii) legislation (*lois*) cited as D. 1955, L. 44. Since 1965 this and the above series have been published as *Recueil Dalloz-Sirey* in three similar parts, again separately paged.

3. *La Semaine juridique* or *Juris-classeur périodique*, cited as J.C.P. or Sem. jur., is more recent (1927). It, too, has three parts, each of which is arranged by numbers rather than pages: doctrinal articles, jurisprudence, and legislative texts (for example, J.C.P. 55.2.8505).

4. *Gazette du Palais*, cited as Gaz. Pal. or G.P., is a newspaper, founded in 1881, which appears several times a week. The subject matter is

republished in bimonthly editions and these are finally bound as two volumes per annum. While the decisions are published quickly, the annotations are usually only in the form of references.

5. In addition to the series listed above which report cases in all subject matters, there are other specialized reports: *Revue des loyers, Revue des fermages, Droit social, Recueil des arrêts du Conseil d'Etat* (or *Lebon*) and those where civil-law matters are examined particularly from the point of view of the conveyancer (i.e. notarial practices): *Répertoire général pratique du notariat* (*Defrénois*) and *Journal des notaires*.

History. The arrêts or holdings of the French *parlements* of the old regime were not "motivated" (i.e. written reasons were not provided). One author, Lamoignon, gave the following explanation (but it would only have been applicable to the Parlement de Paris): the *procureur-général*, always present, could give an oral explanation to the king of the reasons for the decision. This feature of the old system did prevent, however, the formation of a coherent jurisprudence. Somewhat paradoxically, the revolution, by imposing the duty that judges provide written reasons (in an effort to guarantee individual rights) established, by the same token, the means whereby any tendency towards narrow legalism could be defeated. It is of interest to note, however, that the reports of decisions from the old regime do contain summaries of the parties' pretensions, from which it is possible to infer, at least in part, what the reasons for a decision were. Thus it seems clear the practitioners of the time did use, although certainly to a lesser degree than today, previously decided cases. A number of series of reports were published (for example, the *Répertoire de jurisprudence* by J. N. Guyot [1728–1816]). The oldest series of French reports is *Les Olim*, dating from the thirteenth century 4 vols. (ed. Beugnot, 1839–1848).

Sociology. The jurisprudence might be studied as a phenomenon of social imitation, of hierarchical interaction (the influence of the highest court on the lowest, or again that of the lowest on the highest since the judges at the level of first instance are generally considered to be "closer" to the litigants themselves and more directly aware of social needs). Another possibly fruitful avenue of investigation: to what extent has

French jurisprudence since 1804 been influenced by the social origins of the members of the judiciary? One remark, in any event, not made often enough, is this: what we call the jurisprudence is much less the work of the judges than it is of the lawyers. Their pleadings and conclusions are the stuff from which new systems of interpretation and construction are forged. The judges' role is thus mainly one of choosing between different suggested theses; in France, at least in the civil law, they are not really inventive in their own right.

Legislative Policy. Is it desirable in a modern civil-law system that greater weight be given to the jurisprudence, or should enacted law be so developed that jurisprudence might be rendered unnecessary? During the last century the infatuation for jurisprudence has increased—the evidence lies in the fashion of the case comment (*commentaire d'arrêt*) which has become the preponderant form of contemporary doctrinal literature.

The work of the Cour de cassation has sometimes been compared to that of the Roman praetor because of its suppleness and the supposed facility with which it adapts to contemporary needs. But the weaknesses of the jurisprudence must also be noted: 1. Its *slowness*. A delay of ten years or more may elapse before a controverted question reaches the Cour de cassation and, in the event of a difference between it and the judges on the merits, the bringing into operation of the mechanism of the full court may take a very long time indeed. 2. Its *uncertainty*. The stylized formulae in which decisions are drafted are often very puzzling; it is sometimes more difficult to interpret the jurisprudence than the law, and the difficulty is all the greater in regard to the jurisprudence of the Cour de cassation because of its tendency to qualify its holdings in a way which will not impair future developments. 3. Its *insecurity*. Any change in the jurisprudence amounts to a change in the law with retroactive effect—and one is not, moreover, warned of the change in advance. 4. Its *inability* to bring about any true reforms. The jurisprudence, inevitably, meets a number of formal obstacles (for example, the enactment of a number: the courts could not have been expected to adapt the figure of 150 francs in Article 1341 of the Code Civil [17] to the realities of a devaluated currency); nor can it be creative to the point of establishing an

---

[17] The article required that a writing be produced in regard to the proof of matters in which the sum or value exceeded 150 francs.

administrative system (such as the organization of a system of recordation of births, marriages, and deaths).

A wholly jurisprudential formation of the law would not, moreover, be without inconveniences: litigation dilutes legal realities. What we call, with some conceit, the "needs of the practice" are not always the needs of real social life but only those that have received some expression through the prism of a lawsuit. It need hardly be observed that not all legal relations give rise to lawsuits. It may be that those involved with the law are too poor to go to court (this fact was of some influence on the Code Napoléon, the law of the rich and the middle classes, enacted at a time when there was no legal aid), or too timid, or too reasonable (the law emerging from the jurisprudence is necessarily somewhat pathological). On the other hand, those involved with the law are sometimes too powerful: large corporations can come to compromises and arrangements amongst themselves about which one knows nothing. No one could construct a law on the subject of oil and gas on the basis of the reported decisions on the subject.

Legal Theory. It is a widely held modern doctrinal view that the jurisprudence *is* a source of law and that the only matter open to debate is the *reason* for its obligatory force. Different reasons are advanced: it is based on the *tacit consent of the legislators;* or upon an *autonomous power of the legal professions,* by which term is to be understood not only judges whose judgments constitute jurisprudence and others who conform thereto, but also members of the practising professions who henceforth forego litigating the same points, since the *consensus* of the latter is as important as the decisions of the former. Or is it a *modern form of customary law?* It must, on this point, be observed that the jurisprudence does not recognize itself as a source of law: there would be insufficiency of reasons were a court to cite, in support of its judgment, a line of uniformly and previously decided cases (*jurisprudence constante*).[18] The Cour de cassation only pays heed to the jurisprudence *through* enacted law: it never annuls a decision for inobservation of its own jurisprudence, only for error of law; but the error of law lies in not interpreting as it

18 Civ. 26 March 1941, D.A. 41.194.

does. For these reasons it appears more accurate to say that jurisprudence is no more than an authority in the civil law.[19]

It is nonetheless an authority which jurists, whether notary or judge, must know because it forms part of the total system or science of the law (the Cour de cassation prefers to say because it "forms a whole" with enacted law,[20] but it may be doubted that it would go so far as to say that a private person should therefore be familiar with it by virtue of the principle *ignorantia juris non excusat, nul n'est censé ignoré la loi*). The Cour de cassation itself, moreover, draws a distinction between "settled" and "unsettled" jurisprudence (*jurisprudence assise* and *jurisprudence controversée*), and it is really only the first that is integrated into the legal system. This idea, that the jurisprudence is a source of inspiration for the judge, not a binding rule, is that of the Swiss *Code Civil*.[21] The opposing view, which would make of decided cases a source of law, is very close to the theory of English law in which the judicial precedent is the primordial source of legal rules. To say as much is, however, insufficient to underline the real difference separating the English system of *stare decisis* and the French view. The general idea of the English system is that any decision rendered by a court of law henceforth possesses, in its own right and without the need of any subsequent reaffirmation by later decisions, the status of an obligatory rule for that court and courts of coordinate jurisdiction. Later changes are in principle ruled out. *Stare decisis* was introduced in order to provide a body of fixed rules of law, and thus security, whereas in France the cases are seen as a means of achieving flexibility. From these premises it follows that in the hypothesis where two decisions conflict, the common law would attach greater value to the older decision and it supposes that the later in date has been "incorrectly" decided since it has broken the rule of precedent. There is nothing further removed from the French conception than this, for in France it is the latest decision that will have the greatest authority.

19 *Cf.* GÉNY, METHOD OF INTERPRETATION AND SOURCES OF PRIVATE POSITIVE LAW 146 ff. (J. Mayda transl. 1963).
20 *Cf.* Note by Hébraud and Raynaud, 51. REV. TRIM. DR. CIV. 731, 735 (1953).
21 Article 1, paras. 2 & 3: [In the absence of applicable provisions of law, the judge] decides according to customary law and, in the absence of custom, according to the rules he would establish if he were performing a legislative function. He patterns his decision upon principles recognized in decided cases and doctrinal writings.

Judicial Practice. As an example of a reversal or change in the position of the jurisprudence (*revirement de jurisprudence*), consider the following example. Upon the question, can a person adopt his own illegitimate child, the Cour de cassation at first gave an affirmative answer, and its decision was greeted as an *arrêt de principe* (Civ. 28 April 1841, S. 41.1.274); two years later, however, it held the opposite (Civ. 16 March 1843, S. 43.1.177); finally, in 1846, it returned to its earlier view (Civ. 1 April 1846, S. 46.1.273), this time definitively.[22]

Some idea of the volume of cases coming before the Cour de cassation is suggested by a statistic from 1965: it dismissed 3,100 *pourvois* and quashed 1,420 decisions of lower courts.

SECTION TWO. DOCTRINE

The term *doctrine* designates legal scholarship, the opinions of the authors of legal literature about the law such as they, as theoreticians, understand it. By likening it to the vehicle which it is, rather than examining its particular contents, doctrine may be defined as the *body* of legal writing or literature. Despite its *different forms of expression*, the doctrine thus plays a *role* which raises fewer problems than does the jurisprudence.

I. Forms of Doctrinal Writing. The literary forms of expression of the doctrine in the civil-law tradition have varied.

a) *Nineteenth century.* This was the era of the great commentators of the Code Civil. The code was thought of as embodying the whole of French civil law; it had displaced both Roman law and old French law and had not, at the start of the nineteenth century, given rise as yet to any large body of creative jurisprudence. For the jurists of the time there seemed nothing better than to elucidate its text, to deduce therefrom solutions to problems not expressly envisaged by the code and, in doing so, to use as their sole guide the text itself, the expressed intention of the legislature. Textual interpretation and the search for the legislative intention of the 1804 code (especially through the use of legislative history, *les travaux préparatoires*) are the characteristics of the school of

---

22 [*Translator's note*: Other illustrations drawn from the jurisprudence will be found in SZLADITS, GUIDE TO FOREIGN LEGAL MATERIALS 21, n. 57.]

literal interpretation (*école le l'exégèse*). This tradition left a legacy of commentaries upon the Code Civil, some running into twenty volumes and more. The importance in these works attached to the enacted law itself is evident, even to the point of their formal arrangement: their ordering of the subject matter is that of the code itself (as in the case of Toullier and Demolombe) although all of them did not adopt this arrangement to the extent that the very sequence of the code articles themselves was observed (as in the case of Troplong). Only the *Cours de droit civil* of Aubry and Rau (the fourth edition of which appeared in 1869) made an effort to escape from this framework in order to pursue some greater synthesis, although it, too, equated the study of the civil law to that of the Code Civil in both spirit and letter. It is, however, the only work of the period to have sufficiently resisted the ravages of age to have been republished in our own time.

Aspiring to nothing more than an interpretation of the enacted law, the writings of the exegetical school were normally very uncritical of the Civil Code itself. These authors were politically moderate and satisfied with the social order of which the code, as it were, was the permanent constitution (family, property, contract). They fastened upon what was static rather than dynamic within the code.

b) *Modern Period.* By the close of the nineteenth century, a change took place in the understanding of the role of the doctrine. The taste for studying jurisprudence supplanted the habit of a strictly grammatical study of the texts. The case note or comment (*note d'arrêt*) and the periodic summary of recent cases (*chronique de jurisprudence*) thus came to claim a large part of writers' energies. And, as to basic texts, the style of the long commentary upon the code has been abandoned in favour of explanations of the civil law in its entirety; that is to say, in addition to the code's texts, statutory legislation and, above all, decided cases, are objects of examination. The jurisprudence is criticized and systematized. The new authors make every effort to avoid pure theory and to be aware of the needs of the practice (*i.e.* trial lawyers).

There never was, however, a complete break between the older and the more modern approaches. The last members of the exegetical school (the team which produced the great treatise by Baudry-Lacantinerie) forecast the new method; but contemporary writers, even though liberated from an exegetical approach in respect of the Code Civil, will themselves employ these same methods in regard to newly enacted legislation.

Of the basic works produced, some have been intended for student use (Planiol's *Traité élémentaire* of 1899, the works of Colin and Capitant, and Josserand) whereas others were destined to be practitioners' texts (the *Traité pratique* of Planiol and Ripert, the *Cours* of Beudant and Lerebours-Pigeonnière). These texts were most often the collective production of a team of writers: the growing complexities of the law have required the development of branches of specialization. This same phenomenon explains the appearance of specialized treatises (such as those on civil liability) and the proliferation of various monographs. Among the latter the doctoral theses, or at the least the best of them, have gained an important place: they assemble large masses of documentation on specific points and, even if the analyses they contain are not in depth, they therefore accomplish basic research essential for later scientific study.

Contemporary authors are certainly not narrow technicians. Their approach to legislation and jurisprudence is essentially critical. Today, as in the past, they remain politically moderate but not in exactly the same way. They endeavour to reconcile antagonistic social forces, and attempt to bring to bear in their work consideration of social interests and postulates of humanism (such as the supreme dignity of the human person). They are profoundly affected by the belief that law can develop, and only ask that it be directed into the proper channels.

II. *Role of the Doctrine.* a) *Doctrine is certainly not a source of civil law.* This means that a judge is never bound either by an isolated doctrinal view (expressed either at the level of an instant case in the form of a legal opinion upon consultation, or abstractly and in advance in the form of a text) or by a unanimously adopted view of doctrinal writers (what in the middle ages was known as *communis opinio doctorum*). Moreover, even if a judge does adjudicate in a manner indicated by the doctrine its mere citation is insufficient; he must adopt, and as his own, all the reasoning upon which it is based.

b) *But the doctrine certainly is an authority in civil law.* The doctrine serves as an inspiration to the judge, an influence among others to which he will attach a greater or lesser weight according to the circumstances

Authorities in Civil Law: France | 107

(more, normally, to a unanimous rather than an isolated view, more to a recent opinion than to an older one, etc.). No doctrinal view is rejected out of hand or a priori; any opinion may, with time, eventually become the law. It is only to be expected, however, that greater weight will be given in the courts to jurisprudence than to doctrine; the former, by way of the processes already described, may establish the adherence of the lower courts within the judicial hierarchy. The doctrine, on the other hand, may be of greatest influence in those areas precisely where there is no established jurisprudence. It has, however, sometimes, happened that persistent doctrinal criticism will prompt the abandonment of established jurisprudential positions.

RELATED QUESTIONS

I. Conspectus of French Civil-Law Doctrine.[23]

A. *The Nineteenth Century.* a) This period, as already mentioned, is dominated by the methods and attitudes of the exegetical school. Its principal representatives, those most orthodox and "classical," are indicated in the following three sections which correspond to the three major phases of the school itself.

First Period (Beginnings 1804–1830)

MERLIN (de Douai), 1754–1838. He revised the RÉPERTOIRE UNIVERSEL ET RAISONNÉ DE JURISPRUDENCE of J. N. Guyot (1728–1816), published at the end of the Old Regime, and added much material of his own. He was intimately familiar with the former law, since he practised law during the Old Regime, and with the new Code Civil, since he was one of its architects in the days of the revolution.

C. B. M. TOULLIER (1752–1835). DROIT CIVIL FRANÇAIS SUIVANT L'ORDRE DU CODE was begun in 1811 but not completed by the fourteenth volume.

The jurists of this period, trained under the legal system of the Old Regime which drew upon a multiplicity of sources, were much less dry than those of the subsequent period. Since, moreover, they were in the position of having to defend the Code Civil at the time of the post-Napoleon restoration of the monarchy, they were still very much aware

---

23 [Translator's note: For further particulars, see *id.* at 86 ff.]

of its political significance (the treatise of Toullier, for example, begins with a chapter devoted to political theory).

Second Period (Apogee, 1830–1880)

A. DURANTON (1783–1866). He was responsible for publishing the first really important commentary, COURS DE DROIT FRANÇAIS SUIVANT LE CODE CIVIL (22 vols.; 4th ed. 1825–1844). His clarity and good sense are especially appreciated.

C. DEMOLOMBE, professor at the Université de Caen, left a course of lectures, COURS DE CODE NAPOLÉON (31 vols.; 1845–1882), although he did not get beyond article 1386; Guillouard continued his work. Today he is criticized for having been much less precise and concise than Aubry and Rau, and much less rigorous in his analysis. The fact is that he tempered his opinions with numerous exceptions and qualifications, and in that he may well be much closer to the true mode of French legal thought—which is far from geometrical. He had, at least once in his life, a generous impulse, but it dates from his youth: his theory that the proof of natural filiation may be made upon proof of possession of the status.[24]

C. AUBRY (1803–1883) and C. F. RAU (1803–1877). They were professors at the Université de Strasbourg before becoming, upon the annexation of Alsace-Lorraine, *conseillers* in the Cour de cassation; this explains, in part, their exceptionally great and continuing influence on the jurisprudence of the court; had Demolombe been named in their place, it is conceivable that the evolution of French law in the nineteenth century would have been different. The first edition of their COURS DE DROIT CIVIL was really a translation of the manual by the German professor at Heidelberg, C. S. Zachariae (1812–1894) (the Code Civil was in force in part of Germany). The subsequent editions—especially the fourth, in eight volumes (1869–1879)—showed no traces of these origins, although there is still something Germanic about their work: their inclination to theoretical developments (for example, the celebrated theory of the patrimony); their abstract and categorical attitudes (despite the presence of ample citations of jurisprudence in the notes); and a style seemingly made up of formulae, of great precision but little attraction. A fifth

---

24 Cf. Vol. V of his *Cours*, nos. 477 ff. He proposed it for the first time in 1835 (1 REV. DE LÉG. ET DE JURISPD. 427).

edition, published as DROIT CIVIL FRANÇAIS, completed in twelve volumes in 1922, is much sought after because of the notes by E. Bartin. The seventh edition was extensively revised by Paul Esmein.

Third Period (Transition, 1880–)

G. BAUDRY-LACANTINERIE (1837–1913). PRÉCIS DE DROIT CIVIL, 1882; TRAITÉ THÉORIQUE ET PRATIQUE DE DROIT CIVIL, published in twenty-six volumes under his editorship, starting in 1895, and continued by the SUPPLEMÉNT by Bonnecase (6 vols., 1924–1935).

On the whole the exegetical writers were mainly technicians and little influenced by the popular movements or sentiments of their times (the problems of the child-mother, the natural child, divorce, and the poor debtor) and any of the reforms of the law touching upon such romantic subjects were accomplished quite apart from any influence of theirs.

b) It is, therefore, all the more apposite to indicate that there were some dissident movements.

1° *Politically dissident* writers were F. LAURENT (1810–1887), a Belgian (the Code Civil is in force in Belgium), a staunch liberal in the Belgian tradition, who wrote PRINCIPES DE DROIT CIVIL FRANÇAIS (33 vols.; 1876–1878); he sometimes resorted to an exaggerated literalism of interpretation in support of his views. E. ACOLLAS (1826–1891), is the sole representative of the political left, a political persuasion so noticeably absent in the French nineteenth-century school. He was a prominent radical but no more than that, and his ideas are now very much out of date. He was, however, named dean of the Paris Law Faculty by the *Commune*, and, although he was wise enough not to accept it, his nomination gained him no credit among jurists of the time. This is regrettable because his MANUEL DE DROIT CIVIL, COMMENTAIRE PHILOSOPHIQUE ET CRITIQUE DU CODE NAPOLÉON (4 vols.; 2nd ed. 1874–1875) is, from the teaching point of view, very remarkable.

2° *Technically dissident* writers were R. T. TROPLONG 1795–1869. His *cursus honorum* (he was first president of the Cour de cassation and speaker of the senate in the Second Empire) suggests that he was a conformist and his DROIT CIVIL EXPLIQUÉ SUIVANT LES ARTICLES DU CODE (28 vols.; 1st ed. 1833–1856), based upon the work of Toullier, is as exegetical in its form as might be imagined. But, as to substance, the work is far removed from the tradition of the exegetical school. The numerous contradictions for which he has been criticized are explained by the fact that he thought of the law as a relative, rather than an absolute, science. His imagination (he has also been criticized for this) often led him to see well into the future (for example, he suggested that the lessee or tenant farmer had a real right [droit réel] or property interest in the land leased, and this, it has transpired, is the tendency of present legislation). Sainte-Beuve, the literary critic, who knew something about such matters, was a greater admirer of Troplong than were jurists themselves.

The group which published La Thémis, an ephemeral legal review (1819–1831), propounded a view of law that went well beyond the work of simple exegesis; they called upon all the resources of the historical, philosophical, political, and economic sciences in their studies.

B. *The Twentieth Century*. The basic philosophy of contemporary civil-law writers, sometimes called the contemporary scientific school, is found in the large methodological works of François Gény, 1861–1959, professor of law at the Université de Nancy: MÉTHODE D'INTERPRÉTATION ET SOURCES EN DROIT PRIVÉ POSITIF (1899), and SCIENCE ET TECHNIQUE EN DROIT PRIVÉ POSITIF (1915–1924). [The former has been translated into English by the Louisiana State Law Institute as METHOD OF INTERPRETATION AND SOURCES OF PRIVATE POSITIVE LAW (1963).]

a) *Teaching Texts*:

M. PLANIOL (1853–1931), TRAITÉ ÉLÉMENTAIRE DE DROIT CIVIL (3 vols.; 1st ed. 1899). The work, entirely revised, has become G. RIPERT & J. BOULANGER, TRAITÉ ÉLÉMENTAIRE DE DROIT CIVIL DE PLANIOL (4 vols.; current ed. 1950–1951). [It was translated into English by the Louisiana State Law Institute as CIVIL LAW TREATISE (3 vols. in 6 parts, 1959).]

A. C. COLIN & H. CAPITANT, COURS ÉLÉMENTAIRE DE DROIT CIVIL (3 vols.; 1st ed. 1944). The work has been completely revised by JULLIOT DE LA MORANDIÈRE (current ed. vol. 1, 1953).

L. JOSSERAND, COURS DE DROIT CIVIL POSITIF FRANÇAIS (3 vols.; 3rd ed. 1938–1940).

R. SAVATIER, COURS DE DROIT CIVIL (3 vols.; 2nd ed. 1947–1951).

Henri, Léon, & Jean MAZEAUD, LEÇONS DE DROIT CIVIL (4th ed. by de Juglart, 1967).

G. Marty & P. Raynaud, Droit civil (Vol. 1 in 3 parts, 1967; Vol. II, 1962; 2nd ed. 1967).

b) *Major Treatises*:

M. Planiol & G. Ripert, Traité pratique de droit civil (14 vols.; 1st ed., 1925–1934; 2nd ed., 1952–1957). The individual volumes have been reedited by various writers.

C. Beudant & P. Lerebours-Pigeonnière, Cours de droit civil français (16 vols.; 1934–1953). An enlarged edition of a course of lectures of Charles Beudant delivered at the end of the last century.

c) *Digests*:

Répertoire de droit civil de l'encyclopédie juridique Dalloz (5 vols.; 1953–1955).

d) *Journals*:

Revue Trimestrielle de Droit Civil (Rev. Trim. Dr. Civ.), a quarterly founded in 1902 is, at the present time, the only periodical devoted entirely to civil-law doctrine.

Revue Critique (R.C.) and the Revue Général de droit (R. G.) ceased publication in 1940.

Revue International de Droit Comparé (Rev. Int. Dr. C.), the Bulletin de la société de législation comparée in 1949, is of great interest to the science of the civil law.

II. *Role of the Doctrine*. In Roman law, the doctrine, that is to say the writings of classical jurists, was truly a source of law (cf. R. Monier, Manuel élémentaire de droit romain [1970 reprint of 6th ed., 1947], Vol. I, nos. 69 ff.). What today is called doctrine in France was understood differently historically. Sometimes the doctrine is a static element of the law (in the form of custom, or tradition) and sometimes a dynamic element of the law (it produces a new legal theory, an invention). It seems possible that in Roman law the doctrine successively assumed both these roles (Justinian's Digest, 533 A.D., consisted of a catena of passages from authoritative jurisconsults). In contemporary French law, doctrine is thought of as essentially creative (with the consequence that twentieth-century authors are preferred to nineteenth-century writers). The opposite view of the role of doctrine is expressed in that rule of propriety, found in some form or other almost everywhere, that no living author should ever be cited. Muslim law provides one explanation: so long as an author is alive, one can never be assured he won't change his opinion.

SECTION THREE. THE METHODOLOGY OF THE JURISPRUDENCE AND THE DOCTRINE

To fulfill their role of helping to find solutions to legal problems, jurisprudence and doctrine have a *methodology*, a method of interpretation in the large sense. And whereas the *principles* of this method may be very much debated, the daily *practical rules* of interpretation are less so.

I. Principles of a Method of Interpretation. As opposed to the classical method of interpretation, that of the exegetical school, there have grown up several modern and so-called scientific methods.

A. *Principle of the Exegetical Method.* Contrary to what one might be tempted to suppose, it is not the literalism but rather the psychologism of this school that is its main characteristic. In the beginning, no doubt, there was a strict adherence to the text of enacted legislation. But the texts were never read in the manner of parchment scrolls deciphered by the orientalist; to say that the exegetical school was one of literal or purely grammatical interpretation would not sum up its flavour. The law is seen rather as a declaration, a manifestation of intention. The law speaks: what does it *intend* to say, that is, what did the legislators intend to say? The matter of interpreting the law is not, from that moment, any different from that of ascertaining the intention of the deceased as found in his last will and testament. Beyond the text itself, therefore, the controlling element is the legislative intention which the interpreter (the judge, the lawyer) must seek out.

This intention can be sought first in the *travaux préparatoires* or the materials of the legislative history of the legislation, where it may well have been directly expressed. If this path is insufficient, one will resort to surmise: what is it likely that the legislators intended? This may be induced from the whole body of the legislation, from its general spirit (since it may be assumed that the legislators did have a coherent intention); it may also be appreciated on the basis of the consequences to which any interpretation may lead (the legislators, again, will not have intended to bring about absurd consequences). In a word, then, in this method, the law is always treated as a legal intention, and therefore a reasonable one.

B. *Principles of the Modern Methods.* The modern methods are in agreement in their criticism of the classical method; they all hold that to attempt to ascertain legislative intention in either the texts or the *travaux préparatoires* is too uncertain. But there is not much agreement among them as to what to put in its place. Several systems are proposed.

1. *Search for Social Purpose.* The meaning of legislation must be determined with the aid of two elements, the literary form in which its text is cast and the social purpose in view at the time of its enactment (which could be something more objectively determinable than legislative intention). The literary words are the fixed part (in no case can a text be made to say the opposite of what it said originally); the social purpose is the changing element, since the same purpose may be attained by different means which the legislators might not have had in mind at the time of enactment.

2. *Historical Method.* More correct, perhaps, would be "evolutionary" method. When interpreting a text one has the right to adapt it freely to the social needs of the time: what would be the intention of the draftsmen of the law had they been working today? The relevant perspective in the interpretation of the Code Civil is not, therefore, the intentions of the lawmakers of 1804 but those of today. In this view a text could be attributed different meanings, varying from one moment of its application to another, or even be found to say the opposite of what its text actually embodies.

3. *Free Scientific Research.* A text of law cannot, through interpretation, be stretched to cover all cases; at some moment it must be recognized that there is no longer any law available for interpretation—that there is a gap in the law. At such times one is entitled to move from interpretation to free scientific research. The judge or lawyer must, as though he were performing the task of the legislators, come up with a solution by relying on whatever there may be as an aid, whether historical, rational, sentimental, or utilitarian considerations—from all of which a rule of law may emerge.

II. Practical Rules of Interpretation. There is a certain number of traditional formulae, rules of thumb, maxims, operations, or tools of interpretation (in the broadest sense) which, since they were constantly used by classical interpreters of the last century, are linked, more or less easily, to the fundamental idea that legislation is an expression of reasonable intention. Although a number of them have been questioned by the proponents of the modern methods of interpretation, they are nonetheless used regularly in practice. Some idea should therefore be given of the principal examples.

A. *Tools of Interpretation.* 1. *Analogies, or reasoning by analogy.* In one sense, this involves more than interpretation, since the idea is to extend the law's application to some hypotheses or subjects which it has not expressly mentioned; one is, as it were, passing from the known to the unknown. When a law has spoken on one matter, it is said to be applicable to other similar matters. The analogy is thus the metaphor of the law. For example, if one says that nullity of marriage *resembles* divorce, it might be concluded, by analogy, that article 301,[25] a text enacted in respect of divorce, is applicable in nullity of marriage as well. It can be objected that the comparison is not a true one, but this is so if the comparison is only intuitive. If there is a similarity of purpose between the existing rule and the solution to be introduced, it is admissible to say that the same reasons should produce the same legal effects (*ubi eadem est legis ratio, ibi eadem est legis dispositio*). This is the argument *a pari*.

2. *A contrario argument.* When a text expressly says one thing, it is deemed to deny the contrary (*qui dicit de uno negat de altero*); when one thing is included in a provision of law, it operates as an exclusion of things differing from it (*inclusione unius fit exclusio alterius*). For example, Code Civil article 6 provides that one cannot derogate, by private agreement, from laws of public order.[26] One may, however, reverse the proposition: private agreements may derogate from laws that are not of public order. In this example, however, one is working from an excep-

---

25 Article 301, *Code civil*: If the spouses have made no settlements upon each other, or if those stipulated appear insufficient to assure the maintenance of the spouse in whose favour the divorce was granted, the court may order that maintenance be paid out of the property of the other spouse, which amount shall not exceed a third of the income of such other spouse. The maintenance may be cancelled when it is no longer necessary.

26 Article 6, *Code civil*: No one can by private agreement contravene laws of public order and good morals.

tional provision (the limitation of public order) to return to a general principle (the freedom of contract). And the argument *a contrario*, it is usual to observe, is only conclusive in such conditions. Otherwise, it would be dangerous. For example, from what is said in article 102, to the effect that "the domicile of every Frenchman is at the place where he has his principal establishment," it was concluded, in the last century, that foreigners had no domicile at all.

3. *Argument a fortiori*. This occurs in the case where one extends a provision of law to a situation not specifically anticipated therein but because the reasons for which it was originally enacted in the first place are found again with even greater force in such other situations. For example, according to Code Civil article 1421, paragraph 1, the husband may dispose of community property; it is admitted, therefore, a fortiori, that he is able to gather in the revenues therefrom, a much less serious act. *Qui peut le plus peut le moins.*

B. *Maxims of Interpretation.* 1. Exceptions must be strictly construed (*exceptio est strictissmae interpretationis*). Textually admitted exceptions are formally indicated in legislation by expressions such as *however* and *nevertheless*. There are others, however, which are virtual or implicit, flowing from the nature of the provision itself (such as those establishing some special privilege, incapacity, forfeiture, or civil penalty because the general law rests upon the precepts of equality, capacity, and freedom). The maxim means, first of all, that the exceptions admitted by the law itself must be kept within the bounds of their literal terms, but also that the interpreter does not have the power to allow yet other exceptions not anticipated by the text. The jurisprudence has not, however, always been faithful to this principle; for example, the courts extended the incapacity of the "prodigal," assisted by a judicial adviser, well beyond the terms of former Code Civil article 513.[27] The reason is that provisions which are only seemingly exceptional may also be viewed as but fragmentary applications of a contrary but only implicit general principle (thus, in the previous example, under article 513, such principle

---

[27] Former article 513, *Code civil*: A prodigal may be prohibited [by the court] from being a party to actions, from entering into compromises and settlements, from borrowing, receiving any movable capital, and from giving receipts therefor, from alienating property or constituting it as real security, without the assistance of an adviser appointed by the court. (This article was abrogated by the law of January 3, 1968, creating a new general regime of incapacity for incapables of major age.)

was that the appointment of a judicial adviser established a general incapacity).

2. Where the law draws no distinction, distinctions are not allowed (*ubi lex non distingui, nec nos distinguere debemus*). The interpreter has no authority to restrain or limit the application of some text framed in general terms. For example, Code Civil article 457 requires that the authorization of the family council be obtained prior to the sale of lands belonging to a minor person;[28] it would be inadmissible to introduce a distinction to the effect that lands of little value could be sold without such authorization.

3. When the reason for the law ceases, the law itself ceases (*cessante ratione legis cessat ejus dispositio*). A law must not be made to apply to situations which, even though apparently envisaged upon a literal reading of its letter, are nonetheless excluded by reason of its spirit. This maxim may seem to contradict those preceding, but can be reconciled by limiting its application to hypotheses where the contradiction between the spirit and the letter of the law is obvious, and where any overreaching of its visible intent is manifest. Thus, for example, former Code Civil article 452 used to provide that the personal property of the minor had to be sold at the start of his tutorship; it was considered that they were of little value and that it was preferable to invest the proceeds in real estate productive of income. If, however, there was income-producing personal property, the basis for the provision no longer existed and, in that event, article 451 was not applied.[29]

RELATED QUESTIONS

General Bibliography. The literature on the subject of the different methods of interpretation in France and in other countries is immense. The basic work is that of F. GÉNY, MÉTHODE D'INTERPRÉTATION ET SOURCES EN DROIT PRIVÉ POSITIF, 1899.

---

28 The family council, normally composed of persons related by blood or marriage to the minor, or others such as friends and neighbours interested in him, is presided over by a judge (C.C. arts. 407 ff.); its approval is required for most dispositions of the minor's property by the tutor (C.C. arts. 456 ff. as modified by the law of December 14, 1964 and decree of November 5, 1965).

29 The whole subject of the tutor's administrative powers over the minor's property was revised by the legislation cited above.

Philosophy. Studies on legal logic have been numerous during recent years but have developed in two opposite directions. One stream has been devoted to the effort of adapting to law the research accomplished in modern logic and its mathematical formalism (cf. G. KALINOWSKI, INTRODUCTION À LA LOGIQUE JURIDIQUE, 1965). On the other hand, the Belgian School of Charles Perelman, adopting a more literary point of view, sees in legal logic a theory of argumentation, debate, and persuasion. (Cf. C. PERLEMAN, & L. OLBRECHTS-TYTECA, TRAITÉ DE L'ARGUMENTATION, 1958; in English, see his THE IDEA OF JUSTICE AND THE PROBLEM OF ARGUMENT, 1963).

Sociology. All methods of interpretation derive, in the final analysis, from the same idea: law is an expression of intention, of human and reasonable will and, as such, is always discoverable by an interpreter through the use of his own intelligence; men can always come to an understanding with each other. This rational conception (*ratio legis*) was, doubtless, the position of Roman law, and it also seems to have been accepted, although in quite another context, by St. Paul (2 Cor. 3, 6: the letter killeth, but the spirit giveth life)—and from this, perhaps, derives the medieval canonical presentation of the law as a *spiritus mobilis*. This familiar idea should not, however, lead us to forget that there is another more primitive, more fixed, notion according to which the legal text has an almost sacred quality. The law may well be an expression of intention, but it is not necessarily comprehensible by man; methods of interpretation are not, therefore, necessarily rational. They are, rather, processes of divination, according to the letter of the law rather than an explanation of its spirit (cf. the method of the Hebrew *agada*, the process of counting the numerical value of the letters contained in a word). Nor can it be assumed that literalism is totally foreign to contemporary methods: the English notions of interpretation are more literalist than psychological. (Thus the greater unwillingness to use the materials of legislative history or *travaux préparatoires*, a rule established in England in the seventeenth and eighteenth centuries partly because of the identification of English law with divine law. Thus, legislation is to be interpreted literally because it is literally inspired—can this influence be traced, through the Reformation, to the Old Testament?)

Legal Theory. There are few traditional rules of interpretation that could not be put into question today. Thus, for example, the rule that exceptions must be strictly interpreted: one can say that the exceptional legal provision is a rule made for a specific series of cases and, since it has its own social purpose, its meaning must be interpreted in the light of such purpose. Inversely, however, one can also argue that all law is "exceptional" since all law, in the end, is an evil.

Judicial Practice. The jurisprudence has always held that *travaux préparatoires* do not prevail against a text whose meaning is clear, Civ. 22 Nov. 1932, D.H. 33.2; Paris, 9 Jan. 1947, D. 47.141. There are, too, limits put upon the use of analogies: v. for example, Civ. 12 Feb. 1951, G.P. 51.1.260 (one cannot reason, in all family law disputes, as one would in a divorce case). The principle that exceptional provisions must be strictly construed has been affirmed several times by the Court of Cassation, for example, Req. 26 July 1928, S. 29.1.70 where the status of special statutes (*lois spéciales*) in relation to the general law (*droit commun*) was considered.

ABBREVIATIONS

D.	Dalloz
D.A.	Dalloz analytique
D.C.	Dalloz critique
D.H.	Dalloz hebdomadaire
D.P.	Dalloz périodique
G.P.	Gazette du Palais
J.C.P.	Juris-classeur périodique
R.C.	Revue critique
R.G.	Revue général de droit
	Recueil Dalloz
	(i) "Chronique doctrinales"=D. 1955 chron. 5
	(ii) jurisprudence=D. 1955 J. 229
	(iii) legislation Clois=D. 1935 L. 44
Rev. Int. Dr. C.	Revue International de Droit Comparé
S.	Sirey
Sem. Jur.	La. Semaine juridique
R.T. or Rev. Trim. Dr. Civ.	Revue Trimestrielle de Droit Civil

VI

Supereminent Principles in French Law*

René David
PROFESSOR OF LAW, UNIVERSITY OF AIX-EN-PROVENCE,
PROFESSOR EMERITUS, UNIVERSITY OF PARIS

English translation by Michael Kindred,
Professor of Law, Ohio State University

Having spoken of legislation, custom, judicial decisions, and legal scholarship, we might seem to have exhausted the sources of French law. Certain supereminent principles, however, must also be considered. Such principles have a double role. First, they help fill any gaps which exist in legislation in that limited area of French law where, to borrow Gény's term, one can use "free scientific research." And second, in exceptional circumstances these supereminent principles can help correct existing legislation. The law serves a particular ideal; its goal is the realization of our conception of social order and justice. Whatever the applicable rule of law might seem to be, we would not apply it if its application directly and indisputably contradicted the requirements of social order and justice, as those notions are understood in our society. In such a case, supereminent principles are used to correct the poorly conceived rule and avoid its application. In both roles, such supereminent principles would seem essential to any legal system. They are necessary if one is to realize the system's full potential and avoid making it too formal. They insure that the system serves effectively the goals we set for it.

Let us first examine the problem of gaps in the law. According to Article 4 of the Civil Code, a judge cannot refuse to decide a case because of the silence, insufficiency, or ambiguity of the law. And Article 185 of the Penal Code sets a modest fine and five to twenty years' prohibition from holding public office for any judge, court, or administrative au-

---

* Excerpt from DAVID, FRENCH LAW: ITS STRUCTURE, SOURCES, AND METHODOLOGY (La. St. L. Inst. transl. 1972), 194–207.

thority who, for any reason whatsoever, including silence or ambiguity of the law, fails to settle the parties' dispute.[1] The judge, whether civil, penal, or administrative, thus must always give a decision when a case is brought before him. He can decide that he lacks jurisdiction, but if he accepts jurisdiction, he must settle the substance of the matter by his decision.

Legislation and custom, however, may be insufficient and not tell him how to solve the problem. Moreover, since prior judicial decisions and writings by legal scholars are not true sources of law, a case cannot be decided simply by citing their authority. If the judge finds that there is a gap in the legislation that is not filled by custom, how can he settle the dispute? In truth this problem is usually avoided in French law. In both private and public law, although through two different techniques, judges seldom (if ever) see any need to call upon these supereminent principles, because the legal system that the judge is applying never has any gaps.

In the branches of French law that are codified, we have already discussed the technique that is used: it is that of a somewhat forced interpretation of legislative texts.[2] In the arsenal of code articles at his disposal, the judge can always find a rule to cite in support of his decision. The existence in the codes of very general formulae, such as Civil Code Article 1134 for contracts, Article 1382 for delicts, and Article 544 for property, practically guarantee the judge a basis for his decision. Only very exceptionally will he base his decisions on an equitable principle, such as the one that prohibits unjustified enrichment.

The situation is different for the administrative judge. He has no code and so will often give decisions without citing any legislative text in his support. In such a case, he ordinarily simply asserts the existence in French law of the legal rule he applies; he does not think he needs to justify his assertion by invoking a supereminent principle of law. Writers, in their commentaries, have been less circumspect and have argued that the decisions of the administrative courts are in fact based on certain supereminent principles.

Moreover since 1940 the Council of State has changed its approach

---

[1] VOUIN, PRÉCIS DE DROIT PÉNAL SPÉCIAL, NO. 403, p. 415 (1953). A list of the abbreviations used in this chapter appears on page 132.

[2] See VI RIPERT, TRAVAUX DE L'ASSOCIATION HENRI-CAPITANT POUR LA CULTURE JURIDIQUE FRANÇAISE 68 (1950).

and has abandoned its reluctance to be bound by principles, no matter how general and consequently ambiguous, and has repeatedly asserted in its opinions the existence in French law of supereminent principles, that dominate its decisions. It has required that the government, in its regulations and conduct, conform to the general principles thus stated, so that these principles, independent of any legislation or custom, seem to dominate modern French administrative law.[3]

Supereminent principles thus do come into play and have a definite role in supplementing and thus perfecting the French legal system. But by the use of two different techniques—forced interpretation of private law legislative texts and in public law the more elementary technique of simply asserting the existence of a legal rule—their role remains somewhat disguised. Except for the general principles of law that are recognized by administrative court opinions, reading French judicial opinions will not reveal their importance or content.

A different question is whether supereminent principles can go beyond the filling out of the legal system and also act to correct a rule that, at first sight, seems to be part of the legal system but whose application in the case at hand would contradict the requirements of public policy and justice. The judge, whether civil or administrative, may follow the usual reasoning processes using legislation and custom and decide how a particular dispute should be solved. Is this solution absolutely obligatory, or can the judge change or set aside the application of this rule by invoking supereminent principles?

This question will immediately suggest to lawyers the distinction in Roman law between civil law and the praetorian law, or that in England between common law and equity. Let us state at the outset that there is not, and never has been, in French law anything comparable to these distinctions.[4] Nevertheless, techniques do exist by which French courts can avoid a solution that seems to be required by legal rules, but is unjust or seems to have serious inconveniences for the society.

A first supereminent principle that one might think of is resort to the concept of equity. At first glance, this technique seems to be ill-regarded in France. The word *equity* has a bad press in France; French lawyers

---

3 On these principles, see JEANNEAU, LES PRINCIPES GÉNÉRAUX DU DROIT DANS LA JURISPRUDENCE ADMINISTRATIVE (1954).
4 See Dawson, *Remedies of the French Chancery before 1789*, in FESTSCHRIFT FÜR ERNST RABEL 99–140 (1954).

immediately associate it with the idea of arbitrary action. "God save us from the equity of the *parlements* [prerevolutionary courts]" is a formula that is often cited and continues to influence the minds of lawyers and judges. Aside from the few exceptional cases where the legislator himself has referred to equity, a litigant has no chance of success if he simply argues the equity of his position to the judge. The French judge decides in law, not in equity.

Still, it is clear that French courts are not, and cannot be, indifferent to the equitable posture of litigation before them. To use these equitable factors effectively, however, one must present the argument in a different way and rely upon a principle that the judge will be inclined to utilize. Wherever the teleological method of statutory interpretation is required in order to interpret a particularly broad concept used by the legislator, or even where it is just authorized, parties can make considerable use of equitable arguments. The judge who has to decide whether the cause for a contract is immoral (Article 1133, Civil Code), or whether a testator was of sound mind (Article 901, Civil Code), or whether an expense of an emancipated minor is excessive (Article 484, Civil Code), or whether a condition in a donation is immoral (Article 900, Civil Code), or whether there are extenuating circumstances in the case of a penal offense (Articles 463 and 485, Penal Code) can give very considerable weight, in fact, to equitable considerations. This will also happen where he must evaluate certain kinds of conduct and their consequences in order to decide a case. To decide that a person has committed a fault or to evaluate damages caused, particularly exemplary damages, in the situation envisioned by Civil Code article 1382 certainly requires a judge to weigh equitable factors carefully.

In public law, we should recall the government's discretionary power to enforce or not enforce the rights of society or of a particular government agency against individuals. We have already discussed the system of "discretionary prosecution," which is part of French criminal law. Tax authorities, too, can grant taxpayers extra time for the payment of their taxes; in some cases the government can even compromise on the amount of penalty owed by a person. Such rules and administrative practices allow equity to play a role in French law that is not apparent if one considers only the legislative texts.

Supereminent Principles in French Law | 123

There are other approaches that can make a judge consider the equitable posture of a case, in addition to those mentioned above. Some of these are based upon ancient tradition, as in cases where there has been fraud. Ordinarily it is a poor argument to tell a judge that equity is on your side, but the contrary can be true if you argue that you have been defrauded. The Latin adage *fraus omnia corrumpit* ("fraud spoils everything") has continuing validity in France. French judges readily apply it in certain types of situations, even though no general code text articulates it.[5] The effective scope of the adage, the conditions in which it can be invoked, and its effects are in fact quite imprecise. There are cases where its application is traditionally excluded. This is true of marriage, where, according to Loisel's picturesque phrase, "One deceives if he can" (*Il trompe qui peut*). Other rules prevent its application because they are recognized as being eminently formalistic, such as rules establishing formal requirements, fixing time limits, and establishing particular required procedures.[6] But there is not total agreement on the scope of this exclusion. The adage *fraus omnia corrumpit* seems to be available against statements in public registers like the commercial register and the registry of mortgages.[7] According to a recent decision, it is there to protect the victim of the fraud and not to punish its author.[8] Unlike rules of equity, it acts in rem rather than in personam and thus can even be invoked against third persons in good faith. It has been applied in the areas of persons (invalidation of acts performed by an interdicted person prior to his interdiction), succession (invalidation of an ill-considered partition of a succession), obligations (liability of the person who helps a debtor violate his contractual obligation), matrimonial relations (invalidation of acts performed by the husband in fraud of his wife's rights, particularly pending a divorce hearing), and private international law (the so-called theory of fraud on the law).

5 RIPERT, LA RÈGLE MORALE DANS LES OBLIGATIONS CIVILES 287 ff., particularly 314 ff. (4th ed. 1949).
6 See the general report of Paul Roubier on legal technique and method since the Civil Code of 1804, in VI RIPERT, TRAVAUX DE L'ASSOCIATION HENRI-CAPITANT POUR LA CULTURE FRANÇAISE 48–49 (1950).
7 PICARD, LES BIENS, Vol. III of PLANIOL & RIPERT, TRAITÉ PRATIQUE DE DROIT CIVIL FRANÇAIS, NO. 650.
8 Cassation Chambre Civil 10 May 1949 (D.1949.277, note by Lenoan; S.1949.J. 189, note by Bulté; J.C.P. 1949.4972, note by Becqué).

Another way to make a judge consider equitable factors in reaching his decision is to invoke the doctrine of unjustified enrichment.[9] Here again the courts hide behind a Latin maxim: *Jure naturae aequum est neminem cum alterius detrimento et injuria fieri locupletiorem* ("By the law of nature it is not just that anyone should be enriched by the detriment or injury to another").[10] This adage comes from the *Digest* and has always been the basis for several doctrines and rules of French law: unauthorized management of another's affairs, undue payments, expenses incurred on the property of another, the idea that one who fights to avoid a loss should be preferred over one who fights to hold a gain (particularly with respect to the creditor's action to invalidate transactions in fraud of his right). It is only recently, however, that the doctrine has been held to state a general equitable principle that can justify recovery by an impoverished person in cases not specified by the code. The doctrine of abuse of rights is certainly the most important tool available. It has completely changed the relationship between law and equity in France in recent years.

Nowhere do the French codes state that persons' rights have limits that their holders cannot exceed. The idea seems to have been foreign to the codes' drafters. Eighteenth-century legal philosophy was the source of inspiration for these codes, and it exalted the role of the individual, the independence of his will, and the natural rights of men. Both the Declaration of the Rights of Man and of the Citizen and the civil code are based on these ideas and seem to consider a person's rights as his absolute prerogatives. *Neminem laedit, qui suo jure utitur* ("He who exercises his right injures no one").

Since the beginning of the twentieth century, French private law has been influenced by Jhering's ideas and by doctrines developed in French public law to the effect that the government and its agents have functions to fulfill rather than, in the strict sense, rights to assert. Civil, commercial, and procedural law all have reacted against the idea that a person's rights are absolute. The principle has been proposed that an individual must not abuse his rights. Because French courts always feel that they must have a legislative text on which to base a new doctrine, they used Civil Code Article 1382 in this case. A person commits a fault

9 Dawson, Unjust Enrichment (1951).
10 Pomponius, *Digest*, L. 17, *De regulis juris*, 206.

and becomes liable for damages if he abuses his rights. The doctrine of abuse of rights, for this reason, is covered by French writers in books on delictual liability, although the principle is in fact a general one. Because it dominates all French law and is applied throughout the legal system, some people think it should be placed at the very beginning of the civil code with the other general principles that are presented as being applicable to all French private law.[11]

Sometimes it has been argued that the doctrine of abuse of rights is the private-law equivalent of the doctrine of abuse of power in French administrative law. Such an analysis makes it seem that the doctrine has completely revolutionized the French legal system. Individuals could no longer act freely in their own interest; they would simply have social functions and "rights" granted to help them fulfill these functions. In other words, personal rights would exist essentially for the good of society and not for the benefit of their holders; their use would be conditioned and limited by the social interest that they are designed to serve. An individual could not abuse his right, in the sense that he could not divert it from the social goal that defines its scope and justifies it.

This socialist conception of rights prevailed in the civil code of Soviet Russia.[12] In France it was articulated by the illustrious public law lawyer Léon Duguit and has also had its private law advocates, the most important of whom was L. Josserand. But there have always been reservations. Even its most fervent supporters have always admitted that in addition to "functional rights," which must be used in conformity with certain social goals, French law also recognized "power rights," over the exercise of which no supervision is allowed.

---

11 Examples of this approach are found in the Swiss Civil Code (art. 2) and the German B.G.B. (sec. 226). RIPERT, LA RÈGLE MORALE DANS LES OBLIGATIONS CIVILES, 158–66, recalls that Saleilles proposed embodying the theory of abuse of rights in the Civil Code by inserting a new article in the preliminary book of the code immediately after the present Article 6. The Commission for the Reform of the Civil Code expressly recommended that this be done: VI TRAVAUX DE LA COMMISSION 14–26 (1950–51), and Article 147 of the proposed new Civil Code.

12 Russian Civil Code, art. 1: "The rights of citizens are protected by the law, except for situations where they are exercised in contradiction with their social-economic function." Also see Article I of the Law of July 18, 1950, in the Polish Democratic Republic: "The provisions of the law are to be interpreted and applied in conformity with the basic structure and goals of the people's state," and Article 3 of the same law: "No one should use his rights in contradiction with the principles of communal social life in the people's state."

The socialist conception has had a very considerable legislative effect. Individual freedom has been restricted in order to prevent the exercise of rights in specific ways thought contrary to society's interest. This legislative initiative has been particularly important in labor law (limitations on the freedom of contract in order to benefit workers, limitation on property rights in order to benefit the national economy), but they have also profoundly affected civil and commercial law.[13] Except for these legislative steps, however, French private law has remained faithful to the civil code conception of personal rights.

The theory of abuse of rights that the French courts have developed is only apparently analogous to the administrative-law theory of abuse of power. Abuse of power has nothing to do with morality or equity. Rather, it is one aspect of the idea of exceeding one's power: the question asked is whether the government agent, acting as he did, can be objectively considered to have acted in the public interest that limits his power. The French doctrine of abuse of rights, on the other hand, has a definite moral basis. To know whether a person has abused his rights, one asks whether he has used them so as to constitute a fault, i.e., wrongful behavior. The fault can consist in having acted with the sole intention of injuring someone else; or it can, and increasingly does, consist in having acted in disregard of the interest of society or of another person. But in the doctrine of abuse of rights, it is always personal conduct that must be evaluated, and the approach is always subjective: the question is never what are the objective limits of a right and have they been exceeded, as it is in the doctrine of abuse of power.

Because of this basis, the doctrine of abuse of rights introduces an equitable evaluation into litigation. To decide whether or not a person has abused his right is to decide whether or not he has committed a fault, and no matter how one may try to define the notion of fault in objective terms, it remains essentially a moral concept to which the law gives legal effects. Equity has a similar moral basis, with the difference that it leads one to consider the relationship as a whole, with special attention to the person injured, whereas the search for and evaluation of fault center principally on the person causing the injury. The theory of

---

13 SAVATIER, DU DROIT PRIVÉ AU DROIT PUBLIC À TRAVERS LES PERSONNES, LES BIENS, ET LA RESPONSABILITÉ CIVILE (2nd ed. 1950).

the abuse of rights, because of its moral basis, is frequently used to satisfy equitable needs.

A judge may be tempted to depart from legal rules or avoid their strict application by other than equitable factors. He may feel the same need where a solution dictated by the strict application of the law seems to him to violate society's interests. In such a case, he will use the notions of public order (*l'ordre public*) and good morals (*les bonnes moeurs*).[14] The two concepts are generally tied together and are used by the French codes in several articles, the most general, and therefore important, being Civil Code Article 6, which states that "one may not, by private agreement, depart from laws based on public order or good morals."

When a judge must decide whether or not an agreement violates public order and, if so, whether the consequence should be invalidity of the agreement, he will decide the case by applying legislation, i.e., Articles 6 and 1131. Thanks to the general formulae used by the code, he can satisfy the requirements of public order and good morals as they appear and as he understands them at the moment of his decision. Public order and good morals can be invoked at any time, even beyond the already broad scope of these articles. The judge can use these notions to avoid deciding a case in a way that he finds unacceptable.

This use of the notion of public order varies according to the branch of law in question.[15] It is used most frequently, and probably excessively, in private international law, where it is divorced from the concept of social morality. The principles of private international law may lead to the conclusion that a particular foreign statute is applicable to a case. Courts frequently, however, refuse to apply the statute and apply French law in its place by deciding that the foreign-law rule violates French public order.[16]

14 On these two concepts and the relationship between them, see MAULAURIE, LES CONTRATS ET L'ORDRE PUBLIC: ETUDE DE DROIT CIVIL COMPARÉ (France, England, USSR) (1953).
15 Julliot de la Morandière, "Cours de doctorat sur 'l'ordre public,'" 1930–31, 1931–32, 1950–51 (mimeographed); "L'ordre public en droit privé interne," ETUDES DE DROIT CIVIL À LA MÉMOIRE D'HENRI-CAPITANT (1937), 381.
16 LEREBOURS-PIGEONNIÈRE, DROIT INTERNATIONAL PRIVÉ NO. 379, has shown that the notion of public order is utilized in private international law in two series of cases: (1) to avoid rules of foreign law regarded in France as being contrary to morality or natural justice; (2) to defend and impose solutions of French law that are in fact disputed within France itself.

In internal law, the notions of public order and good morals are used to invalidate objectionable agreements by invoking Civil Code Articles 6 and 1133.[17] Here public order and good morals are simply general provisions that supplement other legislative rules. Where an agreement violates a statute, it would suffice to call it illegal and invalidate it as such. Even in such cases it is common to invoke Articles 6 and 1133 in addition to the particular provision violated and to assert that the agreement violates public order and good morals. This characterization places an additional stigma on the agreement in question, as it insists that the invalidity is not just a matter of legal technique, but that it is required and justified by society's interest. Even in the absence of a special statutory rule to which one can refer, an agreement can be invalidated simply by invoking the general formulae of Articles 6 and 1133.

Public order and good morals, moreover, are general concepts, overriding principles, that can be invoked to exclude the application of a particular legal rule, even beyond the framework of Articles 6 and 1133, which deal only with the invalidation of private agreements. In internal law, however, the courts, aware that abuse of these concepts would destroy all legal security, use them with moderation. As with equity, an advocate who wants to convince a judge to utilize the concepts of public order or good morals should try to articulate more precisely the principle whose protection is being invoked and to cite an established line of judicial decisions that has accepted the role and efficacy of these concepts in such cases.

In this connection, we should mention again the cases discussed above where equity may be relevant: both the importance of equity and the idea of good morals can be invoked to support particular applications of the adage *fraus omnia corrumpit* and use of the doctrines of unjustified enrichment and abuse of rights. Other adages that are unrelated to equity can be used in connection with the concept of good morals. This is true of *in pari causa turpitudinis cessat repetitio* ("he who is an equal cause of the evil loses his remedy"), by virtue of which invalidation of an agreement may not lead to restitution of performance already made where the invalidation is based on a violation of social morality. The concept of

17 *L'ordre public* in internal law is very different from *l'ordre public* in private international law. Moreover, there is not even a single concept of *"loi d'ordre public"* in French internal law. It is necessary to distinguish between the various consequences that follow from use of the concept.

public policy, separated from social morality, is relevant to Article 645 of the Civil Code, which provides, "In a dispute between landowners for whom [running water may be useful], the court decides the case by reconciling the interest of agriculture with the respect due to ownership."[18]

In all these areas, French law may give an impression of being imprecise. The theories of abuse of rights, public order, and good morals may seem imprecise, in danger of compromising the security of legal relationships. The French lawyer, however, will share neither this impression nor this fear. His conception of legal rules allows for some flexibility both in their application and in their expression. His own intuition and a study of judicial decisions will give him a feeling for the cases where he may be able to convince a judge to consider equitable factors, public order, or good morals. Except for a few established doctrines, of which we have discussed the most important, there are few cases where these considerations can have any effect. Tradition and judicial decisions provide important guidance and points of reference with respect to such cases.

There are in fact certain "equitable rules" and "rules of public order" in French law that could, and perhaps should, be defined with greater precision than is done in the codes.[19] If this were done, we would see that only a very narrow area remains where the general notions of equity, public order, and good morals have any role and where ambiguity is, consequently, greater than usual.

The way the courts use the concept of public order does not create much uncertainty. Foreign lawyers are likely to get a false impression if they study, as they often do, the concept of public order as it is used in private international law. For example, in the French law of contracts public order is quite a stable and precise concept. Only in the last few years has it been invoked alone without the support of an additional

18 See also, concerning partition of successions, Code Civil, art. 832 (June 17, 1938, revision): "In the formation and composition of the shares, the separation of immovables into small parcels and the division of [industrial and commercial] establishments must be avoided." "Insofar as it is possible to avoid fragmentation of objects of the estate and division of enterprises, each lot should, as much as possible, be composed . . . of movables and immovables, and assets and liabilities of equal value."

19 RIPERT advocates more precise definition in his LA RÈGLE MORALE DANS LES OBLIGATIONS CIVILES, 181.

text justifying its use in the particular case in question. Good morals, certainly, is a concept traditionally more independent of statutory law, but here too the courts have developed a number of doctrines that guide the jurist. The uncertainty that remains cannot be avoided in any country. The French courts have often rejected pleas, sometimes urgently pressed, that equity be allowed to prevail over law, or that considerations of public order should determine a decision. Thus in civil and commercial law, they have refused to invalidate or modify contracts on the grounds of changed circumstances. And the administrative courts have been able to develop an administrative law that guarantees individual rights and freedoms without succumbing to the argument that public order requires that the claims of the government must always prevail.

To this list of supereminent principles, composed of equity, public order, and good morals, we must add certain general legal principles that have been articulated by the administrative courts since 1940. We have already discussed these eminent general principles, which the Council of State has affirmed are part of our legal system.[20] In some cases, however, these principles have a role that goes beyond filling in legislative gaps and compensating for the absence of an administrative code. Sometimes they fulfill a function much like that of equity, public order, and good morals. Let us read how an eminent member of the Council of State explains why that court has found it necessary, since 1940, to elaborate these principles. The principles were not mentioned before 1940 primarily because it was unnecessary:

> To mention principles directly inspired by and tied to the democratic system in a country where this system was neither disputed nor endangered by those who governed, principles whose existence was so obvious that the courts had no reason to restate them and had only to apply them. . . . But in 1940 the Vichy government was formed and immediately sought to undermine the system upon which French life had been based for so many years. Then came the liberation, which was accompanied, as could be expected, by sufficient public unrest to be a matter of legal concern. Most important, the liberation left intact some of the newly created organisms, strongly imbued with the ideas of the preceding system that created them. Now, faced with this "setback to public liberties," this threat to the very foundation of the traditional French system, the Council of State changed its approach completely

---

20 See DAVID, FRENCH LAW 130, 195, and in this volume, page 120.

and set about developing its theory of the "general legal principles," which it had previously refused to do even though its decisions had been impregnated with them.[21]

The quoted passage is clear: the Council of State utilized the idea of general legal principles not simply or even principally in order to systematize its case law, something that it has always been somewhat reluctant to do, but in order to limit the application of legal rules emanating from other parts of the government and to correct these rules. Certain opinions handed down by the Council of State using general legal principles confirm this conclusion. Thus, the Council of State has affirmed the possibility of appeal for exceeding powers (excès de pouvoir), in conformity with general legal principles, against an administrative decree that the law declared "could not be appealed in either the administrative or regular courts."[22] It proclaims principles such as equality of individuals in the eyes of public officials in order to limit the apparently discretionary powers given to prefects by legislation. It fixes the limits for the exercise of the executive branch's regulatory power.[23]

The members of the Council of State who have written on this question have endeavored to show that these general legal principles are only a broad interpretation of the written law and in no way endanger the supremacy of the written law. The truth seems to be that, since the Council of State has the wisdom to limit its use of these concepts, the general legal principles do not threaten the supremacy of the written law in the administrative law area any more than the use by the regular courts of the principles of public policy and equity threaten the supremacy of legislation in the civil law area. Nevertheless it seems to us, as it does to the majority of writers,[24] that alongside the general principles that constitute an expansion and systematization of principles posed by the legislator, there is another category of general principles, whose character

---

21 Letourneur, Les Principes généraux du droit dans la jurisprudence du Conseil d'Etat, in CONSEIL D'ETAT, ETUDES ET DOCUMENTS, NO. 5, pp. 19, 21–22 (1951); see also Cassin, Le Conseil d'Etat gardien des principes de la Révolution française, in REVUE INTERNATIONALE D'HISTOIRE POLITIQUE ET CONSTITUTIONELLE 54 (1951).
22 Council of State, February 17, 1950, Ministre de l'Agriculture v. dame Lamotte.
23 On all these points, see JEANNEAU, LES PRINCIPES GÉNÉRAUX DU DROIT DANS LA JURISPRUDENCE ADMINISTRATIVE, passim, but especially 52–54, 59–60, 63, 160.
24 Id. at 218 ff.

is reforming rather than conforming. These principles aim at insuring the supremacy in French law of those conceptions of order and justice as opposed to purely formal law, that we regard as the foundation of our society. The general principles, when seen with this function, can be used to "neutralize some legislation," to "rank legislative law beneath judicial law."[25] The law is not an end in itself; it serves the conception that we have of our social life and of justice. An attachment to formalism must not lead us to sacrifice the means to the end. The strictness of the law must be relaxed if its strict application violates what we believe justice requires. The appeal to general legal principles by the administrative courts and the use of concepts such as equity, public order, and good morals by the regular courts are required by our very conception of law. The use of these general principles and broad concepts is based in itself on an awareness that positive law is not an end in itself and is not sufficient to accomplish the final goal of the legal system—justice. This technique provides a means of incorporating into the legal system broad value-oriented norms, which some will call basic concepts of the society and others will call natural law.[26]

25 These terms are borrowed from MM. Rivero and Vedel; see II JEANNEAU, LES PRINCIPES GÉNÉRAUX DU DROIT DANS LA JURISPRUDENCE ADMINISTRATIVE 146.
26 Id. at 220, 254. Jeanneau analyzes the approaches taken by M. Hauriou, J. Rivero, and L. Duguit.

ABBREVIATIONS

B.G.B.	Bürgerliches Gesetzbuch (German Civil Code of 1900)
D.	Dalloz
J.C.P.	Juris-classeur périodque
S.	Sirey

VII

The Open Legal Development: Germany

Karl Larenz
PROFESSOR OF LAW, UNIVERSITY OF MUNICH

English translation by Kate Wallach, Professor of Law and Comparative Law Librarian, Louisiana State University

[*Translator's introduction.** Karl Larenz teaches civil law, civil procedure, and legal philosophy at the University of Munich. Among his many contributions to legal scholarship are treatises on the German Civil Code (General Part and Obligations) and the philosophical treatise from which excerpts dealing with the development of the law by doctrine and jurisprudence are here presented in translation.

The translation, it is hoped, is true to meaning; it is not a literal, word-for-word translation. A few explanations may be helpful. The German word *Rechtsprechung* has been translated *jurisprudence*. There is a distinction between the common-law "case law" (judicial decisions) and the value of these decisions in the civil-law system. Thus, jurisprudence, as referred to in the following translation, should not be understood as legal philosophy.

The English word *law* represents various meanings; law in general is used for the German *Recht*, the French *droit*; *enacted law* or *legislation* for the German *Gesetz*, similar to the French *loi* meaning legislation. Enacted law may refer to an act of the legislature, a statute or a code like the German Civil Code (abbreviated BGB for *Bürgerliches Gesetzbuch*). The German Constitution is called *Grundgesetz* which is usually translated *Basic Law*.

Germany has two court systems, federal (*Bundesgerichte*) and states

---

* The able assistance of John S. Odom, Jr., managing editor of the *Louisiana Law Review* (1972–1973), in editing the translation is gratefully acknowledged.
  A list of the abbreviations used in this chapter appears on page 162.

(*Laender*). The court hierarchy is similar to the American: supreme courts (courts of last resort); intermediate (appellate) courts; and trial courts (courts of first instance).

Larenz' *Methodology of Legal Science* [*Methodenlehre der Rechtswissenschaft* (2nd ed. 1969)] consists of two parts, each containing five chapters. In the first part, "Historical-critical part, legal theory and methodology in Germany since Savigny," Larenz discusses the legal philosophy of the various schools and their theories about a codified legal system: (1) Savigny's methodology; (2) Legal conceptualism (*Begriffsjurisprudenz*) of the nineteenth century (Puchta, Jhering, Windscheid, Binding, Wach, and Kohler); (3) Legal theory and methodology under the influence of positivist concepts (Bierling, Jhering, Heck and Stoll, Buelow, Kantorowicz, Isay; Ehrlich, Jerusalem, and Kelsen's pure theory of law); (4) Departure from positivism in legal philosophy in the first half of the twentieth century (Stammler, Rickert, Lask, Radbruch, Sauer, Binder, Schoenfeld, Reinach, Welzel, G. Husserl); (5) Contemporary methodic endeavors.

The second part, "Systematic Part," deals with (1) Legal theoretical foundation; (2) Application of legal rules to facts; (3) Interpretation of enacted laws; (4) The (open) development of the law by legal science (doctrine) and jurisprudence; (5) Formulation of concepts and the system of legal science.

The translated passages are all taken from chapter four of the second part (pages 341–412). Some of the footnotes have been omitted because they refer to German cases and statutes which are not generally available and are not helpful to a reader who is unfamiliar with German law.]

1. THE (OPEN) DEVELOPMENT OF THE LAW AS A CONTINUATION OF STATUTORY INTERPRETATION

Even though statutory interpretation is its primary task, a dogmatic legal science oriented to the practice of law has never really limited itself to mere interpretation. It is generally recognized that no matter how carefully a statute is drafted, it cannot contain a rule for every possible case which arises; in other words, every statute has unavoidable gaps. Allowing the judge to fill the statutory gaps, so that he may reach a just decision, has almost always been considered one of the most important tasks of legal science. Beyond this, the conflict existing between the legal, ethical, and teleological meaning of a rule on the one hand, and its expression in the words of the text on the other, often compels the one who applies the law to transgress the limits of the meaning of the words and, thereby, their interpretation in the narrower sense. This happens quite frequently in the belief that the process is still merely interpretation. Actually "the transgression of the limits" results not only in actual clarification or preciseness of the statutory text but also in deviation from the text by way of addition or correction. We are dealing here with a methodically directed legal development.

Interpretation and dogmatic legal development are not of a different nature but are two stages of one process. This is especially evident in that the same (subjective and objective) teleological criteria which apply to statutory interpretation also control legal development. The methodically directed legal development is only the continuation of the "real" interpretation beyond its immanent limit, the possible meaning of the words. However, this would not be possible if, conversely, simple interpretation "by itself" were already the beginning of legal development, even if not so conceived by the interpreter. This is so because it transforms a previously uncertain expression into certainty, and fixes one of several possible interpretations as the "'suitable" and authoritative one. Judicial interpretation of a norm does not simply preserve the status quo (factually, as an applied rule). True, the interpreter intends to find the one and only meaning in the text, which anybody can discover, adhering to the proposition that there can be only one normatively "correct" meaning. But as long as it has not yet been ascertained, it is not yet "in existence" as far as law practice is concerned. In most cases, the result of interpretation cannot be anticipated with the same certainty as that of an arithmetical problem. Achievement of that certainty requires many complicated deliberations, as well as critical evaluations and analyses. In this sense, interpretation is a "creative" activity. In the dialectic process of application of the law, which consists of the constant adjustment of the law to the general legal conscience, the law may at first appear already complete, something merely prescribed and applied as simple "subsumption." Viewed from this aspect, a legal interpretation may appear to be simply the explanation of something already in existence, not a creative activity. Only at the stage of "open" legal development does the judge himself, through applying it to varied human transactions, become conscious of the other aspect of this dual process—the change which the law experiences constantly—as a factually applicable norm. Unnoticed by him, it had long existed in the result of his activity. Viewed from its result, judicial statutory interpretation, just like clarification of an "uncertain" standard, is a "concealed" legal development. Without any break, interpretation can be continued by open legal development.

Interpretation as a creative activity inseparable from legal development is not new, since it was common knowledge of the legal philosophers in the twenties; we recall Radbruch, Sauer, Binder, and Schoenfeld. If one understands interpretation (as we do) as the acquiring of knowledge, then it is in contrast to a "naive" *erkenntnis*-theoretical realism which sees knowledge as only a receptive act, a copying of something already in existence. Applying this theory to legal science, one has to limit it to simple interpretation, and interpretation itself to the mere rethinking of the legislator's thoughts, something already "in existence"—an empirical exploration of legislative intent. This limitation is still taken for granted by so many jurists because *erkenntnis*-theoretical realism is considered "natural" by most people. Knowledge is indeed a creative process, impossible without action and spontaneity on the observer's part. One does not necessarily understand this in the Neo-Kantian sense, according to which science creates its object by a process of recognition, and forms the given, inorganic matter according to a system specially applicable to this thought process. Even if this process is conceived as a dialectic in which the object's inherent structure becomes progressively recognizable, so that the person can become conscious of it through a methodically directed thought process, this process is always creative, because it demands of the thinking subject a free action aimed at acquisition of knowledge. In all sciences (to quote Engisch) one is concerned not with mere rendition of an already existing object, but with the end result: a correct decision. This is especially applicable to the interpretative sciences, such as legal science. Even where the interpreter merely follows the thoughts of the statute's author, he does not simply remain passive; he rethinks and reformulates these thoughts in a different context, one unknown to the author. The interpreter must go beyond the author's thoughts since the author could not have anticipated all possible consequences and because a legal norm only experiences final certainty by application to unforeseen cases. With reference to its object, legal science (as Radbruch has expressed it first) is reproductive as well as productive, imitative as well as creative. In this way, these two motives in their lively application penetrate each other constantly, and though they may differ in ideas, they are in fact indivisible. At each stage (as Betti has observed) spontaneity of subject interpretation is needed.

Legal science is "productive" not only in an erkenntnis-theoretical sense but also in a practical way because it directly influences the practice of law. It is (as Engisch points out) "the most unique advantage of legal science among the cultural sciences that it does not walk with or behind the law, but helps with the formulation of the law as well as with life in and under law." Legal science can do this because its knowledge transcends what is considered the law of today, and courts and legislators accept it insofar as it corresponds to the needs of the time and to the general legal conscience. The identification of law with enacted law and the will of the legislator may: (1) strengthen the power of the state, the political will of the ruler, or the volonté générale to implement the ideology of a ruling party, or (2) guarantee minimum legal security to prevent judicial arbitrariness and to make all decisions predictable. Such a period or such a government will question the judge's authority to utilize "open" legal development and will even limit interpretation as narrowly as possible as it contains elements of "concealed" legal development. Under the aspect "prohibition of denial of justice" (as it prevailed in nineteenth-century Germany and is today recognized as customary law) filling statutory gaps was recognized principally as a jurisprudential task. However, under the influence of formal-logical thinking (negation of teleological interpretation) and the subjective theory of interpretation, legal science strived to maintain priority for binding the courts to the law by narrowly limiting the concept of gaps. Where the judges were prevented from developing the law openly by this binding force of the law, they did so indirectly. So begins (as Esser explains) "the play at hide-and-seek which keeps secret not only the open judicial development of the law as a source of law but also the productive character of interpretation." Where the judges are obligated to the legal order and to the idea of the law (as in Germany at present), they can rely on understanding and can openly exercise their authority to develop the law methodically, even without express statutory authority. They correctly understand that being bound by the law gives them conditional authority and requires only that they give preference to being bound by "law" as a "whole," an expression of the idea of law. The departure from positivism in German legal philosophy and the emphasis on "law," besides enacted law in the Basic Law,[1] point in the same direction.

One cannot overlook the dangers to legal unity and security and to the judge himself—e.g., the dangers of loss of authority due to provocation by political criticism and unconscious abuse of power. It is in the interest of both the administration of justice and the individual judge himself to use the authority of developing the law very carefully, by methodically developed means and in conformity with the general legal conscience as well as with recognized legislative or supereminent principles of the legal order as a whole. Insofar as this is done without transgressing any inherent limits, one can perhaps discern an improvement in legal development in this freedom of the courts with regard to legislation. In Germany this is perhaps the most important step since the completion of the "codification."

The Supreme Court (Bundesgerichtshof), in a decision of the first civil senate, dealt for the first time extensively with the court's authority to develop legislation. It was argued that the Basic Law denied such an authority to the judge since it placed him without reservation under the "law" in Article 97. The Bundesgerichtshof (BGH) stated: "The principle of placing the judge under the law does not mean that the judge is bound by the law as a norm which can no longer be developed. Correct application of positive law requires further development of positive law to reach an equitable decision. This task of the courts has found clear expression in Article 20, section 3 of the Basic Law which emphasizes that jurisprudence is bound by legislation and law. Therefore, one cannot speak of any limitation of judicial authority with regard to enacted law imposed by the Basic Law." The Great Civil Senate has ruled that, in spite of the "unequivocal wording," an "amended, but meaningful limitation of a penal norm" was justified to give proper effect to the statute.

[1] Basic Law article 20, § 3. Doctrine is divided on the importance which should be attributed to *enacted law* and *law*. . . . To us, the relation of *enacted law* and *law* is that of a part and the whole, whereby the whole is more than the sum of its parts and takes precedence over any single part. The judge is also bound by the law to the extent that it is a part of the entire legal order, provided that it is not in conflict with the idea of law. In the absence of enacted regulation the judge is bound by the law as a whole, including its unwritten principles and the immanent supereminent inherent principles of evaluation.

In a legal memorandum the first Civil Senate has announced the following guiding principles: "The principle of separation of power does not preclude the formulation of judge-made law when the judge, through development of general principles derived from either the legislature and the legal order, or general values, finds and applies them. But he would violate his duties if he undertook or if he created generally binding law on his own volition simply of necessity."

The highest social court (*Bundessozialgericht*) has declared with succinct brevity: "The development of the law is the duty of each senate, not just of the great one. It is constantly exercised." However, by way of limitation, the court added that the judge can only create law if there are gaps in the enacted law or the legislator has failed to provide law according to his obligation under the Basic Law (as had long been the case with regard to equality in family law). In a later decision, the court reemphasized that among the legitimate duties of a judge is the supplementation and (with certain limitations) the correction of enacted law, as well as interpretation of the applicable law.

The Constitutional Court has stated: "This type of law-finding through filling of gaps—namely the concretisation of an abstract legal principle—has increasingly become a genuine judicial task in the modern law-and-order state." One could find many similar decisions. In legal theory, the courts' authority to find the law in such a supplemental and amending fashion has basically become undisputed, although there still remain many doubts as to limitations.

How German judges today conceive their responsibility for the continuity and development of the law, their duty to the law and to justice, and the necessity for scientifically reasoned interpretation and development of the law, is vividly expressed in the words of Bruno Heusinger upon his taking leave as president of the German Supreme Court on March 30, 1968. They are here presented as the self-appraisal of the German judiciary:

The highest jurisprudence, that of the Supreme Court, characterizes the law by emphasizing two special tasks: safeguarding both the uniformity and the development of the law. The Supreme Court, within its jurisdiction, has to provide a uniform application of the law throughout the Republic of Germany. That can only be achieved if the Supreme Court does not, without necessity, decide a similar case differently today than it did yesterday or the day before. This continuity is not reprehensible conservatism, but simply indispensable to guaranteed stability of the law.

A high court should neither adhere too closely to tradition nor be too conservative. It should constantly be aware of changes in the world and adjust the law to these changes within the framework of the statutes.

The act of judging is also action. The life of the judge is an active life, not a contemplative one. The decisions of the courts, whether by shaping or changing, influence the passage of life, personality, family relations, and property. This distinguishes judicial decision from the tranquility of theoretical research. A judge, considering himself bound by the law, can only inadequately excuse his self-reproach for rendering a decision which he considers unjust, by saying that this injustice needs to be suffered for the sake of the higher legal good found in stability of the law. Every judge constantly experiences for himself the extent to which he is inescapably driven to decide cases under the awareness of his immediate responsibility to the parties involved to render a just decision, as well as to implement the law faithfully. But suppose that in a concrete case harmonization cannot be achieved. The judge would destroy himself if he could suppress his dislike for this situation. One should not despise a judge who, overburdened with daily pressures, seeks to relieve his conscience by retreating to general principles or by resorting too liberally to presumptions or to skills of interpretation.

Basically there is no room in the legal order of our state for such a "free law" or "kadi" justice. Jurisprudence can only exist by scientific application. Theorists and practitioners depend closely on each other. Although science—the systematized knowledge of or, at least, the pursuit of truth—has become a kind of magic word for mankind today, my thoughts are not concerned with this phenomenon. I am only dealing with the following: the core of jurisprudence is equality; deepest harm comes to justice where similar cases are treated differently. A high court, which has the duty to guarantee uniformity of law, is especially faced with the inevitable necessity to classify each case within a gapless and uncontested system. This is a simple command for integrity. We can only maintain ourselves when what we consider to be the law in a single case endures tomorrow and the next day, and is permanently adapted into our entire legal order. As judges, we do not usurp any legislative power, but we are at the same time very conscious that in this framework there is great opportunity for creative jurisprudence, for shaping our legal order.

2. THE FILLING OF STATUTORY GAPS

[*Translator's note*. Section two of chapter four deals with the filling of statutory gaps (legal development *praeter legem*). Larenz discusses (a) the concept and types of statutory gaps; (b) the filling of "open" gaps especially by analogy; (c) the filling of "concealed" gaps especially by "teleological reduction"; (d) the "teleological extension" and "teleologically founded statutory correction"; (e) the relation of determination of gaps and filling of gaps; and (f) the meaning of the gap-filling norm. Gaps which cannot be filled?]

3. THE CHANGE OF A STATUTORY NORM AND THE DEVELOPMENT OF NEW LEGAL INSTITUTIONS (DEVELOPMENT OF THE LAW EXTRA LEGEM BUT INTRA JUS)

[In the previous section] we discussed cases in which the enacted law, measured by its own intent and teleology, was found incomplete and therefore showed gaps. The law requires and makes possible supplementation from its own context. The norm which fills the gap is still, at least indirectly, founded on the legislation derived from its teleology. Jurisprudence and doctrine have not stopped here. In many cases they have changed an enacted law or created new legal institutions which the statute did not contain, without any requirement of the teleology of the statute or its underlying values and principles. Involved herein is a legal development which is not *contra* but *extra legem*, which is compatible with the purpose of the law, but goes beyond the recognized purpose of the legislation; in any event, the changes are not simply oriented to the values underlying the statute. To talk here of filling gaps would require the extension of the meaning of gaps beyond its recognized limits.

A conflict arises on the basis of the following considerations: in cases of gaps in an enacted law which are caused by its own context and which can therefore be deduced from its text, the judge must always fill them since he has to apply a statute according to its meaning. He is bound by the legislative text and its inherent teleology. Where the legislation (according to its underlying intention and according to its own purpose) cannot be considered incomplete, and where the judge wants not only to go beyond the text (the "possible" meaning of its words) but also to go beyond the inherent meaning and purpose of the legislation, a special justification is required. As we shall explain at the end of this chapter, this exists only in a state of emergency (*Rechtsnotstand*) which would threaten the idea of justice. Even in this case, the judge has to be guided by objective standards such as the "nature of the thing" or legal ethical principles. Legal development must conform to basic principles of the legal order (constitutional conformity) and to comparable rules in existing regulations; it must be incorporated into the heart of this legal order. It must remain within the frame of the legal order although it exceeds the enacted law and its principles of evaluation (*extra legem*, but *intra jus*). The judge who acts in this manner must justify his action within the framework of the legal order. He can act neither simply according to his subjective reasoning nor "arbitrarily"; he needs certain standards which enable him to proceed in a methodically safe way. Here the methodical means for filling gaps—individual analogy, teleological reduction, and extension—are no longer sufficient, because the judge goes beyond the teleology of the enacted law.

Thus, one cannot speak of a gap in the BGB because it does not contain any regulations on transfer of movables for security (*Sicherungsubereignung*). Although one may see in Article 223, section 2, a formal starting point, it does not by itself justify using the form of possession under BGB article 930 (*Besitzkonstitut*) to transfer property for security purposes. This obviously contradicts the purpose of Article 1205 (transfer of possession). The civil code has no provision for chattel mortgage in its modern form as a substitute for pledge without possession—neither for individual things nor for composite things—not because it was overlooked but because it did not conform to the codifier's plan. The drafters of the BGB did not want to create a chattel mortgage of which a third person could have no knowledge. Therefore, the absence of a nonpossessory chattel mortgage is not a gap in the code at all. There is no incompleteness which contradicts the plan of the code.

By the same token, liability for *culpa in contrahendo*, at least in its modern extension, cannot be deduced from the code unless, perhaps, by total analogy. Such liability represents a change in the code's delineation between delictual and contractual liability and its favorable treatment of the latter, especially in view of BGB article 278.

The same applies to contracts for the benefit of third persons which extend contractual protection to a third party and to Doelle's theory of "social contact." Likewise, the principle of "abuse of right" finds its formal origin in BGB article 242, but it actually goes beyond Article 226 which is considered unduly narrow. In the field of damages, undoubtedly, the causal connection between the cause of liability and further effects of damages (for which the wrongdoer is liable) must be limited by equitable considerations or in some other way; the code does not refer to it at all. In all these cases, the code is not incomplete, but within the general legal conscience it does not provide the legal institutions which are recognized without any indirect enacted law.

Abandoning the legal fiction that the code controls these cases, we realize that jurisprudence and doctrine are influenced not only by value standards deduced from the code, but in actuality the determining factor is the need of the business community. Sometimes this results from the nature of the thing. Sometimes there is a legal ethical principle which is not included in the code (or only to a limited extent) which has acquired validity as part of the general legal conscience. Certainly, all these factors are present in statutory interpretation and in filling gaps, but here they are considered only within the limits of either the text of the legislation or the immanent teleology of the law. Sometimes they transgress these limits and lead to a change of the law and to new legal institutions. These respective viewpoints are not exclusive but often supplement each other, and they will be illustrated by some examples. The examples are classified in three groups in the order of the importance of each viewpoint; this does not preclude some measure of influence by the other two viewpoints.

a) *Development of the law with respect to the urgent demand for a legal transaction (Rechtsverkehr).* The classical example of a new law created by an urgent demand of the business community is the chattel mortgage. Originally it came into use through *Kautelarjurisprudence* as a temporary means to achieve what could not be done under the code for a pledge of movables without possession. This was done by applying the *Besitzkonstitut* which is a form of transfer of property. It has gradually developed into a legal institution of its own, hereby enlarging the "closed circle" of rights in rem under the BGB. If one accepts the basic validity of the chattel mortgage in its present form as undisputed customary law, it is necessary to consider how to treat this property (which has been transferred only for security purposes), in its relation to other creditors of the same debtor. Furthermore, there arise the questions of (a) "definiteness" of "composite things" (with their changing component elements); (b) the retention of ownership (*Eigenthumsvorbehalt*) by the supplier of the goods; and (c) the rights of the secured creditor against the debtor, e.g., the use of the goods not covered by any contract provision. These questions could be solved by an analogous application of the provisions on pledge, and some legal scholars adopted this doctrine to the extent that there is no conflict in the apparent secured owner receiving "more" rights than in a regular pledge; the purpose is to prevent a fictitious transaction.

Such a far-reaching analogy not only affects the "formal" ownership status of the debtor, but also makes an important factual difference. Possession, and with it the opportunity to use and often also a limited power of disposition, as retained by the creditor, makes an obvious difference and also changes the structure of the security device vis-à-vis the nonpossessory lien. Henrich Lange correctly points out that the lien of the BGB is a "typical single lien on goods which can be obtained without securing short-term credit," whereas the security transfer typically involves a transfer in toto to secure a longer-lasting credit transaction, which is in this sense a *Mobiliarhypothek* (a mortgage on movables). Although related, the institutions are not the same when viewed in the light of their normal purposes. In the case of long-term credit, it is in the interest of the creditor that the debtor retain the opportunity to manage the pledged goods. Since the debtor has possession for a long time, there may be seizures by other creditors so that the creditor needs the protection of section 771 of the ZPO (code of civil procedure) which the jurisprudence has applied but which the theorists withhold because the analogy to mortgages goes too far. ZPO article 805 fails to adequately protect the creditor because it permits premature termination of the long-term credit transaction and may deprive the debtor of the chance (through the continuation of his business) to obtain the means of repaying the credit. It is generally accepted that only when the goods which have not been transferred for security are insufficient to satisfy another creditor, must he be able to refer the security creditor to ZPO article 805.

From this limited discussion, and what is methodically important, it appears that the solution of a single problem, namely the applicability of ZPO article 771 or 805, started with the typical purposes of security transfers, and that one attempts to discover the legal consequences of this legal transaction without any consideration of either the formal-legal determination of the right "property" or "lien-like right." Furthermore, Paulus' explanation of the different legal "functions" of property is important. On the one hand it includes the authority to dispose, on the other it is part of the patrimony as an object of liability for the debts of its owner. Paulus argues that in a chattel mortgage these functions are temporarily separated. The transferred goods are not removed from his patrimony, as becomes particularly evident in the case of the debtor's bankruptcy . . . when a moratorium prevents other creditors from seizing these goods in individual bankruptcy proceedings. However, the power to dispose of the goods, which at first was limited to a certain period, then passes onto the security creditor. He is only morally bound not to use it in a way which would be in conflict with the agreement. After his claim becomes due, the security creditor can demand by owner's action (BGB article 985) satisfaction of his claim. His obligation to the security creditor to obey the provisions on sale of liens depends on the contract. If the contract is silent, some would apply articles 1235 ff. by analogy; perhaps one should take into consideration that the creditor's pre-maturity position is rather weak, compared with the position of a lien-holder with possession, and may therefore deserve a more liberal treatment—unless he violates the duty to protect the interest of the debtor (to maximum realization).

Regardless of which position is taken on any of these questions, it is clear that neither the simple subsumption of the chattel mortgage under the property provisions in rem, nor in some respect justified analogy to liens can do justice to the peculiarities of this new type of law. One can only reach meaningful results if one starts, as in modern doctrine, with the typical purpose of the transaction and considers the various functions which property performs in our legal order as a means of coordinating a person's disposition and liability. . . .

b) *Development of the law with regard to the nature of the thing.* The *nature of the thing* was already mentioned among the objective-teleological criteria of interpretation, spoken of by the positivists only reluctantly because it reminded them of the disapproved natural law. *The nature of the thing* does not exist in any doctrine based exclusively on law, on a general abstract theory of law, nor in legal science (which is oriented on a formal logic of legal relations), like the pure theory of law. It also confused Neo-Kantianism. Sociological jurisprudence alone has access to it, because *the nature of the thing* means not a norm which is separated from life but, in a way, life itself. Of course, it does not mean facts alone but only facts as they are related to and expressed in human relations of social value or purpose and their resulting objective-teleological structure. For the positivist, "order" is the result of normative formation and a will to create order. Those who talk about *the nature of the thing* mean that things, especially human relations, already contain (in part before formulation of norms) a certain idea which requires order. It is necessary to recognize this order which corresponds to its "nature" (its objective purpose, its *telos*) and to build the law with it. Heinrich Dernburg has expressed this very clearly: "Human relations, although more or less developed, carry with them their measure and their order. This inherent order is called nature of the thing. Those requiring an institutional method mean nothing else fundamentally." Those who see law founded in the sense of (human) being—and this applies particularly to any ontological interpretation and to Hegel's metaphysics—must insist that the enacted law does not ignore the nature of the thing, but rather uses it as a rule of conduct and develops it under given circumstances. Where it obviously fails in this task, science and jurisprudence have to correct it to provide a just order. One should not overlook that the nature of the thing does not provide complete regulation but only the fundamentals and elements. To achieve certain results which must conform to the prevailing legal order, it is necessary to consider further methodical aspects, such as the pertinent principle, analogy, or comparison of cases.

[*Translator's note*. Larenz then discusses nonregistered societies (*nicht rechtsfaehige Vereine*) as an example of the code's failure to deal with the nature of the thing and where doctrine and jurisprudence have provided the needed correction and extension of the rules in the BGB.]

The contrast between the nature-of-the-thing approach and that by formal-logical subsumption becomes apparent in the theoretical treatment of the bilateral contract. According to the objective legal definition of a bilateral contract, each party obligates itself to perform in exchange for a counterperformance (*do, ut des*). Therefore, basically nobody promises more than performance in exchange for counterperformance. The parties can agree that one has to perform first, but where no such agreement is reached, then according to the nature of the thing each party's obligation to perform is limited to performance on payment and delivery. Whoever demands performance due him must at the same time offer his counterperformance. Prevailing opinion differs: it assumes that everyone is entitled to performance by the other unless the contract contains a limitation, and the other party can counteract only with an equitable defense. Actually, the code (BGB article 320) permits such a defense based on a bilateral contract in case no counterperformance was received, but only as a procedural device providing the right to refuse performance. Even though this defense must be brought through the claiming opponent, the defense of nonperformance is not an equitable counterclaim, but only a procedural form of a right to performance founded on the nature of the thing, a limitation by contents. Therefore, according to prevailing opinion, the plaintiff met by this defense must prove the prerequisites of an unlimited claim to content; each can, by notice, place the other in default (unless one is obliged to perform first) if he is willing and ready to render his own performance.

The correct understanding of the bilateral contract helps in an understanding also of the balance theory in an action based on enrichment, another example of the way in which the nature of the thing affects a change in enacted law through jurisprudence contrary to the intention of the legislator.

This "theory," prevalent in jurisprudence but disputed by doctrinal writers, states that by performance of a void bilateral contract according to the provisions of BGB articles 812 ff. in a case (either from the beginning or because of novation of the original obligation into a pecuniary obligation under BGB article 818, section 1 or 2) where comparable performances have to be exchanged, the only one who owes performance is the one who in the end has been enriched "in balance," and he owes no more than this balance. In case of unequal performances, according to this theory, each party can only request return of his performance upon return of the counterperformance. This leads to the following result: e.g., the vendee who no longer had the object of the sale (nor the value received for it) can no longer be held to performance under BGB article 818, section 3. Neither can he demand the price which he has already paid, with the exception of a possible balance, because he must account for the value of the received object. The balance theory means that no longer can the party which does not have to return anything, because it no longer has the object or its countervalue, demand the full value for its own performance. It also imposes the danger of loss on the one who has not suffered any loss, a result inevitable under the interpretation of the codal provisions. According to this interpretation there is no settlement on a legally defunct obligation but only an exchange of performances received without consideration, or their value, up to the amount of the still existing enrichment. The void contract is legally a "void"; there is no consideration for either performance. Each performance creates an independent enrichment claim by the performer against the receiver with no connection between the two claims (Zweikondiktionentheorie; two conditions theory). But this interpretation of the code is in conflict with actual circumstances, or "with the nature of the thing." Although the contract may be void, the parties have made performances in its fulfillment; they intended and willingly agreed not to make single performances, but to exchange their performances even though the contract is void. Only if one considers the whole exchange of performances as a unity can he deal equitably with the intention of the parties and the factual events. Weintraub, the leading proponent of the balance theory, correctly sees its justification not in an ad hoc–developed concept of enrichment or in analogy to adjustment of benefits in damages, but in the "unity of the factual relation," the economic connection of the mutual performances. Here, as in the case of chattel mortgages (Sicherungseigentum), one should not contrast alleged economic considerations with legal ones. All these cases concern the concept of the legal structure which, in turn, is determined by the typical meaning of the facts of life, by the nature of the thing. Where the code has bypassed it, it will eventually prevail in legal transactions and in jurisprudence, even if indirectly.

In some cases the balance theory leads to results which conflict with other equitable principles of our legal order which have a higher rank, and that is one reason why it is opposed by some legal writers. The result is unworkable for reasons of value considerations where minors or incapacitated persons are involved or in cases of fraud where the party who asks for return of his counterperformance at full value is no longer enriched by what he received. In these cases I believe the balance theory should not be applied. The incapable, partially incapable, or deceived person should be protected at the cost of his opponent.

c) *Development of the law with regard to a legal ethical principle.* Legal ethical principles are guiding standards in the creation of legal norms[2] and have inner convincing power which makes them formative factors

[2] But not themselves "highest" norms or legal principles.

in legal development. They are, in contrast with legal technical principles based on their usefulness, "ideas," not only in the sense of a subjective image, but as objective, imaginative legal truths as well. As such, they owe their validity not to an act of the will, a "norm," but to their own immediately apparent quality of justice which is reflected in the general legal conscience during the debate and formulation of enacted law and in the jurisprudence. This does not preclude their asserting themselves at different stages of the development of the "objective spirit" with different intensity (or not at all) and thus taking their part in historical change. At another place I have said: "They, the principles, are forms of expression, trends, tendencies of the objective spirit which influence the general feeling for justice and find their reflection (*Niederschlag*) in enacted laws and in jurisprudence."[3] As "legal truths" they are thus relative as far as the entire content of the respective legal conscience is concerned, which itself is only a "legal" conscience insofar as it is a conscience of those principles in which the (one and general) legal idea appears and is concretized.

We have mentioned earlier some examples of these principles—in the discussion of objective-teleological criteria of interpretation. They determine to a considerable extent not only interpretation but also the supplementing of gaps, inasmuch as they—by way of total analogy, or by discovery of a fundamental principle of a norm, *ratio legis*—can be recognized as inherent in the norm. You may remember the "teleological reduction" of a principle of superior rank. The "internal value" of these principles, their extent and their "'effect," are quite different and subject to historical change. The determining factor is not that these principles could be fitted into a firm system in a logical and noncontradictory way. Quite frequently there is a conflict of principles, such as that today in obligations law between the fault principle and the principle of objective distribution of damages. Although the limits for the application of one or the other principle can usually be found in positive law, they can be shifted through interpretation of norms and even more by newly created institutions. These shifts reflect a change of the general legal conscience. Seldom is any principle so firmly established that a single case could be decided by it alone. Rather, a further development of the principle is

[3] FESTSCHRIFT FÜR ARTHUR NIKISCH, 301.

needed to determine its exact limits, or, differently stated, positivation through legislation or jurisprudence. The principle becomes positive law to the extent that such a positivation has been achieved. . . .

The development of the law which transforms enacted law, which transgresses the immanent teleology of the statute *extra legem* on the basis of a legal ethical principle, occurs not when such a principle (or a new phase or variation of its application) is deduced from the enacted law, but when it is discovered independently of it—even where, as a starting point, one of the general clauses is used and first expressed in a convincing way. The occasion is usually a case or series of cases which can be solved neither by means of statutory interpretation nor by filling of gaps corresponding to legal conscience. According to Esser, legal principles not yet positivized break through "in a leading case and cross the borderline of consciousness into judicial thought." Thus, at first only subconscious principles are formulated by doctrine or by a court in a leading case and gradually find general recognition as part of the current legal conscience. What Doelle has called a "legal discovery" is probably just the first formulation of such a principle or a subsequent consequence of such a principle which enabled it to become incorporated into "general legal conscience." After consciousness follows formulation of the principle and explanation in a leading case, the delineation of its applicability (with regard to other principles or to unchangeable positive legal norms) and finally its adoption as a firm "doctrine." Thus the following were developed from the "fundamental principle" of "good faith" during the last decades: the doctrine of abuse of right, forfeiture, frustration of contract, and, especially in connection with the doctrine of "personal community of interest" in labor law, the "obligation to provide welfare services." In all these areas we are dealing—regarding the period in which our code was enacted—with new experiences which, although covered as valid by BGB article 242, actually far exceed the legislator's intent or a reasonable interpretation of the code.

As an example we take *culpa in contrahendo* to demonstrate how such a doctrine progresses in its development. Jhering, who first started the doctrine in 1861, describes at the beginning of his article how he arrived at it. For years, when lecturing on error, he had great difficulties in one respect: "whether the party in error was liable to his opponent for damages caused by his fault." The sources seemed to demand a negative answer; but the "inequity of such a result is obvious." Jhering's legal ethical conscience was not satisfied by the resultant application of the corpus juris. He gave several examples to show those results and asked himself what was peculiar to these cases as contrasted with other cases. He discovered that they were distinguishable because culpa occurred "in connection with an intended contractual transaction." That provided the decisive understanding: these were cases of "culpa in the formation of contracts—*culpa in contrahendo*." Only then—and this is especially noticeable in Jhering's report—did he turn to doctrinal writing. He searched for and found "a number of other cases in which the same facts were repeated, and among them to my delight also one (!) in which the need for an action, but without sufficient reasons (!) was already recognized by doctrine. The most important discovery for me, however, was that Roman law itself in two cases had recognized liability, namely in the case of sale of a res extra commercium and in the case of a nonexisting inheritance." Jhering stated triumphantly that his theory had entered "solid foundation of sources" and it was now only necessary by way of interpretation and analogy to discover "in the decisions of the sources their more hidden than expressed content as will be attempted here."

From this report of Jhering's there is no doubt how the doctrine was discovered. At the beginning, there was his legal ethical evaluation, followed by factual analysis, and from it was derived the principle: liability for *culpa in contrahendo* in "intended contractual transactions" according to the principles of contractual obligations. He found subsequent confirmation in the sources. But this in and of itself was not sufficient, and he attempted "by application of the two cases which he had found in the sources to determine and to substantiate the theory of *culpa in contrahendo* as a general principle." In other words, he discovered the inner reasoning or the justification for such liability in the thought: "The one who contracts, enters from the strictly negative circle of duties of extra contractual transactions into the positive sphere of contracts." In modern terms that means: increased duties characteristic of parties to a contract are already created by the act of entering into a contract. This was at first nothing but a presumption, a *petitio principii*, even though everything else was already a finding. Gradually, however, the idea succeeded and was acknowledged by doctrine and became part of the general legal conscience. Although the BGB has not adopted it in these general terms, jurisprudence tried to realize it by means of a fictitious precontract (protective contract) or by other artificial means in individual cases. But in 1923 Stoll connected it with good faith and succeeded in formulating it so convincingly that the "doctrine" of "liability for *culpa in contrahendo*" similar to contractual liability has become a "firm part" of our law of obligations. This history of the origin of the doctrine (which is now generally accepted) confirms what Esser has said about it: "At its beginning is not the hidden wisdom of the code, which only has to be coaxed into talking, but the case to solve it with the help of the code evidently contradicts the legal conscience. In attempts to discover an equitable solution, first one finds, still without realization of its importance, a principle, then looks for suitable passages in the positive law in which one believes it has been expressed, although only in individual cases, and then justifies the principle with the code by 'legal analogy.' Actually, legal ethical principles justify the enacted laws as much as *the nature of the thing* and factual contexts; and where such a principle appears for the first time and is thereafter recognized in doctrine and jurisprudence, it happens because the principle convinces people and not because the enacted law so 'wills.' "

Today's treatment of contracts for the benefit of third parties is similar. The underlying principle is simply an extension of the precontractual relationship. Entering into business contracts creates increasing duties of care and protection, not only with regard to the potential contracting party but also with regard to those third parties who are clearly involved in the preparation or execution of the (intended) contract. They are subjected to the same dangers as the contracting parties. He justifiably relies on security to the same extent as the parties do. Reliance on the code (BGB articles 328 ff) as well as justification with additional contractual interpretation are nothing more than an emergency measure; if one dispenses with them, one clearly recognizes a development of the law which is demanded by the general legal conscience.

The use of *jurisprudence constante* by the *Bundesgerichtshof* (Supreme Court) to recognize the general right of personality and other private rights under BGB article 823, section 1, illustrates development of the law due to the priority rank of a legal principle. The BGB and the private-law system based on the code contained very few, narrowly defined private personal rights such as the right to his name and his portrait (likeness); furthermore, it protected the human private sphere indirectly by way of BGB article 823, section 2 (reference to criminal-law provisions on violation of honor) and BGB article 826. There can be no doubt that the civil protection of personal rights is insufficient in many respects. The legislator did not intend to recognize a comprehensive "general right of personality." Such a wide and uncertain clause would conflict with the well-balanced system of defining torts in BGB articles 823 ff. For this reason a total analogy is inappropriate. Rather than resorting to individual analogy (recognition of a right on personal letters analogous to copyright; right to one's own words analogous to rights on a person's likeness), the BGB with a keen sweep has recognized the right to the person as part of the general legal order, and has done so by reference to the Basic Law (articles 1 and 2) as the outranking norm. It is true that the Basic Law, through the Bill of Rights, not only protects the individual from the power of the state, but also, by its inherent recognition of undeniable values, sets a standard for the relations of individuals among themselves which determine interpretation and development of private law. But contrary to the BGH, this does not answer the question how the rights of the individual are to be protected from interference by third persons, as heretofore, by granting of individual specific rights of personality and by reference to protective norms or by a general norm or by a combination of both. The legislator of the Basic Law refrained from making such a choice. The BGH decided to provide private protection of rights of the personality in as comprehensive a way as possible, not because the Basic Law necessitated it (as in the case of carrying out the provisions on equality in the marriage law) but for urgent ethical and legal pedagogical reasons which prevailed over any dogmatical and methodical considerations, before the desirable legislative changes could be accomplished. In the *Herrenreiter case*, in spite of the express statutory limitation of a claim under BGB article 253, there was recognized a demand for incorporeal damages basically for any violation of the right of personality, using its own judgment in contrast with the code to resolve an as yet unanswered question. One may now ask what are the limits of judge-made development of the law.

d) *The authority of the courts to develop the law by statutory changes.* Under prevailing doctrine the judge has the authority to fill gaps and to interpret the law. He is bound by the framework of the law and he can only evaluate the law itself, although in practice there is a difference. Those cases can also be considered as a development within the framework of the law itself where this same law contains a general principle, like good faith, and this is then developed by reference to a special legal issue, through case comparison, concretization, and "strengthening" into a doctrine and new legal institutions. But it is not unusual for the courts ... often under the guise of fictitious reasoning, to have limited, enlarged, or changed a legal norm by applying extralegal measures, like *the nature of the thing* or an ethical principle which is generally recognized, independent of the law. The only positive justification for judicial law finding which not only supplements but actually changes the law, is the vague formula of the constitution (article 20, section 3) that jurisprudence is bound by statute and law. Since the courts themselves have to interpret this formula, they actually have to define the limits of their own authority to develop the law. To avoid arbitrariness, it must be possible to clearly define these limits on the basis of the concept, the specific task of jurisprudence and the constitutional position of the judge as the bearer of jurisprudence.

The task of jurisprudence is the realization of the law in the decision of each single case. The judge is bound by the statute which is a symptom of the law. The law which has to be realized is not always already prescribed in statutes, in other norms (customary law), or in exemplary decisions, but has to be discovered by him through a process of creative judgment and methodical reasoning. He has to allow himself to be guided by principles of evaluation which have been expressed in the legal order itself, its immanent principles, and lastly by the idea of the law itself—rather than by mere judgments of utility (which are the task of the legislator), or by his personal attitude and personal evaluation (which would represent only a part of the community, a single group or a certain ideology). Finally, it is important that the result conform to the general legal conscience, or, expressed differently, to the spirit of the legal order. The legal conscience grows in time, and with it the law. The "general legal conscience" is at each moment of its development richer in content than that of the statute. It contains new insights into the law; legal ethical measures; and clarified, or very newly expressed, concrete legal ideas which have not yet been expressed or have been expressed only suggestively in the statute. At first, the judge bound by the statute can consider the development of the legal conscience only by statutory interpretation and filling gaps left by the statute's own teleology. He thus reconciles the statute with the legal conscience of the time and develops it constantly. Beyond this, for jurisprudence to fulfill its task of realizing law, it must be possible to apply an idea which has not yet materialized as a statute but has been accepted into the "general legal conscience" under special, narrowly defined conditions, and thereby change the statutory rule where otherwise a legal state of emergency would impair the idea of the law. Such a situation occurs when the legal order does not satisfy a particular need in legal transactions (situations) which is considered "imperative" or when the nature of the thing or a legal ethical principle is neglected in a manner that is considered "intolerable" by the general legal conscience. Clearly the "legal emergency" must be evident, and one cannot count on timely legislative action.

In the interest of their own power, the courts should take very seriously the limits of their authority. An "unavoidable public need" whose non-satisfaction would lead to a "legal emergency" might perhaps have been present in the case of "transfer of property for security reasons." Nevertheless, it is questionable whether it would not have been better if jurisprudence had forced the legislator into action by refusing to approve it (as a circumvention of the law).... A clear case of "emergency" was the Supreme Court's regulation of inflation.... The extension of the protection of the person—not necessarily by recognition of a "general right of the person"—e.g., in cases of publication of a letter or a secret recording not authorized by the author, is an urgent ethical demand of our time, where the Supreme Court was correct in not waiting for legislative relief. Awarding relief for "intangible damages" in case of violation of personal rights presents a different situation. There ... the "general legal conscience" did not react so clearly that legislative action could not or should not have been awaited.... To decide a case of such a disputed question of legal policy is the task of the legislator. The courts should not anticipate his action.

In areas where it might have created new law for constitutional principles not yet fully realized in statutory law the Constitutional Court has shown remarkable restraint. It has said that it could not apply a law as if it existed where for its full realization legislative determination of its content was needed. This would anticipate the creative freedom of the legislator. It could only determine that the legislator has not fulfilled his duty to create such a law. In creating and forming a new legal institution, care must be taken to prevent any radical change to the existing legal order ... both to sustain the cohesiveness of the legal order and to control the correctness of the change.

4. THE SIGNIFICANCE OF "PRECEDENTS" FOR THE INTERPRETATION AND THE DEVELOPMENT OF THE LAW (PRECEDENTS AS SOURCES OF THE LAW?)

"Precedents" are decisions in which the same legal issue to be decided has already been decided by a court in another case. "Precedent" is not the final decision in the individual case, but is the opinion of a particular court on an issue which has to be posed in the case to be decided in the same or comparable manner. One has to distinguish two possibilities here. It must be noted that if the question is how a certain legal norm is to be interpreted, then it is a general question which is to be treated uniformly for all similar cases. . . . But if the court is faced with the task of applying a broad general clause like *good faith* or *tolerance* (equitable demands) to a certain case where the facts may control the decision, the given answer is not one which can be generalized as a firm rule. It has, rather, because of the considerations of the individual circumstances of this single case, immediate validity only for this case. The individual case does not set a rule but serves as an example, an orientation for comparable cases. We know that this is the way to clarify concepts and solidify value judgments.

Precedents of both kinds play a most important part in court practice and especially in judicial development of the law. Decisions of the highest court which—because of the importance of their legal issues—are published, are usually followed by the lower courts. But even the highest court is reluctant to deviate from its own decisions, although it frequently limits or modifies some of its rules in later decisions. Since the courts will probably follow the precedents of the high court, the attorneys of the parties, of business firms and associations rely on them. Consequently, precedents, especially those of *jurisprudence constante*, are viewed after a certain time almost as "valid law."

Whether or not precedents, at least those of the supreme court, are "valid law" cannot be answered with a simple yes. If one understands "validity of the law" simply in the sense of a sociological value concept, or whether a preponderant chance exists that the courts, the administrators, and finally practice will actually be guided by precedents, the question has to be answered affirmatively. But if one understands "validity of the law" in a normative sense, meaning whether the courts and the people are bound to follow precedents as legal norms, then one has to answer negatively. In our legal order the judge is bound by statutes and customary law, but he is free to interpret the statutes and develop the law according to their meaning, obeying only his own consciously formed conviction. Thus he is bound not by precedent but by the "correct" interpretation or concretization of the norm expressed in the statute. Each judge must decide in each case whether the interpretation or concretization of the norm contained in the precedent is correct, because the precedent cannot replace his responsibility for the correctness of his decision. The judge is therefore not only justified, but obligated to deviate from a precedent when he is convinced that it either contains a wrong interpretation or development of the law or that the question, although correctly answered at the time of the decision, must now be decided differently because of normative or circumstantial changes. Germann[4] states that by retaining precedents "in spite of the knowledge that they contradict meaningful interpretation of the law, perhaps because they are based on illegal, independently created law," the law may be openly disregarded and its function as guarantor of equality and security undermined. The judge may not rely, sight unseen, on precedent, but must form his own judgment, at least when he has any doubt as to its correctness. In such a case a mere reference to the precedent without reasoning pro and con is insufficient.

The German Supreme Court, in contrast to the former *Reichsgericht*, extracts, in the form of a leading theory, the answer to a doubtful or controversial question. Undoubtedly, this involves the danger that this kind of theory may be separated from the rest of the opinion, and thereby from the actual basis of its formulation, and considered an established rule. The court which had in mind only the single case when it formulated its rules is not in a position to evaluate the possible consequences of its theory for all future cases. Therefore, the court frequently deviates in later cases from a theory, or modifies it by introducing new distinctions.

4 PRAEJUDIZIEN ALS RECHTSQUELLE (1960), 43.

If the court could not do so, it would soon be enmeshed in the snare of its own theories and would hinder a sensible and meaningful development of the law. Each theory is only valid when the case to be decided does not contain any elements which were not considered for the formulation of the theory but which should be considered under the law. The theory should be considered only together with each decided case.

The formation of a new rule of law by judicial developments is a gradual, step-by-step, experimental process. A thought, which first appeared only incidentally in the decision, becomes a supporting foundation in another decision, although not yet integrated into the legal system and thus defined or limited in its scope. Total integration occurs only gradually by application to new cases or by limitation, until out of the totality of these decisions a complex rule can be deduced which, because it conforms to the general idea of the legal order and has been accepted into the general legal conscience, can be accepted as a valid law. ... Through premature adherence to single precedents, or acceptance of theories without criticism or citations only partially pertinent, this process can be hampered or even misguided. Precedents, whether expressed in the form of theories or not, do not have the same legal or representative authority as statutes, and do not enjoy any normative validity.

Nevertheless, if one does recognize precedents as sources of the law, particularly in Swiss literature, one's concept of "source of the law" becomes important. Juristic positivism equates law with legal norms in a statute or customary law. It assumes that the process of creating a law is completed with the statute or with customary formation of the norm. Today we realize that the norms are applicable through a constant process of interpretation and concretization. This process is effected with competent cooperation of legal science, particularly through jurisprudence. A practical knowledge of the application of the law requires a study of the jurisprudence. Therefore, the precedents are a source of legal determination (judgment) but not a source of directly binding legal norms. Esser is correct in stating that they neither create any original source of law, nor have any normative contents apart from the dutiful concept (solely carried by conviction of correctness of the law of each individual judge), but are only a "medium of judicial determination." In general, the courts understand legal norms as they appear in the "medium," by transmission of precedents, of *jurisprudence constante*. But the correctly interpreted norm in the precedent is their only binding force, and the correctness of a precedent is always subject to new examination by each judge.

A *jurisprudence constante* can obtain binding force, equal to a law, by being strengthened to a customary law, but time alone is insufficient to prove itself constant. Although it evidences a strong indication of its correctness, the absence of objection in legal literature is not enough since no consensus of jurists can effectuate recognition of legal norms. Rather, the rule must be recognized by the people who obey the rule, understanding that they thereby follow a demand of the law. Adherence to the rule must be supported by the general conviction that obeisance is legally required, that to disobey it is a "wrong." It is not sufficient that the participating groups of businessmen have accepted a certain jurisprudence. Using this kind of measure, one could accept affirmatively the formation of customary law by jurisprudence, especially where legal ethical principles are applied, e.g., in the field of security of transactions and contractual obligations, the obligations under social security, and loyalty in labor law. These general principles especially need to gain normative power, as will be shown later, without lengthy prior application supported only by general legal conviction. They will hardly reach customary law status when the rules are concerned with mere legal technicalities . . . e.g., interpretation of a tax law or rules of prescription. In these cases, as Esser pointedly remarks, "the rule-building force of the decisions of the high court, even if recognized by scientific opinions, is not based on creation of customary law but on the continuous factual correctness and agreement with living legal conviction." Esser feels the court must be able to examine these at all times. Strengthened ideas of the law, solidified by long-lasting jurisprudence, could not supersede the statute but could aid in its interpretation. The ideas must be constantly examined. Fundamentally this means that the judge is only bound by the statute and by customary law, not by precedent as such.

When the courts nevertheless rely on precedents to a wide extent, then there must be legal reasons, aside from reasons of convenience. The reasons of convenience are obvious: if a judge of a court of original jurisdiction reexamined all that the appeal court undertook in a precedent to reach a certain interpretation of a statute, it would amount to an unjustified expenditure of time and effort. A carefully considered and reasoned opinion of the highest court has a certain factual presumption of correctness. This presumption, however, does not free the other courts from their duty to form a judgment of their own, when they have any doubt as to its correctness. It is not unusual that the appeal court's opinion differs from that of the Supreme Court.

One reason for the adherence to precedent is uniformity of jurisprudence in the total sphere of the legal order. Uniformity of jurisprudence is a recognized, if not the foremost, purpose of an appeal. The Great Senate and the Combined Great Senates of the *Bundesgericht* and recently the Combined Senate of the higher *Bundesgericht* (which took the place of the originally envisioned Supreme *Bundesgericht* [Constitution article 95]), were created for appeal. The legislator no longer attempts to promote uniformity by forcing lower courts to follow precedents. Even the decision of the Great Senate or the Combined Senates of the *Bundesgericht* (which can only decide legal questions) is only binding for the Senate before which the particular case is pending, and not in future cases. The Senate has to resubmit the question anew to the Great Senate or to the Combined Senates only when it wants to deviate from the previous decision in a new case. This procedure clearly indicates that the legislator attaches great importance to uniformity of jurisprudence, but prefers to give the courts the opportunity to later correct an interpretation which they once held to be correct or a development of the law.

The concept of uniformity of jurisprudence requires that like things be decided in a like manner. This postulate, as Germann has pointed out, applies only to the extent that the answer in the precedent on a question of law was really the *ratio decidendi* of the case. So-called *obiter dicta*, remarks of the court of a more incidental nature which do not really support the judgment, should not be considered precedent at all. Observing this limitation, one can say that a court should only deviate from a precedent or from *jurisprudence constante* where compelling reasons indicate that the precedent is incorrect, not in cases of doubt alone. If the judge is convinced the precedent is wrong, he is not impeded from deciding differently by the postulate, "the same treatment for the same case," since the postulate that correct decisions have to be made is even more important. Otherwise, by detour via principle of equality, one would eventually be bound by incorrect precedents, a position alien to our legal order. The precedent would have a representative power of law.

However, one may ask whether the fact that the highest court has decided a certain legal question in a certain way, carries its own weight. We must remember that there are a few rare cases in our history of jurisprudence where a decision of the highest court was accorded legal validity when it was rendered for the first time because the legal ethical postulate corresponded to general legal conviction. It would be unfortunate if the court at the next opportunity would change its own decision. This would not only weaken the security of the law in the traditional sense (the predictability of decisions), but also would tremendously shake the confidence in jurisprudence where a question of fundamental importance is involved, the answer to which establishes a legal ethical principle. Probably the high court would never withdraw a decision of such fundamental importance and consequence (e.g., the recognition of a right of personality or social security in the labor contract) except in case of contravening legislative action. However, the court must retain the freedom to deviate from a prior decision in certain details, because such development can only be brought about gradually in each individual case. But in the principal question, the court cannot overrule itself when the decision corresponds to general legal conviction. In these cases the courts are indirectly bound by the high court's precedent because of the "reliability principle" which can be compared with the binding force of customary law. I understand this to be a principle which prevents the courts from disappointing the confidence in the continuity of a jurisprudence supported by general legal conviction. This principle, forbidding deviation from a fundamental decision, lends normative power to the decision. It can only be applied where the fundamental decision is a responsible interpretation of the law or is an admissible judicial development of the law. It carries only as far as the decision expresses a general legal ethical principle corresponding to an established or developing general legal conviction.

In summary, it can be said: precedents, even those of the highest court, are neither binding on the court rendering the decision nor on any other court. The correctness of their interpretation of the law or its development is subject to reexamination by the court in each new case. Unification of jurisprudence and equality of judgments favor adherence at least to precedents of the higher court; these principles, however, yield to the demand for correct interpretation and development of the law. A customary law is created through *jurisprudence constante* only when a rule has been formed which is obeyed by the people because they feel they are thereby adhering to a demand of the law. A precedent of the highest court indirectly binds another court under the principle of reliance. This requires adherence to a basic principle in a decision which expresses general legal conviction and which conforms to justifiable judicial interpretation of the law. In such a case, formation of a customary law is not necessary; the recognized principle, even without further development, enjoys normative power.

ABBREVIATIONS

B.G.B.	Bürgerliches Gesetzbuch (German Civil Code of 1900)
B.G.H.	Bundesgerichtshof (German Supreme Court for Civil and Criminal Matters)
ZPO	Zivilprozessordnung (Code of Civil Procedure)

VIII

The Italian Legal Style III: Interpretation

John Henry Merryman
PROFESSOR OF LAW, STANFORD UNIVERSITY

1. THREE KINDS OF INTERPRETATION

There are certain similarities between the judicial functions in Italy and in common-law jurisdictions. In each the court is required to decide a concrete case according to authoritative rules, and in each the process of identification, interpretation, and application of the rules in the context of the case is for the judge. Interpretation is necessary whether the authority to be applied be judicial or legislative in origin, and in a sense the same problems are faced by the judge regardless of the source of the norms he must seek to bring to bear on the problem before him. In both systems a simplistic view of the judicial process as mere mechanical application, in the one principally of precedents and in the other principally of statutes, continues to influence the thinking not only of laymen but of a large segment of the profession. And in both systems the literature on the nature of the judicial process is extensive. In the United States one talks about the judicial process; in Italy the discussion is of the interpretation and application of statutes (*interpretazione ed applicazione della legge*).

But the apparent similarities in the judicial processes themselves mask differences in emphasis and outlook. Like and unlike multiply at various levels of comparative analysis and from different perspectives. In fact the act of interpretation is the point at which doctrine and law intersect. It is the focus, the culmination, of the forces represented by the formally recognized sources and institutions of law and the prevailing attitudes toward them that have so much to do with their actual force and effect.

Hence all that has previously been said about doctrine[1] and law[2] takes on new meaning when considered in relation to interpretation.

Judicial interpretation is only one of three kinds of interpretation traditionally discussed in continental works on the subject, the others being "doctrinal interpretation" and "authentic interpretation."[3] Doctrinal interpretation is the work of scholars. Authentic interpretation is performed by the formal source of the statute itself, the legislature. The special significance of doctrinal and of authentic interpretation at specific periods in the history of the civil-law system is generally unfamiliar to common lawyers, and a brief discussion provides useful background for an explanation of current theories of judicial interpretation in Italy.

There was a lengthy and highly creative period in the history of Roman law in which the opinions of legal scholars were authoritative. These scholars, who came to be called jurisconsults, would give opinions in concrete cases, and their opinions would become the explicit bases for decisions in those cases. Such opinions were frequently written down and collected and had a certain power as precedent. Doctrinal interpretation was a vital—perhaps the most vital—force in the evolution, explanation, and preservation of the law.[4] It played a somewhat similar role after the Revival,[5] in the *jus commune* of the medieval period,[6] and in Germany after the Reception.[7] Each of these periods, in its own way, represents a kind of golden age of doctrinal interpretation.

In the later Empire the authority of doctrinal interpretation and the prestige of scholars declined.[8] The culmination of this trend was the command in the *Corpus Juris Civilis* that no commentaries on it should

1 Merryman, "The Italian Style I: Doctrine," 18 STANFORD LAW REVIEW 39 (1965) [hereinafter cited as Merryman, "Doctrine"]. A list of the abbreviations used in this chapter appears on page 201.
2 Merryman, "The Italian Style II: Law," 18 STAN. L. REV. 396 (1966).
3 See, e.g., Rotondi, "Interpretazione della legge," 8 NOVISSIMO DIGESTO ITALIANO 893, 897–98 (1962).
4 For good discussions see BONFANTE, STORIA DEL DIRITTO ROMANO 397–430 (4th ed. 1958); GROSSO, LEZIONI DI STORIA DEL DIRITTO ROMANO 403–30 (4th ed. 1960); WOLFF, ROMAN LAW: AN HISTORICAL INTRODUCTION Chap. 4 (1951) [hereinafter cited as WOLFF].
5 On the Revival of Roman legal studies see VINOGRADOFF, ROMAN LAW IN MEDIEVAL EUROPE Chap. 2 (3rd ed. 1961); WOLFF 183–90.
6 See WOLFF 204.
7 On the Reception see WOLFF 193–206. Wolff mentions the practice of referring legal problems to scholars at 204.
8 For discussion of some of the reasons for this decline see WOLFF Chap. 5.

be written and that judges, when in doubt about the meaning of a law, should refer the matter to the Emperor. He alone, in Justinian's own words, had the authority "to make and to interpret laws."[9]

Napoleon's despair at the appearance of commentaries on his code is well-known.[10] For a brief period in France after the revolution courts were required to refer questions of the meaning of laws to the legislature for interpretation.[11] Similarly various early efforts at codification in Italy during the eighteenth century contemplated referral of problems of interpretation to the prince for authoritative solution.[12] In modern times Italian courts, unlike those in France and Germany, have been forbidden to cite the works of legal writers in their opinions.[13] Both in the *Corpus Juris Civilis*[14] and in Europe during the age of codification and reform [15]

---

9 The relevant provision is CONSTITUTION Tanta 21. On contemporary interpretation of that ban on commentaries see WOLFF 180–81. As to earlier imperial legislation limiting the authority of doctrine to a few named writers, see the "law of citations," CODEX THEODOSIANUS, 1.4.1–3, discussed in WOLFF 159–62.

10 See, e.g., the statement quoted in Friedrich, *The Ideological and Philosophical Background*, in I THE CODE NAPOLEON AND THE COMMON-LAW WORLD 15–16 (Schwartz ed. 1956), and the remark attributed to him when he was informed that the first commentary on his civil code had been published: "Mon code est perdu," quoted in GÉNY, METHOD OF INTERPRETATION AND SOURCES OF PRIVATE POSITIVE LAW 16 (J. Mayda transl. 1963).

11 The reaction in France is usually described as being based in part on antagonism toward the courts, in part on hostility toward Roman and feudal law, and in part on a rationalistic brief in the possibility of creating a clear, simple, coherent, complete statutory system. It led to such laws as the Decree of August 16–24, 1790, Article 12, reserving to the legislative assembly the power to interpret the laws. Later the Tribunal de Cassation was established as a nonjudicial organ to give authoritative interpretations binding on the courts (Law of November 27–December 1, 1890). For a thorough discussion see GÉNY, METHOD OF INTERPRETATION AND SOURCES OF PRIVATE POSITIVE LAW 49–56 (J. Mayda transl. 1963). On the development of the *Corte suprema di cassazione* in Italy see CALAMANDREI, LA CASSAZIONE CIVILE (1920).

12 See the discussion of this aspect of the compilations of King Vittorio Amadeo and his eighteenth-century successors in SCHUPFER, MANUALE DI STORIA DEL DIRITTO ITALIANO 575–76 (1895). See also Statuto Albertino art. 73 (1848) (first promulgated as a constitution for Sardinia and Piedmont and later employed as the constitution of unified Italy): "Interpretation of the laws, in a manner obligatory for all, belongs exclusively to the legislative power."

13 DISPOZITIONI PER L'ATTUAZIONE DEL CODICE DI PROCEDURA CIVILE art. 118 (1942). The same rule existed under the 1865 Code. See IV MORTARA, COMMENTARIO DEL CODICE E DELLE LEGGI DI PROCEDURA CIVILE 93–94 (3rd ed. 1910).

14 See the complaint about commentators on the *edictum perpetuum* in CONST. Tanta 21 and in WOLFF Chap. 6.

15 See discussion in SCHUPFER, MANUALE DI STORIA DEL DIRITTO ITALIANO 612–34.

the number and diversity of doctrinal points of view and the mass and varying quality of doctrinal writing were described as evils to be corrected by compilation and codification.

From this point of view the great periods of codification at two widely spaced periods in the long history of the civil-law system were, to some extent, reactions against the doctrine. The *Corpus Juris Civilis* and the codifications in eighteenth-and nineteenth-century Europe were, in a sense, attempts at a massive "once for all" authentic interpretation. They were intended to substitute legislation for doctrine and were accompanied by the hope, and sometimes by the admonition, that doctrinal interpretation of the new law was to be avoided.[16]

Hence doctrine is excluded from the *numerus clausus* of sources of law in Italy, as it is generally in civil-law jurisdictions;[17] doctrinal interpretation is not authoritative in any formal sense. To the foreign observer this might seem to indicate that the work of legal scholars is irrelevant to the Italian legal process. In fact it is not. As has been pointed out in an earlier article on doctrine and as is further developed below, it dominates the Italian legal process. Realistically speaking, the law in Italy is to a large extent what the scholars say it is. It could hardly be otherwise. Laws must be interpreted. Authentic interpretation, reference back to the lawmaker, has never been and could never be a more than sporadically useful solution to the problems inherent in the interpretation and application of statutes in concrete cases. Continental judges are severely restricted by a traditional view of the judicial process (happily perpetuated by scholars) and by their lower stature to a relatively narrow interpretive function. Someone has to do the job. The scholars, who draft the codes, who develop the conceptual structures within which the law operates, who write the doctrine and teach it to their students, and who have the great scholarly tradition of the civil law behind them, do it. Their formal authority is nil; their real authority is great.

16 The point should not be overstated. The reaction against doctrine was only one of a number of forces at work in either period. The fact remains, however, that it was a force. See the authorities cited in Notes 14 and 15 above.
17 See the discussion in Merryman, "The Italian Style II: Law," 18 STAN. L. REV. 396 (1966).

2. THE FOLKLORE OF JUDICIAL INTERPRETATION

Like the American, the Italian legal system operates in an atmosphere of assumptions which, although demonstrably unsound, tend stubbornly to persist because they are firmly rooted in the culture.[18] This kind of folklore serves a variety of functions, some laudable and others regrettable. Although it exists in most exaggerated form in the lay mind, it tends, somewhat refined, to dominate the thinking of the profession itself. Alternately idealized and caricatured, it becomes the starting point of much scholarly discussion. One who would begin to understand the conventional terms of scholarly discourse about interpretation in Italian law must first become familiar with the folklore. It takes different forms, depending on whether one contrasts the work of judges with that of scholars or with that of legislators.

From the time of the Roman jurisconsults on, the history of Continental law has been one in which the role of the judge is unfavorably contrasted with that of the scholar-jurist. Jurisprudence (in the Continental sense: the reports of judicial decisions) follows and is dominated by the doctrine, just the reverse of what is generally thought to be the natural order of things in common-law jurisdictions. The civil-law judge

18 ARNOLD, THE FOLKLORE OF CAPITALISM (1937), is a delightful, penetrating discussion of the way some of these assumptions operate in the United States. For discussions and criticisms of the Italian folklore see ASCARELLI, L'idea di codice nel diritto privato e la funzione dell'interpretazione, in STUDI DI DIRITTO COMPARATO E IN TEMA DI INTERPRETAZIONE 165 (1952); Ascarelli, "Giurisprudenze costituzionale e teoria dell'interpretazion," 12 RIVISTA DI DIRITTO PROCESSUALE 351 (1957); Bianca, "L'autonomia dell'interprete: A proposito del problema della responsabilità contrattuale," 10 REVISTA DI DIRITTO CIVILE Pt. 1, p. 478 (1964); CALAMANDREI, La Funzione della giurisprudenza nel tempo presente, in VI STUDI SUL PROCESSO CIVILE 89 (1957); Cappellitti, L'attività e i poteri del giudice costituzionale in rapporto con il loro fine generico, in III SCRITTI GIURIDICI IN MEMORIA DI PIERO CALAMANDREI 83 (1958); Meneghello, "Il Formalismo nella interpretazione giuridica," 15 JUS (n.s.) 226 (1964) [hereinafter cited as Meneghello]; Torrente, "Il Giudice e il diritto," 16 RIVISTA TRIMESTRALE DI DIRITTO E PROCEDURA CIVILE 1,261 (1962). Not all criticism of the folklore is recent. For an earlier realistic discussion of judicial interpretation in Italy see Pacchioni, "I Poteri creativi della giurisprudenza," 10 RIVISTA DEL DIRITTO COMMERCIALE Pt. 1, p. 40 (1912). There is a good brief discussion of the problems of interpretation in French law in STONE, THE PROVINCE AND FUNCTION OF LAW 149–65 (1961). Stone refers repeatedly to the work of François Gény, whose most important book is cited in Note 10 above. Gény wrote in reaction against the extremes of the folklore of judicial interpretation in France at the turn of this century.

is not a hero-figure (or a father-figure), as he tends to be in England and the United States. The great names of the common law are those of judges, but the great names of the civil law are those of scholars.

In Italy, under the influence of the assumptions of the traditional legal science, this contrast between the scholarly and the judicial functions has assumed the particularly sharp form already discussed.[19] The scholar is the scientist, and the judge, at best, merely the engineer. The scholar provides the systematic, scientific legal structure that the judge accepts and applies. The work of the scholar is creative and exalted; that of the judge, although important, is on a lower plane. The judicial function is not really a creative one. Jurisprudence is not only dominated by doctrine, it attempts to imitate it, with consequences that will be discussed below.

This attitude, fundamental to the folklore of interpretation, has some interesting by-products. The literature on interpretation, produced out of the abstractness, conceptualism, and cultural agnosticism that characterize Italian legal science,[20] is rendered even more unreal by the fact that it is produced by persons who have no experience in the business of deciding cases.[21] The scholars having, so to speak, occupied the field, the judge, who might be able to supply useful insights into the judicial process, abandons it to them on the theory that they are better qualified than he.[22] The more exalted role of the doctrine, as compared with the jurisprudence, leads naturally to the emulation of the one by the other. The form and style of Italian judicial opinions is closely imitative of doctrinal writing. The way for the young judge to get ahead is to write opinions that show his ability to move easily in the doctrinal *ambiente*. Both in the writing and in the publication of opinions the abstractness and conceptualism of the doctrine are prominent. The factual emphasis,

---

19 See Merryman, "Doctrine," 45–46.
20 Id. at 45–46, 49–61.
21 "It is one thing to interpret, it is another to talk about interpretation," Meneghello, 227.
22 Since World War II, some Italian judges have joined in the growing Italian trend toward reconsideration of the folklore of judicial interpretation. In particular, the articles by Torrente and Meneghello, mentioned in Note 18 above, are the work of judges. Andre Torrente is president of a section of the Supreme Court of Cassation: Bruno Meneghello is a Tribunale judge. Even if these judges espoused a traditionally limited view of their power and responsibility, the mere fact that they were entering into the dialogue would indicate that some change in attitude toward the role of judges was under way in Italy. In fact they both argue for broader recognition of the creative part judges play in the legal process.

the concreteness, which common lawyers associate with judicial writing is absent in the Italian. Opinions often contain no coherent statement of the facts of the case, and even those that do are seldom published with the facts intact. Instead, at the point where the facts might be found, one encounters the disheartening term "*omissis*," signifying that a part of the opinion is omitted. The emphasis, rather than on the facts, is on production of the polished maxim (*massima*), and this abstract and conceptual statement, divorced from the factual context out of which it arose, may be the only part of the opinion to be published.[23]

The folklore of the strict separation of legislative and judicial power leads to an even more extreme oversimplification of the interpretive act and a further diminution of the stature of the judiciary. The attitude, whose origins have previously been indicated,[24] has at its base the dogma that only the legislature can make law. With its companion assumptions that the code is complete and that the legislature can enact laws whose meaning is clear and simple and whose application is certain, this premise makes the judge into a kind of expert clerk. Interpretation is not a problem because the meaning of the statute in application is obvious. While the doctrinal folklore admits that the judge must interpret and tells him how to do so, the legislative folklore, at the extreme, denies that there is any interpretive function.

23 For extensive discussion and criticism of these characteristics of the preparation, publication, and use of *massime* and judicial opinions see the following writings by Gorla: "Contratto a favore di terzi e nudo patto," 5 REVISTA DI DIRITTO CIVILE Pt. 1, pp. 585, 598–603 (1959); "Lo Studio interno e comparativo della giurisprudenza e i suoi presupposti: Le reccolte e la techniche per la interpretazione della sentenze," 87 IL FORO ITALIANO Pt. 5, p. 74 (1965); "La Struttura della decisione giudiziale in diritto italiano e nella 'Common Law,'" 9 GIURISPRUDENZE ITALIANA Pt. 1, p. 1 (1965); Nota, 87 IL FORO ITALIANO Pt. 1, p. 430 (1965).

This practice is clearly related to the abstractness that is typical of, although it is not restricted to, Italian legal scholarship. See Merryman, "Doctrine," 45–48. One Italian colleague puts part of the responsibility on codification, with its tendency to simplification and abstraction of facts—to reduction of concrete facts to the abstract legal *fattispecie* of the norm. See Merryman, "Doctrine," 49–50. The attempt is to reduce legally relevant facts to the minimum in the interest of: abstract order at the expense of pragmatic concreteness, the rule at the expense of the exception, the category or class at the expense of the individual.

In reaction to all this, which is related to the waning traditional legal science, one hears talk among contemporary Italian scholars of the importance of the facts, of concreteness, of the need to preserve the exception from the rule. The work of Professor Gorla is particularly important in this connection.

24 See Merryman, "Doctrine," 52–55.

This attitude has as an obvious corollary the denial of any legal effect to a decision beyond the case itself. The dogma of strict separation of powers and the doctrine of *stare decisis* are clearly incompatible. For the decision of a judge to be binding in future litigation would encroach on the legislative monopoly on lawmaking. Hence precedent is not binding in Italian law. The apparent inconsistency between this attitude toward judicial precedent and the constant insistence on the value of certainty in the law leaps to the eye of a common lawyer.[25] To him certainty means foreseeability of result, and *stare decisis* is a means by which this is guaranteed. But in Italy the emphasis on certainty has its historical origins in distrust of the judiciary and sums up the judgment that lawmaking should be kept out of the hands of judges. Certainty is endangered by the growth of judicial power, and hence of judicial arbitrariness. So the need for certainty becomes an argument *against* the doctrine of *stare decisis* and, by extension, against lesser degrees of influence of the decision beyond the case itself. Foreseeability of result is of course important, but it is guaranteed in other ways. The legislative folklore sees it as following from the clarity and simplicity, and hence the certainty, of legislation. The doctrinal folklore finds it in legal science, in the structure erected by the doctrine for the guidance of the judge. If the judge is able, he will, by following the directions provided by the scholars, arrive at the same result as would another judge in the same kind of case.

One who mentions the readily demonstrable fact that Italian judges sometimes reach different results in otherwise indistinguishable cases receives the candid admission that this is true. From a fundamentalist point of view, however, there are only three possible explanations: (1) One (or perhaps both) of the judges was mistaken. (2) The legislation is imperfect. (3) The doctrine is imperfect. The remedy is to get better judges, who will not make such mistakes, or to improve the legislation or the doctrine, whichever is at fault.[26] *Stare decisis* is not an admissible approach to the problem.

---

25 For a discussion of the emphasis on certainty in Italian doctrine see Merryman, "Doctrine," 61–63.

26 "Almost everyone, however, thinks that different opinions and opposing solutions are due to contingent factors, to imperfect formulation of the statutes, to lack of preparation of operators of the law and above all to their lack of logical rigor. It is considered a perfectly clear truth that every fact has its own objective reality for whose discovery it is enough to know how to avoid deceptive appear-

The Italian Legal Style III: Interpretation | 171

The net image of the judicial process is one of something mechanical and automatic, of slot-machine jurisprudence. Applying juridical logic—the way of legal thinking supplied by the folklore[27]—the judge is driven inexorably to the proper decision. As a prominent Italian jurist has described it:

> There is everything in the statute: all is foreseen in advance. The legal order (it is said) does not have lacunae. The legal system is like an immense cabinet, in which each pigeonhole contains the provision for a certain fact situation: the work of the judge consists above all in the qualification of the facts found, that is, in finding which among the thousands of fact situations foreseen by the law is that to which the facts found correspond. Once having found this coincidence, the judge need do nothing except open the little box in the pigeonhole (which is the article of the code that applies to the case) and find inside, like a prescription, the ready solution. This is the famous logical mechanism according to which every decision can be schematized in a syllogism: the major premise is the statute, the minor premise is the facts: it is enough that the facts coincide with those contemplated by the statute for the conclusion to come out by itself.[28]

This kind of thinking has its equivalent in the United States. Common lawyers have their own folklore of the judicial process and their own theory of automatic decision.[29] The most striking difference is Italian relegation of the judge to inferior status, as the operator of a machine designed and built by scholars and legislators.[30] Some of the consequences of this attitude are discussed below. Here it should be observed that it

---

ances; it seems perfectly logical that each norm have, of necessity, one and only one meaning and that differences concerning it can only be the fruit of sophistry and equivocation, which can only be eliminated by correct reasoning. In substance, given a well-drafted law and a certain fact, it is supposed that any judge, young or old, conservative or progressive, educated or ignorant, in any part of the globe, now or a hundred years ago, should arrive at the same conclusion." Meneghello, 228.

27 For a thorough criticism of "juridical logic" see CALOGERO, LA LOGICA DEL GIUDICE E IL SUO CONTROCCO IN CASSAZIONE (2nd ed. 1964). For an excellent discussion in English directed toward French practice, see STONE, THE PROVINCE AND FUNCTION OF LAW 149–65. For the same author's discussion of fallacies of the logical form in common-law reasoning see 166–212.

28 CALAMANDREI, La Funzione della giurisprudenza nel tempo presente, in VI STUDI SUL PROCESSO CIVILE 89, 95 (1957). Meneghello, 228, speaks of "an electronic calculator. Inside the machine there is a program made up of substantive and procedural legal rules; introducing the facts, in their proceduralized form, and pulling a lever, the decision issues forth."

29 For a discussion and references, see Merryman, "The Authority of Authority," 6 STAN. L. REV. 613, 621–29 (1954).

30 In fact it is common practice in Italy to refer to judges as "operators of the law." See, e.g., the quotation from Meneghello in Note 26 above.

seriously affects judicial prestige. The tendency is to think of a judge as just another kind of civil servant. Judicial appointment is not a reward for distinguished academic or government service or for eminence in practice, it is not the crowning achievement, the ultimate recognition, that it often is in the common-law world. Judges tend to think of themselves as the folklore pictures them and, through operation of the principle of self-justifying expectations, to conform to the folkloric model.[31]

3. THE PRACTICE OF INTERPRETATION

It is unlikely that Italian jurists have ever had much confidence in the extremes of the folklore. Although one sometimes finds suggestions that such a view of the judicial process existed among Italian scholars in the nineteenth century, these turn out on investigation to be straw men. The folklore does not represent an accurate picture of Italian thought about interpretation in the nineteenth century or in the twentieth. What has varied is the degree of awareness of the breadth of the chasm betwen folklore and practice and the degree of willingness to talk about it openly. At an earlier time it might have seemed more important to act as though the folklore were valid, but it is doubtful that many thoughtful scholars ever really believed in it.

It is too obvious that the practice is sharply different from the folklore. For one thing, the illusion of the self-applying statute, the legislative norm that is so clear its application is an automatic process, was long ago

---

31 To the same effect in Germany and France see Von Mehren, *The Judicial Process in the United States and Germany—A Comparative Analysis*, in FEST-SCHRIFT FÜR ERNST RABEL 67 (1954); Von Mehren, "The Judicial Process in the United States and France—A Comparative Study," 22 REV. JUR. U.P.R. 235 (1952).

Under Article 135 of the Constitution of 1948 judges of the Constitutional Court may be chosen from among professors of law and practicing lawyers, as well as from the judiciary. Some members of this court have been appointed from outside the judiciary. By article 106 of the Constitution (and by law before 1948) professors and practicing lawyers are eligible for appointment to the Supreme Court of Cassation. No such appointments have been made since 1948, and there were very few before that date. By Article 104 professors and lawyers are represented on the *Consiglio superiore della magistratura*, which is a kind of supreme judicial council for the nation.

The growing importance of the Constitutional Court and the practice of appointing professors and lawyers to it may indicate that the prestige of judges of that court will, in time, approach that of judges in the United States and England. There is much less evidence on which to base a prediction that the same kind of transformation will take place elsewhere in the Italian judiciary.

dispelled by the facts. The most obvious practical objection is that ever since 1865 the Italian courts have been busily engaged in hearing and deciding disputes whose resolution depends on the meaning to be given to a legislative norm. Such litigation is frequently appealed, and reversals of lower-court decisions are far from uncommon. Hardly a norm in the civil code has escaped the need for judicial interpretation to supply a meaning that was unclear to the parties, to their counsel, and to the judges themselves.[32]

Likewise, the dogma that the code is complete (no lacunae) and coherent (no conflicting provisions) fails to survive even a cursory glance at the jurisprudence. The books are full of decisions in which the court has had to fill gaps in the legislative scheme and reconcile apparently conflicting statutes. The claim of legislative prescience becomes nonsense in view of the constant appearance of new problems, clearly unforeseen by the legislature, demanding judicial solution. Although the text of the statute remains unchanged, its meaning in application often changes in response to new social pressures. The ideal of certainty in the law becomes an illusion in the face of the uncertainty that exists in fact, where determination of the rights of parties frequently must await the results of litigation.

The evidence is overwhelming. The Italian judge is not, in practice, relieved by clear, complete, coherent, prescient legislation from the necessity of interpreting and applying legislative norms. Like his common-law counterpart, he is engaged in a vital, complex, and difficult process. He must characterize problems and select and apply norms to them that are seldom, if ever, clear in the context of the case, however clear they may seem in the abstract. He must fill gaps and resolve conflicts in the legislative scheme. He must adapt the law to changing conditions. The code is not self-evident in application, even (or, rather, particularly) to the thoughtful judge.

But, according to the folklore, the judge need only turn to the doctrine to find the systematic guidance that will relieve him of the uncertainties of interpretation. Here again the facts belie the hypothesis. Despite the best efforts of judges to follow doctrinal instructions, otherwise indis-

---

32 The amount of accumulated published judicial interpretation of codes and other legislation in Italy is impressive. For an introduction to Italian case law, see GRISOLI, GUIDE TO FOREIGN LEGAL MATERIALS: ITALIAN 32–47 (1965).

tinguishable cases are frequently decided differently by different Italian courts, and often the same case will be decided differently on appeal. The scholars themselves are frequently in disagreement not only about important elements of the doctrine but also about the proper result in concrete cases. The doctrine is not monolithic; there are wide variations in point of view within it. But even where the scholars appear to speak with a single voice their words must be interpreted by the judge. The doctrine may not so much clarify the judge's problem as complicate it.

Thus, despite the best efforts of the scholar and the legislator, the judicial decision in Italy is far from automatic and the application of the law to the case far from mechanical. There is too much litigation turning on questions of law to be explained away as the intransigence of parties, the maintenance of lawyers, and the ineptitude of judges. The code is not clear, certain, complete, and coherent; interpretation is necessary, and the doctrine is not a sure guide to interpretation. The judge plays an important role in the creation and evolution of Italian law, a fact which the jurisprudence amply demonstrates.

4. THE TENSION BETWEEN FOLKLORE AND PRACTICE

The greater the scope of judicial interpretation the greater the de facto power of the judge. And the greater his power the greater his responsibility. According to the folklore, judicial scope, power, and hence responsibility are all sharply limited. In practice they are substantial. The tension thus created is the source of serious problems for the Italian legal process.

Consider the judge who is persuaded by the folklore. He must decide hard cases; he must make law. But, unaware of what he is doing, he is liable to do it all wrong. Unconscious of his lawmaking power, he decides irresponsibly. Putting his faith in an omniscient legislature and the infallibility of judicial logic, he sets major and minor premise together and watches the decision trot forward, not recognizing it as his own. In this process of inadvertent lawmaking the product is bound to show the signs of its origin.

Consider the judge who is aware of his lawmaking power but unwilling to take the responsibility it entails. The folklore becomes his refuge. Faced with the opportunity to contribute to a better method of solving a social problem before him, he instead selects a more traditional interpretation, pleading that his hands are tied. It is not for him, a mere judge, to change the law, even if change is obviously desirable and the change is one that might more appropriately be made by evolutive interpretation than legislation. And so he adds judicial to legislative *immobilismo*, blocking the development of the law in the name of the separation of powers, certainty, and other traditional verities.[33]

Consider the thoughtful judge, aware of his power and willing to accept the responsibility of its conscious exercise. He must clothe his work in the traditional costume, conceal what he is doing behind the camouflage of the folklore, or run the risks of reversal on appeal, of castigation by scholars, of injury to his career. The folklore tends to limit what the good judge can do.

These problems are intensified by the fact that prior decisions, contrary to the folklore, do in practice have some effect on future cases. Cases are in fact reported, sometimes fully, more often in highly abbreviated form. Courts do in fact cite prior decisions, or *massime* from them. Although a formal doctrine of *stare decisis* does not exist, an informal practice that closely resembles it does. This fact, which makes every decision a precedent, increases the lawmaking power of the judiciary and magnifies the tension between the folklore and the practice of interpretation.

This tension helps to explain some of the peculiarities of the Italian use of precedent. The idea that a judicial opinion is a third art form, which has its own characteristics and can stand on its own feet, seems unacceptable. Instead the opinion is disguised so as to look as much as possible like doctrine and legislation. The abstractness of Italian opinions and the frequency of the "*omissis*" where the facts might be found have already been mentioned. The published opinions of the Supreme Court of Cassation and the lower ordinary courts thus read more like excerpts from treatises or commentaries on the modes than the reasoning of a court in deciding a concrete case.

Most opinions of the Supreme Court of Cassation are not published even in this form. Instead, brief abstract statements from them, indistinguishable in appearance from typical legislative norms in the codes, are the normal form of publication of judicial decisions. These *massime*, divorced completely from the facts of the cases and from the reasoning of

---

33 On *immobilismo* see the discussion of the Calamandrei thesis in Section 10 below.

the court, go into a general repository of similar *massime* called the *massimario*. There, looking much more like a collection of statutes than judicial precedents, they stand available to the lawyer or judge, who will sometimes apply them to cases quite different from those out of which they arose.

All the dangers of the use of headnotes and dicta that seem so real to the common lawyer are encouraged by the Italian practice. A formal doctrine of precedent being inadmissible, precedents are made to look like statutes and, like statutes, are generally phrased and generally applicable. The way of someone who wishes to restrict a *massima* to its original context is very hard. If the opinion is published, the facts are probably omitted. He must go to the opinion in the files of the court to find the complete text, but even this will frequently contain only an incomplete statement of the facts. He must then go to the record and the pleadings in order to find them. In the nature of things this leads to constant use of the bare *massima*. The process of reconstructing the facts is too difficult.

5. THE PROBLEMS OF INTERPRETATION

Italian jurists are aware of the inadequacy of the folklore as a model of the legal process. They are conscious of the disparity between folklore and practice and of the difficulties the resulting tension creates. The discussion about interpretation is an ancient one in Europe and goes on in Italy today against an extensive background of European and, recently, American thinking and writing. Interrupted by the years of Fascism, when some Italian jurists espoused traditional theories as a defense against executive interference in the judicial process,[34] it has become particularly lively again since establishment of the Republic of Italy, enactment of the Constitution of 1948, and creation of the Constitutional Court.

The debate about interpretation can be put in terms of three more or less classic problems: (1) The problem of interpretation in the strict sense—of the unclear norm, (2) the problem of lacunae—of the nonexistence norm, and (3) the problem of evolution—of the norm whose meaning changes while its text remains constant. To these a fourth, rationalization of the use of precedent, should be added. All of these draw attention to the variation that exists between folklore and practice, and

---

34 See the discussion and authorities cited in Merryman, "Doctrine," 62.

all involve reexamination of the traditional distribution of power between legislator and judge.

The problem of interpretation in the strict sense assumes, as is abundantly clear, that it is not always obvious how a norm should be applied to a case. The judge is faced with a choice of possible interpretations and, by exercising that choice, runs the risk of making, rather than applying, law. Under a strict doctrine of separation of powers he should not decide, but it is settled law in Italy that he must. The judge is not permitted to say *non liquet*, the law is not clear, and dismiss the action.[35] He must interpret the applicable norm.

The problem of lacunae is distinguished from that of interpretation in the strict sense by rather sharply (and, it would seem, sometimes artificially) contrasting the existence of an applicable unclear norm with the nonexistence of any applicable norm. Here again the judge should not decide, according to the orthodoxy of interpretation, but here again he must. The problem of interpretation is to supply meaning to the norm; that of lacunae is to supply the norm.

The range of points of view about these problems is very wide, from the simplistic discussion in the *manuali*, through various ingenious attempts to rationalize folklore and fact, to frontal assaults on traditional views.[36] The serious contemporary discussion can be summed up as a polemic between those who seek to mediate between fact and tradition and those who attack tradition in the name of fact. But before turning to

---

35 CODICE DI PROCEDURA CIVILE art. 55 (1957); CODICE PENALE art. 328 (1959); TORRENTE, MANUALE DI DIRITTO PRIVATO 27 (5th ed. 1962).

36 Recent critical discussions of the folklore of judicial interpretation are cited in Note 18 above. For a more traditional discussion by an established and highly respected scholar, see BETTI, INTERPRETAZIONE DELLA LEGGE E DEGLI ATTI GIURIDICI (1949). Rotondi, "Interpretazione della legge," 8 NOVISSIMO DIGESTO ITALIANO 893 (1962), is a representative brief statement of the traditional view. For an excellent discussion of newer (at the time) Continental trends in the theory of interpretation and conscious rejection of them in favor of a traditional view of the judicial process, see Ferrara, "Potere del legislatore a funzione del guidice," 3 RIVISTA DI DIRITTO CIVILE 490 (Milano 1911). For a reaction to the trend toward realism in discussing the judicial process in Italy, see Tedeschi, "L'insufficienza della norma e la fedeltà dell'interprete," 8 RIVISITA DI DIRITTO CIVILE Pt. 1, p. 536 (Padova 1962).

For examples of discussions of interpretation in the *manuali*, see 1 DE RUGGIERO & MAROI, ISTITUZIONI DI DIRITTO CIVILE 45–56 (9th ed. 1961); TORRENTE, MANUALE DI DIRITTO PRIVATO 21–27 (5th ed. 1962): TRABUCCHI, ISTITUZIONI DI DIRITTO CIVILE 36–44 (13th ed. 1962).

this current debate it is necessary to consider Article 12, Provisions on the Laws in General, which states:

Interpretation of statutes. In interpreting the statute no other meaning can be attributed to it than that made clear by the actual significance of the words according to the connection between them, and by the intention of the legislature.
If a controversy cannot be decided by a precise provision, consideration is given to provisions that regulate similar cases or analogous matters; if the case still remains in doubt, it is decided according to general principles of the legal order of the State.[37]

The first paragraph is the legislative instruction to the judge on interpretation in the strict sense; the second is a similar instruction on the problem of lacunae. The meaning of the first paragraph, in particular, seems to be clear enough: the judge applies the applicable statute according to its literal meaning and legislative intent; other approaches to interpretation are prohibited. However, this provision is a statute and, like other statutes, is itself subject to interpretation. This interpretation about interpretation has led to some interesting products.

For one thing, it seems to be generally conceded that: "To be applied to the concrete case the legal norm must be interpreted.... Application of a legal norm that has not been interpreted cannot be logically conceived.... Even the most perspicuous and clearly formulated norm needs interpretation."[38] This being true, "the actual significance of the

---

[37] This provision reproduced, with some modification, a similar provision in Article 3 of the Preliminary Provisions of the 1865 Civil Code. That, in turn, was based on a provision of the Albertine Code which was, in turn, taken from the Austrian Civil Code of 1811, arts. 6–7. On the nature of the modifications see Note 49 below.
  Neither the French *Code Napoléon* nor the German *Buergerliches Gesetzbuch* contains equivalent statutory directions to the judge on interpretation. However, the doctrine on interpretation in those countries is substantial, particularly in Germany. For excellent discussions and introductions to the literature, see the articles by Von Mehren cited in Note 31 above. There is a good discussion of French practice in DAVID & DEVRIES, THE FRENCH LEGAL SYSTEM 113–21 (1958).

[38] Rotondi, "Interpretazione della legge," 8 NOVISSIMO DIGESTO ITALIANO 896 (1962). All of the discussions cited in Note 36 above make this point with varying degrees of emphasis, as do those cited in Note 18. The statement of Meneghello, 226, is particularly good: "If the norms are clear and the facts simple and incontrovertible, application becomes a quasi-automatic function, but if problems are presented an intellectual effort is necessary to resolve them. It might seem that the first case is normal and the second the exception, an almost pathological legal condition, but reflecting a bit it becomes clear that in

words" being an illusion, "the intention of the legislature" becomes the key to meaning. Here, however, it seems long since to have been settled that the reference is not actually to legislative intent but to the "intention, spirit, objective content of the norm itself."[39] For legislative intent substitute personification of the norm. Or, as another writer has put it: "It is usual . . . to compare the norm to fruit which, detached from the tree, assumes its own identity, distinct from the tree that produced it."[40] The actual occasion for its enactment—the *occasio legis*—is irrelevant. What the interpreter seeks is the *ratio legis*.[41] Some of the consequences of this universally accepted interpretation of the first paragraph of Article 12 of the Provisions on the Laws in General will appear below. Here it will only be observed that one of its results is to deprive the words *no other meaning . . . than* of much of their potential effect by opening the door to other methods of interpretation than a search for the literal meaning or the actual legislative intent. All norms are unclear, and the norm can have a different content than that which the legislator had in mind.

6. LACUNAE

The second paragraph of Article 12 contains three important concepts: lacuna (no "precise provision"), analogy, and general principles of the legal order of the state. The first sums up the problem and the latter two the methods of solving it.[42]

A great deal of ingenuity has gone into consideration of the problem of lacunae, some of it for the purpose of demonstrating that it does not exist. It will be recalled that the problem offends the folklore by positing both the incompleteness of legislation—the existence of lacunae—and the judicial creation of norms to fill the gaps left by the legislature.

---

the conditions we have called normal, professors, judges, lawyers, universities, courts, reviews, textbooks, reports, etc. would be completely useless and that effectuation of public ordering would be a simple administrative and police affair."

39 Rotondi, "Interpretazione della legge," 8 NOVISSIMO DIGESTO ITALIANO 896 (1962).
40 TORRENTE, MANUALE DI DIRITTO PRIVATO 23 (5th ed. 1962).
41 Ibid.
42 For an excellent critical introduction to the topic of lacunae and to the extensive literature on it, see Bobbio, "Lacune del diritto," 9 NOVISSIMO DIGESTO ITALIANO 419 (1963).

Three theories have achieved some prominence as proofs that there are no lacunae. One of them distinguishes between legislation and the legal order as a whole. There may be lacunae in a code or *testo unico*, the reasoning goes, but not in the legal order, a much broader category of which legislation forms only a part. Legislation, in other words, is not always complete, but the legal order is.[43] That order includes not only the specific group of statutes under consideration in the case but all the norms in force, whether in legislative or other form.

Two other approaches, which closely resemble each other, insist on legislative completeness. There are no lacunae, according to the first, because every norm has a double effect: to govern some activity and to leave the ungoverned activity unaffected. There are only two possibilities: either the law applies to the activity in question or it does not. There can be no lacunae, taken as lack or insufficiency of legal regulation, because where the law applies there is no problem and where it does not the activity is legally indifferent. The banks of a stream are not lacunae in the stream.[44] The other hypothesis supposes that every specific norm is accompanied by an unexpressed general norm that excludes, by negative implication, what the specific norm does not include.[45] The first may be summed up as assuming as a general proposition that all that is not expressly governed is legally irrelevant; the second that all that is not expressly forbidden (or permitted) is legally permitted (or forbidden).

It has been argued, in response to these two latter theories, that they constitute an extension of the principle *nulla poena sine lege*, usually restricted to criminal law, to all law. But the Italian legal order does not admit such broad application of the principle. In fact there are not just two possible aspects to the norm, but three: the area regulated, that not regulated, and that similar to the area regulated but not legally irrelevant or governed by any general principle of negative implication. The interpreter, in the absence of a "specific provision," has not one but two possible courses of action: the argument by analogy and the argument *a contrario*. The choice between them is a problem of interpretation in

---

43 See id. at 419–21.
44 Santi Romano, Osservazioni sulla completezza dell'ordinamento statale (1925).
45 See Donati, Il Problema delle lacune dell'ordinamento giuridico (1910).

the strict sense, and the true lacuna comes into being only on rejection of the argument a contrario.[46]

Once a lacuna is found to exist, the interpreter is told to try to decide the case first by recourse to analogic interpretation, by reference to "provisions that regulate similar cases or analogous matters." Theoretically this requires the judge to draw from the "similar cases or analogous matters" the legal principle inherent in the legislative norms that govern them and apply it to the case before him. The assumption that such broader principles are implicit in specific norms leads to the conclusion that the law, even though not complete, is self-sufficient. The process is called "logical expansion." Lacunae are filled from within the legislative scheme rather than from without. Analogic interpretation is a process of auto- rather than hetero-integration, and so there is no need to resort to the creative power of the judge.[47] This is on the whole the prevailing view.

If analogy fails, then the interpreter, according to Article 12 of the Provisions on the Laws in General, decides the case according to "general principles of the legal order of the state." The principal dispute over the interpretation of this expression is between those who would find such general principles outside the positive legal order—in natural law or some other type of ideal system[48]—and those who would stay within it. The terms of the statute are loaded in favor of the positivists—the judge is not to look to general principles of *law*, but to general principles of *the legal order of the state*—and theirs is the dominant view.[49] Thus the process of drawing broader principles from specific legislative norms is merely a first step; such principles themselves contain equally valid but more general implicit principles, and so on up the scale.

46 Bobbio, "Lacune del diritto," 9 NOVISSIMO DIGESTO ITALIANO 421–22 (1963).
47 Id. at 422–23.
48 For a representative statement of this view, see DEL VECCHIO, Sui principi generali del diritto, in I SCRITTI SUL DIRITTO 205 (1958).
49 In the Preliminary Provisions of the 1865 Code, Article 3, the reference was to "general principles of law." The same terms were used in Article 14 of the Albertine Code. But in Article 7 of the Austrian Civil Code of 1811, which is the source from which the Italian provisions were drawn (see Note 37 above), the reference was to "the principles of natural law."

In Article 1 of the Swiss Civil Code the judge is instructed, in the absence of an applicable legislative provision, to look first to the customary law and, failing that, to apply the rule he as a legislator would adopt.

This process of logical expansion is, of course, the fundamental method of the traditional legal science.[50] The general principles of Article 12 of the Provisions on the Laws in General and the conclusions of scholars as a result of their scientific study of the law consequently are identical under this view of the meaning of Article 12. The scholar, by his work in bringing such principles to light, is engaging, at least indirectly, in the judicial process and hence making his contribution to the law in action. The judge, in the process of interpretation, is contributing to the science and hence performing a scholarly function. But since both are merely drawing forth principles that are implicit in the legislation, they are not making law. The dogma of strict separation of powers is preserved.

7. EVOLUTIVE INTERPRETATION

The neatness with which all of this fits together may account in some measure for the massive uniformity one encounters in the standard discussions of interpretation. Since the Second World War, however, attacks on this image of the judicial process have multiplied in number and intensified in force.[51] They have concentrated on a problem that is not expressly governed by Article 12 of the Provisions on the Laws in General and has not yet been discussed here: evolution of the meaning of a textually constant statute. Like that of lacunae, the problem of evolutive interpretation is an ancient one, and the contemporary discussion in Italy goes on against a background of centuries of thinking and writing.

The extreme folkloric view would be that evolutive interpretation is not a permissible judicial function. If law can be made only by the legislator, only he can change it. This formulation is now generally repudiated in favor of theories which justify evolutive interpretation, the dispute shifting from its legitimacy to its nature. In a very general way it may be said that two points of view are in conflict. One, the most widely held, argues that the judge, even in evolutive interpretation, merely interprets the statute. The lawmaking power remains in the legislature under this view, and the folkloric model of the legal process is thus preserved. The other view is that the judge makes law when he interprets evolutively. This necessarily leads to a drastic reformulation of the Italian legal

---

50 See Merryman, "Doctrine," generally and at 43–48.
51 Some of the most important of these are cited in Note 18 above.

process. What appears on the surface to be a kind of scholarly quibble is really the focus of a much more far-reaching and significant discussion.

Those who take the conservative view marshal a number of arguments. One, which explains some but not all evolution in statutory applications, posits a kind of interdependence of laws. The statute is not interpreted alone, isolated from other statutes, but in the context of the statutory scheme of which it is a part. The obvious necessity for this kind of interpretation, which none would question, is proof of the organic, interrelated nature of the body of laws. But, like all the law, this corpus of legislation is in constant flux, and a change in one part of it affects the others. Thus the meaning of a law whose text remains constant will change as a result of legislation not directly affecting it; every legislative act has some amending effect on existing legislation. Evolutive interpretation merely recognizes and effectuates legislative change.[52]

8. THE BETTI THESIS

Such a theory does not purport to rationalize all evolutive interpretation with the orthodoxy of the strict separation of powers, but the one about to be considered does. It finds recent and effective expression in the work of Emilio Betti, probably its most resourceful and sophisticated advocate.[53] Its effect is to explain how a judge may properly give a statute a meaning different from what it appears to say, without making law. Perhaps the prime example of such drastic interpretation is found in the interpretation of Article 12 of the Provisions on the Laws in General itself. It will be recalled that the first paragraph of that statute says that "no other meaning" can be given to a statute than "that made clear . . . by actual significance of the words . . . and by the intention of the legislature." As has already been pointed out, this statute is also subject to

---

52 Rotondi, "Interpretazione della legge," 8 NOVISSIMO DIGESTO ITALIANO 898–99 (1962).

53 For a biographical sketch of Professor Betti, see 2 NOVISSIMO DIGESTO ITALIANO 383 (1958). His principal work on legal interpretation is INTERPRETAZIONE DELLA LEGGE E DEGLI ATTI GIURIDICI (1949). He is also the author of a unique two-volume work, TEORIA GENERALE DELLA INTERPRETAZIONE (1955), in which he discusses the interpretive process in general and a wide variety of specific "types of interpretation" (philological, historical, translative, dramatic, musical, etc.). Legal interpretation is discussed in Volume I, at 801–66. His works are serious, impressively erudite, and not easy to read. A good summary of his views on evolutive interpretation is presented in Betti, "Interpretazione della legge e sua funzione evolutiva," 10 Jus (n.s.) 197 (1959).

interpretation. The theory to be discussed interprets it to mean that statutes may be interpreted by other means than resort to the literal text and legislative intent and that the resulting effect may be something quite different from what the words seem to say and what the legislature seemed to intend. This interpretation of Article 12 then becomes the rationale of interpretation of other statutes.

In barest outline the reasoning is this: [54] By "the intention of the legislature" is meant the *ratio legis*, or reason of the law, rather than the *occasio legis*, or occasion for the law. The statute has a life of its own, a life given it by the legislature. It imports not only the specific norm but also a larger content, of which its legislative form is only a partial representation. This "surplus of content" includes a value content. Latent in the text are legislative consideration and valuation of conflicting social interests. These, being a part of the norm, must be found by the judge. Since the enactment of the statute, society has, inevitably, undergone change. So, as a second step, the interpreter must determine whether and how the play of these social interests latent in the norm has been affected by changed conditions external to it, and the new interpretive result will follow from this process. Just as the logical content of a statute varies with changes in other statutes —by external legislative change—so its value content varies with external social change. Logical expansion of the norm, by finding the broader legal principle of which the norm is only a partial expression, leads to solution of the problem of lacunae. "Axiological expansion," by discovering the social values of which the norm is a partial expression leads to solution of the problem of evolution.

In the conclusion to the article from which this explanation has been drawn Betti states:

> I have presented criticism and ideas which, on the one hand, are opposed to those of persons who would attribute to the judge a task that cannot be that of the judge, the task of setting norms, and on the other seek to justify in the interpretation of the judge an effect, and therefore an evolutive function, that is not limited, should not be limited, to the pure recognition of the literal sense but must extract from the entire order all that excess of content not only logical but especially axiological, *of value content*, that is inherent in general principles of law and in all those supreme values that have found only partial expression in individual norms.

54 This description is drawn from Betti, "Interpretazione della legge e sua funzione evolutiva," 10 Jus (n.s.) 197 (1959).

It is as necessary, therefore, to be sufficiently clear-sighted about the evolutive function of interpretation of statutes (and, in general, of interpretation directive of conduct in conformity with the preestablished system) as to remain aware of the tie of subordination that always binds the interpreter to the objectivity to be interpreted, in this as in other fields of the spirit. The contradiction between evolution and subordination (which imports conservation) is only apparent.[55]

9. THE ASCARELLI THESIS

A number of Italian scholars have taken a substantially different view of the nature of evolutive interpretation and, indeed, of the entire interpretive function. The names most often mentioned are those of Tullio Ascarelli[56] and Piero Calamandrei,[57] the former a commercial lawyer and the latter a proceduralist. Both were towering figures in the postwar Italian legal world, and both have had substantial influence on contemporary Italian legal thought.

Ascarelli denies the univocality of norms.[58] To him the problem is not to apply the norm to the exceptional hard case, but to any case. It is always equivocal, and indeed its abstractness, which permits a kind of stability in the fact of change, also permits its application to concrete changing reality. The norm is merely a *text* which the judge must interpret. It

---

55 *Id.* at 215. For another example of a traditional rationalization of evolutive interpretation by an eminent Italian scholar, see SANTI ROMANO, Interpretazione evolutiva, in FRAMMENTI DI UN DIZIONARIO GIURIDICO 119 (1953).

56 For a biographical sketch of Ascarelli, see 1 NOVISSIMO DIGESTO ITALIANO 1021 (1958). In addition to his work as a commercialist Ascarelli, since deceased, became deeply interested in comparative law during his stay in Brazil (from 1938 until the fall of Italian Fascism). A stimulating collection of his writings on comparative law is contained in ASCARELLI, STUDI DI DIRITTO COMPARATO E IN TEMA DI INTERPRETAZIONE (1952).

57 For a brief biographical sketch of Calamandrei, see 2 NOVISSIMO DIGESTO ITALIANO 664 (1958). For a more substantial biographical appreciation by a student and disciple of Calamandrei, see CAPPELLETTI, IN MEMORIA DI PIERO CALAMANDREI (1957). Two of Calamandrei's shorter books have been translated into English: EULOGY OF JUDGES (1942) and PROCEDURE AND DEMOCRACY (1956).

58 This statement of Ascarelli's views is based on Ascarelli, "Giurisprudenza costituzionale e teoria dell'interpretazione," 12 RIVISTA DI DIRITTO PROCESSUALE 351 (1957); "In tema di interpretazione ed applicazione della legge (lettera al prof. Carnelutti)," 13 RIVISTA DI DIRITTO PROCESSUALE 14 (1958). For the reaction of a more traditionally inclined major Italian jurist to Ascarelli's thesis, see Carnelutti, "Postilla," 12 RIVISTA DI DIRITTO PROCESSUALE 363 (1957); "In tema di interpretazione ed applicazione della legge (risposta al prof. Ascarelli)," 13 RIVISTA DI DIRITTO PROCESSUALE 22 (1958).

only becomes a norm, in the sense of a binding rule, on interpretation and application to the concrete case. Once applied, that application becomes just another text, a point of beginning for new formulations.

He also attacks the view that denies the influence of the judge's values in interpretation, saying: "It is vain to deny the weight of the interpreters' values, that it is they in fact who determine eventual new interpretations, new norms, genuine development in the law even as to texts remaining literally unchanged, that the law changes . . . in an inexhaustible process in which legislator, judge and jurist participate."[59] To talk of the declarative nature of interpretation is to overstate the admitted need for continuity in development and to deny the actual nature of evolutive interpretation.

Ascarelli also rejects the notion of a surplus content of the norm, whether logical or axiological. To him the interpreter begins with an inevitably equivocal text and achieves a norm which is the confluence of his value judgments, traditions, hopes, prejudices, and general conceptions, under the directing influence of the "vectors" of general principles and legal categories.

Ascarelli concludes by arguing that much effort is misdirected into trying to establish or to maintain the fiction of the univocal norm, into disputes about the nature of given institutions, and hence about nonexistent problems, in the search for certainty. In place of all this he believes efforts should be directed toward making the judge more aware of what he is in fact doing, so that he can consciously examine and more objectively and explicitly evaluate the presuppositions and values which actually influence his interpretation.

This exposition of Ascarelli's thesis has been so summarily exposed because of its similarity to the commonplaces of American legal realism and hence its familiarity to the American reader. Its influence in Italy has been substantial, but it is rather abstractly developed and hence just as applicable, on the whole, to any civil-law jurisdiction. The Calamandrei thesis, while also valuable outside Italy, is primarily concerned with Italian practices and problems, is illustrated by description of Italian cases, and is much less abstract in tone. In addition, Calamandrei goes beyond As-

---

59 "In tema di interpretazione ed applicazione della legge (lettera al prof. Carnelutti)," 13 RIVISTA DI DIRITTO PROCESSUALE 14, 17 (1958).

carelli by suggesting how Italian judges should go about consciously employing their creative power.

10. THE CALAMANDREI THESIS

Calamandrei's concern is with the Italian Constitution of 1948.[60] Even today that document is far from fully effective, but in 1955 it was less so.

Only a part of its provisions, perhaps less than a half, have been actuated: in place of all the others, since the law, like nature, abhors a vacuum, old laws have been left in force; hence it is difficult to orient oneself in this uneven panorama, where venerable archaeological ruins stand beside new construction projects still encumbered with scaffolding, and where heterogeneous legal sources corresponding to three different historical periods live together in disconcerting promiscuity: some norms of a constitution of democratic inspiration with socializing tendencies; some pre-Fascist laws of liberal inclination; and many Fascist laws with a strongly authoritarian mark. The jurist who goes in search of the road in this landscape devastated by a still recent cataclysm, and who, according to his function, asks nothing other than to be faithful and obedient to the laws of his country, finds himself bewildered and uncertain: he hears laws that speak to him of liberty, others that talk of authority; on one side he encounters provisions that seem to exalt free private initiative, on the other, provisions that place the accent on social solidarity; here he comes across the needs of regional autonomy and of decentralized administration, and there the reaffirmation, by way of old organs still in force, of a traditionally centralized system; on the one hand he reads the program of a rigid constitution where individual rights are secured under the armor of the principle of legality, on the other he encounters in full effect the preeminence of those discretionary powers by which rights of liberty were transformed into flaccid rights, reduced in substance to desires without any legal guarantee.

How ought the jurist to conduct himself before such a disparity of voices, in such uncertainty of contrasting conceptions? And what can be the function of the jurisprudence in that clash between the old and the new?

Calamandrei thus puts two problems: why does the situation he describes exist, and how should it be remedied? He finds both the principal fault and the principal hope of correction in the judicial process.

He finds Italian judicial practice "rich in dialectic virtuosity" but, as a result, "less sensitive and open to the human requirements of the individual case than in other countries, particularly those of the common law. One must admire certain decisions that are "monuments of legal doc-

---

60 This discussion is based on his famous article, "La funzione della giurisprudenza nel tempo presente" (1955), in 6 STUDI SUL PROCESSO CIVILE 89 (1957). All of the quotations and paraphrases in the text are taken from that article.

trine," but they leave one with a feeling of discontent and unease, "a secret question that does not find an answer in that display of erudite dialectic." He quotes a judge who told him: "We decided unanimously, because juridical logic required it, but when we parted we were all full of sadness."

This juridical logic is the most valuable instrument of justice, so long as it remains an instrument, but it becomes its own most dangerous enemy when allowed to dominate. At present formal logic has got the upper hand. This is perhaps a secular legacy of the scholastic tradition, "not yet exhausted in our university education, in which jurisprudence was nothing but a chapter of logic, understood as the art of language." Even today, after so many centuries, the way in which an Italian judge approaches a case is essentially different from, almost the reverse of, the approach of an English or American judge. With them the fact is what counts: justice is justice to the extent it is adequate to the case; the solution for the case is sought not in general criteria but in the equity that is better adapted to concrete circumstances, not in abstract logic but in social values.

"In our jurisprudence," on the other hand, "it appears that everything is a question of abstract logic." Even where the judge has interpretive functions to perform, "this work of supplemental jurisprudence is . . . traditionally considered not as work of creation," but as mere interpretation, "as research, among general and abstract statutes, for something that is already there by intention of the legislature" to be "discovered and recognized," not created. "Our jurisprudence is essentially conceptual." Application of the statute to the case means discovery within the norm of those narrow and more detailed norms that are already there. The judge is like one who patiently seeks to sort out the individual fibers of a rope. The rope is the law and the ever smaller threads the jurisprudential *massime*. "But rope and thread are logically of the same fiber." The judge in disentangling the threads adds nothing of his own except his patience and precision. "The jurisprudence in our reports is prized not as dispenser of justice adequate to the requirements of the individual case, but as revealer of *massime* good for the future," to be used by other judges and lawyers in their search for the useful formula.

"Think, oh colleagues, on the form our work as lawyers takes when we prepare an argument: our work consists not only in tracking down in the legislative chaos the statute that best serves our thesis, but in going with our little lamp into the jurisprudential forest that has grown up around each statute, in search of the jurisprudential *massima* that accommodates itself most to our case." The *massime*, that "by force of inertia are confirmed by other judgments," in fact acquire authority similar to that of statutes, "and neither lawyer nor judge can free himself of them."

"I confess to you . . . my diffidence, which sometimes approaches terror" of juridical logic. "I have the suspicion that in general we jurists . . . abuse the logic: even in the field of justice we have inherited, perhaps from medieval scholasticism more than the Roman *aequitas*, a tendency toward systematic architecture: we build castles of concepts to provide a dignified dwelling for justice, and we do not notice that little by little they are transformed into barred prisons from which she is unable to free herself."

Think about how *massime* are formed in practice. In origin they are the result of an inductive process, from an individual case to a judgment that claims a general character. Even though it is claimed that the legal order is complete, the statutes cannot foresee all the cases that reality, much richer than the most fervid imagination, brings before the judge. Thus, even in a system of legality, every law leaves a certain margin of discretion to the judge within which he becomes, even if he does not realize it, a "creator of law." Even the most precise and minute law leaves to the judge, in the reconstruction of the facts and in the search for the relation between the facts and the precept, a certain freedom of movement and choice. Here the judge must find the answer not in the statute, "but in his conscience." The system of legality is not the abolition of judicial choice, but its control and rationalization.

The Italian judiciary, according to Calamandrei, does not employ this power of controlled choice with courage and resolution. The judge shrinks from openly stating that he has, within the limits of the statute, decided for reasons peculiar to the case. Instead he feels the need to disguise this and to draw a general principle from it, a *massima* that seems appropriate for application in future cases. "His conscience is not at peace" if he does not transform the unique case into terms typical of juridical logic and "draw from that case a general principle of which his decision can appear to be an application." By force of inertia it is applied by other judges in future cases. But since the specific facts and reasons for the original decision are not included in it, since it has been "logic-ized," a *massima* that was born to justify the decision of a certain case is made, out of regard to formal coherence, to apply to a case in which the facts and considerations of equity and policy are quite different and perhaps opposed.

Calamandrei argues that cases would not be decided in this manner if the judge did not give the effect of law to the logical constructions of his predecessors. Juridical logic can be compared to an instrument the old portrait painters used when exact reproduction of the subject was highly valued. It was a wooden frame with a network of silk threads at right angles. By using this to view the subject it was easier to obtain the exact proportions. The syllogisms of the jurist serve a similar purpose. But if the number of threads is increased too much, and the apertures through which justice is viewed made too small, at a certain moment justice, behind the tangle of the jurisprudence, can no longer be seen.

Even in a system of legality, he goes on, the statute offers the judge the means to interpret creatively. Evolutive interpretation, analogy, and general principles are windows which open on the world. By using them the judge can, within the limits of the law, keep the law abreast of changing times. There are periods of relative social stasis in which it is possible and right for the judge to remain faithful to the statutes, but there are also times of rapid transformation in which the judge should have the courage to be a precursor, a standard-bearer. Italy finds itself in such a period, but there is much legislative inertia. Hence it is even more important that the judge should exercise his creative function. But almost always "we find ourselves before another inertia . . . a waiting contest . . . between the legislative and judicial powers . . . a kind of connivance in immobility." Someone proposes an urgent reform in parliament, perhaps a change in one article of a statute. The competent minister replies that this ought to be left to evolutive interpretation by the judges. But when one knocks on the judge's door he hears the reply that the laws are written and that the judge can do nothing but wait until the legislator decides to change them.

> Now I think that this ostentatious immobility of the judges before the neglect of the legislator, in which they almost seem to enjoy applying to the letter the decrepitude of old laws no longer corresponding to the changed needs of society, does not correspond to the useful and trustful cooperation between powers that there should be in a democratic regime.
> I understand that in an authoritarian regime . . . the judges . . . might limit

themselves to applying the statutes as dictated, without adding or taking away anything, in order to leave all the responsibility in [the legislator] . . . especially when infamous laws, like those of racial persecution, are involved. But in a free regime, in the presence of a constitution in which the judiciary is a power placed on the same plane as the legislative, this agnostic attitude of the jurisprudence, this kind of ironic relish that one sees between the lines of certain judgments in putting into evidence the inadequacy of the statutes and of making all the blame fall on the inertia of the legislature . . . no longer conforms to the constitutional duties of the judiciary.

The constitution, with its programmatic provisions, is not addressed solely to the legislature to transform into statutes. It is also addressed directly to the judiciary so that, through the openings provided by general principles and evolutive interpretation, it can bring the new social demands that the constitution embodies and consecrates into effect in its decisions without waiting for the legislature. The much-discussed distinction between preceptive and programmatic constitutional norms,[61] which has served to prevent realization of the document's most essential dispositions, should not be considered an obstacle by the judiciary. Instead these provisions should serve as orienting principles in judicial practice.

Thus, even if the legislature remains inert, the judges can make the spirit of the constitution live in their decisions. They can transform it in their daily work into the reality of human relations. This does not mean abandoning the spirit of legality. To be inspired by the constitution in order to refuse to apply old formulas is the true democratic legalitarianism. A free and autonomous judiciary, courageously inspired, ought to be proud to perform such a function.

The United States Constitution, originally composed of only a few written articles, has been strengthened, developed, and perfected day by day by the dedicated and courageous jurisprudence of the Supreme Court. It can be said that "in America the Constitution has become, through a labor of almost two centuries, a monument created by the judiciary." The Italian judiciary can do the same.

This, then, is the Calamandrei thesis. Judicial interpretation is creative, and hence the judge is responsible for the conscious exercise of his power

---

61 Programmatic norms, in Italian constitutional doctrine, are those held to require governmental action in order to produce effects. Preceptive norms, on the contrary, establish operating rules. The distinction is similar, in effect, to that drawn in the United States between self-executing and non-self-executing norms.

as law-maker. That power must be exercised within the limits imposed by the principle of legality, in the interest of continuity, but it must also be exercised with careful regard for individual justice in concrete cases. The glorification of juridical logic and the production and use of *massime*, which contribute to the extremes of the logical-formal conception of interpretation, lead to judicial irresponsibility, to unjust decisions, and to immobility in the law. The law must adapt itself to new social demands; judges can aid in such adaptation, indeed it is their function to do so. The agnostic, formal, conceptual structure of the traditional doctrine, which rejects such social values as unscientific and avoids direct encounters with the justice of the concrete case, is inadequate as a sole source of analogy and general principles. The values which ought to guide the interpretive process are not found in the doctrine, but in the new democratic constitution of Italy, and the judges ought to draw on that document in their daily work.

In other words, Calamandrei argues, as do others such as Ascarelli, for a conscious redistribution of power and responsibility between judge and legislator. But unlike others he goes on to advocate deliberate utilization of the constitution as a source of analogy and general principles. Not only are traditional attitudes about interpretation brought into question; the whole dogmatic doctrinal structure, with its assumptions about the nature and functions of law, its methodology of logical expansion, and its paraphernalia of abstract concepts, is accused of inhibiting judges from the proper performance of their true role. Whereas Betti builds a model of the legal process that rationalizes fact and folklore, Calamandrei proposes an entirely new model which, in the name not only of fact but of individual and social democratic values, is incompatible with traditional attitudes toward doctrine, legislation, and jurisprudence.[62]

This brief exposition of the Betti, Ascarelli, and Calamandrei views does not summarize the current discussion of interpretation in Italy. It is merely an indication of three of the most important landmarks in a great

---

62 Meneghello, "Il Formalismo nella interpretazione giuridica," 15 Jus (n.s.) 226 (1964), arrives at similar conclusions by an even more drastically realistic route, calling on contemporary thought about linguistics, the nature and area of applicability of the scientific method, the limitations of scientific certainty, Heisenberg's Uncertainty Principle, Gödel's Proof, Wittgenstein, Russell, and Whitehead.

sea. Of the three, Betti is by far the most nearly representative of the way Italians currently think about the judicial process. The more realistic theses of Ascarelli and Calamandrei are widely discussed, but usually for the purpose of refutation. Only a minority, although a growing one, holds similar views.

11. PRECEDENT

According to the traditional doctrine, judicial decisions are not a source of law.[63] One way to put this proposition is to state that judicial decisions are not binding precedents in subsequent cases; another is to say that decisions of courts affect only the parties and have no effects *erga omnes*. However the matter is put, it is obvious that the traditional Italian view of precedent is an organic part of the traditional view of the legal process, with its emphasis on legislative supremacy and a sharp separation of powers. The judicial function is limited to the interpretation and application of the law. If the decision of a court is a precedent or is otherwise effective beyond the limits of the case, it is engaging in a function reserved to the legislator.[64]

This theory of the limits of the judicial process, like other aspects of the folklore of judicial interpretation, is in conflict with the facts in Italy. A decision by the Constitutional Court that a law is unconstitutional, although made in the context of a concrete case, does have *erga omnes* effects; the law is, as a result, invalid.[65] The decision is binding not only on other Italian courts but throughout the Italian legal process. The same is true of a decision by the Council of State that a regulation or other administrative act is invalid.[66] It is, of course, quite possible to consider these powers of the Constitutional Court and the Council of State exceptional, to distinguish them from the judicial function in general,

---

63 See the discussion of sources of law in Merryman, "The Italian Style II: Law," 18 STAN. L. REV. 396 (1966). The sharpness of this distinction between sources and nonsources is similar to the distinction in the legal folklore of the United States between primary and secondary authority. For a discussion, see Merryman, "The Authority of Authority," 16 STAN. L. REV. 613, 619–28 (1954).

64 See, e.g., Rotondi, "Interpretazione della legge," 8 NOVISSIMO DIGESTO ITALIANO 897 (1962).

65 See discussion and authorities cited in Merryman, "The Italian Style II: Law," 18 STAN. L. REV. 400–401 (1966).

66 Id. at 401.

and to argue that elsewhere in the Italian judicial process the decisions of courts have no effects beyond the case in which they are rendered.

There are other factors, however, that call the validity of the folklore into question. The Supreme Court of Cassation is the highest court of judicial, as distinguished from administrative and constitutional, jurisdiction. It is at the apex of that part of the Italian judiciary most like common-law courts in function. Article 65 of the 1941 Law of the Judiciary places the obligation of assuring the "uniform interpretation of statutes" and the "unity of national law" on the Supreme Court of Cassation. At an earlier time there were five such courts, all on the same level of authority, and considerable disparity existed among their interpretations. A principal argument for a single such court was the desire for an authoritative final voice on the interpretation of the law, and the statute cited expressly confers that function on the Supreme Court of Cassation. Even though the decisions of that court are not "binding" in theory, few judges would knowingly adopt a different interpretation. They may not be bound, but the pressure to conform is irresistible.[67]

It is also relevant to note that the Procurator-General may, under Article 363 of the Code of Civil Procedure, attack a civil decision in which the government is not a party "in the interest of the law." The purpose of such an attack, which does not affect the interests of the parties to the case, is to avoid allowing an erroneous "precedent" to remain at large. Although this procedure is hardly ever used, it exists *in posse* and clearly implies that decisions have effect as precedents.[68]

Finally, and most important of all, Italian courts regularly cite and apply *massime* and decisions (of lower courts, as well as of the Supreme Court of Cassation) in their opinions. The practice is widespread. Whatever the folklore may say about the value of precedent, the fact is that courts do not act very differently toward reported decisions (and *massime* from them) in Italy than they do in the United States. When an Italian judge cites a prior decision, he presumably thinks that it is relevant in some way to decision of the case before him.[69] It is true that, as the Italian

---

67 For a good discussion of this function of the Supreme Court of Cassation, see II CALAMANDREI, LA CASSAZIONE CIVILE 48–85 (1920).

68 *See id.* at 104–30.

69 For a discussion of the assumptions implied by a citation, see Merryman, "The Authority of Authority," 16 STAN. L. REV. 613, 614–16 (1954).

The Italian Legal Style III: Interpretation | 195

discussions of precedent uniformly point out, he is not formally bound by the prior decision. He is, however, affected to some extent by it.[70] To that extent the prior decision is, in realistic if not in formal terms, a precedent.[71]

It is an interesting fact that Italian scholars generally have not focused on these matters. The literature on the question of whether the judge makes law for the case when he interprets statutes is, as was shown above, extensive. The literature on whether he makes law beyond the case, by creating a precedent that will affect the actions of persons or organizations and the decisions of courts in future cases, is not. Most discussions of interpretation say little or nothing about precedent. The reader is told that precedent in Italy, in contrast to common-law countries, is not binding, and the matter is left there.[72]

One writer, Colesanti, probing more deeply into the effect of decisions as precedents, distinguishes between the normative effect of a case or *massima* and its "interpretive value."[73] Its normative value is limited to the case itself, but its interpretive value gives it life beyond the case, a power to "impose itself on the critical perception of a future judge" and to be useful to him in the solution of new cases. It is legitimate to "distill from the particular facts the rule valid for the decision of future cases." In this way, over time, a mass of "decision-rules" is formed. Their normative

70 For an enumeration and discussion of the variety of reasons why judges use authority, even though not "bound" by it, see *id.* at 612–29.
71 In addition to the views of Calamandrei discussed in Section 10 above, see II CALAMANDREI, LA CASSAZIONE CIVILE 57–85 (1920), and the articles by Gorla cited in Note 23 above. And consider the following statement by TORRENTE, MANUALE DI DIRITTO PRIVATO 21 (5th ed. 1962): "Judicial interpretation . . . especially if it is contained in decisions of the Cassation, which is the supreme judicial organ, or is repeatedly accepted in the pronouncements of lower judges, has notable importance for other judges who are called on to decide analogous controversies; they will not depart from them, or they should not depart from them, unless they are convinced of the wrongness of the principle that was affirmed in other decisions. One speaks in this connection of *auctoritas rerum similiter indicitarum*." To the same effect, see CAPPELLETTI & PIERILLO, CIVIL PROCEDURE IN ITALY 49 (1965): "Although Italian law does not formally embrace the principle of stare decisis, court decisions . . . do have persuasive authority."
72 See, e.g., Rotondi, "Interpretazione della legge," 8 NOVISSIMO DIGESTO ITALIANO 897 (1962).
73 Colesanti, "Giurisprudenza," 7 NOVISSIMO DIGESTO ITALIANO 1101, 1102 (1961).

import does not extend beyond the cases decided, but their value "on the level of interpretation" does. In this way they assume authority as "precedents."[74]

Such "decision-rules," he continues, exist in the presence of a tendency toward uniformity of decision. When a new case arises there is a strong probability that the same basis of decision will be invoked, leading to a series of conforming decisions. The mere fact that a rule has been applied in a previous case gives it a certain "authority," satisfying the drive toward certainty in the law by a "constant jurisprudence." On the other hand, the freedom of the judge to decide whether or not to apply the old *massima* allows the case law to develop, to be refined, to meet new demands. An inherent problem in the use of *massime* is the tendency to allow them to have normative effect. But "our legal order, inspired by the principle of legality, and on the other hand permitting no limitation on the judge but the statute, forbids conferring normative effect, even indirectly by way of *massime*, on the jurisprudence. . . . [The *massime*] have their effects on the level of interpretation and their survival is conditioned on their persuasive force."[75]

It is apparent from this discussion that such a distinction between the normative effect and the interpretive value of *massime* and decisions is a fairly subtle one. Colesanti himself recognizes that it is not carefully observed in practice and that the tendency is to use *massime* and decisions much as they are used in common-law countries. He concludes that the theoretical differences between the value of precedent on the continent and in the common law tend to obscure substantially similar practices. The folklore of the Italian judicial process demands that decisions and *massime* be freely evaluated by the judge; in practice they are treated as normative not only by subjects of the law but by judges themselves.[76]

12. CONCLUSION

Although the views of a Calamandrei or an Ascarelli are far from dominating contemporary Italian thought concerning interpretation, one can observe that great changes in the Italian judicial process—and hence in the

---

74 *Id.* at 1102–1103.
75 *Id.* at 1103–1104.
76 Colesanti also discusses the problems created by the abstractness of *massime*

entire legal process—are under way. A variety of factors is at work. After almost two hundred years the specter of the pre-French Revolutionary judge walks less often and with less effect.[77] The years of self-imposed restraint under Fascism are over, and a democratic constitution is in existence and in partial effect.[78] Attitudes toward the separation of powers are becoming more flexible.[79] There is a constitutional court, manned by judges who have the power to override the legislature, and some of this heady liquor filters down to the lower courts in the form of a power to declare a constitutional objection "not manifestly unfounded."[80] The tension between folklore and fact continues to grow, and despite the ingenuity of apologists for the traditional view, folklore is losing its grasp while the power of fact increases. There is a new concern for individual justice, achieved at the expense of dogmatic certainty, and a concern for the implementation of social policy by judges as well as legislators. A younger generation of scholars and judges, many of them students of such men as Ascarelli and Calamandrei, is beginning to fill the university chairs and the bench. New concepts and attitudes enter through windows opened by comparative legal study and by Italy's participation in international organizations, refreshing the stale air of a house long closed against the common-law world. Although many Italian scholars still seek to rational-

---

and the tendency to treat them as normative in situations dissimilar from those out of which they arose, thus supporting the criticisms of Calamandrei, described in Section 10 above, and of Gorla (see the articles cited in Note 23 above).

77 See Merryman, "Doctrine," 54–55 for an explanation of the effect of this specter on continental legal thought in the nineteenth century.

78 Although the constitution was enacted in 1948, a number of its provisions are still ineffective because of the lack of implementing legislation. The most obvious examples are the failure to enact laws concerning collective labor contracts under Article 39 and the failure to establish the regional governments contemplated by Articles 114–33.

79 One author, as early as 1934, argued that judicial review of the substantitive validity of legislation was not inconsistent with the separation of powers, properly conceived. ESPOSITO, LA VALIDITA DELLA LEGGE (1934). See also the interesting discussion of the separation of judicial and legislative powers in BATTAGLIA, I GUIUDICI E LA POLITICA 3–13 (1962).

80 Cassandro, "The Constitutional Court of Italy," 8 AM. J. COMP. L. 1 (1959), contains a description of the Constitutional Court and of the role of lower courts in referring questions to it. For an extensive discussion of the Constitutional Court and its interpretive function see Cappelletti, L'attivatà e i poteri del guidice costituzionale in rapporto con il loro fine generico, in III SCRITTI GIURIDICI IN MEMORIA DI PIERO CALAMANDREI 83 (1958).

ize contemporary judicial practice with a traditional model of the legal process, employing such devices as "logical expansion," "axiological expansion," and the "interpretive value" of precedent, there is increasingly general recognition that Italian judges have broad interpretive power and that reported decisions and *massime* have effect as precedents. The dispute is less about the facts than about the characterization to be given the facts and the conclusions to be drawn from them.

EPILOGUE: TOWARD A NEW ITALIAN STYLE

Doctrine, law, and interpretation, as the terms have been used throughout this article, are merely names for different aspects of the same process. The work of the scholar, the legislator, and the judge does not go on in isolation; each affects and is affected by the other. Together they comprise only a part, although a very important part, of a legal process that extends far beyond them, to the limits of the culture of which that process is itself only one manifestation.

Certain themes have constantly recurred throughout this discussion. Of these, the orthodox doctrine and the constitution may be taken as particularly significant because they are symbols of the forces of tradition and of change. Prior to 1948 the traditional legal science was the Italian constitution in a very real sense. It dictated a model of the legal process to which scholars, legislators, and judges conformed. Norms and concepts came to mean what the doctrine said they meant, and the doctrinal view of fundamental institutions like property and contract operated as a limitation on government in the interest of nineteenth-century liberalism. Culturally agnostic, rigidly "scientific" and dogmatic, it excluded not only Catholic natural law but every form of secular idealism, functionalism, utilitarianism, and pragmatism, and every intrusion of history or sociology, as nonlegal. It supplied general principles of law and a judicial method and dominated legal education in the universities. It influenced every aspect of Italian legal life. A variety of forces lay behind the doctrine and gave it its character, and some of these have been described. But the doctrine was the medium through which these forces acted, and after a time it developed its own independent momentum.

If the doctrine has been the stronghold of the forces of tradition, the Constitution of 1948 is the banner of the *avanguardia*. It represents the exuberance of release from long years of repression under Fascism and the accumulation of decades of frustrated desire for reform. It embodies principles of individual and social justice of the sort the traditional doctrine rejects. It establishes the institution of judicial review of legislation for the first time in Italy, destroying the dogma of legislative supremacy and increasing the status of the judiciary. It redefines fundamental legal institutions in terms quite different from those of the doctrine. It provides a basis for theories of interpretation which are more realistic and more value-conscious than the older model. It provides an alternative source of analogy and general principles of law. It is both cause and symbol of a modernizing revolution in Italian law.

That revolution is part of a much broader transformation. "It has become a cliché to speak of a post-Fascist cultural renaissance in Italy."[81] The Italian industrial development since 1945 is frequently spoken of as a "miracle."[82] Names like Antonioni, Dolci, Fellini, Ferragamo, Ferrari, Fiat, Lampedusa, Mattei, Michelangeli, Montessori, Moravia, Nervi, Olivetti, Pavese, Pininfarina, Pucci, and Quasimodo are familiar symbols of the creative energy that was released on the fall of Italian Fascism. To this force add an open society, a democratic polity, a mixed economy, and the reaction to economic, social, and cultural isolation that finds expression in contemporary Italian internationalism. The resultant can have important consequences not only for specific legal institutions but for the legal order as a whole.

The response of that legal order is determined to some extent by its traditional view of itself. A doctrine that excludes the "nonlegal" from the attention of scholars, teachers, and judges can expect to experience a kind of subversion. A Betti, for example, must smuggle the jurisprudence of interests into the traditional view of the legal process by positing a "value content" of the norm and a process of "axiological expansion." It would be a mistake to underestimate the extent to which legal change of this kind has taken place in Italy. But an extreme form of legal purism and a rigid conceptual legal structure (which have survived beyond their time by making a virtue of insensitivity to what was going on in the culture of which they were a part) also invite open attack. I have referred

---

81 HUGHES, THE UNITED STATES AND ITALY 236 (Rev. ed. 1965).
82 Id. at 219.

throughout these articles to a representative selection from among the many legal scholars, judges, and lawyers who are today calling for a conscious, deliberate reformulation of the Italian legal process.

That reformulation is already under way, and something can be foreseen of the directions it will take. Specifically, the future would seem to hold an expanded role and greater prestige for Italian judges. In part this will come about through deflation of the bloated conception of the legislature that has loomed over Continental legal thought since 1804. In part it will flow from reconsideration of the nature and the rigidity of the separation of powers. And to an important extent it may follow from recognition of the broader doctrinal role that can be played by a creative judiciary whose decisions have precedential effects, leading to a more equal sharing by judges and scholars in the conscious development of the law.[83]

The result, however, is not likely to be a facsimile of the legal process in the United States. The new Italian style will continue to be part of a separate legal tradition, and no matter how familiar the words look, the music will be different. Those comparative lawyers who predict unification of the law across the historical and cultural boundaries that separate the common law and the civil law are likely to be disappointed. They expect unison when they should be seeking harmony.[84] The study of each other's law by jurists in the United States and Italy can be mutually stimulating; it can open the way to communication between elites in both societies; it can lead to mutual understanding, mutual respect, and mutual accommodation of differences. It seems quite possible for us to learn

[83] Colesanti, "Giurisprudenza," 7 NOVISSIMO DIGESTO ITALIANO 1106 (1961). An opposite trend seems to be taking place in the common-law world with its very brief history of academic legal scholarship. In the United States, in particular, legal scholarship exercises a growing influence. See Merryman, "La funzione della dottrina nel diritto degli stati uniti," 19 RIVISTA TRIMESTRALE DI DIRITTO E PROCEDURA CIVILE 246 (1965).

[84] "Civil law and common law represent, therefore, not only the two main legal systems of Western civilization, but also two fundamental trends of human nature. It would be childish to try to find out which is better." Pekelis, "Legal Techniques and Political Ideologies," 41 MICHIGAN LAW REVIEW 665, 692 (1943); also in LAW AND SOCIAL ACTION 42, 74 (1950).

It is interesting to note that the various treaties creating the European communities use such terms as "harmonization," "coordination," and "approximation," but not "unification" of national law. See Polach, "Harmonization of Laws in Western Europe," 8 AM. J. COMP. L. 148 (1950); Stein, "Assimilation of National Laws as a Function of European Integration," 58 AMERICAN JOURNAL OF INTERNATIONAL LAW 1 (1964).

from one another, but there is no apparent reason why this should be taken to mean that we ought to sing the same tune.

I have tried to say something useful about the way Italians think about their law, emphasizing those features of the Italian style that might appear odd to a common lawyer and trying to explain why what seems odd is not or, if it is, how it got that way. In the process I have said very little about the substance of Italian law. But I am confident that one who has read these articles will be in a good position to understand the substance of Italian law (and of the law in other civil-law countries) [85] when he does encounter it, whether in the form of doctrine, law, or interpretation.

85 Particularly in Latin America. Legal thinking in many Latin American nations is similar to that in Italy. Latin America shares the legal tradition of which Italy is the source and the archetype. The influence of contemporary Italian legal scholarship in Latin America is substantial. To those in the United States and Canada who see "real understanding between English America and Latin America" as essential to "the unity and survival of the Western civilization" (Pekelis, "Legal Technique and Political Ideologies," 41 MICH. L. REV. 692 [1943]) the study of Italian law has an additional value.

ABBREVIATIONS

Am. J. Comp. L	American Journal of Comparative Law
Mich. L. Rev.	Michigan Law Review
Rev. Jur. U.P.R.	Revista Juridica de la Universidad de Puerto Rico
Stan. L. Rev.	Stanford Law Review

IX

Judicial Decisions and Doctrine in Scots Law

David M. Walker
REGIUS PROFESSOR OF LAW, UNIVERSITY OF GLASGOW

It is well known everywhere outside England that the law of Scotland evolved separately from English law, subject to different influences and having a quite distinct literature, content, and approach, and that it is today one of the mixed systems, originally largely civilian in content and approach but in modern times increasingly subject to influence by English law. This is so not least because since 1707 legislation for Scotland has been made by British (1707-1800) and United Kingdom (1801 to date) Parliaments sitting in London and composed as to roughly eight-ninths of English members, and because since 1707 ultimate appeal has lain to the House of Lords, a tribunal composed until 1857 exclusively of English lawyers and still, even when hearing Scottish appeals, normally composed as to a majority of English lawyers. Apart from these factors there has been a natural tendency to look to English books and cases for guidance in default of native authority. What, then, have been (and are) the roles of judicial decisions and of doctrine—the published writings of legal scholars—in the formulation and development of major doctrines of Scots law, and in determining the decisions of courts today?[1]

When the College of Justice, of which the main component is the Court of Session, the still existing supreme court, was instituted by King James V of Scotland in 1532, he ordered one of the Lords of Session to keep a journal of decisions. Whether or not this stimulated it, there was

[1] For further accounts of the subject see WALKER, THE SCOTTISH LEGAL SYSTEM (3rd ed., 1969) and DAVID, INTRODUCTION A L'ÉTUDE DU DROIT ÉCOSSAIS (1972). A list of the abbreviations used in this chapter appears on page 220.

apparent in the sixteenth and seventeenth centuries a common practice among judges and leading lawyers of maintaining manuscript collections of notes of decided cases.[2] Sometimes these contained also a mixture of notes of points of law and abstracts of statutes. The earlier ones were chronological, but the later ones were digested under headings and must have been written up from earlier notes. Both kinds were known as Practicks, from practice, or uniform practice in the decision of cases, based doubtless on the natural wish to do as had been done before, the word later coming to mean practical notes on law. Of these, the most notable surviving specimens are, of the earlier kind, Sinclair's *Practicks* (covering 1540–1549) and Maitland's *Practicks* (covering 1550–1580). And of the later, digested, type are Balfour's *Practicks* (covering 1469–1579), published in 1754; Spotiswoode's *Practicks* (1541–1637), published 1706; Hope's *Major Practicks* (1608–1633), published 1937–1938; and Wallace's *Law Repertorie and Collection* (1660–1680) unpublished). These all contain numerous cases, noted briefly. (Hope also wrote a smaller *Minor Practicks* which, despite the title, contains no reference to cases or other authority and is in fact a concise manual of Scots law.)

From the first kind of Practicks developed the later collections of decisions and from the second developed the treatises and textbooks. For the period prior to 1660, Practicks are of the first importance as sources of our knowledge of Scots law of the time; Balfour's *Practicks*, in particular, has repeatedly been cited as an authority since it first circulated in manuscript copies. But as early as 1621, Lord Durie was collecting the decisions and those were published in 1690, the first book recognisable as a volume of decisions.

The existence of these collections of notes of decisions must have influenced the Court of Session to have some regard to consistency in decision and to its own course of practice. As early as 1622 the Court reached a decision "contrair to the decision made, 22 November 1621, in the action *Muckall against Stuart*; But the Lords declared in time coming they would decide, where the like question occurred, conform to the last decision."[3]

The first systematic legal treatise in Scotland is Craig's *Jus Feudale*

---

2 The appendix to this essay gives the full titles of all the books of decisions and of writings referred to in the text.
3 Carmichael v. Learmonth (1622) Durie 28.

(c. 1603) a learned disquisition on feudalism and a still valuable discourse on the land law, which is still founded on strictly feudal principles. It is the earliest reasoned examination and statement of Scots law and Craig presents it as a system embodying the spirit of the civil, canon, and feudal laws, all parts of the common heritage of Western European law. The main sources referred to are the Books of the Feus, the Roman law, and the canon law and some of the great commentators thereon such as Bartolus, but reference is sometimes made to Scots statutes. The *Jus Feudale* cites only seventy-three cases, of which only a few have been identified by later scholars; they are cited as instances only and there is no indication at all that they were regarded as in any sense authorities.

Later in that century an event of capital importance occurred. James Dalrymple, Lord President of the Court of Session, resigned on religious grounds in 1681 and took refuge in Holland, not returning till 1688, when he was reappointed, being created Viscount Stair in 1690 and holding office until his death in 1695. Since he had become a judge he had assiduously collected decisions of the court and these, covering the period 1661–1681, were published in two volumes in 1683 and 1687. They were the first volumes entitled *Decisions of the Court of Session* to be published (other *Decisions* of earlier date were published later), and mark the transition from Practicks to collections of decisions. But, more important, just before he fled he published his *Institutions of the Law of Scotland, Deduced from Its Originals, and Collated with the Civil, Canon and Feudal Laws, and with the Customs of Neighbouring Nations*, a work on which he must have been engaged for some years. He published a revised and enlarged edition in 1693.

It is noteworthy that he followed Justinian in calling his work *Institutions* and in dividing it into four books dealing respectively with original personal rights, original real rights, the transfer of both, and the judicial ascertainment and enforcement of both, each subdivided into titles and sections, and also that he set out to state on a philosophical, historical, and comparative basis the law of the country. In the dedication to the first edition, he said, "Our law is for the most part consuetudinary." In the preface to the second edition he stated that he had

> . . . made indexes of all the decisions which had been observed by men of the greatest reputation and did cite the same. But considering that the ancient

decisions were before these trodden paths, which have since come to be fixed customs, and that there were not authentic copies of these old collections, I thought fit, in this edition, only to relate to the later and more authentic and useful collections. . . . I have omitted no material decision of the Lords that I found, especially where they were contrary and seemed to be inconsistent, that judges might not be overruled by adducing some decisions, where others about the same time were opposite.

Clearly, there was already a feeling that decisions should be consistent with other decisions on the same points, but decisions were evidence of custom and usage and no more.

In the book[4] he set out his understanding of the influence of decisions: "But there is much difference to be made betwixt a custom by frequent decisions and a single decision, which hath not the like force [especially if it be invested with many circumstances of fact: but such as are more effectual if they be in any abstract point of law].[5] Yet frequently agreeing decisions are more effectual than acts of sederunt themselves which do easily go into desuetude." Decisions accordingly are sources of law subordinate to equity and ancient custom, influenced by the civil canon and feudal laws, and to statutes. They declare and exemplify equity and custom, but are not sources having any authority.

Shortly thereafter, in 1684, Mackenzie produced his *Institutions*, a small handbook as compared with Stair's large treatise, but set out on the same plan. It probably served as a students' textbook, for it went through nine editions in seventy-five years. In it he says[6] "Our unwritten law comprehends the constant tract of decisions past by the Lords of Session which are considered as law, the Lords respecting very much their own decisions, and though they may, yet they use not to recede from them except upon grave considerations." Not long after that, Dirleton in his *Doubts and Questions in the Law* (1689)[7] under Descreets of the Lords of Session raises the question: "Whether the sentence of the Lords of Session should be considered as Laws, and if notwithstanding thereof, these who are of another opinion, may in cases occuring thereafter, vote according to their own Opinion?" Clearly already by this time some people regarded decisions of the Session as laws, and doubted whether in a subsequent case judges were not bound to follow the prior decision.

4 I, 1, 16.
5 Words in brackets in first edition, absent from second edition.
6 *Inst.* I, 1, 10.
7 P. 40.

From the latter part of the seventeenth century onwards there was a steady series of volumes of *Decisions*, frequently collected by judges. These provide a sometimes overlapping coverage from 1661 to 1822. Thus Lord Kames published two volumes of *Remarkable Decisions* covering 1716–1752 and a volume of *Select Decisions* covering 1752–1768, and Lord Kilkerran a volume of *Decisions* covering 1738–1752.

From the early eighteenth century the Faculty of Advocates was accustomed to charge one of their number, and latterly several, with noting and later publishing a report of the most remarkable cases decided in the Court of Session.

In 1760 they began to publish the Faculty Decisions or Faculty Collection, from the year 1752, a series which ran to 1841. Since then reports have been published regularly, in steadily improving form. From 1821, a series of annual volumes commenced, at first concurrently with and, since 1841, replacing the periodical volumes containing several years' cases. From 1821 to 1907 they were known and cited by the editor or chief reporter's name. In 1907 they were taken over by the Faculty of Advocates and published as Court of Session cases. This series continues to the present.

Forbes in his *Journal of the Session* (1714) containing the decisions from 1705 to 1713 narrates[8] how circumstances "roused my curiosity to dig in the Records, or otherways for so great a Treasure of Standard Law."

Some complain we have too many Collections of Decisions . . . but the Decisions of Judges . . . are applications of that Rule [viz. Law is the Rule of Right and Property] in various Cases, and the best explanations thereof, where it is obscure or doubtful. They furnish Notions of things for determining parallel cases, without the Expence of that Time and Thought imployed in hitting upon them at first. . . . It's ridiculous to think that the Subject of Decisions is exhausted; when we daily see so great Variety of cases, out of which the rich invention of Lawyers do always discover something new, that fall not directly under former Procedents, but must be determined by Analogy.[9]

Forbes later became professor of law at Glasgow and wrote a brief *Institutes of the Law of Scotland* (1722). In the preface he observed[10]

8 P. xlv.
9 P. xvii.
10 P. iii.

that great alterations had been made in the law of Scotland since Mackenzie wrote, "and several points controverted in his Time are now cleared up and established by a Tract of Uniform Decisions." In the text,[11] he lists the foundations of the Municipal Law of Scotland as including "7. Some old Books. . . . 10. Acts of Sederunt, and Decisions of the Court of Session." Dealing with these foundations individually he notes [12] "Decisions of the Lords of Session, sometimes called *Practiques* are the Determinations or Resolutions upon particular Points of Right, or form contested before them. Which, if they continue uniform for some considerable Time, have the force of a Law."

By 1741 decisions were sufficiently regarded for Henry Home, later Lord Kames, to publish his two-volume *The Decisions of the Court of Session Abridged and Digested under Proper Heads in Form of a Dictionary*. He observed in the preface:

In Scotland where we have so little written law and where our judges depend, in a great measure, upon practice and precedent as their guides, it must be an useful design to digest the decisions of our sovereign courts into one body. . . . There are eminent men among us who . . . chuse to talk with little regard of our decisions. . . . I know not if a treatise concerning the advantages that may be reaped from our decisions, and concerning the proper weight that ought to be laid upon them, would tend to remove such prejudices. Till such a work is produced, the following short hints may be of use.

In the first place, Decisions upon arbitrary questions, points of form and such like, ought to have the utmost weight and authority. . . . As to cases which ought to be determined from principles universally agreed upon, I acknowledge that decisions ought there to have no authority.

But he goes on to point out that such decisions are not useless. Most of our knowledge of law is by induction, which can be exercised in such cases, and by induction from many cases a general rule is formed.

In the eighteenth century also there commenced the textbook on smaller distinct branches of the law as distinct from the general treatise embracing the whole legal system. Thus George Dallas published a *Systems of Stiles* (i.e. conveyancing forms or precedents) (1697 and 1733), Forbes wrote on *Elections* (1700), *Bills of Exchange* (1703), *Justices of the Peace* (1703) and *Church Lands and Tithes* (1705), J. Carruthers published a *Compend or Abbreviat of the Most Important Ordinary*

11 P. 5. Prelim., III, pr.
12 Prelim., III, 10.

Securities (1702) and Andrew Birnie another book of the same name (1709), Spotiswoode an *Introduction to the Knowledge of the Style of Writs* (1708) and other books.

As already suggested, Mackenzie's short *Institutions* was probably the original students' textbook on Scots law. A volume of *Notes for the Use of Students of Municipal Law in the University of Edinburgh Being a Supplement to Mackenzie's Institutions*, by Alexander Bayne was published in 1731. His successor, John Erskine (professor, 1737–1765) for long used Mackenzie but in 1754 he published his *Principles of the Law of Scotland in the Order of Sir George Mackenzie's Institutions of That Law*. This replaced Mackenzie and reached its ultimate (twenty-first) edition, much altered by editors, in 1921. It states: [13] "An uniform tract of the judgments or decisions of the Court of Session is commonly considered as part of our consuetudinary law . . . but decisions, though they bind the parties litigating, have not in their own nature, the authority of law in similar cases; yet, where they continue uniform, great weight is laid on them . . . where a similar judgment is repeated in the court of the last resort (*i.e.* the House of Lords) it must have the strongest influence upon the determinations of inferior courts."

The eighteenth century produced two major treatises, one of the second and one of the very first order of importance. In 1751–1753 Andrew Mac-Douall, Lord Bankton, published in three volumes his *Institute of the Law of Scotland in Civil Rights after the General Method of the Viscount of Stair's Institutions*. He says therein: [14]

The decisions of the Court of Session serve to explain our laws and ascertain our customs, in the same manner as the judgments of the sovereign courts of other nations do theirs. Where there is a tract of such judgments and precedents uniform upon the same point, it is justly esteemed as law, and ought to be followed in all time thereafter in parallel cases; but otherwise the rule is, that *non exemplis sed legibus judicandum*. Not one or two precedents, but the prescription of the law is to govern the decisions of courts of justice.

Then in 1773 there was published posthumously John Erskine's *Institute of the Law of Scotland* to the composition of which he had devoted his retirement. Erskine's is the second great classical treatise on Scots law. It lacks the philosophic depth and breadth of Stair, but is a careful, reasoned, and accurate statement of the law.

[13] I, 1, 17.
[14] I, 1, 74.

Erskine[15] deals with written and unwritten or customary law, and under the latter head states:

> An uniform series of decisions of the Court of Session, i.e. of their judgments on particular points, either of right or of form, brought before them by litigants, and anciently called "Practics," is by Mackenzie accounted part of our customary law. Thus far may be admitted, 1st, that their more ancient decisions, from which it appears that any particular usage had then acquired the force of law, may be properly brought in proof of that custom, if it have not afterwards lost its authority by an immemorial and universal usage to the contrary; and 2ndly, that great weight is to be laid on their later decisions, where they continue for a long time uniform, upon points that appear doubtful. But they have no proper authority in similar cases; because the tacit consent, on which unwritten law is founded, cannot be inferred from the judicial proceedings of any court of law, however distinguished by dignity or character; and judgments ought not to be pronounced by examples or precedents. Decisions, therefore, though they bind the parties litigating, create no obligation on the judges to follow in the same tract, if it shall appear to them contrary to law. It is, however, certain, that they are frequently the occasion of establishing usages, which, after they have gathered force from a sufficient length of time, must from the tacit consent of the state, make part of our unwritten law. What has been said of decisions of the court of session is also applicable to the judgments pronounced upon appeal by the house of Lords: for in these that august court acts in the character of judges, not of lawgivers; and consequently their judgments, though they are final as to the parties in the appeal, cannot introduce any general rule which shall be binding either on themselves or inferior courts. Nevertheless, where a similar judgment is repeated in this court of the last resort, it ought to have the strongest influence on the determinations of inferior courts.

The position at the turn of the eighteenth into the nineteenth century can be found by sampling the cases reported in the *Faculty Decisions* about that time. It was clearly common practice to cite as well as statutes, cases reported in the older private reports and in the earlier volumes of *Faculty Decisions*, and the institutional writers. On some topics there was reference to the commentators on the civil law, particularly Voet and Vinnius. Cases and the views of the text-writers seem to have ranked equally, as valuable evidence of accepted and settled practice. But as the judges did not express or write opinions (or at least are not reported as having done so) but merely reached a decision, it is difficult to know precisely how they evaluated the cases and books cited to them.

The importance of decisions was, however, clearly on the increase, so much so that W. M. Morison was moved to produce his consolidated

---

15 *Inst.* 1, 1, 47.

Dictionary of Decisions, reprinting in over seventeen thousand pages, usually bound in nineteen volumes, followed by *Synopsis* and *Supplement*, most of the cases contained in the older reports. The work was continued by M. P. Brown's five-volume *Supplement* containing most of the cases omitted by Morison, and a *Synopsis* in four volumes of the cases in Morison's *Dictionary*, Brown's *Supplement* and some other collections. The reports of about 1800, moreover, frequently record the citation to the bench of unreported cases.

The enormous importance of the institutional writings in systematising the law can also be seen from these cases of about 1800. Each is not merely a decision, but a decision of a point arising under and in relation to a head or subhead in a body of law analytically classifiable under, e.g., insurance, damage to property, marriage, constitution, testament, superior and vassal, and so on.

In the nineteenth century the series of reports continued and the volumes swelled as the practice developed of reporting the opinions of the judges, which themselves rapidly became longer, frequently tediously long, but more informative.

It has been suggested [16] that until the nineteenth century the only recognized sources of Scots Law were statute and custom, but custom meant learned custom, the practice developed by the jurists and through judicial practice determined in a course of judicial decisions. It included much Roman law, canon law, natural law, and feudal law. Until the mid-nineteenth century judges, by decisions, and jurists, by their writings, were partners in developing the learned custom of Scotland.

David Hume, professor of Scots law at Edinburgh, 1786–1822, in his *Lectures*,[17] stated the position about 1820, as being that the repositories of the common law were

> . . . first, those collections of reports, those statements of the decisions of court, which have been laid before the public from time to time, by our lawyers or our judges; secondly, the writings of those learned and eminent persons, skilled in the law, who have digested and published in different shapes their notions of what they understood to be the principles of law, and the rules of our municipal practice. The delineations of doctrine given by such men, when they are explicit and in unison with each other, have justly

---

16 Smith, "Authors and Authority," 12 JOURNAL OF THE SOCIETY OF PUBLIC TEACHERS OF LAW 3, 9 (1972).
17 I, 14.

much weight as evidence of the strain and tenor of our common law; and they are quoted in that view, by our pleaders, as of little inferior authority to the judgments even of Court.

This is significant. It appears that, since Erskine had written, judgments had begun to be regarded not as evidence of custom, but as authority, and treatises also to be of authority but of lesser authority.

Bell, Hume's successor in the chair of Scots law at Edinburgh (1822–1843) published a *Treatise on the Law of Bankruptcy* (1800) expanded into *Commentaries on the Laws of Scotland and on the Principle of Mercantile Jurisprudence*, which rapidly attained the rank of an authority and reached its eighth edition in 1870. In 1829 he published a *Principles of the Law of Scotland*, intended for the use of his students; in the preface he states his trust that students "may find this book of some use as a Repository of Authorities on all the important questions of Law." It takes the form of short paragraphs containing plain statements of points, followed by references to statutes, institutional writings and textbooks, including Blackstone and Pothier, and cases, including some English ones. He also published three volumes of *Illustrations*, notes of decided cases, intended as a companion to his *Principles*, for the use of students.

By the fourth edition Bell had added many more references and many more were added by editors. The last (tenth) edition of 1899 had more space devoted to references to authorities than to text, and long before this Bell's *Principles* had been recognised as an authoritative text and of institutional authority.

Neither book discusses the question of the authority of decisions or of textbooks, but the growing weight of citation of cases in the footnotes of successive editions makes it clear that they had been accepted as authorities.

The published *Lectures* of John S. More, Bell's successor as professor of Scots law (1843–1861) observe[18] that "the decisions pronounced by Courts of Justice are very superior to any other kind of legal authority. . . . The great advantage which such decisions must possess over the opinions, even of the most learned jurists, given in the retirement of their closets, must be very apparent; and it is chiefly by such decisions that the jurisprudence of any country can be built up and consolidated into a firm and consistent system."

18 P. 6.

But by this time the doctrines of precedent had become settled in England. Holdsworth maintained [19] that the modern doctrine of precedent was settled in the latter half of the eighteenth century but it had certainly not spread to Scotland until the nineteenth century.

But as the nineteenth century progressed the authority of judicial decisions rose, parallel with the development of the doctrine of *stare decisis* and of the hierarchy of authority of precedents, and the authority of juristic writings declined. This tendency has been accentuated as time passed by the facts that the jurists of undoubtedly "institutional" standing (Craig, Stair, Mackenzie, Bankton, Erskine, and Bell) are long dead; their works have not even been reedited for nearly a century, and in most cases longer, and they do not, and have not for years, supplied guidance on many modern problems; and many of the standard textbooks, such as Fraser's *Husband and Wife* and McLaren's *Wills and Succession*, are also now about a century old and too frequently have not been replaced by modern standard books. (Indeed one might cynically remark that any author will be dead by the time the courts have awakened to the fact that his book is a standard work.)

By this time also the reported decisions themselves evidence the practice of the courts in Scotland.

Thus in *Virtue v. Alloa Police Commrs.*[20] a bare majority of a bench of seven judges of the Court of Session took the view that the principle laid down by the House of Lords in a Scottish appeal, *Duncan v. Findlater*,[21] and accepted and applied, albeit reluctantly, thereafter by the Scottish courts, was inconsistent with the rule laid down by the House of Lords in two English appeals, *Mersey Docks Commrs. v. Gibbs* and *Mersey Docks Commrs. v. Penhallow*[22] in which *Duncan v. Findlater* was possibly misunderstood, and that the later rule, though pronounced in an English appeal, should be followed. The dissenting view was that the judgment of the House of Lords in an English appeal could not be a binding precedent on the Scottish court.

In *Houldsworth v. City of Glasgow Bank*, the House of Lords held that the Court of Session had rightly held itself bound by a prior House of Lords decision in a Scottish case. Lord Blackburn said, "For when it

---

[19] "Precedents in the Eighteenth Century" 51 L. Q. Rev. 441 (1935).
[20] (1874) 1 R. 285.
[21] (1839) Maclean & Robinson 911.
[22] (1866) L.R. 1 H.L. 93.

appears that a case already falls within the *ratio decidendi* of the House of Lords, the highest Court of Appeal, I do not think it competent for even this House to say that the *ratio decidendi* was wrong." [23] Thus was established for Scotland the rule that even the House of Lords is bound by its own decisions, unless the prior decision can be distinguished.

In Orr Ewing's Trs. v. Orr Ewing,[24] Lord Chancellor Selborne said:

A decision of this House, in an English case, ought to be held conclusive in Scotland, as well as England, as to the questions of English law and English jurisdiction which is determined. It cannot, of course, conclude any questions of Scottish law, or as to the jurisdiction of any Scottish Court in Scotland. So far as it may proceed upon principles of general jurisprudence, it ought to have weight in Scotland; as a similar judgment of this House on a Scottish appeal ought to have weight in England. If, however, it can be shown that by any positive law of Scotland, or according to authorities having the force of law in that country, a different view of the proper interpretation, extent or application of those principles applies there, the opinions on those subjects, expressed by noble and learned Lords when giving judgment on an English appeal, ought not to be held conclusive in Scotland. When a Scottish decision, in apparent conflict with them, is brought to the bar of this House, the first duty of your Lordships must (I conceive) be, to ascertain whether there is any settled rule of Scottish law requiring or justifying that decision. If not, it may still be open to the House to reconsider the points raised, in any new light which may be presented by the view of them taken in the Scottish Court.

Thus there developed in Scotland, largely by analogy with contemporary English practice, a trend encouraged by the common ultimate court of appeal, the modern principle that a judicial decision, if not distinguishable, is binding.

There remain, however, a few respects in which the rules of *stare decisis* are more liberal in Scotland than in England.

In the first place if either Division (normally comprising four judges) of the Inner House of the Court of Session thinks fit it may order a case heard by it to be reargued before a fuller court, usually of seven (but it can be of any number larger than the normal quorum of three), and such a court may overrule a prior decision of either division.

Secondly, the first division in *Beith's Trs. v. Beith* [25] laid down that "if it is manifest that the *ratio decidendi* upon which a previous decision has rested has been superseded and invalidated by subsequent legislation

23 (1880) 7 R. (H.L.) 53, 62.
24 (1885) 13 R. (H.L.) 1, 3.
25 1950 S.C. 66.

or from other like cause, that *ratio decidendi* ceases to be binding" and in reliance on that principle discarded a decision of a court of seven judges of 1875 as having been superseded by the changes in the position of married women effected between 1875 and 1950. "We owe respect to previous decisions of superior or equal authority, but we also owe respect to Acts of Parliament; and if subsequent statutes have deprived a decision of its whole content, we have no duty to echo outmoded and superseded conceptions. . . . There is no need to overrule [the 1875 case] and no justification for so doing. The proper course is simply to cease to follow it."

The present position of judicial precedent can probably be summarised as follows:

1. A decision in point of the House of Lords in a Scottish appeal, or on a matter, such as the interpretation of a statute common to Scots law and England or Northern Ireland, under consideration in the precedent, is binding on the House itself for the future, subject to the power of the House exceptionally to reconsider its own decisions, and on all lower courts in Scotland.

2. A decision of a court of seven or more judges as the Court of Session is generally binding on all Scottish courts.

3. A decision of either (appellate) division of the Inner House of the Court of Session is generally binding on each division and on all inferior courts.

4. A decision of a single judge of the Court of Session or of an inferior court judge does not bind any court but may have persuasive value.

5. Decisions of the Privy Council, English, Northern Irish, Commonwealth, and U.S. courts may be persuasive depending on the status of the particular court and the similarity of the branch of law and principle involved to that of Scotland.

Turning now to the influence of doctrine, or juristic writing, down to the end of the eighteenth century the works of the institutional writers which surveyed the whole field of the municipal law were, with a few exceptions, the only books. There were few instances of textbooks on specific topics or branches of the law. About the end of the century a few more appeared, and the book on a branch of law became steadily commoner as the nineteenth century progressed. Some of these books have been superseded. Some such as Fraser's *Husband and Wife* have long had influence.

The phrase "institutional writers" was clearly originally a generic term for those who wrote general wide-ranging books entitled, in imitation of Gaius and Justinian, *Institutions* (Stair, Mackenzie); *Institutes* (Forbes); or *An Institute* (Bankton, Erskine). But later, out of deference to the value, importance, and formative influence of most of these works, the term "institutional writing" came to be attached to books not thus entitled—such as Bell's *Commentaries* and *Principles* and Hume's *Commentaries on Crimes*—but of comparable standing, and hence to have the connotation of "books of authority," and higher standing than mere textbooks. It is questionable if the rank of "institutional writing" can properly attach to a work unless it deals with the whole field of Scots law, or at least the whole of a major area of that field such as private law or criminal law. Probably no book on, say, contract can ever be rated more highly than merely a standard textbook. In *Fortington v. Lord Kinnaird*,[26] the court pointed out that not all of an institutional writer's works were entitled to that status, and writings not finally prepared for publication by him but later edited and published were only really evidence of professional understanding of the law at the time he wrote. Accordingly Hume's *Commentaries on Crimes* were institutional but his *Lectures*, (published by the Stair Society in 1939–1958) were not. (Nevertheless the *Lectures* have been repeatedly cited subsequently.)

Some modern books seem to suggest that the list of institutional writings has been closed since Bell's *Commentaries* and *Principles* on the civil side and Hume's *Commentaries* and Alison's *Principles and Practice* on the criminal side—that is, about 1840. While the task of treating the whole of the public, private, or criminal law is now an immensely heavier and more daunting task than 140 years ago, and the formative and decisive influence of any juristic writing must now be much less when so many points are regulated by statute or covered by decision it is disheartening for the modern jurist to think that his work can never be a "work of authority." In fact this conclusion seems unfounded. What makes a book a work of authority is its value to and influence on judges and lawyers. If they use and come to respect and accept the formulations of law in a modern book there seems no adequate a priori reason why

26 1942 S.C. 239.

one should not be rated a work of authority, and in spheres of law which have developed within the last 140 years there is no reason why a modern book should not be as authoritative as Erskine or Bell.

Indeed there is danger of excessive deference to the words and ideas of men long dead; in other sciences one can have profound respect for the formative and seminal work of Newton, Lavoisier, and Adam Smith but yet recognise that others, now living, state better these subjects as they have now developed and are applied. Indeed the steadily increasing complication of law in an uncodified system, stated in jumbled statutes and the *rationes* of numerous cases, would be an incomprehensible jumble but for the systematising, arranging, restatement, and criticism of the modern jurist, normally an academic rather than a judge or practitioner. Their work is too little recognised.

But the fact remains that the "institutional writers" stand on a peak. As Lord Normand (Lord of Appeal in Ordinary, 1947–1953) said in a published address: "Stair, Erskine and Bell are cited daily in the courts, and the court will pay as much respect to them as to a judgment of the House of Lords, though it is bound to follow a judgment of the House of Lords whatever the institutional writers may have said." They are as Domat and Pothier were to pre-Code French law, as Voet to Roman Dutch law, as Coke and Blackstone to English law, and as Kent and Story to American law. Their influence on the growth and development of the law has been enormous; it remains substantial in those areas where the law is still largely common law.

The extent of reliance on the institutional writers is naturally tending to decline as the law develops and its emphasis changes; disputes more and more come before the courts dealing with matters not covered by these writers, or matters in which their views have been incorporated into, repeated, explained, or explained away in, later judicial decisions. But in any question of fundamental importance, particularly where there is little or no modern judicial authority, particularly in fields such as land law, where the modern law has been built on and evolved from the law of the seventeenth and eighteenth centuries, reference to the institutional writers is essential. Thus when the question arose whether money paid under mistake of law was recoverable or not, the judge examined the statements in the Roman law institutional writers, the early cases, and modern cases containing *obiter dicta* on the point: *Glasgow Corporation*

v. Lord Advocate.[27] Again when the question arose in 1963 of the ownership of valuable objects found by an archaeological expedition[28] the authorities cited included Roman law, *Regiam Majestatem*, Craig, Stair, Mackenzie, Bankton, Erskine, Bell, McLaren's *Wills and Succession*, Rankine on *Land Ownership*, books on Scottish history, and various cases.

The present attitude of the courts to scholarly treatises may be said to be: the works of the institutional writers are books of authority, having influence on a court about as powerful as that of a decision of either division of the Inner (*i.e.* appellate) House of the Court of Session. The works of a number of text-writers have lesser authority but are cited and discussed in judgments in much the same way as persuasive, or non-binding, judicial precedents; they may be called standard textbooks. A number of current textbooks are achieving recognition as standard. The amount of citation of them is as yet small, and they cannot yet be said to have achieved recognition but they are probably in the course of doing so. It takes some years before some judges appreciate that modern books exist and may be worth attending to, and even citing. Lastly there are lesser works, students' books and the like, which have no authority and are not worth citing to the court, nor are ever likely to be discussed in judgment. In the second category there is sometimes apparent a regrettable judicial tendency for judges to cite the books which were standard in their student days, apparently oblivious of more modern and better books.

The Scottish courts never seem generally to have subscribed to the English view that a writer was never an authority until after his death, because the works of living authors have been and are frequently cited, and more frequently supply the basis for judicial reasoning but are unacknowledged. It remains true that no modern, *i.e.* post-1850, book has an authority to outweigh a decision of the Court of Session, still less the words of an Act, but in default of such authority a statement in a textbook is much better than nothing. Lord Reid has observed extrajudicially:[29] "In the House of Lords at least we turn a blind eye to the old rule that an academic writer is not an authority until he is dead,

---

27 1959 S.C. 203.
28 Lord Advocate v. Aberdeen University, 1963 S.C. 533.
29 Reid, "The Judge as Law Maker," 12 JOURNAL OF THE SOCIETY OF PUBLIC TEACHERS OF LAW 22 (1972).

because then he can no longer change his mind." But some modern judges have not taken a favourable view of the citation of modern textbooks.

It may also be noted that while down to 1900 judges were frequently the authors of collections of decisions or of textbooks or of both, the production of reports is now in the hands of the Scottish Council of Law Reporting and of commercial publishers, and the writing of both standard textbooks and of students' books is in fact mainly in the hands of academic lawyers. In 1960, the Scottish Universities' Law Institute was founded to coordinate and stimulate the efforts of scholars in the universities to produce new standard textbooks, though some important books have also appeared outside of their scheme.

In some branches of law textwriting originating outside Scotland is similarly treated as persuasive. Thus in questions of public international law, apart from classical treatises on the subject, modern works such as Oppenheim, in public law English books on the constitution, the royal prerogative, and similar topics, in international private law the works of Story, Dicey, Westlake, and Cheshire are listened to with respect, in shipping law the texts of Abbott on *Shipping*, Scrutton on *Charterparties*, and Marsden on *Collisions at Sea*, and in commercial matters such classics as Byles on *Bills*, Lindley on *Partnership*, Buckley on *Companies*, Benjamin on *Sale*, but always with a careful eye on whether the learned author's proposition is consistent with the law of Scotland or is one peculiar to English law, in the context of which he wrote. In topics where Scots law and English differ sharply the great English books such as Anson or Pollock on *Contracts*, Pollock or Salmond or Winfield on *Torts*, are rarely cited and then only if the point is one in which there is a rule common to both countries, such as contributory negligence.

On matters such as taxation, patents and trademarks, factory legislation, trade unions, and others where the laws of Scotland and of England are for most purposes identical, English textbooks are regularly used and cited. But there are many matters of English law which differ so markedly from Scots law that their books are never looked at in Scotland and are utterly unhelpful.

In modern practice, apart from statute, both decisions of the courts and books, authoritative and standard, are "authorities" furnishing the rule for the determination of most litigated disputes. "Now the common law must be sought in law books by writers of authority and in judgments of the judges entrusted with its administration. The law books give no assistance, because the work of living authors, however deservedly eminent, cannot be used as authority, although the opinions they express may demand attention, and the ancient books do not assist. I turn therefore to the decided cases." Seven pages later: "In my view, therefore the authorities are against the appellant's contention."[30]

Looking at modern Scottish practice broadly, the first distinction is between cases which are determined by authority and those which may be determined on principle, that is, by application of, or deduction from, or analogy with, a general principle of law which, however, may be found stated or suggested by *obiter dicta*, or in an institutional work or a standard textbook or by the judge's concept of justice and equity.

The term "authority" is used of any formulation of a rule which must be applied unless it can be distinguished, which formulation may be contained in statute, judicial decision, or juristic writing. Thus: "What about authority? There is no authoritative judgment . . . on this topic. I have looked at the textbooks and . . . we were referred to two Outer House [first instance] cases."[31] "There is no authority binding on us. We must therefore deal with the question on principle and with such incidental help as is to be found in Outer House [i.e. first instance] decisions and in the text-book writers."[32] "The authorities which are said to debar us from coming to this decision are [a case of 1680] and a passage in section 627 of Bell's *Principles*."[33] "Four authorities of the highest weight . . . these are Bell in his *Principles*, sections 1632 and 1633; Lord Kyllachy in [a case of 1907] as cited and adopted in [a case of 1935]; Lord Hunter and Lord Murray in [the case of 1935]."[34]

In stating or suggesting "principle" in this sense the courts rely mainly on the institutional writings and, frequently without acknowledgment, on the modern standard textbooks. Scottish principle may, moreover, outweigh English or other authority, unless the latter is binding in the circumstances. Thus "In these circumstances I do not feel any obligation to follow the English authorities in preference to a trend of opinion in

30 Lord Buckmaster in Donoghue v. Stevenson, 1932 S.C. (H.L.) 31, 35, 42.
31 Meadow v. Meadow, 1932 S.C. 475, 480, per Lord Anderson.
32 Donnelly v. D., 1959 S.C. 97, 101, per L. J. C. Thomson.
33 Pettigrew v. Harton, 1956 S.C. 59, 75, per Lord Patrick.
34 Hutchison v. H's Trs., 1951 S.C. 108, 120, per Lord Mackay.

Scotland which, while not authoritative, is uncontradicted."[35] Again "In that state of the law the question is technically open for this Court to determine on principle . . . I have reached the conclusion that the *condictio* does not apply to such a case. My main reason is that the doctrine is an equitable one."[36]

The hierarchy of authorities in current Scots law may be said to be:
1. Statute or statutory instrument or other legislation.
2. Decision of the House of Lords in a Scottish appeal.
3. Decision of the Inner House of the Court of Session, or of the House of Lords in a non-Scottish appeal, or statement in an institutional writer.
4. Decision of an Outer House (single) judge of the Court of Session or of a superior English, Northern Irish, Commonwealth, or other English-language court, or statement in a standard textbook.
5. Proven custom or usage; ideas of equity, justice and reason; analogy from English or other foreign law.

The modern position can be stated shortly as follows: the influence of statute has increased, is increasing, and seems unlikely to diminish; the influence of judicial decisions is very great and considerably outweighs that of any book; among the books statements in institutional writings, where relevant, remain of high authority, and statements in books accepted as standard, of known reputation and quality, of authority lesser but comparable to that of single judges. Lesser books, students' books, and the like are not authorities at all. The influence of the judge and the jurist have been and are the major factors in developing and maintaining law as a systematic structure of rules. Statute amends, abolishes, and adds new rules, but contributes nothing to system or rational structure.

[35] Plank v. Stirling Mags., 1956 S.C. 92, 112, per L. J. C. Thomson, referring to merely persuasive Scottish decisions.
[36] Glasgow Corpn. v. L.A., 1959 S.C. 203, 232, per L. P. Clyde.

ABBREVIATIONS

L.R. H.L.	Law Reports, House of Lords
L. Q. Rev.	Law Quarterly Review
J.S.P.T.L.	Journal of the Society of Public Teachers of Law

Additional abbreviations and a general bibliography appear in the appendix below.

APPENDIX

Works referred to in the foregoing chapter by author's name or abbreviation. For further information on these see McKechnie (ed.), *Sources and Literature of Scots Law* (Stair Society, 1936) or Walker, *The Scottish Legal System* (3rd ed., 1969).

1. SOME OLDER COLLECTIONS OF DECISIONS:

Balfour, James. *Practicks, or System of the More Ancient Law of Scotland* (1754).

Dirleton, John Nisbet. *Doubts and Questions in the Law, as also Some Decisions, 1665–77* (1698).

Durie, Alexander Gibson. *Decisions of the Lords of Council and Sessions, 1621–42* (1690).

Forbes, William. *Journal of the Session Containing Decisions from 1705–13* (1714).

Hope, Thomas. *Minor Practicks, or Treatise of the Scottish Law* (1726, 1734).

———. *Major Practicks, 1608–33* (Stair Society, 1937–38).

Kames, Henry Home. *Remarkable Decisions in the Court of Session 1716–52* (1728–66).

———. *Select Decisions of the Court of Session, 1752–68* (1780).

Skene, John. *Regiam Majestatem: The Auld Lawes and Constitutions of Scotland collected fwth of the Register and other bukes.* 1597, 1609, 1774, and (Stair Society) 1947.

Spotiswoode, Robert. *Practicks of the Laws of Scotland* (1706).

Stair, James Dalrymple. *Decisions of the Lords of Council and Session in the Most Important Cases, 1661–81* (2 vols., 1663–87).

2. MODERN REPORTS (CITED BY VOLUME NUMBER IN SERIES AND PAGE, OR SINCE 1907 BY YEAR AND PAGE):

D. Dunlop's reports (Court of Session Cases, 2nd series, 24 vols., 1838–62).

F. Fraser's Reports (Court of Session Cases, 5th series, 8 vols., 1898–1906).

M. Macpherson's Reports (Court of Session Cases, 3rd series, 11 vols., 1862–73).

*R. Rettie's Reports (Court of Session Cases, 4th series, 25 vols., 1873–98).

*R.(H.L.) Rettie's Reports (House of Lords Appeals from the Court of Session, 25 vols., 1873–98).

S. Shaw's Reports (Court of Session Cases, 1st series, 16 vols., 1821–37).

*S.C. Court of Session Cases, current series, 1907 to date.

*S.C.(H.L.) Court of Session Cases, Appeals to the House of Lords, 1907 to date.

* In these cases the reports of the Court of Session cases and of cases appealed to the House of Lords are contained in the same volumes but paginated separately. Some cases appealed from the Court of Session to the House of Lords are also reported in Appeal Cases or All England Reports.

3. INSTITUTIONAL WRITINGS: THOSE MARKED * ARE OF THE HIGHEST AUTHORITY:

Craig, Thomas. *Jus Feudale,* 1655, trans. Clyde, 1934.

*Stair, James Dalrymple. *Institutions of the Law of Scotland,* 1681, 5th ed. 1832.

Mackenzie, George. *Institutions of the Laws of Scotland,* 1684, 8th ed. 1758.

———. *Laws and Customs of Scotland in Matters Criminal,* 1678, 2nd ed. 1699.

Forbes, William. *Institutes of the Law of Scotland,* 1722–30.

Bankton, Andrew McDouall. *Institute of the Laws of Scotland in Civil Rights,* 1751–53.

Kames, Henry Home. *Principles of Equity,* 1760, 5th ed. 1825.

*Erskine, John. *Institute of the Law of Scotland,* 1773, 8th ed. 1871.

*Hume, David. *Commentaries on the Law of Scotland Respecting Crimes,* 1797–1800, 4th ed. 1844.

*Bell, George Joseph. *Commentaries on the Laws of Scotland and on the Principles of Mercantile Jurisprudence,* 1800, 7th ed. 1870.

———. *Principles of the Law of Scotland,* 1829, 10th ed. 1899.

Alison, Archibald. *Principles of the Criminal Law of Scotland,* 1832, and *Practice of the Criminal Law of Scotland,* 1833.

4. SOME MORE MODERN TEXTBOOKS OF JUDICIALLY RECOGNIZED STANDING:

Fraser, Patrick. *Husband and Wife According to the Law of Scotland,* 1846, 2nd ed. 1876–78.

Dickson, W. G. *Law of Evidence in Scotland,* 1855, 3rd ed. 1887.

Menzies, A. *Lectures on Conveyancing,* 1856, 4th ed. 1900.

McLaren, John. *Law of Wills and Succession,* 1862, 3rd ed. 1894.

Rankine, John. *Law of Land Ownership in Scotland,* 1879, 4th ed. 1909.

———. *Law of Leases in Scotland,* 1887, 3rd ed. 1916.

Goudy, Henry. *Law of Bankruptcy,* 1886, 4th ed. 1914.

Henderson, R. Candlish. *Principles of Vesting in the Law of Succession,* 1905, 2nd ed. 1938.

Gloag, W. M. *Law of Contract*, 1914, 2nd ed. 1929.
Mackenzie Stuart, A. *Law of Trusts*, 1932.

5. SOME CURRENT MODERN STANDARD TEXTBOOKS:
Anton, A. E. *Private International Law*, 1967.
Gordon, G. H. *Criminal Law of Scotland*, 1967.
Gow, J. J. *Mercantile and Industrial Law of Scotland*, 1966.
Miller, I. P. *Industrial Law*, 1970.
Mitchell, J. D. B. *Constitutional Law*, 2nd ed. 1968.
Paton, G. C. H., and Cameron, J. G. S. *Landlord and Tenant*, 1967.
Walker, D. M. *Law of Damages in Scotland*, 1955.
————. *Law of Delict in Scotland*, 1966.
————. *Principles of Scottish Private Law*, 1970.
————. *The Scottish Legal System*, 3rd ed. 1969.

X

The Role of Doctrine and Judicial Decisions in South African Law

Ellison Kahn
PROFESSOR OF LAW, UNIVERSITY OF THE WITWATERSRAND,
SOUTH AFRICA

The South African legal system may be called a mixed one, a hybrid, with its predominant strain Roman-Dutch law, but with an undeniable infusion of English law. In sum, it is a cross-bred jurisdiction, composed of civil and common law, with the former predominating. Even the most passionate legal purist of the historical school, the most articulate of cleaners of muddied legal waters—to change the metaphor—will, if pressed, concede this; and admit that the most he can look forward to is a little further substitution of Roman-Dutch rules for English rules in the pool.

Why this is so is a story that has often been told.[1] It need merely be be outlined here. The settlement of whites commenced in 1652, when the Dutch East India Company, on behalf of the Republic of the United Netherlands, took possession of the tip of Africa, the Cape of Good Hope, originally so called by the Portuguese (*Cabo de Boa Esperanza*), that to Sir Francis Drake was "the most stately thing and the fairest Cape we saw in the whole circumference of the earth."[2]

"John Company" brought with it what was soon to be called *Roomsch-*

---

[1] See HAHLO AND KAHN, THE UNION OF SOUTH AFRICA: THE DEVELOPMENT OF ITS LAWS AND CONSTITUTION Chap. 2 (1960), and THE SOUTH AFRICAN LEGAL SYSTEM AND ITS BACKGROUND Pt. 2, especially Chap. 17 (1968). These two works, hereinafter referred to respectively as SOUTH AFRICA and LEGAL SYSTEM, refer to the principal literature as of the date of publication. For a later helpful analysis, see Hosten, "The Permanence of Roman Law Concepts in South African Law," COMPARATIVE AND INTERNATIONAL LAW JOURNAL OF SOUTHERN AFRICA 192 (1969), where additional references can also be found. A list of the abbreviations used in this chapter appears on pages 270–71.

[2] VIII HACKLUYT, THE PRINCIPALL NAVIGATIONS, VOIAGES AND DISCOVERIES OF THE ENGLISH NATION (1598–1600) 74 (Glasgow ed. 1903-1905).

Hollandsch recht. The term came to be translated into English as Roman-Dutch law, though more accurately (albeit less euphoniously) it should be rendered as Roman-Hollands law. For in truth there was no "Dutch" law, in the sense of a law of the Netherlands as a whole. That "country" consisted of seven provinces loosely linked together in a confederation,[3] through representation in the Estates-General, which dealt with a few matters of common concern, notably foreign affairs, defence and colonies. The Estates-General conferred on the Dutch East India Company its charter. As the most powerful province in administering the company was Holland, it followed that its law became the law of the Cape. In its broad sweep, that law did not differ from the laws of the other provinces; but in detail it had its own particularity.

Roman-Dutch law was the product of a fusion of the law of Holland and Roman law. Roman law first began to influence the local legal system in the thirteenth century. Its impact became increasingly stronger until it swelled into the Reception of the late fifteenth and the sixteenth centuries. Though in theory Roman law was invoked in Holland only *in subsidio*, in practice its rules were frequently adopted, because of the difficulty in proving the local customs and because many of its rules were in fact accepted by the legislature.

When the British captured the Cape in 1806, as was their wont with a territory acquired by conquest or cession that was applying a civilized legal system, they allowed the Roman-Dutch law to continue; and wherever the white man went in southern Africa, he took it with him. Technically it is the legal system of the Republic of South Africa. Wherefore, then, the alien strain of English common law? The answer lies in the natural desire of the British rulers of a newly acquired land with a strange Continental civil legal system and alien method of administration of law to efface them in places with something more familiar. Sir Frederick Pollock once whimsically asked the question why Whitehall always assumed it as axiomatic that it was English and not Scots law[4]

---

3 This, it is believed, is the correct view.
4 Sometimes South African and Rhodesian judges express regret that so little reference has been and is being made to Scots law, with its background more Romanistic than English law. Thus: "It is of some persuasive value to note that in Scottish law, a system which is much more akin to Roman-Dutch than English law," per Beadle CJ in State v. Munyani 1972 (1) S.A. 411 (R.A.D.) at 420. Roman-Dutch law had its influence on Scots law. It must be remembered that in the seventeenth and eighteenth centuries Latin was the *lingua franca* of

that crossed the seas to British colonies. No satisfactory answer can be given for the Cape, no more than it can for any other British posession. That it happened in a moderate way in the peninsula of Africa is undeniable.

At one time, indeed, it seemed possible that ultimately the Roman-Dutch legal system would largely depart. For in 1826 Commissioners Bigge and Colebrook, reporting on the judicial affairs of the Cape,[5] recommended the assimilation of the legal procedure of England, the couching of new enactments in the spirit of the laws of England and the gradual absorption of the common law of England—except, mercifully, the law of property, as the local law there was "so simple and efficient." This was a fate that lay in store for British Guiana in 1917.[6] Attachment to the local legal system proved too strong in the Cape; but much anglicization inevitably took place—either directly, through legislation, or

---

scholars. Lord Macmillan said in Stewart v. London, Midland & Scottish Railway Co. 1943 S.C. (H.L.) 19 at 38–39: "During the seventeenth and eighteenth centuries Scottish students of law, in the absence of opportunities of academic instruction in their own country, resorted in large numbers for their legal education to the great seminaries of civil law in Holland, then at their zenith. Stair . . . was himself in exile at Leyden from 1682 to 1688. Lord President Forbes (1685–1747) was a student at Leyden, and Lord President Dundas (1713–1782) studied at Utrecht. It was on his way to study at Utrecht that Boswell in 1763 enjoyed the august company of Dr. Johnson as far as Harwich. We "import our lawyers from Holland," said Butler to Saddletree in a famous passage in The Heart of Midlothian. From their sojourn in Holland the aspirants to practice in the Parliament House brought back with them not only the principles which they had imbibed from the masters of the Roman-Dutch law but also the treatises of which the law schools of the Dutch Universities were so prolific. No Scots lawyer's library was complete in those days which did not contain the works of Grotius, Vinnius, the Voets, Heinneccius and other learned civilians. . . . [T]he Court of Session, with its predilection for principle rather than precedent, heard many arguments adorned with citations of the Roman law and its Dutch commentators."

See, further, Smith, "Scots Law and Roman-Dutch Law—A Shared Tradition," Acta Juridica 36 (1959; reprinted in his STUDIES CRITICAL AND COMPARATIVE 46 [1962]) and SCOTLAND: THE DEVELOPMENT OF ITS LAWS AND CONSTITUTION 22 (1962); WALKER, THE SCOTTISH LEGAL SYSTEM 48–49 (3rd ed. 1969); Kahn, "Dr. Johnson, Boswell and the Roman-Dutch Law," 71 SOUTH AFRICAN LAW JOURNAL 384 (1954).

5 XVII, THEAL, RECORDS OF THE CAPE COLONY 333 ff.; XVIII id. at 342 ff., 1 ff.; Botha, "The Early Influence of the English Law upon the Roman-Dutch Law in South Africa," 40 S.A.L.J. 396 at 401–403 (1923).

6 Civil Law of British Guiana Ordinance 1916. See Dalton, "The Passing of Roman-Dutch Law in British Guiana," 36 S.A.L.J. 4 (1919). See also Ledlie "Roman-Dutch Law in British Guiana and a West Indian Court of Appeal," 17 JOURNAL OF COMPARATIVE LEGISLATION, n.s., 210 (1971).

indirectly, through judicial decisions and professional practice. In some ways it was reminiscent of the Reception of Roman law in Europe three hundred years earlier.

The lawmaker of the Cape Colony took over English law in several ways. Sometimes it passed a statute modelled, to a greater or lesser extent, on one in force in England: so with company and insolvency (bankruptcy law), negotiable instruments, merchant shipping, patents, trademarks, copyright, and formalities for wills and marriage. Sometimes it simply said, in effect, that South African law was the same as English law: so with evidence and certain types of insurance. And in other cases it passed a statute that introduced to the Cape, admittedly in some instances in a much modified way, the legal rules obtaining in the "mother country": thus with criminal procedure, many aspects of civil procedure, the administration of deceased estates, the freedom of testation. All this activity was perfectly understandable. In the areas covered by this legislation the Roman-Dutch law in general, and particularly at the Cape, a backward colony with but distant relations with the first homeland, was undeveloped or unfit for the commercial expansion of the nineteenth century, or considered cruel or antiquated or unclear or felt—as with the legitimate portion for close relations in the law of succession—to be out of keeping with the current beliefs in "freedom of property" and economic individualism.

Similar laws were passed not only where British rule extended, as with the colony of Natal, but also where the Dutch inhabitants of the Cape set up independent republics, in the Transvaal and Orange Free State. When these republics were conquered by the United Kingdom at the beginning of this century, a retreat could hardly be expected to take place; nor did it occur when all four colonies were united in the Union of South Africa on May 31, 1910; nor has there been much sign of it since May 31, 1961, when all ties with the United Kingdom were cut with the establishment of the Republic of South Africa. All the calls of recent decades to remain true to our Roman-Dutch heritage and to seek guidance in lawmaking, if that be needed, from the civil-law countries of the Continent rather than from England with her common law, have met with little response here—and understandably so. A country whose legal, institutional, economic, and cultural flora have grown in soil so impregnated with legislative nutriment from England is hard put to make any fundamental change. It caused no surprise, for instance, when the recent Company Law Commission, which had ransacked the legal systems of the Western world for guidance, concluded that, by and large, it should draw on recent changes in the English legislation and recommended, in the same vein as earlier commissions, that as far as practicable and making full allowance for divergences between Britain and South Africa as to company activities, the common law, underlying legal concepts, institutions, and functionaries, there should be substantial conformity with the English enactment.[7] So, too, there was no break with the legislative philosophy of the past when our Parliament recently passed acts on the laws of negotiable instruments, interpretation of legislation, patents, trademarks, copyright, and merchant shipping.[8]

The seepage of common-law rules into the Cape Colony and ultimately into the whole of South Africa through judgments and the practice of lawyers was a natural and not a deliberately created phenomenon. Roman-Dutch law ceased to prevail in the Netherlands very early in the nineteenth century, being replaced initially by the Code Napoléon and then, in 1838, by the Dutch Civil Code, based on the French model. The adaptation and development of Roman-Dutch law to meet modern conditions was now entirely up to the inhabitants of southern Africa. The other two Dutch possessions that had been allowed to retain Roman-Dutch law on their acquisition by Britain—Ceylon and British Guiana—legally undeveloped, and with Dutch a lost language, were in no position to help.

From a study of the earliest law reports it is clear that no one intended to be a traitor. But many of the early judges, recruited from England and Scotland, not only had had no systematic training in Roman-Dutch law but were unable to read a goodly portion of the books in which its rules were set out. The two thirds of the works that were in Latin they might cope with, at least as to their meaning translated into English, if not always as to the legal significance of their content; but only one or two of these immigrant members of the judiciary ever mastered the High Dutch language in which the balance were written. Painfully, as the nineteenth

---

[7] See Main Report of the Commission of Enquiry into the Companies Act R.P. 45/1970. See Benade (one of the commissioners), "A Survey of the Main Report of the Commission of Enquiry into the Companies Act," C.I.L.S.A. 277 (1970).
[8] Bills of Exchange Act 34 of 1964; Interpretation Act 33 of 1957; Patents Act 37 of 1952; Trade Marks Act 62 of 1963; Copyright Act 63 of 1965; Merchant Shipping Act 57 of 1951.

century dragged on, some of the major 'old authorities' were translated into English. But even today many important tomes remain only in pristine form. "Persuasive authorities," such as the Pandectists of Germany, were, by and large, closed to the linguistically unaccomplished members of the bench. In any event, many of the "musty manuals of the Middle Ages" were hard to come by. With English as the language of the Cape courts; English legal works readily available; the terminology of English law found in a number of important statutes framed on those obtaining in Britain; English precedents of contracts, wills and other documents to hand; the large body of English case law; the readiness of the Judicial Committee of the Privy Council, the ultimate court of appeal from the Cape, Natal, and then the Union of South Africa to 1950, to find Roman-Dutch legal rules the same as the rules of English law; and many of the early leading advocates trained in England, it is perhaps more remarkable that so large a part of the Roman-Dutch law remained intact and unsullied than that English law had so considerable an impact.

It is no coincidence that, with a few exceptions, English law had greatest influence where the Roman-Dutch law was least developed or most obscure or antiquated: thus with domicile (with the consolation that the common law was built on civil-law foundations) and aspects of choice of law in the conflict of laws; nuisance (at least until recently);[9] agency;

[9] As to domicile, see Webber v. Webber 1915 A.D. 239 at 242, 243, 249, 258; Ex parte Donelly 1915 W.L.D. 29 at 32–33. But in the past the identification with English law has been too dogmatically couched. The two legal systems differ in rules of substantive law that lead to differences in rules of domicile (e.g. as to minors); and it would be an ill day if our courts were to take the rigorous attitude of certain English decisions on *animus manendi* and *animus non revertendi*. On the latter score there are signs that the South African judges have seen the danger: see KAHN, THE SOUTH AFRICAN LAW OF DOMICILE OF NATURAL PERSONS 3 (1972; this work is also published in ACTA JURIDICA [1971]).

English law was, of course, influenced by civil-law authorities in general and Roman-Dutch law in particular, up to the middle of the last century not only in the area of domicile but also in the area of choice of law. A.C. Gutteridge commented: "The English rules of conflict . . . were largely built up, in the first instance, on the doctrines of the Dutch jurists of the seventeenth century—notably on Huber's *De Conflictu Legum*." (*Comparative Law* 44 [1946].) Llewelfryn Davies remarked that "a very noticeable feature of the English decisions on the subject . . . during the latter half of the eighteenth century and the first half of the nineteenth century is the frequency with which the doctrines of Huber and of the Voets are cited and their conclusions followed." (Davies, "The Influence of Huber's *De Conflictu Legum* on English Private International Law," 18 *British Year Book of International Law* 49 at 52 [1937]). See also STORY, CONFLICT OF LAWS §§ 31, 38; LORENZEN, "Huber's De Conflictu Legum"

the formation, discharge through acceptance of an anticipatory repudiation of, remedies for breach of and yet other aspects of the law of contract;[10] certain specific crimes; aspects of the law of delict (tort), notably liability for negligence and the defences in defamation; all but a small portion of constitutional and administrative law (obviously so, as the government of the Cape was on the settled British colonial pattern); and least influence where the old law was clearly developed, systematic, and in conformity with the spirit, mores and sense of justice of nineteenth-century southern Africa, as in the law of property, succession, husband and wife, family relations, the specific contracts (particularly sale and lease), and unjust enrichment. In several of these branches the inheritance of the scientific Roman-law system made for viability.

In the event the legislature, judiciary and legal profession proved pretty canny in what they transported, consciously or unconsciously, from England into the law of southern Africa.[11] Over vast tracts of private law and criminal law (at least with general principles) they rested largely content with what they had received. With much of commercial law they have had perforce to go elsewhere, and the natural destination was England. Sometimes, it must be confessed, unhappily, a draftsman of legislation has proved inept in following the wording of the English prototype, failing to take account of principles of South African law. Thus in the Copyright Act[12] the acceptance of the alien doctrine of con-

---

in his SELECTED ARTICLES ON THE CONFLICT OF LAWS 136 (1947); III Sack, "Conflicts of Laws in the History of the English Law," in LAW: A CENTURY OF PROGRESS 1835–1935, 342 ff. (1937).

10 For example, Novick v. Benjamin 1972 (2) S.A. 842 (A.D.), especially at 853–58 (anticipatory repudiation); Nel v. Cloete 1972 (2) S.A. 150 (A.D.), especially at 160–61, 169–76 (recession on the ground of *mora debitoris*); Farmers' Co-operative Society v. Berry 1912 A.D. 343 and Haynes v. Kingwilliamstown Municipality 1951 (2) S.A. 371 (A.D.) (the remedy of an order of specific performance). The whole of modern South African law of contracts unlawful as being restraint of trade is based on English law, as I have tried to show in my note "The Rules Relating to Contracts in Restraint of Trade—Whence and Whither?" 85 S.A.L.J. 391 (1968). The rules in the "ticket cases" are based on English law. See Central South African Railways v. McLaren 1903 T.S. 727; Turpin, "Contract and Imposed Terms," 73 S.A.L.J. 144 (1956). As far as the measure of damages for breach is concerned, English law is justifiably looked at, for it started off with reliance on Pothier. Indeed, the influence of Roman law on the common law of contract generally has not always been fully appreciated.

11 See Lawson in 33 JOURNAL OF COMPARATIVE LEGISLATION & INTERNATIONAL LAW (3rd series) 101 (1950).

12 63 of 1965 s 19.

version has led to problems; in the Bills of Exchange Act the meaning of "value" has not been made clear and our judges and practitioners are struggling with references to valuable consideration.[13] But the translation or partial translation of English enactments to this country has also at times been a process skillfully accomplished. For instance, there has been a general resistance to making the resultant legislation a code, in the strict sense of being self-contained, not allowing for reference to earlier law. Thus the Insolvency Act,[14] despite its detailed provisions on impugnable presequestration dispositions, has not eliminated recourse to the *actio Pauliana*. And the Bills of Exchange Act has not prevented reference to the old *wisselrecht* where it is on a particular matter.[15]

Undoubtedly there were a number of instances where the alien corn was a potential danger to the future of the native crop—or at least unsightly. Much of it was eliminated after the unification of 1910, which led to the creation of a central court of appeal, the Appellate Division of the Supreme Court of South Africa. Imbued with a sense of duty to make the law uniform throughout the country[16] and able to iron out, where the vagaries of the process of litigation so permitted, the differences of view among the trial courts, frequently composed of men steeped in learning of Roman and Roman-Dutch law (though there were lean periods, as in the thirties), this tribunal made a notable contribution to the protection of what has been called "contemporary Roman-Dutch law," so exposed in its uncodified state, and to its adaptation and development to modern conditions.

To take but two examples of the work of the Appeal Court in the elimination of English law excrescences: in 1919 it exorcised the Cape heresy that the Roman-Dutch requirement of *justa causa* for contract was more or less the equivalent of the valuable consideration of the common law.[17] In the same year it pronounced that earlier courts that had been guided by English rules as to discharge of contract by supervening

---

13 See Froman v. Robertson 1971 (1) S.A. 115 (A.D.); Cowen, THE LAW OF NE-GOTIABLE INSTRUMENTS IN SOUTH AFRICA Chap. 8, especially 93–96 (4th ed. 1966).
14 24 of 1936.
15 Estate Liebenberg v. Standard Bank of South Africa Ltd. 1927 A.D. 502, especially at 507.
16 See, e.g., Webster v. Ellison 1911 A.D. 73.
17 Conradie v. Rossouw 1919 A.D. 279. The other South African courts had never taken the Cape view.

impossibility of performance had erred: the question was governed entirely by civil-law principles.[18]

In two or three instances it may well be that the ultimate tribunal went too far in fitting an English legal figure with a Roman-Dutch garb. The trust may be one of these. If *inter vivos*, it is regarded as a *stipulatio alteri*; if testamentary, by some judges, at least, as a *fideicommissum*.[19] Neither view seems sound.

In the last twenty or thirty years there has emerged a school, growing ever more vocal, that more of the alien crop should be removed, by legal decision if possible, by legislation if necessary. The courts have undoubtedly shown some sympathy for this view. Understandably, the approach is a pragmatic one. In one or two branches of the law the judges have consistently dwelt on the importance of remaining true to "curial practice." In particular, with the specific crimes the Bench is inclined to say that their nature and scope has been settled by judicial practice, and cannot now be changed, no matter that this practice was largely determined by English law. Occasionally the courts will say that *communis error facit jus*. And there are several areas where it is hard to believe that the influence of English law can be removed: the vicarious liability of a master for the wrongful acts of his servant for instance. (It will be of no avail to say that here pretty well the same rules could have been and still could be arrived at by using Continental models built on general delictual provisions in civil codes.) But every now and then some tribunal, especially the highest one, the Appellate Division of the Supreme Court, will give practical expression to a sentiment voiced twenty-five years ago by Stratford ACJ, that "if the decisions [of the past] had disregarded fundamental principles of our law, we might have to reassert those principles even at the cost of reversing judgments of long standing." [20] It is often a delicate matter on which to reach a conclusion. Thus the ultimate court decided that it was too late to call back yesterday and restore the

---

18 Peters, Flamman & Co. v. Kokstad Municipality 1919 A.D. 427.
19 See Estate Kemp v. McDonald's Trustee 1926 A.D. 147; Commissioner for Inland Revenue v. Estate Crewe 1943 A.D. 656; Crookes NO v. Watson 1956 (1) S.A. 277 (A.D.); Commissioner for Inland Revenue v. Estate Merensky 1959 (2) S.A. 600 (A.D.); HAHLO AND KAHN, SOUTH AFRICA 663 ff. and authorities there cited; HONORÉ, THE SOUTH AFRICAN LAW OF TRUSTS (1966).
20 Dukes v. Marthinusen 1937 A.D. 12 at 23.

Roman-Dutch law relating to contractual penalties[21] that had been supplanted, to its chagrin, by English law through judgments of the Cape Court and the Privy Council. In this situation, it was necessary to enact legislation.[22] It was based on Roman-Dutch principles but showed the impress of modern civil law, especially the German Civil Code and the Swiss Federal Code of Obligations—one of the few illustrations of the influence of modern civil-law systems in South Africa. On the other hand, the Appellate Division, after eighty years of blissful belief by practitioners that the English law of nuisance had taken root in South Africa,[23] declared that nothing of the sort had happened: ours is "neighbour law." It was unfortunate, the court in effect conceded, that so little was said of the detailed rules of this branch of law in the Roman and Roman-Dutch texts: our courts would simply have to develop it on sound basic principles.[24] This has left practitioners groping when called upon to advise their clients.

21 Tobacco Manufacturers' Committee v. Jacob Green & Sons 1953 (3) S.A. 480 (A.D.).
22 Conventional Penalties Act 15 of 1962.
  It might be mentioned at this stage that very occasionally the legislature tacitly acknowledges that in the past it had been too greatly influenced by English law. An interesting illustration is afforded by extinctive prescription. The previous Prescription Act 18 of 1943 (itself based on earlier South African legislation) was an admixture of the "weak extinctive prescription" of English law (Limitation of actions) and the Roman-Dutch "strong prescription" that wipes out a debt. The new Prescription Act 68 of 1969 provides for a strong extinctive prescription, going back fundamentally to Roman-Dutch principles but also invoking aid from certain modern civil-law systems for some of the detailed rules.
23 Ever since the decision in Holland v. Scott (1882) 2 E.D.C. 307.
24 Regal v. African Superslate (Pty.) Ltd. 1963 (1) S.A. 102 (A.D.). See Mathews and Milton, "An English Backlash?" 82 S.A.L.J. 31 (1965); Jaffey, "Nuisance: South African, Roman and English," 87 S.A.L.J. 436 (1970).
  In ANNUAL SURVEY OF SOUTH AFRICAN LAW (hereinafter cited as ANNUAL SURVEY) 306 (1963), H. Luntz wrote: "Are we to say now that every [earlier] decision [each one based on English law] is of no authority and that when the matter arises again it must be decided by authorities as obscure as most of those cited by the Chief Justice in the present case and whose availability is confined, perhaps, to the Appellate Division library and one or two others? One does not object to the overthrow of English doctrines which have been grafted on to our law if these are shown to be objectionable in some way and they are replaced by clear, concise principles of Roman-Dutch law. But where a fully worked out system, with hundreds of comparatively accessible precedents, is replaced by an admittedly fragmentary treatment scattered through virtually unknown volumes —a treatment to some extent influenced by procedural remedies which have since fallen into disuse—one cannot but regret the spirit of antiquarianism which seems to prevail."

Another such happening, the revival by the Appellate Division[25] of the Roman-Dutch defence in an action for defamation of absence of *animus injuriandi* (intention to injure), has also caused considerable uncertainty; and only now, after numerous cases and much anguished analysis by jurists, are the lights in this corner of the law beginning one by one to be switched on.

The striking unequivocal pronouncement of the ultimate tribunal that the South African law of estoppel is not that of England may fittingly close this analysis of the responses to the call *petere fontes*. In *Trust Bank van Afrika Bpk. v Eksteen*[26] Steyn CJ rejected the view of the court *a quo* that our law of estoppel must be sought in the first place in the decisions of English courts. True, he said, a series of Appellate Division decisions had taken the view that our law of estoppel is the same as that of England, and in practice more regard is given to English decisions for guidance than to our own authorities. But, continued Steyn CJ, he was in no way convinced that the application of principles of South African law would in all respects lead to the same results as those accepted in England. It is wholly unjustifiable to conclude that South African courts are bound by English decisions. No court, he stressed, not the Appellate

---

25 See Jordaan v. Van Biljon 1962 (1) S.A. 286 (A.D.); Craig v. Voortrekkerpers Bpk. 1963 (1) S.A. 149 (A.D.); Nydoo v. Vengtas 1965 (1) S.A. 1 (A.D.); Benson v. Robinson & Co (Pty.) Ltd. 1967 (1) S.A. 420 (A.D.). See also Maisel v. Van Naeren 1960 (4) S.A. 836 (C.); Hassen v. Post Newspapers (Pty.) Ltd. 1965 (3) S.A. 562 (W.); Wentzel v. S.A. Yster- en Staalbedryfsvereniging 1967 (3) S.A. 91 (T.). Perhaps the last two cases clarify the matter: that one must distinguish between defences based only on the subjective absence of fault, viz *animus injuriandi* (probably limited to jest, mistake, insanity, drunkenness, and *rixa* [justifiable retaliation]) and those based on an objective ground legally recognized (such as justification, privileged occasion, and fair comment), which do not relate to the rebutting of the presumption of *animus injuriandi* that flows from the publication of defamatory material, but concern a ground of legal justification pertaining to wrongfulness and not fault (intent). See, generally, Roberg, "Animus Injuriandi, Privilege, and the Law of Defamation," 79 S.A.L.J. 113 (1962); "A New Concept of Animus Injuriandi," 80 S.A.L.J. (1963); "Animus Injuriandi Without Tears," 82 S.A.L.J. 437 (1965); "Some Light on the Subject of Animus Injuriandi," 84 S.A.L.J. 387 (1967); and "Animus Injuriandi and Mistake," 84 S.A.L.J. 57 (1971); Van der Vyver, "Animus Injuriandi en die Afwesigheid van Wederregtelikheidsbewussyn," 29 Tydskrif vir Hedendaagse Romeins-Hollandse Reg 336 (1966); in 30 *idem* 157 (1967); and "Privilege, Wederregtelikheid en Skuld," *idem* 370 (1967); Joubert and Van der Walt in *idem* 375 (1967).
26 1964 (3) S.A. 402 (A.D.) at 410–11. The judgment is in Afrikaans. It was concurred in by three of the four other judges of appeal sitting in the case. A synopsis in English follows.

Division itself, has the capacity to replace our common law with that of another country: only the legislature can do so. The elementary duty of a tribunal is to apply its own law, and it would be entirely wrong to yield to another legal system, even where its legal principles are the same.

But, went on the Chief Justice, reference to or consideration of the principles of the law of another country is by no means out of the question. A comparative approach, as is apparent from innumerable South African judgments and legal writings, can be a particularly valuable means of getting clarity on the best application, adaptation, and development of our own principles. The exclusion of the fruitful influence of related (nota bene) legal systems would not only be a hopeless task but would be unacceptable, impoverishing shortsightedness. However, it is one thing to investigate another law in order to apply our own more effectively, and an entirely other thing to approach another law as if it were a naturalized part of our acknowledged sources of law.

The impact of this fascinating passage must not be overstated. It has not by any means led to a radical change of attitude in favour of extreme purism. The lawyer looks through subsequent law reports in vain for signs that "through creeks and inlets making, / Comes silent, flooding in, the main." Rather, what the Chief Justice was pronouncing was his credo that the principles, concepts, divisions, and basic rules of our Romanistic-patterned legal system should not be jettisoned or warped by any entry of the common law.[27]

In practice, it does not always prove possible to eliminate the stranger who has settled in South African law. Thus the pronouncement in the *Eksteen* case has not precluded the Appellate Division itself from finding in special circumstances that a particular legal doctrine which emigrated from England has indeed become naturalized in South Africa. So it has been with the agency for an undisclosed principal. Recently [28] our ultimate court was seised of this matter for the first time. It found that the doctrine did not appear to have any warrant in, and was indeed contrary to the basic principles of, the Roman-Dutch law, but that it had been

---

27 See Oliver, "Promissory Estoppel in English and South African Law," 88 S.A.L.J. 321 (1971): "English precedents will still be used in our courts, albeit as persuasive authority and as a matter of comparison. Extensions to the application of estoppel in England and America should be closely studied by our lawyers, not merely from an academic interest but also with a view to their adoption here."

28 Cullinan v. Noordkaaplandse Aartappelkernmoerkwekers Koöperaise Bpk. 1972 (1) S.A. 761 (A.D.).

applied for over a century by our courts, borrowing from English law. Despite the fact that the doctrine had been subject to considerable adverse criticism from writers on Anglo-American as well as South African law, the court decided that it could not now be "thrown overboard," because it had been applied for so long in commercial practice and the declaration of its demise would result in the loss of innumerable supposed rights and obligations. A judicial pronouncement works retrospectively, it emphasized. Thus the court concluded that the doctrine had become so naturalized that it had to be regarded as existing law. Then their lordships had to consider whether the consensuality principle in contract could be further violated by allowing for an agent to act for more than one undisclosed principal.[29] Counsel quoted certain Anglo-American authority that this could not be permitted. Reflecting the recent homeward trend, the court found it unnecessary to consider the comparative material. The problem could be solved, it ruled, by applying the general principles of South African law; and these did not allow for this extension of the doctrine.

Considerable debate, frequently acrimonious, took place for years between jurists professing to belong to different schools of thought. Those labelled by some as pragmatists or realists and by others as pollutionists urged that foreign influences should not be eliminated unless they could be shown to be evil. An attempt to restore the chimerical pure Roman-Dutch law, they argued, would result in legal uncertainty and the loss of numerous valuable importations, by no means all inconsistent with civil-law principles. Others, called purists or antiquarians, according to the taste of the critic, have called for a restoration of the glories of our past. Today most of the bitterness of the dispute has departed and there is broad acceptance, in the words of a middle-of-the-road jurist skilled in Roman and comparative law, that "[f]uture reforms, if any, are therefore bound to be on a realtively small scale." [30]

A great deal of accommodation has taken place. No one will dispute that, in the absence of legislation, binding precedent, or modern custom (including trade usage), when a question of a general rule is involved regard must first be given to the Roman-Dutch authorities. Whereas on a particular issue, these authorities had arrived only at the beginning of

---

29 In the particular case, for himself and two undisclosed principals.
30 Hosten in C.I.L.S.A. 200 (1969).

the road, the Appellate Division has shown in several striking judgments that it is sometimes possible today to build the road to its logical end.[31] If the old writers enunciate a clear rule that has not been abrogated by disuse, then in very exceptional circumstances, delimited by an intuitive feeling, the issue of judicial experience and curial fealty to the received law, a court (particularly the Appellate Division) might modify or reject what they say "in order to keep in touch with the expansion of legal ideas, and to keep pace with the requirements of modern conditions";[32] or in order to produce justice, such as equality of treatment of the sexes.[33] Via this route it is still possible that English law may make an entry or two on to the stage. It is not beyond possibility, for instance, that duress of a third party will be held to be operative, allowing the aggrieved party to cancel, only when it was exercised by or known in advance by the party in whose favour it was exerted, and not in all circumstances, as the Roman-Dutch authorities, in conformity with the civil law, had it.[34] Even so loyal a supporter of our legal heritage as Professor J. C. de Wet advises this, in the interests of legal fairness and consistency.[35]

When it comes to the interpretation of the numerous statutes on mer-

---

31 See, especially, Roberts Construction Co. Ltd. v. Willcox Bros. (Pty.) Ltd. 1962 (4) S.A. 326 (A.D.) (causae continentia principle in jurisdiction); State v. Bernardus 1965 (3) S.A. 287 (A.D.) at 294 (versari in re illicita principle in criminal law). A possible future development in equitable adjustment of loss where a contract is terminated through supervening impossibility. Cf. De Villiers JA in African Realty Trust Lt. v. Holmes 1922 A.D. 389 at 400–402.

32 Per Innes CJ in Blower v. Van Noorden 1909 T.S. 890 at 905 (liability of agent who exceeds his authority). See also Linton v. Corser 1952 (3) S.A. 685 (A.D.) at 695–96 (changed conditions of finance may make it unrealistic to have recourse to the old authorities); Harris v. Harris 1949 (1) S.A. 254 (A.D.) at 266 (nondiscretion to condone the adultery of the plaintiff in a divorce suit produces injustice and is unsuited to our times).

33 For example, Rosenbaum v. Margolis 1944 H.L.D. 147 at 158. But there are numerous decisions in which judges have considered themselves bound by a rule of Roman-Dutch law, however undesirable they have considered it to be: e.g. Lobley v. Lobley 1940 C.P.D. 420 at 434; Van Staden v. Van Wyk 1958 (2) S.A. 682 (O.) at 684; Barnard NO v. Miller 1963 (4) S.A. 426 (C.) at 428.

34 For example, VOET COMMENTARIUS AD PANDECTAS 4.2.4; POTHIER, OBLIGATIONS para. 23. It is a rule observed in a number of civil-law countries today—for instance, France, the Netherlands, and Germany, as well as the state of Louisiana.

35 DIE SUID-AFRIKAANSE KONTRAKTEREG EN HANDELSREG 43 (3rd ed. 1964). Another possibility is that a court may deviate from the old authorities by holding that the debt against which set-off is raised need not be liquidated and the debt which it is sought to oppose to another debt through set-off need not be due. See KAHN, CONTRACT AND MERCANTILE LAW THROUGH THE CASE 280 (1971).

cantile law fashioned on those of England, there has been no quarrel with or deviation from the attitude taken long since by the Appellate Division,[36] that where identical wording is used the decisions of English courts are of great persuasive force, provided they are not based on "legal principles which are foreign to our system of law." Indeed, a judge who, as has been seen, has been in the forefront of those wishing to preserve our Roman-Dutch heritage, has referred to the considerable "persuasive authority" of the view of an English tribunal as to the meaning of English words used in a like context to identical or very similar words to be assigned a meaning by the court.[37]

Fifty years ago the view, adumbrated much earlier,[38] was put forward in detail by a leading academic[39] that while guidance should be sought in the common law for commercial and adjective law, because of its immense influence in South Africa, modern Continental systems, based on Roman law principles, should be tapped for help with private law (particularly the law of obligations) and criminal law. In 1960 a court suggested that regard be had to "those systems of the West and European continent which, though codified, have their roots in the same historical soil as our law."[40] In 1972 the Appellate Division stated: "In seeking to do justice between man and man it is at the least interesting and sometimes instructive to have some comparative regard to the law of other countries, particularly those whose systems have been touched by the greatness of the Roman law."[41]

In South Africa judges—as opposed to academics—up to very recently seldom went for guidance to the laws of European countries. Indeed, the important occasions on which they have done so have been so rare as to impress themselves on every law student's mind: notably contracts

36 Roodepoort United Main Reef G.M. Co. Ltd. v. Du Toit NO 1928 A.D. 66 at 71–72; Estate Wege v Strauss 1932 A.D. 76.
37 Steyn JA (later CJ) in Consolidated Diamond Mines of South West Africa Ltd. v. Administrator, South West Africa 1958 (4) S.A. 572 (A.D.) at 656. Although this statement was made in a dissenting judgment, no one can doubt its correctness.
38 See 27 S.A.L.J. 489 (1910); Krause J in Lever v. Buhrmann 1925 T.R.D. 254 at 258–60. See, further, Hosten in 25 T.H.R-H.R. 27, 29 (1962).
39 The late Professor I. van Zyl Steyn in 48 S.A.L.J. 203 ff. (1931).
40 Per De Villiers AJ, delivering the judgment of the court in Maisel v. Van Naeren 1960 (4) S.A. 836 (C.) at 847.
41 Per Holmes JA, delivering the judgment of the court in Government of the Republic of South Africa v. Ngubane 1972 (2) S.A. 601 (A.D.) at 609.

Doctrine and Judicial Decisions in South Africa | 239

through the post and attempts in crime to commit the impossible.[42] On the other hand, mediately through acceptance by the judges of the views of eminent academics expressed in treatises, particularly with criminal law, and also to a degree with the law of contract,[43] some of the solutions of Continental systems have found their way into our law in the past two decades or so. And there does seem to be, on the part of certain judges of appeal at all events, a tendency nowadays to mention at least relevant Dutch and German legal writings.[44]

As against this, the law reports of late years give the impression that judges are at times hesitant about pronouncing on the state of a foreign law, for they have not been trained in it, and most, like lawyers generally, are not equipped linguistically to cope with the language, save, possibly, where it is Dutch. This is quite apart from a case on the conflict of laws, where, except in circumstances where it is permissible for the parties to agree as to its content, foreign law that is alleged to be the *lex causae* has to be proved through the testimony of a witness *peritus virtute officii*.[45] In fact, however, there seems to be some leaning towards this solution for the adducing of comparative material, at least where it is derived from Continental systems.[46]

42 Cape Explosives Works Ltd. v. South African Oil & Fat Industries Ltd. 1921 C.P.D. 244, the court preferring the expedition theory of the common law; R. v. Davies 1956 (3) S.A. 52 (A.D.), the court finally relying on the "weight of juristic opinion" and "current of judicial decisions" in England and the United States in pronouncing on attempts to commit the impossible; State v. Bernardus 1965 (3) S.A. 287 (A.D.) at 296–97, 302–303. [N.B.: R. in a case reference stands for Rex or Regina, as the case may be, indicating a criminal prosecution. Since the creation of the Republic of South Africa in 1961 it has been replaced by State (in Afrikaans Staat).]

As mentioned earlier, the Conventional Penalties Act of 1962 was based in part on German and Swiss models, but so far the courts have not turned to the laws of Germany or Switzerland for guidance in the interpretation of the statute.

43 Tribute should be paid particularly to the eminent jurist Professor J. C. de Wet and his scholarly contributions to the books DE WET and SWANEPOEL, DIE SUID-AFRIKAANSE STRAFREG (South African Criminal Law) [2nd ed. 1960] and DIE SUID-AFRIKAANSE KONTRAKTEREG EN HANDLSREG (The South African Law of Contracts and Mercantile Law) [3rd ed. 1964].

44 See Caledon & Suid-Westelike Distrikte Eksekuteurskamer Bpk. v. Wentzel 1972 (1) S.A. 270 (A.D.) at 273, 283; Venter v. Birchholtz 1972 (1) S.A. 276 (A.D.) at 283.

45 Schlesinger v. Commissioner for Inland Revenue 1964 (3) S.A. 389 (A.D.), in which it was held that the rule applies also to English law.

46 See State v. Masilela 1968 (2) S.A. 558 (A.D.), where counsel submitted "opinions" on the issue in the laws of Germany and the Netherlands, written by alleged experts on these laws. Rumpff JA (at 574), while agreeing that such opinions were helpful, was opposed to the way in which they were simply handed

The code-directed jurisprudence and doctrine of Continental countries, it has been suggested, makes them less valuable persuasive material than the noncodified common law.[47] The premises of this submission have not gone unchallenged. The easily accessible English law (all South African lawyers can read the language in which it is written), so the reply goes, gives rise to a mistaken sense of familiarity and mistaken belief that on any particular score it is the same as Roman-Dutch law. Transplants from a common-law system on to the essentially Romanistic Roman-Dutch system are less likely to take than those from a civil-law system, with its more closely related structure, concepts and divisions. A South African lawyer would not commence with the code and law reports of the Continental system, but with its legal writings. There he will find guidance along familiar lines and more stress on teleological considerations than in the casuistic English case law.[48]

The answer to this critic may be that reference is not had only to the legal decisions of the countries espousing Anglo-American law. Textbooks and articles are frequently consulted, and most of them are by no means simple synopses of existing curial pronouncements.[49] Nonetheless, there certainly is much to be said for taking a wider sweep for com-

in. Compare a comparative report handed in by consent of the other side in Government of the Republic of South Africa v. Ngubane 1972 (2) S.A. 601 (A.D.). It treated of the solutions to the problem before the court (whether a claim for damages for pain and suffering caused by the delict of the defendant is capable of being ceded before *litis contestatio*) in the laws of the Netherlands, Germany, Italy, Spain, Austria, Switzerland, France, England, and the U.S.A. The report was made by the Institute of Foreign and Comparative Law of the University of South Africa, "by researchers of impressive qualifications, and we appreciate having it before us." The court also had regard to a case cited by counsel as expressing the law of Scotland. Unfortunately, such divergencies of approach were revealed that the court was "unable in this instance to find guidelines from a comparative survey. So in the end we have had to find a solution within the fabric of our own law" (at 610).

It must be said, however, that judges are not so hesitant about looking to the laws of England, the United States and Scotland, though statements acknowledging lack of real acquaintance with these systems seem to be more frequent. To take a very recent dictum of a provincial division: "The English law of torts is not part of our law. When, however, considering the possible extension of our law it is proper by way of comparison to have regard to the principles of English law on this particular issue [whether liability for negligence should be limited to physical injury to person or property]": per Myburgh J in Combrinck Chiropraktiese Kliniek (Edms.) Bpk. v. Datsun Motor Vehicle Distributors (Pty.) Ltd. 1972 (4) S.A. 185 (T.) at 192.

47 Hahlo and Kahn, Legal System 323, 591–92.
48 Hosten in C.I.L.S.A. 202–204 (1969).
49 See, e.g., the review by Sir Alfred Denning (then LJ, now Lord Denning M.R.) of

parative material, particularly in questions of private and criminal law.

Failing binding legislation, precedent and modern custom, then, a judge in principle must apply the Roman-Dutch law. This is frequently referred to as the common law of South Africa. That, however, is a term that has as far as possible been eschewed in this essay, so as to avoid confusion with the common law of the Anglo-American system as contrasted with the civil-law or civilian systems of today, that were subjected to a pervasive Roman law influence through the Reception.

It would be as well at the outset to make the frank admission that it is not so frequently that judges and practitioners find themselves forced to travel the arduous route lined with the old authorities. The facts in issue are normally concerned with the interpretation and application of some piece of legislation or the expansion or adaptation of a rule of law already domiciled in the reported cases. Were recourse to the old writers a matter of everyday need for those involved in the administration of the law, the legal process would be so protracted and expensive that it would collapse under its own weight.

As would be expected, it is in judgments of the Appellate Division that reference is made most frequently to works on the Roman-Dutch law. In the seventy-two decisions of that court reported in the four volumes for 1968 of the South African Law Reports, we are told, the "writings of Voet were cited eleven times . . . those of Van Leeuwen four times; Sande three times; Matthaeus, Grotius and Pothier twice each; Moorman, Van der Linden, Lybrechts, Van Zutphen, Van der Keessel, Van Bynkershoek, Brouwer, Wassenaar, Schomaker, Bort and Barels once each. German pandectists consulted were Windscheid, Glück, Von Quistorp and Dernburg."[50] A nice mixed bag this, with several names that would be unknown even to a legal historian, unless he happened to specialize in what in the Netherlands is called "*Oud-Vaderlands recht*" (old fatherland law). It may fittingly introduce a conspectus of the "old authorities."

There may be said to be five sources of Roman-Dutch law, of which all save the first to some extent span the same territory.[51]

---

an edition of WINFIELD ON TORT in 63 LAW QUARTERLY REVIEW 516 (1947), in which he pays tribute to writers such as Winfield, Pollock, and Salmond for their legal studies on scientific lines, not as mere repositories of statute and case law.

50 Van Niekert in *Annual Survey* 486 (1968).
51 See, generally, ROBERTS, SOUTH AFRICAN LEGAL BIBLIOGRAPHY (1942); DEKKERS, BIBLIOTHECA BELGICA JURIDICA (1951).

First, legislation. It was published in collected form between 1658 and 1796 in nine enormous volumes, the *Groot Placaet-Boeck*.

Second, collections of decisions of the courts. These were all private, there being no systematic reporting of cases in Roman-Dutch times. The most valuable volumes, oddly enough, have only relatively recently been published between 1926 and 1967: the *Observationes Tumultuariae* of Cornelis van Bynkershoek (1673–1743), for long a member of the Hooge Raad van Holland en Zeeland, the highest court of Holland, being a diary of the day-to-day decisions of the tribunal; and the *Observationes Tumultuariae Novae* of his son-in-law, Willem Pauw (1712–1787), also a member of the court. Their great value lies in their affording reasons for the five thousand reported decisions they contain, which the Hooge Raad in its published judgments did not.

How far should these old judicial decisions be taken as correctly representing the Roman-Dutch law? That they have considerable force is undoubted, but attention must be paid to the doctrine of precedent of the time.[52] In the dying days of that system in the Netherlands the Dutch authority Van der Linden [53] wrote that there were three possible approaches to a judicial decision: first, that it had the binding force of a statute; secondly, that it had no authority beyond the parties involved and thus law reports were of no value; thirdly, that if it had been arrived at after due deliberation, it should be followed by another judge unless, after careful consideration and for a convincing reason, he concluded that the correct answer was different. Van der Linden himself subscribed to the third view, which was accepted by the late Mr. Justice J. G. Kotzé, a most learned legal scholar and historian, as the true reflection of the outlook of that period.[54] A similar attitude prevailed elsewhere in the Continent in the precodification era.

Third, collections of opinions of advocates, including university professors of law. The advice on legal points by these jurists had considerable

---

[52] On this see Kotzé, "Judicial Precedent," 34 S.A.L.J. 280 (1917); Scholtens, "Die Rechtsprechung als Rechtsquelle," 37 DEUTSCHE RICHTERZEITUNG 167 (1959); Kahn, "The Rules of Precedent Applied in South African Courts," 84 S.A.L.J. 43 (1967).

[53] VERZAMELING VAN MERKWAARDIGE GEWIJSDEN [Collection of Noteworthy Judicial Decisions] (1803) Voorberigt [Preface].

[54] 34 S.A.L.J. 280 at 284–85 (1917).

influence with the judges of Roman-Dutch days. But, in the words of the Roman-Dutch writer Simon van Leeuwen, "the opinions of jurists are not law with us; for the opinions given by counsel in our Universities or in cities, on consultation and at the instance of individuals, have no such weight as those of the old accredited Jurists: their advice is probably correct, and that is all." [55] This would very likely represent the view taken today, also, as to these opinions reflecting the law of their times.

A number of collections were published, the parties concerned usually being supplied with imaginary names, but the names of counsel being given. In South Africa no such collection has ever appeared, among other reasons because it would constitute a grave breach of professional ethics. Such view as a practitioner has formed may still, in an indirect way, influence the course of the law, by being accepted by the court before which it is advanced.

Fourth, legal dictionaries and encyclopaedias. These are not of great significance.

Finally, and by far the most important for South African law today, treatises by practitioners or academics. Mention can be made of only a few of the most celebrated and influential works, with the dates of publication of the first edition in each case: Hugo Grotius's *Inleiding tot de Hollandsche Rechtsgeleertheyt* (Introduction to the Jurisprudence of Holland) (1631), Johannes Voet's voluminous *Commentarius ad Pandectas* (1698–1704), Simon van Leeuwen's *Roomsch Hollandsch Recht* (Roman-Dutch Law) (1664), Ulric Huber's *Heedendaegse Rechtsgeleertheyt* (Jurisprudence of My Time) (1686), Dionysius Godefridus van der Keessel's *Theses Selectae* (1800) and *Praelectiones Juris hodierni ad Hugonis Grotii Introductionem ad Iurisprudentiam Hollandicam* (first published, with an Afrikaans translation, in 1961–1967) and Johannes van der Linden's *Koopmans Handboek* (literally, Merchant's Guide). Apart from Van der Keessel's *Praelectiones*, all have been published in an English translation.

There are dozens more writers and score upon score of other textbooks, some of general scope, some of specific branches of the law. In theory, preference should be given to analyses of the law of Holland over those of

---

55 CENSURA FORENSIS (1662) 1.1.1.19. Translation by W. P. Schreiner (Cape Town, 1883).

another province, in particular over those of Friesland, where Roman law had a greater impact;[56] and to later writers, who presumably represented the Roman-Dutch law in a phase closer to its end in the Netherlands.[57] But actually no hard and fast rule prevails. If the old writers are in disagreement, one looks in vain for a law of citations.

The judges of South Africa feel fairly free to plump for the view they regard as most equitable, reasonable, convenient, and in conformity with modern times.

There is no distinct geographical limitation on the treatises that may be cited. Roman-Dutch law was but a branch of the great family of European civil-law systems. The writers on the law of the Netherlands had no hesitation in scanning the legal systems of neighbouring countries for material persuasive in reason, equity, convenience, and social utility, and they cited writers from what today are called Germany, Belgium, France, and Italy.

If it came to a simple clash between, say, Voet, the most frequently cited Roman-Dutch writer, and Robert Pothier, the great French academic (1699–1772), several of whose works were translated into Dutch by Van der Linden, we should follow Voet, unless his views are quite out of accord with the mores and conditions of today.[58] Pothier's statement of the law, however, would carry much weight where the Roman-Dutch writers are silent, uncertain, or in irreconcilable conflict. Sir John Wessels, a former Chief Justice of South Africa, wrote: "In the latter part of the eighteenth century, Pothier was regarded, in Holland, as a great authority on the Civil Law, and his treatise on Obligations was for all pur-

---

[56] Van den Heever JA (one of the most learned of South African judges) said in Tjollo Ateljees (Eins) Bkp. v. Small 1949 (1) S.A. 856 (A.D.) at 865–66: "There is a special reason why we should ignore the Frisians. In Friesland the Roman law was received not merely in *subsidio* as *ratio scripta* but as a system which operated *proprio vigore*." But this is an overstatement. The works of Huber should not be, and indeed are not, disregarded. There was in fact not so much difference between the laws of Friesland and Holland.

[57] Perhaps greater use should be made by counsel, judges, and legal writers of the Ontwerp 1820, an abortive draft code intended to reflect the Roman-Dutch law of the Netherlands at its passing. It was rejected by the legislature of the country. While the draft code is well framed (the principal draftsman was the Leiden law professor J. M. Kemper) it has to be treated with a little circumspection. Every now and then what it says simply was not the Roman-Dutch law at its close.

[58] Cf. Van den Heever JA in Geber v. Wolson 1955 (1) S.A. 158 (A.D.) at 170–71. Fagan JA (at 183) put the two on the same level. But this cannot be supported. See Scholtens in 72 S.A.L.J. 357 (1955).

poses regarded as a text-book on the law of Obligations, as also were his treatises on Lease, Sale and Partnership, because both the Dutch Law and the French Law, in regard to these contracts, were founded on the Roman Civil Law." [59]

It can be seen then, that in the ascertainment of the Roman-Dutch law the writings of the jurists from neighbouring countries have considerable influence as *doctrine* of a peculiar historical nature. But writings of a persuasive force do not stop there. Roman law ran through the veins of the Roman-Dutch law. Even today, albeit, apparently, to a diminishing extent,[60] the *Corpus Juris Justiniani* is cited in legal argument and judgments.

South African courts rightly consider themselves primarily under the duty to apply the law of Justinian as the Roman-Dutch authorities understood it, no matter how wrong this understanding be seen today.[61] Accordingly, attention is paid to the *usus modernus Pandectarum*, to the glossators, postglossators, and pandectists (in particular Savigny), rather than to the classical Roman law, the humanists, and the Romanists of today.

It does not follow, however, that the latter should be shunned. Just as the Roman-Dutch writers did not hesitate to rely on the humanists, so South African courts should be prepared to go to them and contemporary Roman law studies when they wish to invoke Roman law as a subsidiary system on their finding the Roman-Dutch authorities silent, vague, or in conflict.[62] Again we encounter an odd form of historical *doctrine*.

To turn to modern text-writers: no one has suggested that their views are a formal source of law. The accepted outlook is that the conclusions and submission of authors of treatises and articles on legal subjects are

59 I LAW OF CONTRACT (2nd ed. 1951) xiii. On the Roman-Dutch law attitude to the use of "the laws of neighbouring nations," VAN DER LINDEN KOOPMANS HANDBOEK 1.1.4 says that great caution should be used and we must "feel perfectly convinced that the law of the neighbouring country and our own agree in this point in analogy" (translation by Henry Juta, 1891).
60 See Lee, "The Disappearing Roman Law," 74 S.A.L.J. 79 (1957).
61 See, e.g., Master v. African Mines Corporation Ltd. 1907 T.S. 925 at 928–29.
62 See Lammers & Lammers v. Giovannoni 1955 (3) S.A. 385 (A.D.) at 396; Beinart, "Roman Law in South African Practice," 69 S.A.L.J. 145, especially at 162 ff. (1952); Van Warmelo, "Roman Law and the Old Authority of Roman-Dutch Law," ACTA JURIDICA 38, especially at 51, 56–57 (1961); Note in 14 T.H.R.-H.R. 80 (1951); and DIE OORSPRONG EN BETEKENIS VAN DIE ROMEINSE REG (The Origin and Meaning of Roman Law) 208 ff. (1959); Scholtens in 75 S.A.L.J. 146 (1958).

only of persuasive force (sometimes inaptly referred to as "persuasive authority").

Writings on the law are regarded as repositories of scholarship and learning to which a judge (usually through initial reference to them by counsel) may look for guidance in formulating or fortifying his views. In this country "scientific discussion" has proved an active formative agency in the analysis and systematization of the law, the finding of principles and concepts and the formulation of rules. The responsibility for the decision on the state of the law, however, is ultimately that of the court. En route it may well jettison the conclusion reached by the most eminent jurist expounded in the most learned disquisition. Take a famous work, H. G. Mackeurtan's *The Law of Sale of Goods in South Africa*. In 1971 [63] Holmes JA had occasion to adopt a view expressed in it, stating: "It is hardly necessary to add that opinions expressed by that learned author have often been accepted by the courts of this country over the last half century." But the following year, in deciding that damages for anticipatory breach of contract are to be measured as at date of performance and not as at anticipatory breach as submitted by Mackeurtan, Trollip JA said: [64] "That view expressed by such an eminent lawyer, is entitled to great respect, but, after carefully considering the problem, I agree with Jansen JA that it ought not to be adopted. The learned author's criticism of the rule fixing the time of performance as the criterion is not convincing." The decision of the Appellate Division that spouses married out of community of property and with exclusion of the marital power may sue each other during their married life as if single persons [65] affords a nice contrast. This vexed question had been the subject of a brilliant analysis by one of the most gifted and scholarly of our academics, Professor J. E. Scholtens, who had reached this conclusion.[66] His course of reasoning and the authorities he relied on were, as was to be expected, taken over almost *en bloc* by counsel who was submitting that this was

63 Cornelissen v. Universal Caravan Sales (Pty.) Ltd. 1971 (3) S.A. 158 (A.D.) at 174.
64 Novick v. Benjamin 1972 (2) S.A. 842 (A.D.) at 861.
65 Rohloff v. Ocean Accident & Guarantee Corporation Ltd. 1960 (2) S.A. 291 (A.D.).
66 "Delictual Actions between Spouses in Roman-Dutch Law," 76 S.A.L.J. 205 (1959). See also "Actions in Delict between Husband and Wife," 76 S.A.L.J. 4 (1959).

the law. Counsel's argument was virtually repeated by Malan JA, delivering the judgment of the court. Although his name is not mentioned in the judgment, it is obvious that the work of Professor Scholtens had an enormous influence in settling this important problem. Perhaps not many illustrations of a court's to all intents and purposes following a detailed analysis of old authority by a jurist can be found; but there are innumerable cases in which judges have expressed themselves in concurrence with an argument of a legal writer.

What follows will be confined to analysis of South African law. But a word or two should be said initially of textbooks and articles on other legal systems. What is being considered is their direct consultation, not at one remove through a comparative treatment by a writer on the law of this country. Where a judge or practitioner looks for guidance elsewhere, obviously he will frequently consult writings on the rules of whatever legal system he is visiting. Hitherto, as has been shown, it has normally been Anglo-American law. To illustrate judicial practice, it would be convenient to concentrate on one topic, the rules pertaining to agreement (offer and acceptance), where there can be no doubt that Roman-Dutch authority is slender in the extreme. A survey of the leading South African judicial decisions shows frequent citation of leading works on the law of contract of England, such as Cheshire & Fifoot, Pollock, Halsbury's *Laws of England* (which probably enjoys a higher reputation in South Africa than in the land of its birth) and Chitty, and that of the United States, such as Williston, Corbin, and the *Restatement*.[67]

When it comes to a South African statute framed on an English model, such as the Companies Act and the Bills of Exchange Act, manifestly there is still a greater tendency to cite and rely on leading works on the English law.

Recourse to and regard for *doctrine* will vary with the legal issue before the court. If it is of a "universal" character, such as one pertaining to

[67] See, e.g., Hersch v. Nel 1948 (3) S.A. 686 (A.D.) at 692, 698; East Asiatic Co. (S.A.) Ltd. v. Midlands Manufacturing Co. (Pty.) Ltd. 1954 (2) S.A. 387 (C.) at 391; Smeiman v. Volkersz 1954 (4) S.A. 170 (C.) at 177; Steenkamp v. Webster 1955 (1) S.A. 524 (A.D.) at 530; Levenstein v. Levenstein 1955 (3) S.A. 615 (S.R.) at 619; Peri-urban Areas Health Board v. Breet NO 1958 (3) S.A. 783 (T.) at 790; Kantor v. Kantor 1962 (3) S.A. 207 (T.) at 209; Godfrey v. Paruk 1965 (2) S.A. 738 (D.) at 743; Venter v. Birchholtz 1972 (1) S.A. 276 (A.D.) at 282.

public international law, where old authority and modern case law is deficient, the output of leading writers the world over may well be scoured. Reference to overseas literature will also be frequent where the issue arises within the national law of South Africa, but it is little worked out in our decisions or in the old authorities, or else is the subject of consideration in the Roman-Dutch manuals, but is still ripe for development and expansion, such as a good deal of the conflict of laws and aspects of constitutional law.[68]

So persuasive has the formulation of a legal rule by an eminent foreign jurist been on a few occasions that it has become embedded in the legal system of South Africa. Thus it has been said that there "can be little doubt that Spencer Bower on issue estoppel has been received into South African case law"; [69] though that happening has been deplored as contrary to the Roman-Dutch law on res judicata and productive of anomalies and injustice.[70]

As far as South African writers are concerned, it goes almost without saying that the influence on judges of what they write depends considerably on the standing of the writer. This standing does not turn much on his position in legal society. Not infrequently he is a judge; there is no strong—though in certain quarters there is some—feeling that the judiciary should confine its comments on the law to the pages of the law reports; and the Bench has made a valuable contribution to legal literature on topics that do not impinge on current political controversy.[71]

---

68 See, e.g., the consultation of works on constitutional law in the important case on passports, Sachs v. Dönges NO 1950 (2) S.A. 265 (A.D.). What is said here is, of course, a widespread phenomenon. Thus, for instance, L. J. van Apeldoorn, writing of the present-day law of the Netherlands, states that the influence of "rechtsleer" (doctrine) is greatest in practice in the terrain of the law where the legislature leaves the judge most in the lurch, viz. that of private international law (Inleiding tot de studie van het Nederlandse Recht 138 [16th ed. 1966]).
69 Zeffert, "Issue Estoppel in South Africa," 88 S.A.L.J. 312 at 314 (1971). The celebrated formulation of Spencer Bower now appears in BOWER AND TURNER, THE DOCTRINE OF RES JUDICATA 152–53 (2nd ed. 1969).
70. Zeffert in 88 S.A.L.J. 312 at 314 (1971).
71 Many of their writings are on peripheral topics, such as criminological and penal reform (Mr. Justice J. H. Steyn of the Cape Bench and—though to a lesser degree—Mr. V. G. Hiemstra of the Transvaal Bench in particular have lectured and published widely on these matters), the legal profession, legal dictionaries, and the conduct of trials (COLMAN, CROSS-EXAMINATION [1970]); legal history (WESSELS, HISTORY OF THE ROMAN-DUTCH LAW [1903]; the author's THE LAW OF CONTRACT IN SOUTH AFRICA [1951] was published posthumously). But there

More often, as is to be expected, the author is an academic, and particularly so today, for the law schools have grown greatly in number and their staffs in complement, and, with every respect to those who have gone before and paved the way, generally in training and overall competency. Practitioners do make valuable contributions, too, but pressure of work often precludes the most brilliant advocates and attorneys from conveying their researches and ideas to paper, other than perhaps an occasional article or note. There is no closed list of writers on law. Public servants, those with legal qualifications who are engaged in commerce, writers of legal dissertations and theses for higher degrees—the works of these and, indeed, all persons legally qualified who have done the necessary research and shown competency in analysis are given polite and careful attention by the judges.

At the risk of oversimplification one may say that the status of legal

---

have been occasional treatises and monographs on substantive and adjective law, for instance, civil practice and procedure, e.g. HERBSTEIN AND VAN WINSEN, THE CIVIL PRACTICE OF THE SUPERIOR COURTS IN SOUTH AFRICA (2nd ed. 1966); company law, HENOCHSBERG, HENOCHSBERG ON THE COMPANIES ACT (2nd ed. 1963); suretyship, CANEY, THE LAW OF SURETYSHIP IN SOUTH AFRICA (2nd ed. 1970); justa causa, KOTZÉ, CAUSA IN THE ROMAN AND ROMAN-DUTCH LAW OF CONTRACT (1922); criminal law and procedure, GARDINER AND LANSDOWN, SOUTH AFRICAN CRIMINAL LAW AND PROCEDURE (6th ed. 1957); criminal procedure, HARCOURT, SWIFT'S LAW OF CRIMINAL PROCEDURE (2nd ed. 1969); HIEMSTRA, SUID-AFRIKAANSE STRAFPROSES (South African Criminal Procedure) (1967); delict, VAN DEN HEEVER, AQUILIAN DAMAGES IN SOUTH AFRICAN LAW, (1944); breach of promise and seduction, VAN DEN HEEVER, BREACH OF PROMISE AND SEDUCTION IN SOUTH AFRICAN LAW (1954); lease, VAN DEN HEEVER, THE PARTIARIAN AGRICULTURAL LEASE IN SOUTH AFRICAN LAW (1943); agency, DE VILLIERS AND MACINTOSH, THE LAW OF AGENCY IN SOUTH AFRICA (2nd ed. 1956); mercantile law, WILLE AND MILLIN, MERCANTILE LAW OF SOUTH AFRICA (16th ed. 1967); water law, several books by C. G. Hall, e.g. HALL, WATER RIGHTS (3rd ed. 1957); servitudes, HALL AND KELLAWAY, SERVITUDES (2nd ed. 1957); hire-purchase, DIEMONT, THE LAW OF HIRE-PURCHASE IN SOUTH AFRICA (3rd ed. 1964); wills, STEYN, THE LAW OF WILLS IN SOUTH AFRICA (2nd ed. 1948); the many volumes in various editions of MAASDORP, THE INSTITUTES OF SOUTH AFRICAN LAW that were published when the author was on the judiciary; municipal law, DÖNGES AND VAN WINSEN, MUNICIPAL LAW (2nd ed. 1953). But it is only fair to say that a few of these works were written originally when the author was in practice, and later editions were published after they had left the Bench. In one or two cases an edition was brought out by another hand when the author was on the judiciary, as with STEYN, DIE UITLEG VAN WETTE, the third and latest edition of which was prepared by Professor S.I.E. von Tonder (1963), Mr. Justice Steyn then being chief justice.

writing in the South African legal scene of today lies somewhere between its current statuses in the legal systems of England and France—not that these statuses today are very different.[72] Professor René David tells [73] us that in France *doctrine* is an important persuasive guide, giving perspective to court decisions, revealing the legal vocabulary and underlying ideas of legislators and of the methods through which law is understood and legislation interpreted. This midway position of *doctrine* in South Africa is possibly a result of our legal system, at least in private and criminal law, being essentially of a civil-law character, and yet, unlike almost all contemporary civil-law systems, not committed to codes; and to the judiciary's following, in a modified way, the English *stare decisis* principle and the English model of almost always in judgments setting out fully the facts found, the detailed methods employed in ascertaining the applicable rules of law and the result of the application of the law to the facts. A South African judgment does not resemble the typical Continental "pared and polished legal syllogism." [74]

In England one gains the belief [75] that in the course of this century greater reliance has been placed by judges on carefully reasoned publications, albeit they have no hesitation in unequivocally declaring that the conclusion of the most eminent writer is wrong if that is their considered conclusion.[76] The same impression is left by an examination of the South African law reports. If this conclusion is warranted, it must in part, if not wholly, be the result of a greater volume of publications and changed methods of legal tuition in which the teacher inculcates in his pupil—the future judge or practitioner—a respect for *la doctrine* or its surrogate,

---

72 See AMOS AND WALTON, INTRODUCTION TO FRENCH LAW 13–14 (2nd ed. 1963): "It would probably be fair to say that French legal writers play the same part as their English colleagues, but on a higher level of authority; they are cited where there is no other authority, they sometimes suggest new developments in the law and prolonged and persuasive criticism by them may change the law." See also MERRYMAN, THE CIVIL LAW TRADITION Chap. 12 (1969), who speaks of the "folklore" that "the legal scholar does the basic thinking for the legal system," and is critical of "the traditional model, which glorifies the scholar, flatters the legislator, and demeans the judge" (at 86, 91).

73 DAVID, LES GRANDS SYSTÈMES DE DROIT CONTEMPORAINS (2nd ed. 1966) *passim*; DAVID AND DEVRIES, THE FRENCH LEGAL SYSTEM 124 (1958).

74 ALLEN, LAW IN THE MAKING 180 (7th ed. 1964).

75 Cf. PHILLIPS, A FIRST BOOK OF ENGLISH LAW 195–96 (5th ed. 1965); R. J. AND M. G. WALKER, THE ENGLISH LEGAL SYSTEM 147–48 (3rd ed. 1972).

76 For example, Shenton v. Tyler [1939] Ch. 620; Button v. Director of Public Prosecutions [1966] A.C. 591.

the teacher's own ideas. That both these phenomena have occurred in South Africa cannot be doubted.

For a country with so small a population and so few judges, the output of legal writing is truly remarkable. Of its some twenty-one million inhabitants, few outside the white group of under four million participate in the administration of the law. In September, 1972, there were seventy-six judges of the Supreme Court (seventy-eight if those in the territory of South-West Africa are added); and, in round figures, 450 practising advocates (the counterparts of the barristers of England, being specialists in litigation and the giving of opinions, dependent on receiving briefs from the attorneys); 3,700 practising attorneys (the counterparts of the solicitors of England, being general practitioners without right of audience before the Supreme Court); and 150 academics in full-time university posts. Even if the public servants and others in the public sector are added—such as magistrates, prosecutors, legal advisers, and members of staff of the training section of the Department of Justice—the number of those engaged professionally in the legal process is very small. Yet the country sports two legal quarterlies of standing, the *South African Law Journal* and the *Tydskrif vir Hedendaagse Romeins-Hollandse Reg* (Journal of Contemporary Roman-Dutch Law); a volume, *Acta Juridica*, produced each year by the Faculty of Law of the University of Cape Town, devoted to monographs and articles of high quality; the *Annual Survey of South African Law*, published by the Faculty of Law of the University of the Witwatersrand, Johannesburg, since 1947, which is a critical review of legislation, case law and the administration of justice generally; several journals of professional bodies and the legal section of the public service; periodicals dealing with specialized topics such as taxation; a host of reviews of law schools, frequently with contributions by staff members; and an impressive range of legal textbooks.

Yet for all this output, there is much ground left for the would-be writer to till. Although there is a great deal to be said for the standpoint that the complexity of law today calls rather for detailed studies on special topics,[77] there is still room in South Africa for full-scale treatises on certain branches of law. On the general principles of contract there is no satisfactory major opus—the two volumes by the former chief justice,

[77] Twining, "Is Your Textbook Really Necessary?" 11 JOURNAL OF THE SOCIETY OF PUBLIC TEACHERS OF LAW, n.s., 81 (1970).

Sir John Wessels, originally published after his death, are sadly dated and unsystematic.[78] The splendid work of Professor R. G. McKerron on delict (tort) [79] does not profess to be an exhaustive analysis. The days of glory of *Mars on Insolvency* [80] are departed. It is beyond the age when facial surgery to restore its lost youth can be undertaken by editors. Despite its reputation and its appearance in a fourth edition in 1972, *Mackeurtan on the Sale of Goods* has far from preempted its field.[81] There are no up-to-date, detailed, scholarly works on the law of property, the law of succession, company law, or constitutional law (at least in English), to mention but some of the most striking examples. But care must be taken not to exaggerate the width of the gaps. There are some splendid, oft-cited studies in depth on certain parts of the law, such as Hahlo on *Husband and Wife*; Honoré on *Trusts*; Burchell, Hunt, and Milton's works in English, and De Wet and Swanepoel's work in Afrikaans, or criminal law; De Vos on *Verrykingsaanspreeklikheid* (Liability for Unjust Enrichment); Cowen on *Negotiable Instruments*; Spiro on *Parent and Child*; Steyn on *Uitleg van Wette* (Interpretation of Enactments); and, of a much earlier period, Melius de Villiers on *The Roman and Roman-Dutch Law of Injuries* (1899). There are also books that, though taking a broader sweep, still are more than mere practitioner's manuals—books that try to analyse and systematize in a constructive and scholarly way. Of this company are De Wet and Yeats's *Kontraktereg en Handelsreg* (Law of Contract and Mercantile Law); Hahlo and Kahn's *South Africa: The Development of Its Laws and Constitution* (in all humility); and— though it is much less critical in tone—Wille's *Principles of South African Law*. And the coverage of specific subjects is becoming ever greater, the leading publishers being willing to sink capital into even the most esoteric topic at the risk of almost certain loss: witness recent analyses of

78 The present edition is the second (1951). Professor R. H. Christie of the University of Rhodesia is preparing a new edition which may well turn out to be a new book. Professor A. J. Kerr's THE PRINCIPLES OF THE LAW OF CONTRACT (1967), while most helpful in parts, is selective and not exhaustive.
79 THE LAW OF DELICT (7th ed. 1970). In any event, the author is out of sympathy with the recent approach of the Appellate Division. There is also a work in Afrikaans, VAN DER MERWE & OLIVIER, DIE ONREGMATIGE DAAD IN DIE SUID-AFRIKAANS REG (Delict in South African Law) (2nd ed. 1970), but this again is not a large treatise. Furthermore, it is heterodoxical in many parts.
80 MARS, THE LAW OF INSOLVENCY IN SOUTH AFRICA (6th ed. 1968).
81 It would be idle to pretend that NORMAN, LAW OF PURCHASE AND SALE (3rd ed. 1961), is a really satisfactory book.

contract in South African private international law,[82] domicile,[83] and the legal position of a company director.[84]

In fine, the situation of legal literature in South Africa is a fairly happy one. It is not difficult to secure publication of a piece of work of satisfactory standard even if it is of a highly specialized character. There are many openings for analysis and research. Thereby writing is encouraged and some of the most able lawyers are attracted to the groves of academe. In the legal journals, reviews of books are often detailed and, if this is called for, sharp, which leads to constant improvement of quality. Finally, a writer justifiably feels that if he has something to contribute it may well, when the time comes, be cited by counsel and (at least if it is couched in polite terms) accepted by the courts. A recent decision [85] of

[82] VAN ROOYEN, DIE KONTRAK IN DIE SUID-AFRIKAANSE INTERNASIONALE PRIVAATREG (1972).
[83] KAHN, THE SOUTH AFRICAN LAW OF DOMICILE OF NATURAL PERSONS (1972).
[84] NAUDÉ, DIE REGSPOSISIE VAN DIE MAATSKAPPYDIREKTEUR (1970).
[85] The recently retired chief justice, Dr. the Hon. L. C. Steyn, in an extracurial address delivered when he was chief justice, made this comment (see 30 T.H.R-H.R. 105 [1967]):

> There is an unmistakable tendency, not a general one, I am glad to say, but in some of the criticisms of our courts, past and current, towards an irritated acidity, a somewhat overbearing snappishness, in short, towards offensiveness; a tendency to belittle and disparage, to make judges look ridiculous. At times the authors I have in mind seem to be as cross as two sticks, and intent upon showing their teeth in no uncertain way. If their purpose is to persuade, let me tell them as plainly as I can that judges are not impressed by this kind of criticism. If you want to persuade, don't disparage. If you do, you have lost your argument before you have started, and your effort is going to be fruitless. If your purpose is not merely to persuade, but also to satisfy your own ego, as I sometimes suspect, you will, if you live long enough, sooner or later find out that you cannot raise yourself by pushing somebody else down. In our profession there is only one way to put your differences, if you want to achieve any results. It is the time-honoured *suaviter in modo, fortiter in re.* Manner is no substitute for substance, and an offensive tone can be a fatal clog on the persuasiveness of any argument, however convincing it would be in better language. If you want to be heard, as you presumably do, don't tell us, in effect, if not in so many words, that we are so ignorant and stupid that we should not be on the bench. In addition, whatever satisfaction you may derive from it, you do your own profession no good service by promoting disrespect for the judiciary.

The present chief justice, the Hon. N. Ogilvie Thompson, in a speech in 1971 said (see 89 S.A.L.J. 32–33 [1972]):

> In almost every difficult legal problem—and there are many such which come before the courts—there exist areas in which there is room for legitimate difference of opinion. If an academic or practising lawyer differs from the legal reasoning in or conclusion of a judgment, it is of course his right to say so. Judges are the last people to regard their judgments as always being infallibly correct. That

the highest court has borne this out. In 1972 the Appellate Division dealt generously with *doctrine* when, for the first time, it was faced crisply with the problem of what a court is to do in the absence of a binding source of South African law specifically on the legal point before it.[86] Holmes JA, who delivered the unanimous judgment of five judges of appeal, accepted the submissions made in Hahlo and Kahn's *The South African Legal System and Its Background*; he concluded that there should be "reference to relevant and analogous material in Roman law and Roman-Dutch law, in decided cases, and in articles by legal writers of repute."[87] (The word "articles" should, no doubt, be read *secundum subjectam materiam* so as to embrace all types of legal writing.)

As was seen, in the classical Roman-Dutch law of eighteenth- and early nineteenth-century Holland the attitude was taken that a judge should follow a previous decision arrived at after due deliberation, unless, after careful consideration, he concluded that there was a convincing

---

others may hold a different view on a particular legal problem is inherent in the procedure of appeal to a higher court familiar to, and accepted by, all lawyers. Rare indeed is the judge who has never been reversed on appeal. But, that apart, judges know the difficulties all too well, and they fully appreciate how instructive and helpful legitimate criticism can be. I would, however, merely at the same time add that, although in the past the fact has not always apparently been appreciated by certain writers, legitimate criticism loses nothing by being courteously expressed. Having said that, I am happy to record that I believe I am correct in thinking that this last-mentioned fact would appear to be more generally recognized today.

One retired judge of appeal, Dr. the Hon. C. G. Hall, has a view which does not appear to be shared by his brethren, all of whom seem to welcome constructive, courteous criticism of their judgment. He said in the preface to the eighth edition of IV A. F. S. Maasdorp's *The Institutes of South African Law* (The Law of Delicts and the Dissolution of Obligations) (1972): "The decisions of the Appellate Division are binding upon all the superior and inferior courts of the Republic. Accordingly no criticism of those decisions is to be found in the four volumes of the Institutes. That field is left clear to those of the university professors who employ this method of displaying their erudition.

Having myself been a member of that honourable tribunal, I take the gravest exception to those legal pundits who decry its decisions and apparently regard them as being the best guesses of the court of ultimate conjecture."

86 Government of the Republic of South Africa v. Ngubane 1972 (2) S.A. 601 (A.D.).
87 At 606. The conclusion was reached that a claim for damages for personal injury (including pain and suffering, disfigurement, and loss of the amenities of life), as contrasted with a claim for patrimonial loss, is not capable of cession before *litis contestatio*.

reason that it was incorrect. At the Cape itself the Raad van Justitie (Court of Justice) gave no reasons for decisions [88] and there could hardly be said to be a principle *stare decisis*.

It was only some time after the First Charter of Justice of 1827 introduced a professionally qualified Bench—the Supreme Court—and English judicial procedure, that a doctrine of judicial precedent can be said to have come into being at the Cape.[89] To all intents and purposes, systematic law reporting commenced in the colony only in 1870; and probably the bonds of precedent even for some years after that were fairly loose in practice. But then in 1880 and 1890 the great chief justice, Sir Henry de Villiers, explicitly stated [90] that lower courts had to follow the Supreme Court unless it were reversed or overruled by the Privy Council; and so should the Supreme Court follow itself, unless it were satisfied that what it had previously pronounced was clearly wrong. The reasons given for this principle *stare decisis* were expediency and its equity in giving expression to justifiable expectations.

There were those who deplored the birth of a doctrine of judicial precedent sired by the Bench. The legal system, they foresaw, would degenerate into one of case law, and the old authorities would become ever more disregarded.[91] Yet the Cape attitude was taken even in the independent South African Republic (Transvaal), with a judiciary headed by a judge so learned in black-letter law, Kotzé CJ.[92]

No change, of course, occurred after the conquest of the South African Republic and Orange Free State by the British in the Anglo-Boer War (1899–1902). By then it had become the orthodox view that a single judge was in principle bound by the *ratio decidendi* of the judgment of a court of two or more judges.

88 See Visagie, "Die Regsbedeling aan die Kaap onder die V.O.C." (The Administration of Law at the Cape under the Dutch East India Company), ACTA JURIDICA 118 at 150 (1963), and REGSPLEGING EN REG AAN DIE KAAP VAN 1652 TOT 1806 (The Administration of Justice at the Cape from 1652 to 1806) 70 (1969).
89 For a fuller discussion of this doctrine than is possible here, see Kahn, "The Rules of Precedent Applied in South African Courts," 84 S.A.L.J. 43–55, 175–93, 308–30 (1967).
90 In R. v. Strydom (1880) 1 S.C. 60 at 61; Jacobson v. Nitch (1890) 7 S.C. 174 at 178.
91 See "J. F. v. O: Some Remarks on the Study of Roman-Dutch Law," in 10 CAPE L. J. 214 (1893); W. R. Bisschop in his introductory note to THE ROMAN-DUTCH LAW AS ADMINISTERED IN SOUTH AFRICA (1912).
92 Brown v. Leyds NO (1897) 4 Off. Rep. 17 at 24. Kotzé CJ cited Kent's COMMENTARIES and Marshall CJ in Marbury v. Madison (1803) 1 Cranch 137 at 163.

Before the unification of the four colonies brought about on May 31, 1960, when the South Africa Act of 1909 [93] came into force, each colony had its own Supreme Court structure. That of the Transvaal may be used as an illustration. The Transvaal Supreme Court had colonial-wide jurisdiction both at first instance (where a single judge sat) and on appeal (where two or three judges sat, according to the circumstances). The Witwatersrand High Court, though having the same judges as the Transvaal Supreme Court, had jurisdiction confined to the area of the goldfields (the Witwatersrand—ridge of white waters) and then concurrently with the Supreme Court and only at first instance. Thus a single judge of either division was bound by the *ratio* of a decision of a single judge of either division, unless he was convinced it was wrong, and was absolutely bound by the *ratio* of a decision of a two- or three-judge court of the Supreme Court. In principle, a two-judge court of the Supreme Court was absolutely bound by the *ratio* of a decision of a three-judge court of that tribunal. Every court was absolutely bound by a decision of the Privy Council that was in point. As between the colonies the judgments of the various courts were only of persuasive force, but naturally considerably so.

The changes produced by the South Africa Act were minimal. The statute created a Supreme Court of South Africa, with the Appellate Division at its apex, clothed with appeal jurisdiction but no original jurisdiction. The superior courts of the four colonies became provincial divisions of the Supreme Courts, lineal descendants of their colonial predecessors, with their satellite local divisions. Each provincial division was virtually an *imperium* of its own. The link between them was simply a common allegiance to the Appellate Division. And so it has basically remained, despite the carving out of the area of the Cape Province of two new provincial (sic) divisions—the Eastern Cape Division in 1957 [94] and the Northern Cape Division in 1969 [95]—and the inclusion in the Supreme Court in 1959 of the South-West Africa Division,[96] also with the status of a provincial division.

---

93 7 Edw. 7 c 9 (1907).
94 General Law Amendment Act 68 of 1957 section 2(1)(a), now superseded by the Supreme Court Act 59 of 1959 section 1(ix).
95 Establishment of the Northern Cape Division of the Supreme Court of South Africa Act 15 of 1969.
96 Supreme Court Act 59 of 1959 section 1(ix). From 1919 it had been the High Court of South-West Africa (Proc. 21 of 1919 [S.W.A.]).

Doctrine and Judicial Decisions in South Africa | 257

The fairly settled rules of precedent of today have emerged out of practice without much supporting judicial reasoning. Even such notable exponents of Roman-Dutch law as the late Mr. Justice F. P. van den Heever, judge of appeal, and the former chief justice, Mr. Justice L. C. Steyn, have emphasized the need to abide by the principle of abiding by previous rulings.[97] Such reasons as have been advanced have all been confined to the public's need for certainty in the law, the protection of vested rights, the giving of expression to legitimate expectations, and the upholding of the dignity of the court. There are, of course, more elaborate and further advantages. The private individual is enabled to plan his actions with some confidence as to their legal effects. The threat of litigation, expensive both to the public and private purse, is reduced, and if it takes place, often it is on a confined issue of fact only. Judicial officers are compelled to keep to settled rules, for they are normally required to give reasons for their decisions, and through their being bound by these rules the possibility is reduced of a wrong decision's being reached through lack of legal knowledge or intellectual capacity or through partiality, caprice, or prejudice. In summary, the requirement *stare decisis* holds out promise of certainty, predictability, reliability, equality, uniformity, economy, and convenience. But these very advantages can be at the cost of the perpetuation of erroneous rules or the lack of adaptation of the law to changing times and mores, the stifling of scientific development. From what follows it will not appear immodest to claim that the doctrine of precedent in South Africa has attained an admirable position between undesirable rigidity and undisciplined looseness. Unexpressed causes of the detailed South African rules of judicial precedent must include the existence from 1827 to 1950 of appeals to the Judicial Committee of the Privy Council, sitting in London, which tacitly, if not expressly, looked to the courts of the country from which an appeal was brought to follow its judgment, but which, on the other hand, did not (as did the House of Lords from 1861 [98] to 1966) [99] regard itself as abso-

---

[97] R. v. Sibiya 1955 (4) S.A. 247 (A.D.) at 265 (Mr. Justice F. P. van den Heever); Fellner v. Minister of the Interior 1954 (4) S.A. 523 (A.D.) at 529 and R. v. Sillas 1959 (4) S.A. 305 (A.D.) at 311 (Mr. Justice L. C. Steyn).
[98] Beamish v. Beamish (1861) 9 H.L.C. 274.
[99] With the historic pronouncement of Lord Gardiner LC that the Appeal Committee of the House of Lords would depart from an earlier decision "when it appears right to do so."

lutely bound by its own decisions; the English nature of so much of legal procedure and practice; the manning of the Bench mainly from the ranks of leading practising advocates, leading to a judiciary that had confidence in itself and its predecessors and that enjoyed the respect of the legal profession, as a result of which a reasonably strict doctrine of judicial precedent appeared natural; and the desire to reach harbour once the turbulent waters of conflicting old authorities had been crossed.

The basic principles of the doctrine of precedent today are twofold: first, a provincial division of the Supreme Court (together with its local division or divisions) is absolutely bound by the *ratio* of the decision of a higher court or a larger court on its own level in the hierarchy, in that order, unless the decision was given *per incuriam* (as, for instance, where a governing enactment or precedent was overlooked) or there is subsequent overriding legislation; secondly, the Appellate Division and a provincial (including a satellite local) division bench of the same size will follow its own past decision unless it is satisfied it is clearly wrong, in which event it will refuse to abide by it and so in effect will overrule it. Lower courts (called inferior courts, and being mainly magistrates' courts) abide by superior-court precedents but do not create precedents of their own.

To follow the detailed rules of precedent in South Africa it is necessary to glance initially at the pyramidical judicial structure. Now that appeals to the Privy Council have gone, at the apex stands the Appellate Division of the Supreme Court, composed of a chief justice and ten judges of appeal. All eleven members must sit in a case involving the validity of an Act of Parliament. Otherwise the court almost always sits with the mimimum number permitted by the governing legislation, the quorum. This consists of five judges in a civil appeal and three[100] in a criminal appeal.

On the next rung are the seven provincial divisions—the Cape; Transvaal; Orange Free State and Natal Provincial Divisions; and the Eastern Cape, Northern Cape, and South-West Africa Division. Three of these, it will be seen, have jurisdiction over only part of a province (the Cape) and the area of one, the South-West Africa Division, is not within the Republic at all but covers an associated territory. The term "provincial" is

---

100 Five when the appeal is from a special criminal court constituted under section 112 of the Criminal Procedure Act 56 of 1955. See Note 101 below.

Doctrine and Judicial Decisions in South Africa | 259

used not to denote geographical boundaries but status, namely, the competency to hear appeals from lower courts and to have local divisions. Every circuit court of a provincial division is a local division; and in addition the Transvaal and Natal Provincial Divisions each has a permanent local division with concurrent jurisdiction over part of its area—the Witwatersrand and Durban and Coast Local Divisions respectively. Provincial divisions and their local divisions have the same judges.

Spoiling this neat pattern is the special criminal court of two or three judges that may be constituted ad hoc to hear charges of treason, sedition, and like crimes.[101] Though also of superior status it is not a provincial or local division of the Supreme Court.

In the area of each provincial division there is a water court [102] with a judge deputed from among the judges of the particular division.

Those are certainly the main, and—except for the court of the Commissioner of Patents [103]—the only superior courts.

The principal lower courts are those of magistrates. There are over 250 magisterial districts, each with a court composed of at least one magistrate, hearing civil and criminal cases with limited jurisdiction. No district crosses the boundaries of provincial divisions of the Supreme Court. In addition the country is divided into several magisterial regional divisions, some of which do straddle these boundaries.[104] A regional division has competency in criminal cases only, but its jurisdiction goes beyond that of a district magistrate's court.

Though appeals from the Appellate Division to the Privy Council ceased to be possible after 1950,[105] past judgments (strictly opinions, as in theory it simply advises the sovereign) of that body continue to have

---

101 Under section 112 of the Criminal Procedure Act 1955. The court was initially constituted by Act 27 of 1914 to avoid the then jury system. That system was gradually reduced in scope and recently was completely abolished, but section 112 was allowed to remain. The draft of the new Criminal Procedure Bill retains the provision.
102 Water Act 54 of 1956 ch. IV.
103 Patents Act 37 of 1952 sections 16–19. See Gentiruco A.G. v. Firestone (S.A.) (Pty.) Ltd. 1972 (1) S.A. 589 (A.D.). The presiding officer is a Transvaal judge deputed by the judge president of the Transvaal.
104 For example, those of the Orange Free State and Griqualand West (in the area of the Northern Cape Division). See Government Notices 794 of 1964, 1651 of 1968 and 1242 of 1970.
105 Privy Council Appeals Act 16 of 1950.

a certain force. Up to 1950[106] all South African courts considered themselves absolutely bound by the *ratio*[107] of a Privy Council judgment, at least (a) where the appeal was from a court in South Africa, or another country (such as Ceylon or Southern Rhodesia) on a matter of Roman-Dutch law—possibly with the reservations that the appropriate authorities had been considered[108] (the Committee rarely distinguished itself as an analyst of the old authorities) and the particular rule had been received in South Africa; and (b) where the issue was the meaning of a provision in a South African enactment and the Privy Council had passed on the meaning of some other legislative provision essentially identical,[109] unless Roman-Dutch principles called for a different interpretation.[110]

Since the abolition of Privy Council appeals these pre-1950 binding decisions have assumed the status of decisions of the Appellate Division. So that court decided in *John Bell & Co Ltd v Esselen*;[111] and in the process it gave to itself the capacity that the Privy Council had, of rejecting a decision of that body it found to be incorrect. As will have become apparent, the Appellate Division will not necessarily invoke that capacity, no more than it will with one of its own decisions. If the call of legal certainty or protection of assumed vested rights is loud and clear, it will probably be heeded, and the past be left undisturbed. Mr. Justice F. P. van den Heever, Rhadamanthus-like, had extracurially condemned

106 See Welsh, "The Privy Council Appeals Act, 1950," 67 S.A.L.J. 227 (1950).
107 *Obiter dicta* could be and sometimes were disregarded: e.g. the view expressed in Eastern & South African Telegraph Co. v Cape Town Tramways Companies Ltd. [1902] A.C. 381 (P.C.) that the rule of strict liability for damage caused by an inherently dangerous thing brought on the land was "not inconsistent with the Roman-Dutch law" (at 393–94). This gratuitous erroneous remark has been condemned on several occasions by South African courts. But a *ratio decidendi* was conclusive: e.g. Le Mesurier v. Le Mesurier [1895] A.C. 517 (P.C.), on appeal from Ceylon, settled common-law divorce jurisdiction in South Africa in the court of the husband's domicile at institution of proceedings: see Murphy v. Murphy 1902 T.S. 179 at 182.
108 Cf. Conradie v. Rossouw 1919 A.D. 279 at 286; McCullogh v. Fernwood Estate Ltd. 1920 A.D. at 208, 217.
109 De Waal NO v. North Bay Canning Co. Ltd. 1921 A.D. 521 at 524, 528, 533; Perm-us (Pty.) Ltd. v. Maeder 1939 C.P.D. 183.
110 Estate Wege v. Strauss 1932 A.D. 76 at 80–81.
111 1954 (1) S.A. 147 (A.D.). It refused to follow a Privy Council decision on appeal from Ceylon, finding that no Roman-Dutch authority had been cited and that the case had been incorrectly decided. The absence of Roman-Dutch authority, it might be pointed out, would probably have justified disregarding the decision even before 1950.

Doctrine and Judicial Decisions in South Africa | 261

the Privy Council's equation[112] of the Roman-Dutch rules relating to the contractual penalty with the English law dichotomy of liquidated damages and penalty, and wished to expel it from Elysium. But when, in 1953, as a judge of appeal he was given the opportunity of so doing, he concluded that it was too late.[113] The removal had eventually to be effected by the legislature,[114] able to move without touching on past transactions.

Privy Council decisions rendered after the abolition of the appeal have only persuasive force in South Africa. Though there is nothing substantial at present to justify this conclusion, such force will as a rule probably be exercised most strongly by judgments from a Roman-Dutch jurisdiction or interpreting an enactment identical to the one before the South African tribunal.

If it be asked what influence the Privy Council appeal had on the elucidation and development of South African law, the answer is little, and of that little, part was baneful. It is improbable that anything will be found in the pre-1950 reports, say, on appeal from Ceylon, that has not already become settled law or been discarded in South Africa.[115]

For all practical purposes today, the ultimate tribunal is the Appellate Division. Some seventy to eighty of its judgments are printed in the South African Law Reports each year.[116] In two statutes the binding force of certain decisions of this highest court is expressed or implied. Section 385 of the Criminal Procedure Act[117] says that if the minister of justice is doubtful of the correctness of the decision of a superior court on a point of law in a criminal case, on his application the Appellate Division may order a special case to be argued before it, its decision to be "for the future

---

112 Pearl Assurance Co. Ltd. v. Union Government 1934 A.D. 560, [1934] A.C. 570 (P.C.).
113 Tobacco Manufacturers Committee v. Jacob Green & Sons 1953 (3) S.A. 480 (A.D.) at 493.
114 Conventional Penalties Act 15 of 1962.
115 See Kahn, "The End of Privy Council Appeals from Ceylon," 89 S.A.L.J. 241 (1972).
116 A few additional ones are sometimes produced in synoptic form in the digest of reports called Prentice-Hall Weekly Legal Service. Such others as are rendered but are not considered worthy of publication by the editors of the reports (almost always because they apply settled law to the facts) are available to lawyers, at the cost of some digging in libraries and government offices. Rare indeed is the occasion in which one of them is cited to the court.
117 56 of 1955. A similar provision existed from 1917.

guidance of all courts." Once or twice in a decade this provision is invoked.[118] Although some nice arguments could be advanced that such a pronouncement, not being based on actual facts, is incapable of producing a *ratio decidendi*, and, furthermore, the expression "future guidance" is sagging at the knees with weakness, no one has considered that the last word on the point will not have been uttered by the Appellate Division. Then section 113 of the Magistrates' Courts Act of 1944[119] states that where a provincial or local division of the Supreme Court in one province gives an interpretation of that act in conflict with the interpretation of a division in another province, the minister may cause a special case to be argued before the Appellate Division, whose "ruling shall thereafter be deemed by all other courts to be the true interpretation of such provision." The section will be seen to be of very limited range; and in any event a reported case of its application cannot be found.

Thus in the vast majority of instances the binding quality of the *ratio decidendi* of a decision of the Appellate Division on other courts cannot be traced to legislation. But there is no doubt that that tribunal expects all lower courts to follow its pronouncements on the law, no matter what the strength of its bench in any case; though the right to criticize is not denied.[120] In two circumstances only is freedom granted from this obligation to follow my leader. The first, and obvious, one is where a subsequent enactment has altered the ruling. The second one is where the Appellate Division acted *per incuriam*, incuria in this context comprehending failure to notice governing legislation[121] and, possibly, creating a precedent *sub silentio*, through failure to identify the particular un-

---

118 Recent cases are Ex parte Minister of Justice: In re State v. Van Wyk 1967 (1) S.A. 488 (A.D.), Ex parte Minister of Justice: In re State v. Grotjohn 1970 (2) S.A. 355 (A.D.) and Ex parte die Minister van Justisie: In re Staat v. De Bruin 1972 (2) S.A. 623 (A.D.).
119 32 of 1944. A similar provision existed from 1917. The wording today is inapt. The Cape Province contains three provincial divisions and the section does not deal with conflicting interpretations among them.
120 See, especially, Collett v. Priest 1931 A.D. 290 at 297; see also Ex parte Sadie 1940 A.D. 26 at 30; Harris v. Minister of the Interior 1952 (2) S.A. 428 (A.D.) at 452; R. v. Lusu 1953 (2) S.A. 484 (A.D.) at 491–92. Lower courts have often acknowledged this duty: e.g. R. v. B & H 1953 (2) S.A. 344 (C.) at 350.
121 This has occurred very infrequently. An illustration is afforded by Natalite Motor Spirit Co. v. Davies 1923 A.D. 1 at 11–13, disregarded for this reason by the Commissioner of Patents (who has the status of a single judge sitting in a provincial division) in, inter alia, Hard Metals Ltd. v. Sandvikens Jernverks Aktiebolaget, reported in PATENT JOURNAL 13–14 (January 8, 1958).

argued and unconsidered point of law that the decision on the facts logically involved.¹²²

It is the *ratio decidendi*, a pronouncement of law, best translated as the principle of the decision, and not any *obiter dictum*, a remark made in passing, that is binding. The difficult question of isolating the *ratio* is beyond the scope of this essay. Suffice it to say that every now and then a lower court finds itself struggling to bring this elusive attribute into focus or to determine whether the *ratio* of one Appellate Division decision is inconsistent with that of an earlier one, with the result (apparently, at least) that the court has overruled itself, or to decide whether the interpretation of enactment A by the highest court binds a lower court in its construction of enactment B that is in similar but not identical terms. Experience—the little of it that there has been—has taught that in case of doubt a judge or magistrate is well advised to find a statement of the Appellate Division *ratio* rather than *obiter dictum*.¹²³

No judicial officer, not even a magistrate, is in principle bound by any *obiter dictum*. Albeit it has fallen from the lips of all members of an Appellate Division court,¹²⁴ it could be disregarded. In fact, however, if it has been carefully reasoned, such a dictum will almost certainly be respected. A judge recently referred to its "massive persuasiveness." ¹²⁵ And a holding or even an *obiter dictum* of a single judge in a special concurring or a dissenting judgment (on an issue not considered by the majority) may in a particular instance prove persuasive. Something turns here on the stature of the judge, the quality of his analysis and the strength of conviction expressed in the wording of the opinion.

Unlike the House of Lords at one time, but like the Privy Council, the Appellate Division has never considered itself as absolutely bound by its own decisions (absent *incuria* or later legislation), for, as it has said,¹²⁶ the Roman-Dutch law does not warrant this attitude. Yet it is generally loath to overrule itself, for meantime lower courts may have followed its ruling, members of the legal profession and public have relied

---

122 For an example of such a precedent, see Ex parte Steyn 1967 (1) S.A. 610 (R.A.D.) at 613. At most it is of weak persuasive influence.
123 See, e.g., Collett v. Priest 1931 A.D. 290 at 298; Pretoria City Council v. Levinson 1939 (3) S.A. 305 (A.D.).
124 Petersen v. Jajbhay 1940 T.P.D. 182 at 185.
125 Miller J in Modelay v. Zeeman 1968 (2) S.A. 792 (D.) at 795.
126 Fellner v. Minister of the Interior 1954 (4) S.A. 523 (A.D.) at 530.

on it, and rights and duties have been believed to derive from it.[127] The Appellate Division normally considers that sound practice calls on it to refuse to reopen a legal question it answered earlier, in the absence of special circumstances; and in all cases when it does reconsider it, it must, before it will change its mind, be quite clear that in the past it had erred.[128] Neither the size of the bench on the previous occasion nor (unlike the position in the United States) the fact that it was split will signify, provided a ratio decidendi can be abstracted.[129] Such a *ratio* requires the concurrence of the majority of members of the particular bench, not a mere majority of the majority.[130]

Criteria of equity are not without influence; our ultimate tribunal will be particularly disinclined to overrule itself where this would disturb legal relationships believed to exist—thus it is unlikely to abandon the rules that a contract through the post is made when the letter of acceptance is posted [131] and that race and faith clauses in wills are valid,[132] but it may well hold that it ruled incorrectly that there is no general action based on unjust enrichment; [133] it will be inclined to overrule itself if its earlier incorrect decision took away rights from some persons, without giving others additional (even though unwarranted) rights, as, for instance, where it unjustly deprived citizens of the franchise.[134] And if its previous conclusion was arrived at without full argument or consideration, the Appellate Division, in common with courts in the United States and many other countries, will not look so askance at a request to it to change its mind.[135]

127 See, e.g., Habib Motan v. Transvaal Government 1964 T.S. 404 at 421.
128 Collett v. Priest 1931 A.D. 290 at 297, 301; Bloemfontein Town Council v. Richter 1938 A.D. 195 at 232.
129 Fellner v. Minister of the Interior 1954 (4) S.A. 523 (A.D.) at 538.
130 Fellner case (see Note 129 above).
131 Kergeulen Sealing and Whaling Co. Ltd. v. Commissioner for Inland Revenue 1939 A.D. 487. This "expedition" theory of contracting through the post has received considerable adverse comment by South African legal writers.
132 Aaronson v. Estate Hart 1950 (1) S.A. 539 (A.D.), the subject of devastating criticism based on Roman-Dutch authorities by C. P. Joubert, "Jewish Faith and Race Clauses in Roman-Dutch Law," 85 S.A.L.J. 402 (1968).
133 Nortje v. Pool NO 1966 (3) S.A. 96 (A.D.), convincingly criticized as contrary to Roman-Dutch law by J. E. Scholtens, "The General Enrichment Action That Was," 83 S.A.L.J. 391 (1966).
134 Harris v. Minister of the Interior 1952 (2) S.A. 248 (A.D.) at 454, 472.
135 Rohrs v. Newmarch 1915 A.D. 108; R. v. Nxumalo 1939 A.D. 580 at 583; Harris v. Minister of the Interior 1952 (2) S.A. 428 (A.D.) at 471; Standard Finance Corporation of South Africa Ltd. v. Greenstein 1964 (3) S.A. 573 at 578.

To *obiter dicta* of its own or one of its members the highest court will pay respectful attention, but consider itself in principle not bound. In practice its attitude will vary with the circumstances. In *Glazer v. Glazer, N.O.*[136] the Appellate Division, after close reasoning based on a minute examination of the Roman-Dutch authorities, concluded that the chances of its holding that a surviving spouse had a maintenance claim against the estate of the first-dying spouse were so slender that it was not justified in condoning a late appeal against the decision of a lower court that no claim lay. *Obiter dictum* this conclusion may be in the strict sense, but it is difficult to believe that the court would consider it other than a firm pronouncement on the law. On the other, a stray remark made en passant by a judge of appeal will be disavowed without hesitation if found to be wrong: as, for instance, happened to the statement that an accused has to establish a defence of intoxication, showing the absence of the requisite intention.[137]

It hardly needs stating that the Appellate Division, no more than a lower court, will not regard itself as bound by one of its decisions where it was overruled by legislation or it was rendered *per incuriam*. Incuria here would include overlooking a governing enactment or one of its own decisions. In the last-mentioned event the attitude taken is that neither the earlier nor the later decision should be given preference, but the one now considered to be correct[138]—an attitude shared by provincial and local divisions within their particular spheres.[139] This seems too restrictive an approach, however. If the court is satisfied that no previous decision of its own is correct, it must surely be free now to make what it considers to be the right pronouncement.

If the Appellate Division is faced only with a decision or series of decisions of superior courts lower in the hierarchy, it starts again with the basic rule that it is untrammelled. In actual fact the matter proves not so

---

136 1963 (4) S.A. 694 (A.D.).
137 R. v. Kaukakani 1947 (2) S.A. 847 (A.D.), disapproved in R. v. Pethla 1956 (4) S.A. 605 (A.D.).
138 R. v. Sillas 1959 (4) S.A. 305 (A.D.) at 511. The court was faced with conflicting decisions in R. v. Banksbaird 1952 (4) S.A. 512 (A.D.) and R. v. Mazibuko 1958 (4) S.A. 353 (A.D.), in the last-mentioned of which the first-mentioned had been overlooked, probably partly owing to incomplete indexing in the reports.
139 R. v. Mnguni 1958 (4) S.A. 320 (T.); Manganese Corporation Ltd. v. South African Manganese Ltd. 1964 (2) S.A. 185 (W.).

simple. As was seen, the highest court from its inception considered that one of its duties was to harmonize the common law (that is, the non-legislative rules), if feasible in accordance with Roman-Dutch legal principles and rules, and to produce uniformity of interpretation of any piece of legislation.[140] If a decision of a lower court is wrong and produces injustice, or is simply wrong and its correction would not work retrospectively, the Appellate Division will not hesitate to reverse or overrule it.[141]

If reversal or overruling would entail the upsetting of past transactions, the Appellate Division will move with circumspection. Sometimes, in order to produce uniformity of law, it will have no option but to uphold the view of some divisions and reject that of others, as happened, it has been shown, with the rejection in 1919 of the peculiar meaning attached by the Cape courts to the requirement of *justa causa* in contract. In other cases essentially the same agonizing decision may have to be made as with the restoration of a rule of Roman-Dutch law, the subject of earlier discussion. In the interests of justice, it may be found necessary to resist the attraction of wiping out the past and putting the law into its correct position. Of a certainty there are many instances—a very recent one, concerned with agency for an undisclosed principal, was discussed earlier—in which the Appellate Division has said that it felt compelled to endorse a catena of decisions of lower tribunals on which the public had relied in making contracts and settling its affairs, no matter that it felt the rule they enunciated was wrong. The longer and more widespread such decisions, the less inclined seems the highest court to declare them incorrect.[142] But every now and then the Appellate Division flatly declares that the lower tribunals went along a false trail, and must be put in the right direction, no matter what the immediate cost to the public. It is easier for it to correct lower courts than itself: with the former the matter is at large; with itself it must be quite satisfied that it was in error.

Each provincial division (together with its related local divisions) continued after union in 1910 to regard itself, so far as other such divisions

---

140 See Webster v. Ellison 1911 A.D. 73 at 92–93.
141 Webster v. Ellison (see Note 140 above); Spencer v. Gostelow 1920 A.D. 617 at 631, 643; Union Government v. Rosenberg (Pty.) Ltd. 1946 A.D. 120; Bydawell v. Chapman NO 1953 (3) S.A. 514 (A.D.).
142 It will be remembered that there is no possibility of a court's declaring its decision to be operative only in the future or only to future acts, facts, events, or transactions.

went, as autonomous as the colonial superior court that was its ancestor. The creation of the three new provincial divisions of the Eastern Cape, Northern Cape, and South-West Africa, in 1957, 1969, 1959 respectively, simply added three more little empires to the original four. None feels under any high duty to follow a decision of one of its fellows. Within each division the same rules obtain as immediately before union. They have already been adumbrated. *In summa*, subject to there being no subsequent overriding legislation or decision and subject to the *incuria* doctrine,[143] a court must follow a larger court and otherwise, unless satisfied it was clearly wrong, a court of equal size.

Looking at the reverse situation, a two- or three-judge court will not feel under compulsion to follow the decision of a single-judge court within its sphere. It will, however, pay it respectful attention—very respectful at times where the judge was of eminence [144]—and may find it of persuasive force. And it will be disinclined to discard a long line of single-court judgments all in accord. In principle, the size of the court being cardinal, the same should hold for a three-judge court in relation to a two-judge court.[145]

Decisions of other provincial divisions (with their linked local divisions) are only of persuasive force; and the larger the other court and the more eminent its members, the more persuasive will its judgment normally be. A judge sitting alone in the Transvaal Provincial Division, for instance, may well reject a decision of a three-judge court of the Cape Provincial Division. This has happened on a number of occasions. But dicta are to be found that judges should bear in mind the desirability of uniformity in the law throughout the country.[146]

A decision of a magistrate's court does not in any way establish a precedent or even have persuasive force, except possibly unofficially within the magistracy itself. A magistrate, however, is bound by the principles behind the exhortation *stare decisis*. He must follow decisions of the

---

143 The *incuria* doctrine was invoked by a court of the same size in Van den Berg v. Scholtz 1938 T.P.D. 129, where R. v. Schoombie 1924 T.P.D. 481 was disregarded as being inconsistent with the Appellate Division decision of R. v. Scheepers 1915 A.D. 337. See State v. Meeuwis 1970 (4) S.A. 532 (T.) at 533–34.
144 As, for example, Mr. Justice Innes. See Botha v. Soocher 1941 T.P.D. 245 at 247.
145 But the matter is not beyond debate. See HAHLO AND KAHN, LEGAL SYSTEM 254.
146 For example, Halse v. Warwick 1931 C.P.D. 233 at 239; R. v. Ndedwa 1959 (3) S.A. 24 (E.) at 28–29.

Supreme Court, in the order of their precedence within his area of jurisdiction. If, as with some regional courts, his area eats into the areas of two or more provincial divisions, it would appear that he should associate himself with the division within whose area he is trying the case.[147] Thus his primary allegiance is to its provincial or local division. If needs be, he must follow one of its single-judge decisions in preference to a full-bench decision of another superior court.[148] When faced with conflicting decisions of benches of equal size in his own area, he should in principle apply the latest one. And finally, if there is no Supreme Court decision in his area, it would appear that he should regard himself as bound by decisions of other divisions, in order of the size of the court, and if two or more courts of the largest size conflict, the latest of their decisions. For in the final resort magistrates' courts belong to a country-wide organization of inferior courts. Primary allegiance to the local superior court should not disguise a secondary allegiance to other superior courts.

Finally, a brief consideration of some odd situations.

The special criminal court composed under section 112 of the Criminal Procedure Act does not fall within the framework of provincial and local divisions and is bound only by the Appellate Division.[149]

Each of the seven water courts is a separate enclave, bound only by the Appellate Division, but following its own earlier decision unless satisfied it is wrong.

There are two special situations where English precedents may still govern. The first relates to evidentiary rules. The Civil Proceedings Evidence Act of 1965,[150] for the rules of evidence it does not expressly state, invokes the "law of evidence . . . in force" on May 30, 1961. At that date each province had its own evidence statute, that of the Cape and Orange Free State referring to evidence admissible in the English High Court,

---

147 Cf. Ex parte die Minister van Justisie: In re Staat v. De Bruin 1972 (2) S.A. 623 (A.D.). (Some regional courts are itinerant.) What if part of the trial takes place in one area and part in another? See De Bruin case at 632. Possibly the critical place is where judgment is delivered.
148 See R. v. Ntoni 1961 (3) S.A. 507 (S.W.A.) at 509; Tshabala v. Johannesburg City Council 1962 (4) S.A. 367 (T.); State v. Sisulu 1963 (2) S.A. 596 (W.); State v. Titus 1963 (1) P.H. H36 (C.); State v. Louw 1966 (4) S.A. 17 (G.W.) at 18.
149 Cf. R. v. Neumann 1949 (3) S.A. 1238 (Sp. Ct.) at 1258.
150 25 of 1965.

that of the Transvaal to the law "in force in the Supreme Court of Judicature in England" and that of Natal to the "rules recognized by the English law of evidence." Faced with the challenge of solving this puzzle, the Appellate Division in 1967[151] concluded that English decisions after this date have no binding force in South Africa and that, as regards earlier decisions, those of the Privy Council take priority over those of the House of Lords, which in some respects seems a strange conclusion, for the Privy Council is not part of the Supreme Court of Judicature.[152] The ruling is of importance, too, with evidence in criminal cases, where the residuary rules are those in force on that May day.[153] With some hesitation, it is suggested that the Appellate Division will be the primary authority to settle the rules of evidence. It will treat pre-June, 1961, Privy Council decisions on a par with its own. Lower courts will be bound, in order, by the decisions of the Appellate Division, of the Privy Council before this crucial day, and then of the House of Lords and the English appeal courts (in that order, and if rendered before that day).

The second special situation relates to old Cape and Orange Free State statutes directing the courts to apply "the law administered by the High Court of England" to "questions of fire, life and marine assurance, stoppage *in transitu*, and bills of lading."[154] The submissions made in the preceding paragraph would equally apply here, save that there will not be a blockade on English decisions from the beginning of June, 1961.

In the fullness of time these old statutes must surely be repealed and the problem of precedent they pose will disappear simultaneously. Possible, but less likely, is a code of evidence for the whole country, which will put an end to the need to refer to English case law. The final prospect is a true Supreme Court of South Africa, the various divisions coming together in a union and no longer looking like an odd confederation. No doubt the statute accomplishing this will state rules of jurisdiction, for in so large a country it would not be equitable for a plaintiff to be entitled to sue in any court he pleases. But it would put an end to each

---

151 Van der Linde v. Calitz 1967 (2) S.A. 239 (A.D.).
152 Nor, of course, is the House of Lords, but its judgments, unlike those of the Judicial Committee, bind the Supreme Court of Judicature.
153 Section 292 of the Criminal Procedure Act 56 of 1955, as amended by Act 92 of 1963.
154 General Law Amendment Act 8 of 1879 (Cape), section 2; General Law Amendment Ordinance 5 of 1902 (O.F.S.), section 1.

provincial division's tendency to regard itself as virtually independent of its fellows in the sphere of, and would thus tighten, the doctrine of precedent. Such legislation would gradually conduce to greater uniformity of legal rules in South Africa, a most desirable object. New rules of precedent would have to be devised by the courts to cope with the situation. Their performance in the past shows that they are admirably fitted for such a task.

ABBREVIATIONS

Willie's Principles of South African Law, ix:
"Since the year 1947 the reports of all cases decided in the Supreme Courts of South Africa, Rhodesia and South West Africa have been reported in one series called the *South African Law Reports*. The reports of cases decided each quarter appear in a separate volume, that for the first quarter of year 1947 being styled 1947 (1) S.A. At the end of each citation the initials of the court giving the decision are placed in brackets, e.g. Essa v. Divaris, 1947 (1) S.A. 753 (A.D.) Today a single initial is used to identify the court, namely C, E, T, W, G, O, N, or D.

Prior to the year 1947 cases were reported in volumes bearing either the names of the courts in which the cases were decided, or the names of the actual reporters. A particular volume was identified, sometimes by its number in the series, e.g., 9 Menzies, sometimes by its date, e.g., 1923 C.P.D."

Reports

A.C.	Law Reports, Appeal Cases (1891 and onwards)
A.D.	Appellate Division
C.	Cape Provincial Division
C.P.D.	Cape Provincial Division (1910–1946)
D.	Durban and Coast Local Division
E.	Eastern Cape Division
E.D.C.	Eastern District Court Reports
G.W.	Griqualand West
O.	Orange Free State Provincial Division
O.F.S.	High Court Reports on Orange Free States (1879–1883)
Off. Rep.	Official Reports of the South African Republic
R.A.D.	Rhodesia, Appellate Division
S.C.	Supreme Court Reports (1880 and onwards)
S.R.	Southern Rhodesia (1910–1946)
S.W.A.	South-West Africa (1919–1946)
T.	Transvaal Provincial Division
T.H.R.-H.R.	Tydskrif vir Hedendaagse Romeins-Hollandse Reg
T.P.D.	Transvaal Provincial Division
T.S.	Transvaal Reports, Supreme Court (1902 and onwards)
W.	Witwatersrand Local Division
W.L.D.	Witwatersrand Local Division (1910–1946)

Journals

Cape L.J.	Cape Law Journal
C.I.L.S.A.	Comparative and International Law Journal of Southern Africa
S.A.L.J.	South African Law Journal

XI

Codification and Case Law in Israel

G. Tedeschi
PROFESSOR OF CIVIL LAW, HEBREW UNIVERSITY OF JERUSALEM
and

Y. S. Zemach
LECTURER IN LAW, HEBREW UNIVERSITY OF JERUSALEM

The purpose of this paper is to discuss, from a historical perspective, the position of case-law and codification in the contemporary legal system of Israel. The system, which is twenty-five years old, is at present undergoing a fundamental revision of legal tenets and techniques, aimed at the eventual establishment of new laws which should conform more closely to national needs and the spirit of the people of Israel.

"Oust the old and replace it with the new,"[1] characterizes the present activity of the emerging Israeli system. After more than two decades of close dependence upon a variety of legal systems of disparate origins, conceptions, and orientations,[2] Israel is diligently engaged in the preparation of new and, it is hoped, independent and original laws. The legislative drive which began more than a decade ago is now reaching a climax of intensity and potency. Statutes dealing extensively with various legal fields are being enacted. Many branches of private and public (criminal, constitutional, and administrative) law are being substantially rewritten by new laws. An all-embracing codification of Israeli laws is no longer a vision for the days to come.

The development of Israeli law through codification certainly constitutes a revolutionary turning point in its legal history. Israel, which as a consequence of the British Mandate over Palestine[3] has been said to constitute "one of the 'oversea colonies' of the common law,"[4] is gradu-

---

1 Leviticus 26:10. A list of the abbreviations used in this chapter appears on page 295.
2 See Notes 9 ff. below and accompanying text.
3 See Notes 5–6 below and accompanying text.
4 Bentwich, "The Migration of the Common Law: Israel," 76 LAW QUARTERLY

ally beginning to deviate, conceptually and technically, from the traditional common-law paths. The new Israeli statutes are no longer grounded —in any case, not exclusively—on English foundations. Moreover, due to its intensive development through legislation, the Israeli system is steadily losing its (English) case-law basis and acquiring a more codificatory orientation, largely influenced by European Continental systems.

This prominent change in Israeli law can only be appreciated in its national context. In essence—along with several other facets of Israel's life—it mirrors the political birth pangs of the nation and the process of laying its legal and constitutional foundations. It is a process of experience, of trial and error. The development discussed in this paper reflects an important period in the legal history of the State of Israel.

The State of Israel came into being on May 15, 1948, after a twenty-six-year British Mandate over Palestine.[5] Great Britain occupied Palestine at the end of World War I, having defeated the Turks who had ruled over the land as part of the Ottoman Empire for several centuries.[6] Immediately with its establishment in 1948, Israel became engaged in an all-out war launched against it by its neighbors, who opposed its existence. Due to the emergency, the new State did not have any prepared laws. To prevent a legal vacuum, the Israeli provisional legislature[7] provided in its first enactment that "[T]he law which existed in Palestine on . . . 14th May, 1948 . . . shall remain in force, insofar as there is nothing therein repugnant to this ordinance or to the other laws which may be enacted . . . and subject to such modifications as may result from the establishment of the State and its authorities."[8]

The law which existed on May 14, 1948, was derived from divergent legal sources, given recognition in Palestine by virtue of Article 46 of

---

REVIEW 64 (1960); and see Baker, *The Reception and Development of Common Law and Equity in Israel*, in INTERNATIONAL LAWYERS CONVENTION IN ISRAEL 1958, 24 (1959).

5 The British Army occupied Palestine in October, 1918. On July 24, 1922, the League of Nations approved the British Mandate over Palestine. See, e.g., N. BENTWICH & H. BENTWICH, MANDATE MEMORIES, 1918–1948 (1965).
6 The Turks occupied Palestine in 1516.
7 Namely, the Provisional Council of the State.
8 Law and Administration Ordinance, 5708–1948 (Israeli enactments are dated by the Jewish and the Gregorian years), § 11, 1 LAWS OF THE STATE OF ISRAEL (English transl.) [hereinafter cited as L.S.I.] 7.

Palestine Order in Council, 1922,[9] and English royal enactment,[10] considered to be the Palestine constitution. The article incorporated in Palestinian law "the Ottoman law in force in Palestine on November 1, 1914," British Orders-in-Council and Mandatory enactments, and "subject thereto, and so far as the same shall not extend or apply . . . the substance of the common law, and the doctrines of equity in force in England." The article provided further that the said common law and equity should be in force "so far only as the circumstances of Palestine and its inhabitants . . . permit," and "subject to such qualification as local circumstances render necessary."

The block of Ottoman law which accordingly stayed in force in Palestine was mostly codificatory in nature, of both Moslem and European origins.[11] The *Mejelle*, the Turkish civil code of 1869–1876, was the notable restatement of Moslem civil-law rules, systematized according to Western techniques and patterns. The *Mejelle* had been considered the core of the Turkish system.[12] Besides extensive provisions on contracts, civil wrongs, action, evidence, and administration of justice, it embodied jurisprudential maxims of general application.[13] Other Ottoman laws such as criminal law, commercial and maritime laws, laws on civil and criminal procedure, were mainly based on French models,[14] especially Napoleonic codes, many of which had been poured into the Ottoman system in the form of a verbatim Turkish translation. These Ottoman laws were construed by the courts in accordance with their historical origins, whether their French prototype or the Moslem religious rules.[15]

The Ottoman law and the Mandatory legislation were, under the in-

9   3 LAWS OF PALESTINE 2569 (Drayton ed. 1934).
10 Promulgated by the King of England, in his capacity as the Mandatory for Palestine, under the British Foreign Jurisdiction Act of 1890.
11 On Ottoman law received in Palestine law, see TEDESCHI, *On The Movement for Reception and Codification in the Neighbouring Countries*, in STUDIES IN ISRAEL LAW 84 ff. (1960); Ginossar, "Israel Law: Components and Trends," 1 ISRAELI LAW REVIEW 382 (1966). On Ottoman law in general, see, YOUNG, CORPS DE DROIT OTTOMAN (1906).
12 For an English translation of the *Mejelle*, see HOOPER, THE CIVIL LAW OF PALESTINE AND TRANS-JORDAN (1933).
13 The land law, on the other hand, was based on Ottoman feudal tenure of land, customs, and Moslem tradition. See, e.g. GOADBY & DOUKHAN, THE LAND LAW OF PALESTINE (1935).
14 See TEDESCHI, STUDIES IN ISRAEL LAW 103. In a very few instances the Ottoman Empire turned to other Continental systems, such as Germany. *Id.* at 103–14.
15 See, e.g., Baker v. Baker, 14 P.D. [*Piskei Din*, Judgment of the Israeli Supreme Court (Hebrew)] 320 (1957); Sweitat v. Attorney General, 11 P.D. 518 (1960).

genuous language of Article 46, to constitute the principal legal system of Palestine. Principles of the English common law and equity, on the other hand, were to be referred to, subject to the said legislation and to local circumstances. In other words, common-law principles were apparently designated as a subordinate legal source from which gaps in the principal system might, in special conditions, be filled. The reality of the British Mandate over Palestine, however, proved to be completely different. During nearly three decades of administration in Palestine, Britain brought about an almost complete Anglicization of the local system. The Ottoman law had been gradually swept aside by English law.

The Anglicization of Palestine's legal system was attained through statutory enactment and judicial lawmaking.[16] At the legislative level, an enormous bulk of Mandatory ordinances [17] and British statutes applied to Palestine [18] replaced or repealed, wholly or in part, Ottoman laws, in particular those modeled on French codes. Ordinances were based on common law or on British statutes, or on British overseas territorial models embodying or codifying common-law rules. Included were, *inter alia*, the ordinances on companies, partnership, bankruptcy, bills of exchange, civil wrongs, criminal code, and interpretation.[19] Laws of evidence as well as civil and criminal procedure were also Anglicized.[20]

16 See, e.g., TEDESCHI, STUDIES IN ISRAEL LAW 166–237; Tedeschi, *Private Law and Legislation Today*, in V SCRIPTA HIEROSOLYMITANA 9, 39–46 (B. Akzin ed. 1958); Tedeschi, *On Reception and on the Legislative Policy of Israel*, 16 SCRIPTA HIEROSOLYMITANA 11 (Tedeschi & Yadin eds. 1966); Ginossar, "Israel Law: Components and Trends," 1 Is. L. REV. 380 (1966); Baker, *The Reception and Development of Common Law and Equity in Israel* (see Note 4 above); Shimron, *The Reception and Development of Common Law and Equity in Israel*, in INTERNATIONAL LAWYERS CONVENTION IN ISRAEL 1958, 43 (1959); N. Bentwich (see Note 4 above); Apelbom, "Common Law à l'Américaine," 1 Is. L. REV. 562 (1962). For historical survey of the Anglicization process, see MALCHI, THE HISTORY OF THE LAW OF PALESTINE 112–96 (2nd ed. 1953).
17 "Ordinance" is the primary Mandatory Legislation enacted in Palestine by its legislature, the High Commissioner in Executive Council: § 17 of Palestine Order in Council 1922, 3 LAWS OF PALESTINE 2574 (Drayton ed. 1934).
18 See, e.g., Copyright Act, 1911, Air Navigation Act, 1920, and other British Acts introduced by § 35 of Palestine Order-in-Council, 1922, 3 LAWS OF PALESTINE (Drayton ed. 1934).
19 1. Companies Ordinance; 2. Partnership Ordinance; 3. Bankruptcy Ordinance, 1936; 4. Bills of Exchange Ordinance; 5. Civil Wrongs Ordinance, 1944; 6. Critical Code Ordinance, 1936; 7. Interpretation Ordinance, 1945.
20 E.g., Evidence Ordinance (of 1924); Civil Procedure Rules, 1938; Criminal Procedure (Arrest and Searches) Ordinance; Criminal Procedure (Trial Upon Information) Ordinance.

Most ordinances[21] contained interpretation clauses referring—with or without qualifications—to the English principles of legal interpretation or to the English construction of their expressions.[22]

By the close of the British Mandate in 1948, most commercial and criminal laws, laws of torts, of procedure, and of evidence, were thus founded on English law. From the Ottoman laws, the *Mejelle*—especially the provisions on special contracts—substantially survived thus constituting the major obstacle before the legislative Anglicization process. Thus an important part of the law of obligations was still governed by the Ottoman law.[23]

English instruments of judicial control of administration and other principles of administrative law were also imported into Palestine law from England. Article 43 of the Palestine Order-in-Council, 1922, established in Palestine a High Court of Justice, vesting it with the jurisdiction "to hear and determine such matters as are not causes or trials, but petitions or applications . . . necessary to be decided for the administration of justice."[24]

In addition to this broad language, another Mandatory enactment,[25] without prejudice to the generality of Article 43, enumerated particular matters within the High Court's jurisdiction, e.g., orders for the release of persons unlawfully detained or imprisoned, orders issued against bodies and individuals exercising public functions by nature of law to do or refrain from doing acts in the exercise of their functions. The combined effect of Articles 43 and 46 of the Order-in-Council was that the Mandatory High Court was given powers parallel to those exercised by the British King's Bench Division on the Crown side.[26] Consequently, the High

---

21 E.g., Ordinances 1–6 enumerated in Note 19 above.
22 See, e.g., § 2(2) of Companies Ordinance; § 2(2) of Partnership Ordinance; § 141 of Bankruptcy Ordinance, 1936; § 2(2) of Bills of Exchange Ordinance; § 2(1) of Civil Wrongs Ordinance, 1944; § 4 of Criminal Code Ordinance, 1936.
23 In addition, Ottoman land law, Ottoman Maritime Code, and fragments of other Ottoman laws, were still substantially in force.
24 Palestine Order-in-Council, 1922 (see Note 9 above). The High Court of Justice was in fact the Palestine Supreme Court, the head of civil courts' hierarchy in Palestine, sitting—in addition to its appellate jurisdiction on judgments of district court in civil and criminal matters—in original jurisdiction as the High Court of Justice.
25 Section 7, Courts' Ordinance, 1940.
26 Cf. Shimron (see Note 16 above), at 54–55; Zamir, *The Jurisdiction of the High Court of Justice*, in STUDIES IN MEMORY OF ABRAHAM ROSENTHAL 225 (Tedeschi ed. 1964).

Court issued orders of habeas corpus, mandamus, prohibition, certiorari, and quo warranto, questioning thereby the legality of administrative and executive acts.[27] Through these vehicles, the entire body of English principles and techniques concerning judicial review of administrative action and judicial control over judicial and semijudicial bodies was applied to Palestine.

The role judicial-made law has played in the Anglicization of the Palestine law was not less effective than that of the legislation. Principles of common law and equity gradually penetrated into all legal fields, whether covered by statutes or not. Common law was considered by the Mandatory courts not only as a subordinate legal source intended to fill *lacunae*, but also as the exclusive and inexhaustible intellectual source from which legal answers should always be derived. The sense of the superiority of common law over the local law hovers over most Mandatory case-law. Common-law principles were applied even where there was no question of a gap in the local law and their application was not required —or sanctioned—by the law. Enactments were generally viewed through English spectacles. Even Ottoman laws—of French or Moslem origin— were sometimes construed in accordance with English principles of legal interpretation.[28] Entire legal branches—such as rules of private international law,[29] quasi contract, and unlawful enrichment[30]—were incorporated into the domestic law through this channel. The equitable doctrine of specific performance, equitable ownership of land,[31] distinctions between liquidated damages and penalty in breach of contract, between lease and license with regard to contractual tenancies, and other common-law institutions were also adopted by the Mandatory courts, not always on firm legal ground.[32] The principle of *stare decisis*, in its Anglo-American form, was also brought in rather surreptitiously without any mention of it in a Palestine enactment.

27 On prerogative orders in England, see, e.g., DE-SMITH, JUDICIAL REVIEW OF ADMINISTRATIVE ACTION 365 (2nd ed. 1968); 11 HALSBURY, LAWS OF ENGLAND 23 (3rd ed. 1954).
28 See, e.g., Ayoub v. Farouqi, 8 P.L.R. 116 (P.C.) (1941); the Privy Council construed §§ 111–12 of the Ottoman Code of Civil Procedure "in the light of the doctrines of English law."
29 See, e.g., Kotia v. Nahas [1941] A.L.R. 357.
30 See, e.g., Agrest v. Fist, [1944] A.L.R. 1944.
31 See, e.g., Hassan Hammad v. Barlassina, 3 P.L.R. 178 (1936).
32 However, Mandatory Courts refused to receive the private trust in Palestine. Eliash v. Director of Lands, 1 P.L.R. 735 (1920–33).

The victims of this excess use of English common law were not only the Ottoman laws, whose disregard could have been defended on the ground that they were on the whole antiquated, but also the local enactments in their entirety. The Mandatory courts' attitude toward them was rather deprecatory. In the background of most cases, even those based fairly on local law, stood the English law. Local law as such ceased to be judicially considered and analyzed. Instead, judges devoted their opinions to dissertations on English law. The net result thereof was the natural contraction and degeneration of the local law, and the painless death of its provisions on the one hand and the domination of common-law jurisprudence on the other.[33]

The upper hand gained by the common law by the termination of British Mandate in 1948 marked a fundamental revolution in Palestine's legal system: namely, the transition of the center of gravity from (Ottoman) codification to (English) case-law. The development of the common law in Israel, on the other hand, is likely to close this historical period. The present process of diminishing the English influence may transfer the basis of the system from (English) case-law back to (Israeli) codificatory law.

What was the law which existed in Palestine on the eve of the establishment of the State of Israel? It was a mosaic of English law, statutory or judge-made law, side by side with remnants of Ottoman laws and religious laws governing matters of personal status.[34] Among the options open to the Israeli legislature were: (1) to continue the existing law; (2) to replace it by the Jewish law; (3) to let the law grow through case-law; (4) to reform the whole system through codification.

The legislature adopted, for the time being, the first course. It was manifest that a new legal system cannot be prepared overnight. For lawyers educated in the English law, it was impossible to function under any other law without a substantial period of transition. Moreover, the com-

---

33 On this aspect, see, generally, Tedeschi, *Private Law and Legislation* (see Note 16 above), at 38–44. The application of common-law principles became in fact the rule, while the local provisions were considered the exception. See, e.g., the Mandatory Supreme Court holding in Hammad v. Barlassina, 3 P.L.R. 178 at 181–82 (1936).

34 See §§ 51–67 of Palestine Order in Council, 1922, 3 LAWS OF PALESTINE 2563, 2581 (Drayton ed. 1934).

mon law was considered especially flexible and adaptable to the conditions of the new, developing community.³⁵

The retention of English law was favored neither by lawyers who advocated the adoption of codification nor by those who wished to revive the Jewish law and apply it to the new Jewish State. Opinions were divided both before and after the establishment of the State, on the status the Jewish law should have in Israel.³⁶ The orthodox religious viewpoint is absolute and unequivocal: the *Torah* is the law of Israel. Because of their divine sanctity and sovereignty, its rules should, in their entirety, have absolute and immutable binding force, to the exclusion of man-made laws.

A second viewpoint emphasizes the national and cultural value of applying the Jewish law in Israel. In this view, the State is Jewish in origin and aspirations. In the language of the Declaration of Independence,³⁷ it was established in the very land in which the Jewish people "first attained to statehood, created cultural values of national and universal significance and gave the world the eternal Book of Books." Israel, it was proclaimed, "will be open for Jewish immigration and for the Ingathering of the Exiles . . . [and] will be based on freedom, justice and peace as envisaged by the prophets of Israel." ³⁸ The revival of the Jewish law would enrich the national life of the new State of Israel. Unlike the orthodox viewpoint, this approach demanded the adoption of a new Israeli code, a secular-civil creation to the extent that conditions permit, based on the fundamental principles of the Jewish law.³⁹ The modern

35 See, e.g., Shimron (see Note 16 above), at 44.
36 On this controversy, see, e.g., SILBERG, PRINCIPIA TALMUDICA 153 ff. (1961) (Hebrew); Tedeschi, *On Reception and on the Legislative Policy of Israel*, 16 SCRIPTA HIEROSOLYMITANA II, 36–44 (G. Tedeschi & U. Yadin eds. 1966); Cohn, *The Spirit of Israel Law*, in INTERNATIONAL LAWYERS CONVENTION IN ISRAEL 1958, 13 (1959); Englard, "The Problem of Jewish Law in a Jewish State," 3 Is. L. REV. 254 (1968).
37 Its full title is the Declaration of the Establishment of the State of Israel of May 14, 1948, 1 L.S.I. 3 (1948) [hereinafter cited as the Declaration of Independence].
38 These principles have become "the people's vision and its credo." Ze'ev v. Gubernick, 1 S. J. [Selected Judgments of the Supreme Court of Israel (English)] 68, 71 (1948) (Smoira, P.). For a similar attitude of the American courts toward the American Declaration of Independence (1776), cf. Youngstown Sheet & Tube Co. v. Sawyer, 343 U.S. 579, 641 (1951) (the Steel Seizure Case).
39 See, e.g., SILBERG (see Note 36 above), at 155. LEVI, ESSAYS ON JURISPRUDENCE 192 (1969). Contra, Englard (see Note 36 above), at 262–63.

Israeli culture will consequently become a new version of the culture of the past.[40]

A third outlook views the Jewish law as merely an intellectual resource, albeit an important one, from which inspiration can be drawn in the process of preparing new laws. Jewish counsel is to be heeded whenever it offers solutions appropriate to modern statutes. Under this approach, Jewish principles are likely to constitute one of the various components of Israeli law, adopted on a rather fragmental, selective, and critical basis.

Alongside the religious-secular split was the division between those favoring an entire reform of law through codification and those desiring development through judicial decision. The latter opinion held that for an emerging system like that of Israel, which is constantly faced with changes, decisional law should precede legislation. Judges can respond to changing needs better than statutes can. Codification cannot be prepared in a vacuum; rather, it should be deferred until some system of judge-made law has evolved. Judges would find the desirable legal direction which would better accord with national conditions and aspirations. Having the benefit of this judicial jurisprudence, the legislature might, at a later stage, enter the picture to consolidate the works of the judges.[41]

Other jurists favor the outright reform of Israeli law through an original Israeli codification which would be based on the national experience and conditions as well as on the experience of other nations.[42] While this codification should certainly benefit from the jurisprudence of other countries, it should not be identified with the principles of any given legal system, nor should it be compelled to make a preliminary choice between reception and independent creation. Codification would satisfy the natural aspiration for an independent national law. Planned legislation is the best vehicle for the molding of a new system, especially one which is constantly undergoing intensive developments. Legislation can be amended whenever late experience or close study calls for amendment. In this context of flexibility and adaptability codification is certainly preferable to judge-made law. The latter is characterized by con-

---

40 Cf. Silberg, D.P. dissenting opinion, in Shalit v. Minister of Interior ("Who Is a Jew" Case), 23 P.D. (2) 477, 503 (1970).
41 For such suggestion, see, e.g., Baker (see Note 4 above), at 42.
42 See TEDESCHI, STUDIES IN ISRAEL LAW 150 ff. (1960); Tedeschi, *On Reception and on the Legislative Policy of Israel* (see Note 36 above), 44–54; Akzin, "Codification in a New State: A Case Study of Israel," 5 AM. J. COMP. L. 44 (1956).

servatism. As the net of precedents spreads, its meshes become progressively tighter and curtail the freedom of the judge. In a developed system of judge-made law the ability of judges to keep pace with the progress of society is naturally more limited than in a codified system.

The champions of codification thus consider the proposal for basing the new system on judicial experience as a totally unhealthy one. A legal system created only on the basis of haphazard judicial opinions would necessarily be so heterogeneous, disjointed, and inconsistent that it would hardly deserve to be called a system of law. The English law itself, which is by origin and subsequent development judge-made law, is of course essentially imperfectly systematized.

Another objection touches the judicial function in general. Judicial involvement—in making law as a main function of the judiciary and not only in filling the gaps of the law—violates the principles of separation of power and is clearly undemocratic. It suggests distrust of the legislature and the imposition of rules which might not reflect the will of the elected representatives of the people, guided by the socio-legal consciousness of the society. Such status accorded to the judiciary runs counter to the modern tendency to regard the legislature as the legitimate interpreter of the will of the people.

By keeping the Mandatory law in force in Israel,[43] the Israeli legislature neither ruled out other options underlying the above-mentioned approaches, nor intended to perpetuate that law in Israel. The conclusion can now be drawn retrospectively. The history of twenty-five years of legal development shows that the new Israeli law is being shaped along the lines delineated by those various approaches. Israel is gradually and cautiously abolishing the Mandatory system—whether based on Ottoman laws, on English and Palestine laws, or on principles of common law—and replacing it by comprehensive laws and codes inspired partially by the Jewish law and influenced by the judicial experience of Israel and other enlightened countries.

The phases leading to this development were as follows. First, during the initial years after the establishment of the State, the process of Anglicization which had developed during the Mandatory period continued. Then came a reaction against this dependence on English law

---

43   1 L.S.I. 7. Cf. the similar laws passed by American states concerning the force of English law in their legal systems, 15 C.J.S., Common Law, 621 § 13 (1939).

and a drive to de-Anglicize Israeli law. This process in turn paved the way for the massive enactment of new Israeli laws which we are currently witnessing.

The establishment of the State of Israel did not bring in its wake an instant change in the key position the English law occupied during the Mandate. The Israeli Supreme Court refused to review the substance of the Mandatory heritage in virtue of the provision of section 11 of Law and Administration Ordinance of 1948,[44] subjecting its incorporation into the Israeli law to "such modifications as may result from the establishment of the State and its authorities." The Court understood "modifications" as referring only to "technical" modifications, without which the Mandatory law could not be applied in Israel, and not to any other modifications based on analysis or consideration of the merits of these laws.[45] Section 11 could therefore constitute no legislative decree for any deviation from the English law. It can be said, however, that at least as concerns common-law principles, the subjective conditions laid down for their introduction in Article 46 of Palestine Order-in-Council has been changed. In the Israeli context the condition should have been read, "so far only as the circumstances of Israel and its inhabitants permit."[46] And what the circumstances of Palestine and its inhabitants permitted is not necessarily the same in the Israeli setting.

For several years after the establishment of the State, however, the English law remained intact. More than that: it began striking its roots in the Israeli system, even to Israeli enactments. The Israeli legislature and judiciary identified law with English law, as if the English version of legal concepts was the only possible version. Even though the new Israeli statutes were originally enacted in Hebrew, Courts said that it was merely a "Hebrew garment" for an English substance.[47] Israeli laws

---

44 Leon v. Gubernik, 1 S.J. 41, 52–53; (Smoira, P.) (1948). The instance given by the Court for such "technical resdification" was the substitution of the word "Israel" for the word "Palestine" wherever it appeared in any law. *Id.* at 53. See, to this effect, § 15(a), Law and Administration Ordinance, 5708–1948, 1 L.S.I. 10.
45 3 LAWS OF PALESTINE at 2580.
46 Paraphrasing Article 46; see Note 19 above and accompanying text.
47 See, e.g., Mituva v. Kazem, 6 P.D. 4, 10 (1952); Lubin v. Municipality of Tel-Aviv, 12 P.D. 1041, 1077 (1958); Bader v. Minister of Interior, 7 P.D. 366, 400 (1953).

were in fact viewed by Israeli judges through English spectacles and interpreted in accordance with English canons of interpretation.[48]

But this heyday of Anglicization of Israeli law did not last. In the early 1950s the legal profession began displaying an increasing consciousness of independence generating a negative reaction against the automatic subjection of Israel law to common-law criteria. Courts began to adopt a more reserved and reluctant attitude toward the application of the common law. Its injection into the Israeli law became selective and pragmatic. English decisions rendered in the pre-State era continued to have force in Israel but were applied and developed in accordance with the new conditions of the State. Post-1948 English precedents, on the other hand, were not considered binding, even though "they are certainly worthy of the courts' attention."[49] "It is inconceivable," said the Israeli Court,[50] "that a sovereign state ... should continue to be subject to the authority of a foreign legal system and to the innovations of judge-made law created by its courts." This attitude, said the Court, was parallel with the American practice concerning English law which had been in force in America before the revolutionary war. American state courts had held after the United States' independence from England, that English law which was in force in 1776 had become integral to the American law, but the subsequent English decisions, though they might have persuasive weight, did not have binding authority.[51]

---

48 See, e.g., Sofer v. Minister of Interior, 10 P.D. 1213, 1220–21 (1956).
49 Cheshin, D.P., in Kohavi v. Baker, 11 P.D. 225, 244 (1957).
50 Id. following Silberg, J., in Jakobovitz v. Attorney General, 6. P.D. 514, 8 P.D. 785, 828 (1954).
51 The Israeli Court cited among other American cases, Chief Justice Marshall in Cathcart v. Robinson U.S. (5 Pet.) 264, 280 (1831):

> By adopting [English statutes] they became our own as entirely as if they had been enacted by the legislature of the State. They received construction in England at the time they are admitted to operate in this country—indeed, to the time of our separation from the British Empire—may very properly be considered as accompanying the statutes themselves, and forming an integral part of them. But however we may respect subsequent decisions, and certainly they are entitled to great respect, we do not admit their absolute authority. If the English courts vary their construction of a statute which is common to the two countries, we do not hold ourselves bound to fluctuate with them.

Cf. Sussman, "Law and Judicial Practice in Israel," 32 JOURNAL OF COMPARATIVE LEGISLATION AND INTERNATIONAL LAW, Third Series, Pt. 3, 29, 30 (1950).

In addition to this judicial attitude toward English law, another relaxation of common-law pressure on the Israeli law was attained through the new Israeli practice of applying for guidance to decisional law from common-law countries other than England, whenever the case-law of the latter systems suggested solutions more appropriate to the developing system of Israel, or treated legal fields which had not arisen or were not adequately developed in England. This practice is neither permissible under nor sanctioned by the statutory dictate to apply the substance of the common law "in force in England."[52]

American opinions are the most quoted by the Israeli courts.[53] While Mandatory courts never cited American cases, Israel regards American authorities as a most important source of guidance. "Apart from the courts of the United States," said one writer, "the Israeli Supreme Court possibly makes more frequent use of American jurisprudence than any other court in the common law world."[54] Even where there are English cases in point, the practice is often to add the weight of illustrative American cases, or to prefer the latter to the former by virtue of their being more developed and richer in examples. American authorities are, consequently, referred to in various fields of private and public law.[55]

The most important influence of American jurisprudence is felt in the constitutional field. American decisions on separation of powers, on justiciability of constitutional matters, and on the universal problem of distinguishing between law and politics for the purpose of deciding whether in a specific constitutional issue the court should exercise its judicial power or abstain, are regarded as highly persuasive, because "the Supreme Court of the United States [as distinguished from the English courts] . . . has considerable experience in examining the boundaries between the respective functions of the three authorities of the State."[56]

---

52 Article 46 of Palestine Order in Council, 1922. 3 LAWS OF PALESTINE 2569 (see Note 10 above and accompanying text; and see TEDESCHI, STUDIES IN ISRAEL LAW 233–34 [1960]).

53 See, e.g., Gorney, "American Precedents in the Supreme Court of Israel," 68 HARVARD LAW REVIEW 1194 (1955); Apelbom, "Common Law à l'Américaine," 1 Is. L. REV. 562 (1966).

54 Apelbom, "Common Law à l'Américaine," 1 Is. L. REV. 565.

55 For illustrative examples, see id. at 567–77.

56 Jabotinsky v. Weizmann, 1 S.J. 75, 88 (1951). The question was whether it was within the judicial power of the Supreme Court of Israel to interfere with the discretion of the president of the State of Israel in the formation of a new

Individual rights in Israel are not inscribed in any Bill of Rights; they are mostly judge-made. The Israeli Supreme Court, sitting as a High Court of Justice,[57] has proclaimed itself "the shield and stronghold"[58] of the individual against the authorities. In discharging this function, they pay significant attention to American cases on civil rights, rather than to English cases.[59] That is because the English judiciary, as one writer has said, has been "slow and reluctant" to interfere in administrative matters.[60]

This accord in prominent constitutional matters between the American and the Israeli practices exists despite the fundamental differences between the legal systems of the two countries. Israel lacks a formal constitution, and its system is founded on the supremacy of its parliament. It might be, therefore, the compatibility of American decisions with the temperament and spirit of Israel's constitutional and national tenets, and not the formal legal framework, which weighs in the balance.

In the wake of these judicial steps, the mandatory application of English common law has been substantially restricted. The Israeli judge-made law has ceased to be "a pure and unadulterated common law and

---

cabinet, and to dictate the manner in which the president had to exercise this "executive and political power." The Court relying, among other American cases, on Chief Justice Marshall in McCulloch v. Maryland, 17 U.S. (4 Wheat.) 316, 423 (1819), Mississippi v. Johnson, 71 U.S. (4 Wall.) 475, 499 (1866), held that the issue was outside the judicial authority. See also Baker v. Carr, 369 U.S. 186 (1962) (the apportionment case) and Powell v. McCormack, 395 U.S. 486 (1969), referred to in National Circles v. Minister of Police, 24 P.D. (2), 141, 164–65 (1970) (involving Jews' right to worship on the Temple Mount in the old city of Jerusalem).

57 § 7, Courts Law 1957, 11 L.S.I. 157 (1957).
58 Yehoshoua v. Appellate Committee, 9 P.D. 617, 632 (1955).
59 See, e.g., Kol Ha'am v. Minister of Interior, 1 S.J. 90 (1953), involving the suspension of two Communist newspapers for publishing highly inflammatory articles concerning a rumored military alliance between Israel and the United States against Soviet Russia. The Court annulled the suspension. Quoting extensively American leading cases on freedom of speech [e.g., Abrams v. United States, 250 U.S. 616 (1919); Whitney v. California, 274 U.S. 357 (1927); Schenck v. United States, 249 U.S. 47(1919), Dennis v. United States, 341 U.S. 494 (1951)], the Court held that absent a clear and present danger that the publication would bring about a breach of peace or weaken the Israeli citizens' will to carry out their national duty of service in the event of war, there was no justification for the suspension of the newspapers.
60 Hausner, *Individuals' Rights in the Courts of Israel*, in INTERNATIONAL LAWYERS CONVENTION IN ISRAEL 1958, 201, 204 (1959).

equity in its English form," and has gradually become "an Israeli branch of judge-made law" developing according to the national needs.[61]

The process of abolishing the dependence upon English common law is significantly furthered by legislative measures. New Israeli laws dealing with various legal fields expressly exclude the application of Article 46 of Palestine Order-in-Council, 1922,[62] through which the common-law principles were introduced into Palestine, by enacting "autarchy" sections.[63] Mandatory Ordinances, still in force in Israel, are being officially issued in a new Hebrew version.[64] The New Version is determined by the Constitution, Legislation, and Juridical Committee of the Knesset (the unicameral Israeli parliament) on the basis of a draft prepared by the minister of justice and examined by a professional advisory board. The New Version becomes, on publication, the sole binding version of the law, "and no other version of that law shall thenceforth have effect, and the plea that the new . . . version differs substantively from the original law shall not be heard."[65] The result is that the original English text, which until the coming into force of the new version had overriding validity, is thenceforward without legal effect, being replaced by the Hebrew text. Modern Hebrew legal language replaces English expressions. More than two dozen Mandatory Ordinances have so far been issued in a New Version.[66] Recently, in 1972, an Israeli law was enacted repealing any legal provision under which a law or its provisions may be construed in accordance with the English law or with English canons of legal interpretation. This repeal applied to all Mandatory ordinances still in force in Israel, whether issued in a New Hebrew Version or not, and its effect is to isolate them from any dependence on the English law.[67]

---

61 Akzin, *Problems of Constitutional and Administrative Law*, in INTERNATIONAL LAWYERS CONVENTION IN ISRAEL 1958, 161, 196 (1959).

62 3 LAWS OF PALESTINE 2569 (Drayton ed. 1934).

63 See, e.g., § 150 of Succession Law, 5725–1965: "In matters of succession, Article 46 of the Palestine Order-in-Council, 1922, shall not apply." 19 L.S.I. 83. § 160 Land Law, 5729–1969, 23 L.S.I. 311: "Article 46 of the Palestine Order-in-Council, 1922, shall not apply in matters of immovable property."

64 Under § 16 of Law and Administration Ordinance, 5708–1948, 1 L.S.I. 7, as replaced in 1964, 18 L.S.I. 67 and in 1969, 1971. See Yadin, "The New Version," 7 Is. L. REV. 277 (1972).

65 § 16(g), Law and Administration Ordinance, 5708–1948, 18 L.S.I. 67.

66 E.g., the Interpretation Ordinance, Bills of Exchange Ordinance, Income Tax Ordinance, Civil Wrongs Ordinance.

67 Consequently the dependence of the following ordinances on English law have

These direct legislative measures, coupled with judicial attitude, significantly freed the Israeli system from its intimate dependence upon English law, statutory or common. The legal system must now stand on its own feet. After a substantial period of patchwork legislation modifying existing Mandatory law or otherwise based on it, the Israeli legislature began taking the long-range view aimed at the establishment of a new, independent, and original Israeli law. Legal-reform committees composed of prominent jurists, mostly chaired by a justice of the Supreme Court of Israel, were set up. Each was assigned the task of investigating the law in a particular field and preparing a draft of a proposed law. Thanks to the Ingathering of the Exiles, committee members usually represent various legal orientations: Anglo-American, West-European and East-European systems, and, naturally, the Jewish law. Such composition is indicative of the comparative study which is being done for this purpose.

While no uniform formula underlying the preparation of the new law can be suggested, some lines can be discerned. The clear purpose is to create independent laws, free of any link with the Ottoman and Mandatory past and construed in their own terms, not being subject to the canons of construction of other legal systems. They should be original, founded on national experience and needs, and inspired by Israeli national ideas and the best elements of contemporary legal systems.[68] The contents of the new laws are therefore drawn in various proportions from the existing statutory provisions which have stood the test of time; from the Israeli case-law, from the Jewish law, from Anglo-American and Continental-European sources, as well as from other legal systems considered relevant to Israel's conditions.[69]

The Jewish law is naturally regarded as an important source for the new Israeli laws.[70] However, Judaic principles are neither exclusive nor con-

---

been severed: Civil Wrongs Ordinance (New Version); Criminal Code Ordinance, 1936; Bills of Exchange Ordinance (New Version); Bankruptcy Ordinance, 1936; Partnerships Ordinance and Companies Ordinance; and see Note 19 above.

68 See, e.g., explanation notes on the Bill for Succession Law and on Agency Bill, cited in M. Elon, "The Sources and Nature of Jewish Law and its Application in the State of Israel," Part IV, 4 Is. L. Rev. 80, 81–83 (1969).

69 In the preparation of the Bill for a Succession Law, for instance, codes of France, Germany, Switzerland, and Italy, and laws of Soviet Russia, Sweden, Brazil, and Egypt, have been used, along with other material.

70 See Notes 37–40 above and accompanying text.

clusive. The Israeli legislation is essentially inspired and affected by Judaic rules and conceptions, but it does not constitute a codification of the Jewish law. While the extent and mode of reception of the Jewish law vary from one law to another,[71] it seems that the general policy of the Israeli legislature in this respect is as expressed by the former attorney general of Israel:

> Whenever there is in Jewish Law a provision which we can adapt to the needs of a modern and progressive community, we gladly adopt it. But our approach to every legislative problem which confronts us is to ask ourselves what would be the most reasonable, the most practicable, the most equitable solution. If we find that solution in the sources of Jewish law, well and good; but any solution, however well established in Jewish law, which would appear to us unreasonable or impracticable or inequitable—we discard unhesitatingly and look for other systems of law for guidance.[72]

The new Israeli laws deal progressively with fields of private as well as public law.[73] Each treats its subject in a codificatory, thorough, and extensive manner. Laws enacted cover areas formerly dealt with by Ottoman, English, and Mandatory enactments, as well as matters traditionally belonging to the sphere of common law and equity.[74]

Civil and criminal laws are being gradually enacted on a piecemeal basis. A substantial body of individual laws, dealing exhaustively with the various aspects of these fields, has already been accumulated. The compilation thereof may eventually constitute the civil and criminal codes of Israel.

A serious body of work replacing the *Mejelle*, the Ottoman civil code, has been created. Most books and provisions of the *Mejelle*, have been substituted by a systematic Israeli legislation. Among others, these laws are noteworthy: the Agency Law (1965); the Guarantee Law, Pledge Law,[75] Bailees Law (1967); Sale Law, Gift Law (1968); Transfer of Obligations Law (1969); Remedies for Breach of Contract Law (1970).

---

[71] For a comprehensive study of the Jewish law elements in the new Israeli laws, see Elon (see Note 68 above).

[72] Cohn, The Spirit of Israel Law, in INTERNATIONAL LAWYERS CONVENTION IN ISRAEL, 1958, 13 at 22 (1959).

[73] For a detailed survey of the present Israeli legislation, see BAKER, THE LEGAL SYSTEM OF ISRAEL (1968).

[74] The Land Law, 5729–1969, 23 L.S.I. 283, for instance, repealed the application of common-law principles and equitable rights to matters covered by the law.

[75] See Weisman, "Principles of the Pledges Law of 1967," 4 Is. L. REV. 417 (1969).

These laws,[76] along with additional ones expected to cover other specific contracts and general principles of contracts, would eventually introduce into the system a new and exhaustive body of Israeli law of contract. To these laws there should be added another important law, the Standard Contracts Law of 1964. Israel is among the first countries to have made standard contracts an object of legislation.[77]

Other extensive laws enacted in a codificatory manner are those concerning the law of property. The Land Law of 1969, is the most impressive enactment in this area.[78] In its 169 sections, it presented to the country new comprehensive rules concerning various aspects of immovable property such as rights in immovable property (lease, mortgage, easement, preemption), cooperative houses, registration, and transactions. The law abolished the mixture of Ottoman and English conceptions and techniques which governed this field for many years, and rid the system of more than a dozen fragmental and inconsistent enactments dealing with real property. Another law enacted in a pure codificatory way is the Succession Law of 1965. It embraces the entire field of succession and treats it exhaustively. Instead of the variegated elements which composed the previous law on succession—Ottoman, Mandatory, and Israel legislation; English case-law; religious and foreign law—the new enactment constitutes "one single unit, homogeneous in conception, language and modes of expression, thereby insuring . . . uniform interpretation and smoother application."[79]

The same mode of legislation[80] is being employed in the criminal

---

76 Certain provisions of the *Mejelle* have been replaced also by other laws: see, e.g., Water Law, 5719–1959; Limitation Law, 5718–1958, and Capacity and Guardianship Law, 5722–1962.
77 See Hecht, "The Israel Law on Standard Contracts," 3 Is. L. Rev. 586 (1968).
78 Cf. Weisman, "The Land Law, 1969: A Critical Analysis," 5 Is. L. Rev. 379 (1970).
79 Yadin, "Reflection on a New Law of Succession," 1 Is. L. Rev. 132 (1966).
80 The discussion in the present article has been restricted to representative examples of laws in which codificatory mode is salient. Many other Israeli laws though important and original, were consequently omitted. On Israeli laws in most fields, see Baker, The Legal System of Israel (1968).
  It is worth mentioning, however, that the field of commercial law is almost completely covered by Palestine legislation, though constantly amended by Israeli laws. The same applies to civil wrongs. The Mandatory Civil Wrongs Ordinance of 1944 is undergoing significant modifications. (See, e.g., Abatement of Nuisance Law, 1961; Repair of Bodily Harms Law of 1964; Defamation Law

field. Israel inherited from the Mandate the Criminal Code Ordinance of 1936, an extensive piece of legislation, comprising some four hundred sections, based substantially on English law. Again, while the whole body of the code was principally kept in force, Israeli laws repealing corresponding chapters and sections thereof, and substituting them by Israeli provisions, have continually been enacted since the early 1950s. While some of the new Israeli laws have been designed to respond to immediate needs, many others introduced an original Israeli viewpoint on various problems in criminal law. Among the numerous laws for the amendment of penal law the following are remarkable: Laws on Age of Marriage (1950); Assault on Police (1952); Abolition of the Death Penalty for Murder; Modes of Punishment (1954); Offences Committed Abroad (1955); on State Security and on Public Servants (1957); on Concealment of Offences and on Bigamy (1959); Prostitution (1962); on Deceit, Blackmail, and Extortion, and on Bribery (1963); Prohibited Games, Lottery, and Betting (1964). The remaining provisions of the Mandatory Criminal Code Ordinance, along with the general principles of the criminal law are awaiting their turn in this reform.

An impressive criminal legislation is the Military Justice Law of 1955, a 546-section legislation, enacted in a codificatory and comprehensive way, covering all problems of criminal law and the military administration of justice.

The criminal procedure is also dealt with in a codificatory manner in the Criminal Procedure Law of 1965. The 226-section law—repealing dozens of previous enactments and modifying others—presents a reform in the criminal procedure formulated with remarkable conciseness.

In the civil-procedure area, several important laws reforming the existing system have been promulgated. Foremost is the 88-section Execution Law of 1967, substituting a new, efficient execution procedure for the old Ottoman-Mandatory one.

A most comprehensive codification is performed in the constitutional field. While in other branches of private and public law the codification was not determined in advance but has evolved later of itself, in the constitutional law the initial desire was to adopt a formal constitution

---

of 1965; Reward for Persons Injured in Saving Life of 1965). However, its major structure has not been shaken.

Codification and Case Law in Israel | 291

for the new State. The Declaration of Independence of 1948 envisaged the enactment of a written constitution, "not later than 1st October, 1948,"[81] a few months after the establishment of the State. That was an extreme departure from the British pattern of an informal constitution founded on unwritten principles and conventions which are sanctified by statutes. While in other fields the British Mandatory laws were kept in force in the new State, this language of the Declaration stated an intention to open promptly a new Israeli page on constitutional law. The aspiration for a formal constitution was not attained on schedule. The War of Independence, on the one hand, and on the other the unbridgeable national controversies over legal and political questions—above all, lack of consensus on the question of the proper status of Jewish tradition and its organs—have militated against the adoption of a constitution.[82] The Israeli legislation resolved in 1950 to gradually enact Basic Laws—each treating a particular constitutional field—whose eventual compilation would form the constitution of the State. Several Basic Laws dealing with State authorities have been enacted: Basic Law: The Knesset (1958); Basic Law: The President of the State (1964); and Basic Law: The Government, the Israeli Executive (1968).[83] Draft Basic Law: Legislation; and Basic Law: The Courts, are at present under consideration in the Ministry of Justice.[84] The most significant provision of the latter law is that empowering the Israeli Supreme Court, sitting en banc as the Constitutional Court, to consider the validity of a regular law, expressly or by implication amending a Basic Law, having not received the majority required by law for the adoption of Basic Laws. This provision is certainly revolutionary in the Israeli system. Though restricted to the examination of the legislative process in a specific matter, in the long range it might

---

81 1 L.S.I. 3.
82 On these controversies, see, e.g., Akzin, "Codification in a New State: A Case Study of Israel," 5 AM. J. COMP. L. 44 (1956); FREUDENHEIM, GOVERNMENT IN ISRAEL 119–47 (1967). It is noteworthy that two prominent justices from both sides of the Atlantic, Frankfurter and Lord Denning, though from different viewpoints, have disfavored the adoption of a formal constitution by Israel: FRANKFURTER, Israel's Tenth Anniversary, in OF LAW AND LIFE AND OTHER THINGS 119 (Kurkland ed. 1965); Denning, Note, in INTERNATIONAL LAWYERS CONVENTION IN ISRAEL 1958, 235 (1959).
83 See Elman, "Basic Law: The Government (1968)," 4 Is. L. REV. 242 (1969). See also Basic Law: Israel Lands (1960).
84 See Klein, "A New Era in Israel's Constitutional Law," 6 Is. L. REV. 376 (1971).

pave the way for the creation of a doctrine of judicial review of the validity of laws.[85]

This important development has been accelerated by judicial attitude. The Israeli legislator enacts Basic Laws but has never explicitly afforded them any special status over other regular laws. Whether Basic Laws constitute a higher law in the light of which other laws can be reviewed is a difficult constitutional question, left to academic controversies.[86] In a prominent case, *Bergman v. Minister of Finance*,[87] the Israeli Supreme Court took the extraordinary step of striking down a regular law due to its repugnance to a Basic Law. The question was that of election to the Israeli parliament. The regular law was found to have deviated from the electoral equality principle laid down in the Basic Law: the Knesset. *Bergman* is the first case in the legal history of Israel, in which a Knesset statute has ever been denied effect. It may be the *Marbury v. Madison*[88] of Israel's constitutional system. The case presented an important question to the legislature: Do you take seriously your Basic Laws? "Sooner or later," said an Israeli observer, the legislature and the executive "will have either to give up playing at Basic Laws . . . or—as they have been served notice—run the risk that the Courts will start drawing conclusions from the fundamental character of these laws."[89] The authorities elected to react promptly and prepared Draft Basic Laws regulating in a statutory form these major constitutional problems.

Another Draft Basic Law in the course of preparation is the Basic Law: Civil Rights. Without a formal constitution and a Bill of Rights, civil rights in Israel are mostly judge-made. For their establishment and protection extralegal sources have been invoked. Natural rights which are "not inscribed in any [statutory] Book";[90] others deriving potency from

85 On the significance of the power for judicial review, see, e.g., SCHWARTZ, AMERICAN CONSTITUTIONAL LAW 9 (1955).
86 See, e.g., Likhovski, "The Courts and the Legislative Supremacy of the Knesset," 3 Is. L. REV. 345 (1968); Rubinstein, *Israel's Piecemeal Constitution*, in SCRIPTA HIEROSOLYMITANA, 201 (Tedeschi & Yadin eds. 1966); Akzin (see Note 61 above), at 196.
87 23 P.D. (1) 693 (1969); for an English translation thereof, see 4 Is. L. REV. 559 (1969).
88 5 U. S. (1 Cranch) 137 (1803); see Nimmer, "The Use of Judicial Review in Israel's Quest for a Constitution," 70 COLUMBIA LAW REVIEW 1217 (1970).
89 Akzin, Comments [on Bergman v. Minister of Finance]4 Is. L. REV. 576 (1969).
90 Bejerano v. Minister of Police, 2 P.D. 80, 82 (1949), involving the right of a

"our whole constitutional system,"[91] and the people's aspirations expressed in the Declaration of Independence,[92] have become the fertile sources for basic individual rights in Israel.[93] The Basic Law: Civil Rights, once it is enacted, would put in writing this important field based on unwritten constitutional tenets. The passage of these latter three Basic Laws might complete the group of Basic Laws, promoting thereby the eventual formation of Israel's constitution as contemplated in the legislation of 1950.

"Break up your fallow ground, do not sow among thorns,"[94] epitomizes the policy followed by Israel for the creation of its new legal system: not nurturing the chaotic, disparate legal sources which the country inherited from the Mandate, but uprooting them and planting in their stead original Israeli laws.

The obvious victims of this reform are the common-law theories and techniques which ruled the system two decades ago. Comprehensive Israeli legislation, mostly of codificatory nature, is progressively permeating important fields of law, transforming the basis of the system from judicial-made law to statutory and codificatory law.

This is well and good. But the enactment of new Israeli laws cannot by itself bring about a secure and stable legal system. The major challenge, once the legislative process is completed, will be to create from concepts, institutions, and techniques, of different sources and orientations, a coherent and homogenous system. The new laws bear Jewish, Continental, English, and many other imprints. The availability of the

---

person to pursue the occupation he chooses, if not prohibited or conditioned by a statute. This right, said the Court, "is not inscribed in any Book, but it arises from the natural right of every person to look for sources of income and to find a vocation from which to derive his livelihood." The case became a classical basis for the provocation of natural rights.

91 Bergman v. Minister of Finance (see Note 86 above), involving "the equality of all before the law."
92 See, e.g., Kol Ha'am v. Minister of Interior, 1 S.J. 90, 105 (1953) (freedom of speech and press); AL. Khouri v. Chief of Staff, 4 P.D. 34, 37 (1949) (freedom of movement); Peretz v. Kfar Shemaryahu, 16 P.D. 2107 (1962) (freedom of religion).
93 On individual liberties in Israel in general, see Hausner (Note 60 above) and Akzin (Note 61 above).
94 Jeremiah 4:3.

best elements of contemporary legal systems has certainly enriched the Israeli laws. However, to make this legal wealth beneficial for the emerging system of Israel, uniformity and certainty as to interpretation and application of the new laws should be developed.[95]

This overall legislative reform presents a great challenge to the Israeli judiciary. The new Israeli laws were formulated in codificatory manner, entirely reshaping the previous law. They were based on the idea of independence, meaning that every law is to be construed in itself, with reference to its provisions and purposes, with no need to depend on external sources. Courts should, therefore, become conscious of the implications of this process. "Real codification," said an Israeli scholar, "means doing what the French have done: once a code comes into effect, one stops applying a pre-code law in the given sphere altogether. Instead, one begins to build up judge-made law, with the code as a starting-point, wherever the latter is insufficient. [This] is done by applying the process of reasoning and analogy."[96]

The interpretation of a new statute under the English canons of construction, on the other hand, would divert the judicial attention from the statute itself and focus it on external historical material, as in the famous mischief rule of the Heydon case.[97] Once this course of interpretation is reverted to, then "farewell to the statute and back to antecedent case law."[98]

Until recently, it has been the practice among students of the common law to deal with its development merely from the vantage point of its migration.[99] It is being depicted as a one-way movement, permanently

---

95 See TEDESCHI, "On the Technique of the Future Legislation of Israel," in STUDIES IN ISRAEL LAW 69–83 (1960); Tedeschi, On Reception and on the Legislative Policy of Israel (see Note 16 above), at 44–54.
96 Akzin (see Note 61 above), at 198.
97 (1584) 3 Co. Rep. 8: "For the sure and true interpretation of all statutes in general . . . four things are to be discussed and considered: (1) what was the common law before the passing of the Act; (2) what was the mischief and defect for which the common law did not provide; (3) what remedy the Parliament hath resolved and appointed to cure the disease of the commonwealth; (4) the true reason of the remedy . . . " For interpretation of the case, see Lord Simonds in Magor and St. Mellows R.D.C. v. Newport Corporation [1952] A.C. 189, 191–92.
98 Akzin (see Note 61 above), at 198.
99 GOODHART (ed.), THE MIGRATION OF THE COMMON LAW (1960).

proceeding forward toward expansion[100] and occupation of additional territories. The contemporary Israeli example, however, marks (at least partly) a contrariwise movement: toward the *emigration* of the common law.

[100] POLLOCK, THE EXPANSION OF THE COMMON LAW (1904).

ABBREVIATIONS

A.C.	Appeal Cases
A.L.R.	Annotated Law Reports
Am. J. Comp. L.	American Journal of Comparative Law
C.J.S.	Corpus Juris Secundum
Is. L. Rev.	Israel Law Review
L.S.I.	Laws of the State of Israel
P.D.	Piskei Din (Judgments of the Supreme Court, in Hebrew)
P.L.R.	Palestine Law Reports
S.J.	Selected Judgments (Israel Supreme Court, in English)

XII

Judicial Lawmaking in Israel

U. Yadin
DEPUTY MINISTER OF JUSTICE AND PROFESSOR OF LAW,
HEBREW UNIVERSITY OF JERUSALEM

Israel is a "mixed jurisdiction." In its legal system elements traditionally found in "common-law" countries intermingle with elements typical of "civil-law" countries. In historic perspective the law of the country has been like a pendulum swinging between these two poles. In the Ottoman period,[1] of which remnants still subsist on the legal scene, the territory would have been grouped among the civil-law countries, what with a civil code[2] derived from Moslem law and a number of other codes adapted from French counterparts, and with almost no reporting of court decisions. During the period of the British Mandate,[3] much of the Ottoman layer was replaced by English law, both statutory and judge-made. The influx of English law proceeded in various ways. The impact may be gauged from the fact that all those who laid down statutory rules and nearly all judges were British[4] and many advocates were English-trained. Law reporting on the English model was developed.

With the establishment of the State[5] the reverse trend set in. It has been gaining momentum ever since, to a minor degree in case law, to a greater degree in legislation.[6] Many of the judiciary and law teachers had their legal education[7]—and indoctrination—in civil law countries,

---

[1] Terminated in 1918. A list of the abbreviations used in this chapter appears on page 310.
[2] Known as the *Mejella*.
[3] 1922 to 1948.
[4] An appeal could be taken from the Supreme Court of Palestine to the Privy Council in London.
[5] 1948.
[6] For the first time by an elected Parliament.
[7] Prior to their immigration to the country.

and so had quite a few of the members of Parliament and the legal profession.[8] Graduates of Israel law schools are increasingly taking their stand on the bench and at the bar. All this makes for a leaning towards civil-law conceptions and approaches.

Most conspicuous is this tendency in a series of statutes enacted since 1962 in the field of Private Law.[9] Conceived and elaborated on a comprehensive plan, they are in the nature of a civil-code-in-the-making which eventually will have most if not all the features for which civil-law codes are typical.

At the same time Israeli law retains many of its ties to English law. Important areas, including torts, companies, bills of exchange, and bankruptcy, are still governed by statutes from the Mandatory period, corresponding closely to their English models.[10] Each of them contains an express provision calling for its interpretation in accordance with English law. It is true that by a recent law[11] those provisions have been stripped of their compulsory character. But ample reliance on English law will certainly continue in the local interpretation of the said enactments. Such reliance seems, indeed, indispensable in view of the fragmentary character of statutes like the Companies Ordinance of 1929.

Moreover, the provision[12] by which the courts were "to exercise their jurisdiction in conformity with the substance of the common law and the doctrines of equity in force in England" so far as statute law did "not extend or apply," was retained in 1948,[13] and is on the statute book to this day.[14] It has been instrumental for introducing into the country many essential rules and doctrines, such as the protection of human rights by way of prerogative writs, the distinction between penalty and liquidated

---

8 These included officials of the Ministry of Justice who are responsible for the planning and drafting of new legislation; the importance of this factor should not be underestimated.
9 They cover—in the order of their enactment—legal capacity, guardianship, succession, agency, guarantee, pledges, bailment, sale, gift, land law, transfer of obligations, remedies for breach of contract, lease and loan, the law of movables, and a so-called general part of the law of contracts (the last one not yet enacted).
10 In the law of torts the Civil Wrongs Ordinance of 1947 is a statutory restatement of English common law.
11 Enacted in 1972.
12 Article 46 of the Palestine Order-in-Council of 1922.
13 Together with all the law which had been in force on the eve of the establishment of the State.
14 Research with a view to its repeal is now under way.

damages, the remedy of specific performance and—perhaps most important—the doctrine of *stare decisis*.[15]

From all this it would appear that the Israeli courts are bound to follow English precedents in many fields. The living law, however, is different.

Over the years the courts have become conscious of their independence from the British supremacy, and have increasingly gone their own ways where English rules appeared incompatible with local conditions[16] or otherwise unacceptable or undesirable. This was the case with regard to the interpretation of the said Mandatory enactments[17] as well as with regard to the application of English judge-made law in the absence of local statute law. It may be of interest to note that in the first, and still leading, case in which that judicial independence was proclaimed[18] the court referred extensively to the corresponding development which had taken place, in its time, in the United States.

This does not mean that English case law has lost all relevance in Israel. The courts have time and again emphasized their high esteem for English decisions, and English cases are currently referred to and often relied upon. But instead of being part of the law of the land, they have become a source of information, inspiration, and guidance; their authority, instead of being binding, has become persuasive.

And a further trend may be observed. The looser the grip of English decisions became, the more did the courts broaden the legal horizon. Alongside English authorities, American and Commonwealth decisions came to be considered, and gradually also other systems of law, modern or ancient—including, of course, Jewish law—were referred to. In some cases the decision was arrived at from a broad comparative analysis. This happened, *inter alia*, in the leading decision on the validity of "value clause."[19]

15 More on this topic will be said later on.
16 A proviso to that effect had already been contained in the above-mentioned Article 46.
17 This had happened in many instances long before the above amending Law of 1972—which shows that that Law did in fact not change the legal position but rather confirmed a change which had already taken place.
18 Cohavi v. Beker, 11 P.D. 225 (1957). "P.D." stands for *Piskei Din* (Judgments of the Supreme Court, in Hebrew).
19 Rosenbaum v. Zeger, 9 P.D. 533, 2 S.J. 10 (1955). "S.J." being a collection of selected judgments of the Supreme Court in English translation.

Judicial Lawmaking in Israel | 299

The breaking away from strict adherence to English precedents opened the way to the creation of what may be called "Israeli common law." The courts, especially the Supreme Court,[20] have created—or enunciated[21] —a great number of rules which have become part of the law of the land. They were often laid down without statutory basis[22] and irrespective of whether or not they could be derived from English law.

Thus, in criminal law the defence of "irresistible impulse caused by mental disease" was recognized;[23] in the law of torts, the Supreme Court returned from the rule in re Polemis to that in Hadley v. Baxendale;[24] in criminal procedure, the "little trial" on the admissibility of confessions was declared to be compulsory although the Criminal Procedure Law of 1965 does not provide so;[25] in the law of evidence, the rules by which evidence is privileged for reasons of state security or other essential public interest were laid down in a decision of the Supreme Court;[26] in public law, the scope of the Supreme Court's competence of review has been defined independently of, and in deviation from, English rules.[27] These are only some examples among many, and instances may be found in every area of law.

A typical matter in point and also an illustration of the attitude towards English case law is the problem of "the matrimonial partnership." In a series of cases, starting in 1965,[28] the Supreme Court has elaborated certain rules to the effect that the marital relationship is presumed to create joint ownership of the spouses in the assets—at least the after-acquired

20 This is the highest judicial tribunal in Israel; it deals with appeals from the five District Courts (courts of general jurisdiction), and with so-called High Court applications which are mainly in administrative matters (corresponding somewhat to the English prerogative writs).
21 The old question whether the courts "create" or only "declare" law has, fortunately, never arisen in Israel.
22 It was, however, held (in Padva v. Friedman, 14 P.D. 427) that they could not be created contra legem, i.e. where a contrary statutory rule exists.
23 Mandelbrot v. Attorney General, 10 P.D. 281 (1956), 2 S.J. 116; Mizan v. Attorney General, 11 P.D. 769 (1957).
24 Malka v. Attorney General, 10 P.D. 1543, 2 S.J. 213; the case was decided in 1956, years before the English Wagon Mound cases.
25 Taksum v. State of Israel, 24 P.D. (1) 95.
26 Ha-Etzni v. Ben-Gurion, 11 P.D. 403, 3 S.J. 365 (1957). The same rules were later restated, in very similar language, by the House of Lords in Conway v. Rimmer (1968) 1 All E.R. 874.
27 Trudler v. Returning Officer, 17 P.D. 2503.
28 Berger v. Director of Estate Duty, 19 P.D. (2) 240.

assets—of each other.[29] These rules were laid down independently of any statutory provisions. In the first of those cases some English decisions to a similar effect had been referred to though not actually relied upon. At the time a further case came before the Supreme Court, the law in England had undergone certain changes at the hand of recent decisions of the House of Lords.[30] When confronted with these decisions, Justice Berinson said,[31] "It is our duty to pursue the path of the rule laid down by this court as to the partnership of assets of a married couple without regard to the swings of the pendulum of English case law."[32]

Justice Cahan remarked, "It is now clear that the rule laid down by this court on the problem of community of assets of spouses can not be based on English case law. This does not destroy the basis of the rule which has crystalised here ... for us the rule developed in the judgments of this court is decisive."[33] And this is how Justice Ezioni put the matter: "Today there is no room to reconsider the rules laid down in the four (previous) judgments. Whatever their source and whatever the developments in the countries from which they were derived, they form today part and parcel of our own case law."[34]

Matrimonial property law may serve also as illustration of *the interplay between courts and legislature*, between adjudicative [35] and statutory law. The Supreme Court repeatedly pointed out that the whole subject should be treated by legislation rather than by case law. From the latest case [36] it indeed appears that the treatment from case to case has brought matters to a sort of impasse from which only the systematic nature and comprehensiveness of a codificatory statute can extricate them. In fact, a bill covering the entire subject has been introduced into, and is at present being debated in, Parliament.

The superiority of statute law over judge-made law is, however, by no means undisputed. In the very case in which the intervention of the legis-

---

[29] See Yadin, "The Matrimonial Partnership," 6 Is. L. Rev. 106 (1971).
[30] Pettitt v. Pettitt (1969) 2 All E.R. 385; Gissing v. Gissing (1970) 2 All E.R. 780.
[31] Afte v. Afte, 25 P.D. (1) 561 (1971).
[32] Id. at 568.
[33] Id. at 572.
[34] Id. at 573.
[35] I owe the term "adjudicative law" to Fuller, Anatomy of the Law 121 (1971).
[36] Afte v. Afte; see Note 31 above.

lator was called for, one of the judges voiced serious doubt as to the "power of imagination of the legislator" and his ability to deal systematically with the infinite variety of fact situations.[37]

In this instance, among others, the courts have been calling for legislative intervention. In others,[38] legislation has been considered necessary in order to "rectify" decisions of the Supreme Court which seemed inconsistent with the "true" intention of the legislator (or of the government!). This has happened especially—but not exclusively—with regard to the interpretation of tax laws and other financial or economic legislation.

A third group of cases are those in which Parliament has adopted and made statutory rules which originally had been pronounced by the courts. This has occurred, *inter alia*, in respect of the privilege of state secrets in the law of evidence. The pertinent rules were first enunciated in a decision of the Supreme Court; they were later incorporated almost verbatim in an amendment of the (Mandatory) Evidence Ordinance.

A case for the development of legal rules from custom through adjudicative law to statutory law is the subject of severance pay. By a decision of 1940[39] the (Mandatory) Supreme Court first gave judicial recognition to a custom, prevalent in local labour relations, under which an employee is entitled, upon dismissal, to indemnity at the rate of his last monthly salary for each year of service. The (Israeli) Supreme Court further elaborated this rule in a series of cases.[40] Eventually, the legislature took over by enacting the Severance Pay Law, 5723–1963.[41]

Returning now to the issue of "Israeli common law" it should be noted that the method by which its rules are arrived at closely resembles the lines on which *the creation of common law* proceeds in England and other parts of the common-law world. I do not propose to go into detailed com-

---

37 25 P.D. (1) 573.
38 Another instance arose from certain rules of Jewish law relating to claims of alimony between spouses which the Supreme Court had to apply and which it felt itself compelled to construe in a way which produced unjustifiable results. Here, too, the court asked the legislator to come to its help: Cohen v. Cohen, 25 P.D. (1) 327.
39 Cohen v. Capun, 7 P.L.R. 80.
40 E.g., Tartakover v. Barnett Brothers, 16 P.D. 969.
41 17 Laws of the State of Israel 161 [hereinafter cited as L.S.I.]. This is the official English translation of the enactments of Parliament.

parison. But some quotations may be in place. They touch upon problems such as (1) the raw material from which the court arrives at its conclusions; (2) the process by which "rights" become legally recognised; (3) the impact of the distinction between *ratio decidendi* and *obiter dictum* and the intimate relation between the facts of the case and the rule of law laid down in it; and (4) the place of dissenting opinions in the fabric of judge-made law.

(1) In a recent case the question arose whether the tenants of defective premises could be held liable for damage caused by the defect and the landlord be thereby exonerated from such liability. Replying in the negative, Justice Witkon said: "When laying down a rule of law on a question for which there is as yet no authority, I think the court may have due regard to practical and factual considerations and to the social implications of its decision. This is the way in which the law is developing in desirable steps in accordance with the time's requirements."[42]

(2) In Cohen v. Minister of the Defence[43] the military authorities had refused to accredit the petitioner as military correspondent. The court declined to interfere because he had not made out a "right" which the court could enforce. In the course of the judgment, however, Justice Witkon pointed out:

It is the task of the court to protect rights . . . I would not say that the right has to be a statutory one, laid down in an enactment. Many times has this court recognised rights which were not referred to in any written rule, but by receiving judicial confirmation acquired form and became recognised in law. Matters of custom or natural justice which only yesterday were still inarticulate and undelineated have been up-graded in this way and enjoy the status of rights. This is judicial development which proceeds alongside with, and does not trespass on,[44] legislative activity, and I would not like to hamper its steps. This power (of the court) is the guarantee of the rights of the individual.[45]

(3) In a case touching upon a surgeon's duty to inform the parents of an infant patient of the risks implied in a certain treatment, Justice Landau, in refusing a further hearing,[46] remarked: "In our system of law the

---

42 Blaliti v. Greek-Catholic Association, 25 P.D. (1) 578, 585.
43 16 P.D. 1023.
44 On this point, see also Note 22 above.
45 16 P.D. 1027.
46 In Israel, when a case has been decided in the Supreme Court by a bench of three judges, a further hearing of the case before the same court sitting with five or more judges (always an uneven number) may be granted.

courts do not engage in pronouncing rules of law for their own sake. The rule of the court derives all its vitality from the facts of the decided case, and has always to be considered in the light of those facts. A rule which was not necessary for the determination of the issue on the facts of the case is nothing more than an *obiter dictum*, and has no force of precedent for the future. Only in this organic way is a body of rules being created step by step, currently to be re-considered in the light of the ever-changing combinations of facts."[47]

(4) Majority judgments and dissenting opinions are frequent in the Supreme Court. When the limits of the power of pardon vested in the president of the State, and the relation between the sentencing function of the court and the pardoning grace of the president were in issue, conflicting opinions came to a head-on crash. Justice Berinson exclaimed: "His (Justice Cohen's) approach to the issue is unacceptable to me and I can find in his opinion scarcely anything to which I could subscribe."[48] To this Justice Cohen replied: "I associate myself with his [Justice Berinson's] grieve on the discrepancy between our conceptions; but I find consolation in the fact that this very diversity is one of the distinctive marks of the judges' independence. . . . . Each judge approaches his judicial task in an individual manner, and what has been said on the bench of the Supreme Court can serve him only as guidance and enlightenment on his own way; it is better that each one be guided by his own faculties and inclinations than that the judges of Israel be like a company of soldiers marching strictly in step at the word of command."[49]

It should be remarked that in spite of this proclamation of faith of a staunch individualist,[50] Justice Cohen is by no means oblivious to the impact of the doctrine of *stare decisis* of which more will be said presently.[51]

One of the fundamental principles of English law—perhaps the most fundamental of all—is the *doctrine of stare decisis*, that cornerstone of

---

47 Dr. Bar-Haj v. Steiner, 20 P.D. (4) 327, 330; see also Gottlieb v. Levi, 25 P.D. (1) 389, Justice Berinson at 391.
48 Attorney General v. M'tana, 16 P.D. 430, 467.
49 *Id.* at 466.
50 In Plonit v. Rabbinical Court, 18 P.D. (4) 141, 156, he denounced as devious the attempt of "counting judges by heads."
51 For a penetrating discussion of the problems involved in the law-making of collegiate courts, especially with regard to judicial policy-making, see Witkon,

judicial lawmaking in the common-law world. It was transplanted from the shores of the Thames to those of the Jordan by British judges operating in Palestine and, technically, by means of the above-mentioned Article 46 of the Palestine Order-in-Council. Two rules thus became part of the Israeli legal system: the rule that inferior courts are to follow the law laid down by courts of higher instance; and the rule that the highest tribunal, too, is bound by its own precedents. But while the former rule has been retained practically unchanged,[52] the latter has been qualified and has thus become different from its English counterpart—at least until 1966 when the House of Lords declared not to be bound any more by its precedents.

In one of the earliest judgments of the Supreme Court, its president, the late Justice Smoira, expressed his conviction that where "truth" and "stability" were in confrontation, "truth" should prevail. This declaration of judicial policy has later received statutory confirmation [53] to the effect that "a rule established by the Supreme Court shall be binding on every court, except the Supreme Court," and has been further elaborated in a long line of decisions of that court.

Today, the basic rule seems to be that expressed by Justice Berinson when he said: "Although constitutionally we are not bound by our precedents, we are not prone to change our 'adjudicated rules.' " [54]

In order to become an "adjudicated rule," [55] a rule has to pass several tests: it must in the previous case (or cases) have been part of the *ratio decidendi*; if it was contained merely in an *obiter dictum*, it cannot aspire to the rank of "adjudicated rule." [56] It must come from a case (or cases) whose facts were sufficiently comparable to those of the case at hand; if the facts are dissimilar, the rule may be avoided by the cases being "distinguished." [57] The rule must have been arrived at after thorough consid-

---

"Some Reflections on Judicial Law-Making," 2 Is. L. Rev. 475 (1967), with further references to Israeli literature on the subject.

52 Its statutory formulation, in Section 33 of the Courts Law, 5717–1957 (11 L.S.I. 157) speaks of the inferior courts to be "guided" and not as being outright "bound" by the rules laid down by higher courts; only in respect of those of the Supreme Court has the term "binding" been used.
53 In the said Section 33 of the Courts Law, see previous note.
54 "Lapidoth" Ltd. v. Shlisser, 23 P.D. (1) 771, 774.
55 The Supreme Court generally prefers to speak of "adjudicated rules" (Halaha psuka) rather than of judicial precedent (takdim).
56 Justice Landau in Bar-Haj v. Steiner, 20 P.D. (4) 327, 330.
57 Ibid.

eration of the issue at hand; if it was adopted "as a matter of routine," "without due examination and reasoning" or "without attention," it ought to be discarded.[58]

On the other hand there is no need of the rule's having been applied in a series of cases.[59] Although frequently more than one previous case is cited, sometimes a single previous decision has been considered sufficient to provide an "adjudicated rule."[60] Again, it seems to be irrelevant whether the rule to be applied comes from a judgment given unanimously or by a majority and whether the court which laid it down was composed of three[61] or a greater number of judges.[62]

When a rule has thus become an "adjudicated" one, the question arises under what conditions would the court be prepared to deviate from or even reverse it. Here, a valuable distinction has been made between "great controversial issues which are subject to the impact of changing times, places and conviction," and cases "in which a technical provision of some statute is at issue and the adjudicated rule is but an attempt to discover the hidden and involved intention of the legislator."[63] A similar distinction has been drawn in England.[64] In cases of the former kind the court would, presumably, be more easily persuaded to reconsider the established rule than in the latter type of cases where mostly one construction put on a statute is as "good" as the other. Reconsideration will be especially indicated where the previous solution of "one of the great issues" has in the meantime "become obsolete in the eyes of the great majority of the enlightened public."[65] Contrarily the court will be all the more inclined to stand by its previous rule, especially in matters of procedure, where it is to be assumed that interested parties have for

58 Justice Berinson; see Note 54 above; this is what in England is called a decision "per in curiam."
59 This is in contrast to Continental doctrine where *jurisprudence constante*, "ständige Rechtssprechung" is required.
60 State of Israel v. Susman, 22 P.D. (2) 1029.
61 This is the general practice in the Supreme Court.
62 This sometimes happens on the regular hearing of an appeal, and is invariably so in "Further Hearings."
63 Justice Witkon in Triefman v. Victor, 18 P.D. (1) 366, 368.
64 By Lord Reid in Jones v. Secretary of State for Social Services, (1972) 1 All E.R. 145, 149. His words have been cited by President (Chief Justice) Agranat in the case mentioned hereafter (Note 65 below).
65 Per President Agranat in Eisik (Schick) v. The Minister of the Interior, 26 P.D. (2) 33, 43. It goes without saying that the genuine representative and mouthpiece of the enlightened public is—the judge himself.

some time been adjusting their steps to that rule.[66]

A useful illustration of the way in which *stare decisis* is practised in Israel, its limitations and problems, is the recent case of Bella Eisick, the reputed wife[67] of one Schick, who changed her family name to his. The minister of the interior disallowed the change[68] because he thought it would mislead people to believe the two to be lawfully married to each other. A similar first case, that of Tova Stand, had been decided in 1965 in favour of the minister by a court of three in a very short opinion of one of them.[69] In 1966 a second case, that of Alisa Smulon, came before a court of five and was decided, again in favor of the minister, by a majority of three to two.[70] When Bella Eisick tried her luck, the order was discharged in the first place because she had not yet applied to the minister himself.[71] On this occasion the majority of the court of three declined to go into the merits, but the dissenting judge[72] gave a detailed opinion in favour of the petitioner.[73] After she had received the same reply from the minister, she came back to the Supreme Court. Her new petition was heard by three other judges. One of them[74] discarded the *Smulon* rule as having been laid down per in curiam and held for the petitioner. The majority[75] considered the two previous cases as having created an "adjudicated rule" and decided the case in favour of the minister for this reason alone.[76]

A number of questions arise. Were the fact situations in the three cases sufficiently similar to warrant the final conclusion? Was *Stand* a "precedent," considering its scant reasoning and the fact that Justice

66 Cf. the Susman case; see Note 60 above.
67 That is, living with him as—and being considered by the public to be—his wife, although for some reason or other the two are not legally married. These unions are relatively frequent in Israel.
68 He is authorised to do this under the Names Law, 5716–1956, 10 L.S.I. 95, Section 16.
69 Tova Stand v. Minister of the Interior, 19 P.D. (1) 501 (J. Berinson).
70 Alisa Smulon v. Minister of the Interior, 20 P.D. (4) 645; in this case the name had been changed after the death of the reputed husband; this time Justice Berinson joined in the minority opinion, explaining his change of position by the dissimilarity of facts.
71 As provided by the Names Law, Section 24 (see Note 68 above).
72 Justice H. Cohen.
73 Eisick (Schick) v. Minister of the Interior, 25 P.D. (1) 544.
74 Deputy President Susman.
75 President Agranat and Justice Cahan.
76 President Agranat added some reasons on the merits but he emphasized that his decisions were based exclusively on *stare decisis* (see Note 65, at 47–49).

Judicial Lawmaking in Israel | 307

Berinson joined in *Smulon* the opposite faction? Was *Stand* essential for the creation of the adjudicated rule, or was *Smulon* sufficient in itself for that purpose? And again: what if Justice Susman was right in saying that part of a relevant section of the Names Law [77] had been overlooked in *Smulon*? What if it could be shown, in the light of Justices Cohen and Susman's argumentation, that the rule in *Smulon* was only an *obiter*, as has happened on other occasions? [78] Moreover, does the issue in these cases revolve on the interpretation of certain statutory provisions—as it does at first view—or is it "one of the great controversial issues," involving —as it also does—one facet of the legal position of presumed wives?

These questions, to which this writer has no answers, tend to show how complicated the "simple" doctrine of *stare decisis* is liable to become in its practical implementation.

In the foregoing parts of this survey the judicial process has been described mainly against the common-law background. It now remains to show how the courts have reacted to *the new legislation in private law*.[79] Faced with these civil-law-inspired statutes, did they approach them in the same manner as they approach statutes of the common-law type and apply to them the same canons of interpretation? Or did they adjust their process to the different type of statutes and employ methods of interpretation closer to those prevailing in civil-law countries?

It seems too early for a hard and fast answer to these questions. The new statutes have so far come before the Supreme Court only in a relatively small number of cases. Maybe they are too recent; maybe they gave less rise to litigation. But where problems of the method of interpretation did come up, it appears that the court did correctly appreciate the spirit of the new statutory law and its divergence from statute law of common-law vintage.

Whereas Article 46 of the Palestine Order-in-Council [80] proceeded from the assumption that the local statute law [81] was fragmentary and therefore in need of complementation from an extraneous source of law,[82]

77 Section 6 dealing with the family name of a woman upon marriage.
78 Boronovski v. The Chief Rabbis of Israel, 25 P.D. (1) 7.
79 See Note 9 above.
80 See Notes 12–14 above.
81 At the time of its enactment this was the Ottoman legislation.
82 Namely, English common law and equity.

the new Israeli legislation is based on the contrary assumption. It aspires to create law of its own, autonomous and not dependent on complementary rules from without.[83] Accordingly some laws of this category[84] expressly exclude the application of the said Article 46 to matters of their subject, and it may be assumed[85] that the said provision does not apply to this group of statutes even where its application is not excluded *expressio verbis*.

The courts were thus left without the convenience of falling back on English case law.[86] And indeed, English authorities are seldom referred to and nowhere "followed." There are even cases in which not a single English, Commonwealth, or American decision has been mentioned.[87]

Instead the courts have, time and again, emphasized that the construction of these statutes was to proceed primarily by scrutinizing the statute itself and exploring the presumed intention of the legislator.[88] In one of the cases to this effect, Deputy President Silberg said: "We must solve this problem from within the law itself and squeeze it, be it smoothly or obliquely, into the language of the Law."[89]

As regards the legislative history, and especially the explanatory notes which accompany the bills and the debates on them in Parliament, the courts rely on them to a greater extent than they do in respect of statutes of the common-law type.[90] Where they seek inspiration from other systems of law, they turn more frequently and in more detail to Continental law, and feel themselves more at liberty to consult authorities of Jewish

---

83 Further on this point, cf. YADIN, *The Law of Succession and other Steps Towards a Civil Code*, in STUDIES IN LEGISLATIVE PROBLEMS 104 (1966).

84 The Law of Succession, 5725–1965; the Land Law, 5729–1969; and the Law on Remedies for Breach of Contract, 5731–1970; are closest to codification in the Continental sense. See also the Prescription Law, 5718–1958; the Pledges Law, 5727–1967; the Guarantee Law, 5727–1967; the Transfer of Obligations Law, 5729–1969.

85 This proposition has been disputed by some writers.

86 See Russo v. Russo, 24 P.D. (1) 657, where the "independence clause" of the Succession Law was considered.

87 Boker v. Anglo Israeli Management and Trust Co., 25 P.D. (2) 121, an elaborate judgment of a court of five in a complicated question of property law.

88 Estate of Finkelstein v. Finkelstein, 22 P.D. (1) 618; Russo v. Russo, see Note 86 above; Federation of Agricultural Workers v. Farmers Association, judgment of the Central Labour Court of 12 February 1972; *and see* Note 98 below.

89 The Finkelstein case, see Note 88 above, at 619.

90 The case of the Federation of Agricultural Workers, (see Note 88 above) is a good example in point.

Judicial Lawmaking in Israel | 309

law. In the Boker case,[91] for instance, Polish and especially Austrian law was examined in considerable detail[92] by the judge who delivered the leading opinion of a unanimous court of five,[93] and Jewish authorities were also referred to by him.[94] A certain increase, as compared with previous practice,[95] in citation of the writings of local jurists[96] may also be observed in this group of judgments.

Finally, comparison of the new statute with the previous one of common-law provenience has been disqualified as a tool of interpretation. When for the construction of the Arbitration Law, 5728–1968[97] counsel based his contention on a comparison with the (Mandatory) Arbitration Ordinance, the court reacted as follows: "The Arbitration Law of 1968 is not a copy of the Arbitration Ordinance with certain amendments or omissions from which at times conclusions might be drawn with regard to the intention of the legislator or the construction of the statute. The Arbitration Law is an independent statute, to be construed from within and not by means of comparison with the Arbitration Ordinance."[98]

The features here pointed out somehow remind the comparative lawyer of the methods prevalent in Continental case law. It would, however, be misleading—or at least premature—to evaluate this group of cases as an outright break from the general lines of Israeli judicial law-making. The most that can be said with confidence is that civil-law as well as common-law elements are present in them.

My description of the judicial process in Israel appears to reveal two trends: one that mainly follows the common-law method and one that tends more towards the civil-law method. Whether and how far these two trends are parallel, conflicting, or complementary is hard to say; it depends largely on the point of view of the observer. Moreover, my account may have overemphasized the peculiarities of the cases dealing with the

---

91 See Note 87 above.
92 From Austrian law: two statutes, judgments from 1908, 1938, and 1963; and five learned writers were cited.
93 Justice Kister who had his legal training in his time in Poland, cf. Note 8 above.
94 Justice Kister is also an expert in Jewish law.
95 This, however, was never as strict in Israel as it is (or was) in England. A writer does not have to be dead in order to be cited in an Israeli court.
96 Law review articles, comments on judgments, etc.
97 This statute is beyond the field of Private Law, but also belongs to the new, codificatory legislation.
98 Per Justice Mani in Dar v. Hamami, 25 P.D. (1) 396, 398.

new, codificatory type of statutes and thus overestimated their impact on the canons of interpretation. Anyway, insofar as different paths are being followed, it may be assumed that they are more likely to merge than to diverge. Instead of two separate methods, a unified one, containing elements from both, may be expected to develop. Israeli law may thus become a "mixed jurisdiction" also with respect to judicial law-making. But these are speculations on the future, beyond the scope of this essay.

ABBREVIATIONS

P.D.	Piskei Din (Judgments of the Supreme Court, in Hebrew)
S.J.	Selected Judgments (Israel Supreme Court, in English)
L.S.I.	Laws of the State of Israel
All E.R.	All England Reports
Is. L. Rev.	Israel Law Review
P.L.R.	Palestine Law Reports

XIII

Stare Decisis, Doctrine, and Jurisprudence in Mexico and Elsewhere

Woodfin L. Butte
PROFESSOR OF LAW, UNIVERSITY OF TEXAS

Whatever is done, positive law can never entirely replace the use of natural reason in the affairs of life. The needs of society are so varied, social intercourse is so active, men's interests are so multifarious, and their relations so extensive, that it is impossible for the legislator to provide for everything.

It is then, to the course of decision (*la jurisprudence*) that we leave (1) rare and extraordinary cases which cannot enter into a reasonable legislative plan, (2) details too variable and contentious to occupy the legislator, and (3) all those objects which it would be a useless effort to anticipate, or of which premature anticipation would be dangerous.

It is for experience to fill progressively the gaps we leave. The code of a people makes itself with time: properly speaking it is not made.
—M. Portalis et al.*

For the purposes of this study, we may define

(1) "Stare decisis" as "the English doctrine of a rule established by the binding authority of a single case;"[1]

(2) "Doctrine" as "the ensemble of published studies by jurists as to the creation of law and the interpretation of laws;"[2] and

(3) "Jurisprudence" as "in a broad sense ... the ensemble of decisions

---

* Portalis, Tronchet, Bigot-Préameneu, and Maleville, "Discours Préliminaire," in I Locré, La Législation de la France 251, (1827), being an explanatory statement presented by the drafting commission with their draft of the French Civil Code. Quoted and translated by Von Mehren, The Civil Law System 57 (1957), also by Stone, Recent Trends in English Precedent 2 (1945); other translations in this paper are the author's.
[1] Goodhart, "Precedent in English and Continental Law," 50 Law Quarterly Review 40 (1934); reprinted London, 1934, pp. 8–9. A list of the abbreviations used in this chapter appears on page 330.
[2] II Dalloz, Répertoire de Droit Civil 243 (1952).

rendered by the courts; in a limited sense, the series of decisions relative to a specific point of law."[3]

On these definitions, common views were developed, and often and eloquently expressed over the past century, as to the "source of law" to be used in deciding cases. These common views were to the effect that, in deciding each pending case,

(a) Specific and unambiguous statutory provisions of the forum must of course be followed, under any legal system (unless the constitutionality of the statutory provision be itself in question, in which case different and differing considerations would apply, depending on the constitutional system of the country concerned).

(b) In the absence of clearly controlling statutory provisions, English and other common-law courts would look first for an applicable "precedent"—as many cases as possible, but if necessary only *one* case squarely in point—which would be taken as binding determination of the question or questions of law with which it had dealt, and would control the new decision to be rendered.[4]

(c) This rule was of course modified in the sense that a court would show respect to but not consider itself bound by a decision of a court of lower hierarchy or—as in a federal system—a decision of a court of another state in the federation. The United States Supreme Court for a century left the federal courts not bound by decisions of state courts as to questions of "general common law,"[5] only to reverse this rule in 1938 and decide that federal courts are bound to apply to each case the rules of law which would be applied to that case by the courts of the state in which the respective federal court is sitting.[6]

(d) In the absence of any "precedent," English and other common-law courts were left on their own, and must look where they could for guidance: doctrinal writings, logic, custom, "the better rule of law," and

---

3 III Dalloz, Répertoire de Droit Civil 18 (1953).
4 "If the point has already been decided in a prior case, then the English System applies the doctrine of precedent in a different and much more technical sense. ... The prior case, being directly in point, is no longer one which may be used as a pattern; it is one which *must* be followed in the subsequent case. It is more than a model; it has become a fixed and binding rule." Goodhart, "Precedent in English and Continental Law," 50 L. Q. Rev. 40, 41 (1934).
5 Swift v. Tyson, 41 U.S. (16 Pet.) 1, 10 L.Ed. 865 (1842).
6 Erie R.R. v. Tompkins, 304 U.S. 64, 82 L.Ed. 1188 (1938); Klaxon v. Stentor Elec. Mfg. Co., 313 U.S. 487, 85 L.Ed. 1477 (1941).

more lately "Restatements of the Law." That many of them were uncomfortable in this chilly freedom is shown by the lengths to which they often have gone to analogize and interpret and extrapolate from existing decisions to find the all-sustaining "precedent," and the formulary terminology by which they still *"find the law to be"* rather than *"decide that the law shall be."*

(e) In the absence of a clearly controlling statutory provision, courts in civil-law countries were instructed—in a fascinating variety of statutory guidelines which, for the most part, are quite devoid of helpful intellectual content—to decide the case not on the basis of what they thought was right and just, but (giving a general interpretation to the variety of statutory provisions mentioned) to decide the legal question "according to the general rules of law" or as the judge would decide if he were the legislature.[7]

---

[7] The following are a few more or less random examples:

France, Civil Code, art. 4: "The judge who refuses to judge a case, on the pretext of silence, obscurity, or insufficiency of the law, can be found guilty of denial of justice."
"The judge is the servant of the law . . . he must search out what the legislator would have desired if he had foreseen the case. But, especially when the texts of the law are getting old, the judge must not limit himself to searching out the thought of the legislator, at the time when he drafted the law. The 1804 Code can not be interpreted in our days in the spirit of the beginning of the 19th Century. . . . Logical reasoning will not be his only method; he must be broadly inspired by present social needs, equity, the teaching of History and of Comparative Law. As we already know, obligated to judge in the silence of the law, he completes the law, adapts it and prepares its evolution." I JULLIOT DE LE MORANDIÈRE, PRÉCIS DE DROIT CIVIL, par. 206 (1963).

Spain, Civil Code, art. 6: "When there is no law exactly applicable to the point at issue, local custom will be applied and, in its absence, the general principles of law."

Argentina, Civil Code, art. 16: "Obedience will be given to the principles of analogous laws; and if the question is still doubtful, it shall be decided by the general principles of law, taking into consideration the circumstances of the case." Velez Sarsfield, in his notes to his code, cites this provision all the way back to the Justinian *Digest* and to the *Siete Partidas*. Under the *Partidas*, if the judge was absolutely stumped, he could refer the case to the "sovereign," who would decide.

Mexico, Civil Code of Federal District and Territories, art. 19: "Judicial controversies of a civil nature are to be resolved according to the letter of the law or its juridical interpretation. In the absence of a law, they will be decided according to the general principles of law."

Switzerland, Civil Code, art. 1: "In the absence of an applicable legal provision, the judge decides according to customary law, and in the absence of a custom, according to the rules which he would establish if he were called on to act as legislator."

(f) In looking for help, civil-law courts tended to look first to doctrinal writings of recognized jurists. These writings are commonly organized like the codes themselves, as commentaries on the code provisions; and a good commentator will pose and discuss, by way of elucidating each article of the code, hypothetical questions which quite often include the very problem the court has before it or one so nearly on the point as to indicate a clear path for determining what the legislative intent must have been.

(g) As a secondary recourse, the civil-law court would look for such things as accepted interpretation or supplementation of statutory provisions by customary law; and it was in this frame of mind that the judge would check to see whether he could find enough consistent court rulings on the point at issue to constitute "jurisprudence." He seldom could, for few civil-law countries had until quite recently any really helpful indexing systems for finding decisions bearing on a given point of law.

The reader will already have discerned the thesis of this paper. It is: The supposed differences between "judge-made law" (the civilian's derogatory description of the common-law approach) [8] and "code law"

Portugal, Civil Code, art. 10, par. 1, 3: "The cases not foreseen by the law will be decided following the rule applicable to analogous situations.... In the absence of an analogous case, the situation will be resolved according to the rule that the interpreting authority would establish, if he were to legislate within the spirit of the system."

Brazil, Introductory Law to Civil Code (1942), art. 4: "When the law is silent, the judge will decide the case in accordance with analogy, customs, and the general principles of law."

Art. 5: "In the application of the law, the judge will keep in mind the social purposes to which it is directed and the requirements of the common good."

Code of Civil Procedure (1939), art. 113: "The judge may not, on the pretext of a lacuna or obscurity of the law, decline to render decision." Art. 114: "Whenever he is authorized to reach a decision on equitable grounds, the judge will apply the rule which he would establish if he were the legislator."

Chile, Civil Code (Andrés Bello's great code of 1855), art. 3: "'It is only for the legislator to explain or interpret the law in a generally obligatory manner. Judicial decisions have no binding force except with respect to the cases in which they are actually handed down."

Art. 24 (arts. 19–24 are rules of statutory interpretation). "In cases to which the foregoing rules of interpretation cannot be applied, doubtful or contradictory passages will be interpreted in the manner which may seem most in accord with the general spirit of the legislation and with natural equity."

[8] I heard two Latin American law-school deans, just back from a State Department visit to the United States, explain carefully to one of their students that when a judge is called on to apply a statute that conflicts with a judicial decision, he is

grew out of historical accident, and developed by habit into some pretty fundamental differences in thinking. Those differences, however, were never really basic, and are now becoming even less so as what is "basic" is increasingly judged by what is "practical" or "sound." The old reliances on "stare decisis" and "doctrine" and "jurisprudence" are changing in relative strength and emphasis on both sides of the line, so that the differences which strongly separated civil and common law in the past are tending to become blurred and to disappear.

But having thus stated our thesis, let us elaborate a little.

There is a fundamental difference in the way the civilian and the common-law lawyer *think about* their respective systems of law. The civilian believes, almost as an article of faith, that a single, complete, coherent, and logical system of law to govern all the relationships of man to man is possible (in fact, that it already exists in at least a metaphysical sense), and that the human mind is capable of thinking it out and working it out and putting it down on paper. The common-law lawyer, by and large, simply doesn't care whether such a system exists or not. He is busy deciding cases, with the aid of judicial precedent and with or without the aid of statutory enactment of rules in particular areas. If from this process scholars can begin to see bits and pieces of a system emerging, he is interested in it as a potentially useful tool; but he does not regard the discovery or the development of such a complete and logical system as essential or even as particularly important to him in his continuing task of achieving justice in an infinite number and variety of individual cases.

This difference is of fundamental importance. It shows up first, today, in the law-school curriculum. One wonders how the French or Latin American law professor can spend four years talking about his own civil code, until one reads the textbooks or sits in the lecture and hears the article-by-article exposition and the endless classifications and subclassifications which seem to have little practical importance and thus, we are apt to feel, no importance at all. The civilian professor uses hypothetical cases in the classroom as freely and as imaginatively as does his common-law colleague, but for a completely different purpose. The civil-law

---

bound to follow the decision. The same two deans liked to tell of a visit to Washington, where their North American professor-host, standing on the Capitol steps, said "In here they think they make the laws, but over there [indicating the Supreme Court building] they amend them!"

classroom is a quiet laboratory in which the professor is painstakingly *building*, before the eyes and into the minds of his students; a hypothetical case is drawn in to show how neatly and precisely the building blocks are fitted together as the edifice grows. The common-law classroom, by contrast, is likely to give the impression of a chaotic place where the professor is gleefully destroying any lingering idea his students may have that a building is possible, and each new hypothetical case is introduced to show that the rule we just learned in the last case won't apply to this new one.

This educational process unquestionably produces lawyers whose mental habits are different. The common-law lawyer—we must not push this metaphor too hard—sees a jumble of blocks all over the floor, or at best a number of heaps of blocks with little signs on top saying "contracts," "torts," and so on. It is his task to dig around in these heaps until he finds as many blocks as he can on which to rest his particular problem. The civilian sees in his mind's eye the complete and carefully constructed edifice, with each block in its proper place. It is his task to examine the edifice to see where in its structure his own problem will fit precisely, and if not precisely then most neatly and logically.

This characteristic mental approach of the civilian has very long roots. The Romans probably started it about 300 B.C. when prominent men began to study law and give free legal advice to gain public esteem or to further their political careers, when they achieved a label—*jurisprudentes* or *juris consulti*—and when the judges, who were often laymen, began to turn to them for advice as to how to decide cases. The authority of their writings grew throughout Roman history, and a great mass of excerpts from them was ultimately immortalized in Justinian's *Digest*.

During the Dark Ages in Western Europe—say the sixth through the tenth centuries A.D.—the complete and sophisticated system of law which the Romans had developed was not so much lost as it was simply unnecessary for the primitive agrarian economy which was about all the Western Europeans had. Interest in law as a system was thus left largely to a few teachers and to the timeless hands of the church, whose monks and institutions were permitted to keep the Roman law as their personal law after the conquest.

What came out of this process was not exactly the same law that went into it. One can imagine that as the brandy was aged and fortified in the casks in the monastery cellar, the law was mellowed and refined in discussions around the refectory table upstairs. It is certain that the Roman law which was "rediscovered" in the Middle Ages contained generous infusions of canon law and ethical and moral concepts with which the Romans were unfamiliar: *pacta sunt servanda; abus de droit;* reasonable price; restitution in kind. It is equally true and understandable that the Roman law which was rediscovered was even more strongly conceptual in nature than in the days of the *juris consulti*: an authoritative body of rules, drawn from authoritative concepts handed down ex some sort of cathedra, authoritatively interpreted by a select body of learned specialists.

Even after the "rediscovery" and the reawakening of a need for and consequent interest in a general body of law, it took two centuries of work by scholars—glossators, postglossators, humanists—to work the Roman law around into something that was useful to medieval Europe and could actually be used to decide cases. Again, it was the scholars rather than the judges who established themselves as the authoritative source of interpretation. The sharply different focus of the common law also has deep roots, but in political more than legal history.

In Western continental Europe, through these centuries, there was almost no unifying political authority. In sharp contrast to this, William the Conqueror and his successors very soon established and consolidated their political authority in all of England. As a result, the establishment of law and the administration of justice were in the king's hands. The judges on the bench were the king's judges, based at Westminster and riding circuit throughout the realm, constantly checking, when they got home, with each other and with the members of the bar who rode with them. They brought no unified system of law with them from France; they found no unified system of law in the land which they had conquered. Intensely pragmatic, they decided cases and, having done so, tried to remember to decide subsequent cases the same way. The king's law and the king's justice, and the rules which were so developed, were "common" to the entire realm—the "common law" of England. They simply were not interested in concepts or in the idea of a complete and coherent system. And through the control which they still exercise over the training and calling of new practitioners to the bar, this pragmatic approach—deciding each new case the way we decided the last one like it—has become as deeply ingrained in common-law thinking as the search for a coherent whole has become for the civilian.

Historically, just as the upheavals of the Wars of the Roses caused Britain to "miss" the Renaissance, so the upheavals of the Norman Conquest caused Britain to "miss" the rediscovery and ultimate reception of Roman law.

But within the past fifty years there have been fundamental changes on both sides of the line. Some of these changes are:

1. The tremendous growth of positive statutory law in the common-law countries, thus restricting the area within which the judge and his precedent-giving forebears are free to roam.

2. The veritable flood of reported decisions, "key-noted" and collated and annotated and "Shepardized" with all the computerized skill of a technological age, in which the common-law lawyer—especially the North American lawyer—is becoming literally swamped and which is drowning his ability to think for himself. The British barrister may still produce an important opinion or brief three pages long with two or three citations; you are paying to find out what he *thinks*, not how diligently he can research "case law." But the North American lawyer's search for "controlling precedent" forces him into a long and closely reasoned analysis of scores of more or less relevant decisions, often with no clearly defined opinion to be reached at the end. It is small wonder that a North American client often finds he can get better advice from a personal consultation with his lawyer, where this sort of process is impossible and the lawyer has to *think*, than from a written opinion which could increasingly well have been turned out by a computer. The same observation goes for many court opinions, and the judge who is wise enough and courageous enough (or, his critics would say, lazy enough) to look at what he ought to do this time, rather than engage in a sterile search for what somebody else did last time, has been roundly denounced as an undisciplined rebel or hailed as "a creative and innovative thinker," depending on one's point of view.

3. The sharp improvement in indexing methods in civil-law countries, which has enabled "jurisprudence" to be readily (well, more or less readily) found and brought to the court's attention.

Until quite recently, and even today in many countries, civil-law courts

Doctrine and Jurisprudence in Mexico | 319

—even courts of last resort, whose decisions are in many countries the only ones regularly published—have been inhibited by the common statutory admonition to the effect that they are to "decide the case before them without making any general declaration for the future."[9] The result has been that in many countries courts of last resort have handed down as a matter of practice decisions that are quite useless as precedent or even as a contribution to the formation of "jurisprudence." In the reported decisions of a good many of these countries, the facts are not even stated, on the reasonable ground that the parties know them and that the court is not to assume that anybody in the future will be interested in them. Even when the facts are stated or can be inferred, the court is likely in its decision to make reference to arguments in counsel's briefs, or to portions of the opinions of the lower court or courts, which are available only in the original record in the files of the court.[10]

Indexes of court decisions have until quite recently been nonexistent or grossly deficient. In almost every civil-law country, one had to go through each volume of the reported decisions to find what was in it; the idea of abstracting by subject-matter in a single place decisions published over a period of time in many volumes either never occurred to anybody or, if it did, was tried sporadically and inexpertly for a few months or years and abandoned.

Even in going through each volume of decisions, one notices that the quality and reliability of its indexing fluctuates widely from country to country and from period to period. Many indexes are limited to a table of cases. Others feel that one listing of a case by subject matter is enough (it's in the index!) regardless of how many subjects the decision deals with.[11]

9 France, Civil Code, art. 5. Chile, Civil Code, art. 3. Mexico, Ley de Amparo, art. 76: "Decisions rendered in amparo actions will deal solely with the persons . . . who have brought the petition . . . without making a general declaration with respect to the law or act which provoked it."
10 To the particular exasperation of the foreign student who wants to read the decision fast to find out what the "law of the case" is, courts are likely to rely on code provisions cited by article number only!
11 Some forty years ago, I was running down for Professor Borchard rules on tort liability of the state in Spain, and I was reduced to leafing through the pages of reported decisions, volume by volume, in the Bar Association library in Madrid. On turning up one beautiful decision, squarely on his point, I checked out of curiosity to see how it was listed in the volume's index and why I had missed it there. I found it: "Thumb, left, loss of." Things in Spain are much improved since then.

But this is changing everywhere, and has changed radically in some countries. The reason for the change has simply been response to a felt need. When a lawyer in a civil-law country happened to find a previously decided case that supported his position, he would joyfully cite it to the court and rest his argument on it; and in a surprising percentage of decisions, he would win his case on it. Courts whose attention has been directed to a previous decision in point invariably cite it in their opinion with respect, and often give it controlling effect on their own disposition of the case before them. And this is true even if the previous decision is the only one cited, clearly not enough to establish a "jurisprudential" rule.

The generally accepted relevance of "jurisprudence," not as having any binding effect in itself but in the sense of a series of decisions evidencing the existence or the development of an accepted rule of customary law to interpret or to fill a lacuna in statutory rules, has already been pointed out.[12] This respect for prior decisions is nothing new in civil-law countries, and has on occasion even been statutorily sanctioned.[13] But what we emphasize here is what authors have frequently noted, the tendency of civil-law courts to try to find out whether a point at issue in a given case has already been dealt with in even one prior case, and if it has to give that case great weight in its decision.

4. Last of all, one is tempted to remark a decline in the number and (with all respect) in the intellectual quality of commentaries that can rank with the "greats" of the past century. (There are exceptions, of course, which it would be invidious to single out by name; our apologies go to their authors). If this writer had to assign a reason for what he conceives to be this decline, it would be that present-day commentators tend to think of themselves too humbly as research craftsmen for the profession, rather than as independent scholars and thinkers whose writings will be properly accepted among the "sources"of law. This is true in both the common-law and the civil-law worlds. In North America, (a)

---

12 Portalis, "Discours Préliminaire" in I LOCRÉ, LA LÉGISLATION DE LA FRANCE 251 (1827), quoted in the headnote to this essay.

13 For example:
   Mexico, Law on Amparo (1935), arts. 19–96. (Five consistent decisions of the Supreme Court or its chambers constitute *jurisprudencia* binding on all lower courts, though it may be modified by the court itself.)
   Argentina, Constitution, art. 95; Law 13; 998, art. 28. And see I BORDA, DERECHO CIVIL ARGENTINO 76 ff. (1965).

actual or potentially great commentators are also the compilers of casebooks and teaching materials, and are too busy reediting these so they will be up to date with changing court decisions to have time to rethink and renew their truly constructive work of commenting on the law; (b) in some fields like "choice of law," too many scholars of comparable stature have turned out overlapping and contradictory analyses and "guidelines," the result being more confusion than help; and (c) too many scholars who a century ago would have written authoritative treaties are now turning out "practical" material like ALR annotations and "Restatements of the Law," both of which are based on a deification of the "Decided Case." In France, there is some feeling that the definitive commentaries have already been written and that it would be presumptuous for younger men to try to replace or improve on them; so they devote themselves to writing "Notes" on reported decisions (many of them first-rate, too; but the emphasis is still on the reported decision, not on the comment), or popularized *"Ce qu'il vous faut savoir"* practice manuals for the do-it-yourself lay lawyer.

The cumulative effect of these factors has been to make the common-law and the civil-law decision-reaching processes more alike: the flood of decisions is making *stare decisis* self-defeating to the common-law lawyer; and the ability to find decisions is making the civilian more conscious of their importance as jurisprudence.

But overriding all these factors is a major shift in judicial attitude:

5. A growing sense of independence on the part of judges, and a willingness to decide cases on their own. This also is true on both sides of the common-law/civil-law line. Part of it is due to the sense of frustration judges feel in attempting to find help for their decision-making from the traditional sources. Common-law judges are so engulfed in a flood of "precedents" that the rule of *stare decisis* is impossible to apply; the judge's choice among precedents becomes essentially result-oriented and the judge knows that he, not "precedent," is determining the outcome of the case.[14] The civil-law judge, while respecting and increasingly

---

14 Wasn't it Mr. Dooley who, at the turn of the century, referred to the United States Supreme Court as having "wan eye on the Constitution an' the ither on the iliction returns"? Incidentally, the United States comes off better than Britain in the eyes of one Latin American lawyer: "While in the [English] law, respect for precedent is as noted, strict, by contrast in the United States, the role of precedent is more or less similar to that which it has in countries with codi-

relying on the decisions he can now find, has not forgotten that he is not *bound* by them. Both judges live in an atmosphere of rapid and radical social change which frees them from the imposed thought patterns of the past. "Stability" and "predictability" have lost their magic, and are viewed more as hamstringing progress than as protecting a desirable social order. Judges are thus increasingly unwilling to reach a decision which they feel is socially wrong, even though the sources they would hitherto have consulted—precedent, doctrine, jurisprudence—all point one way.[15] It is true that not many courts today are called on to make so great a leap as the French Court of Cassation made in the *Guissez* case in 1896.[16] But there are many fields in which judges have now rebelled against authority and reached what they felt was a just decision, and have said so, when a half-century ago they would have "felt themselves compelled" to bow to "authority" even though it forced them to do an injustice in a particular case.

With the assistance of a young Mexican attorney [17] we have checked to see to what extent these observations are confirmed by experience. We chose Mexico simply because it is one of the states whose reports are on

---

fied laws; judges follow it if they find no good reason to pull away from it, in which case they leave it aside without hesitation. In this matter North American common law has demonstrated much greater flexibility than English law and a great adaptability to changing economic and social conditions." I BORDA, DERECHO CIVIL ARGENTINO (1965).

15 Even the House of Lords has thrown off the shackles it had put on its own freedom to change its mind in London St. Tramways Co. v. London County Council, (1898) A.C. 375. On July 26, 1966, the lord chancellor, Lord Gardiner, made the following statement: "Their Lordships regard the use of precedent as an indispensable foundation upon which to decide what is the law and its application to individual cases. . . . Their Lordships nevertheless recognize that too rigid adherence to precedent may lead to injustice in a particular case and also unduly restrict the proper development of the law. They propose therefore to modify their present practice and, while treating former decisions of this House as normally binding, to depart from a previous decision when it appears right to do so." 116 NEW LAW JOURNAL, 1102, 1116, 1131.

16 Guissez, Cousin et Oriolle v. Teffaine, Ch. civile, 16 June 1896, D. 1897. I. 433 (note Saleilles), S. 1897. I. 17, (note Esmein); quoted and translated in VON MEHREN, THE CIVIL LAW SYSTEM 379, (1957). This is the famous case in which a tugboat employee was killed by a boiler explosion; the Court of Cassation read art. 1384 of the Civil Code in such a way as to open the door for imposition of a presumption of fault against the "guardian" of *anything* which caused damage, a plain perversion of the clear intent of the legislature as expressed in the code provisions involved. The "felt need" was the same which led to the development of *res ipsa loquitur* in the common law.

17 Lic. José A. Rodríquez of Monterrey.

our shelves, complete, and because we have no reason to expect Mexico's experience to be very different from that of any other civil-law state. Our method was first to skim a few cases in Volume I of the *Semanario Judicial*,[18] then to read the first hundred civil cases decided by the Supreme Court in 1900, the first hundred decided in 1930, and the first hundred decided in 1968.

In Volume I, for 1871, we note, first, a practice of printing first of all as to each case the report and recommendations of the *promotor fiscal*, a government attorney who has, among other responsibilities, the right to comment on questions presented to the Supreme Court for decision. This report commonly contains a brief but complete narrative of the facts, a reference to pertinent legislation (which at that time in Mexico was quite likely to be a citation to the *Siete Partidas*) and a summary recommendation of what the *promotor* thinks the court's decision should be.

Then may come the decision of the trial court in an amparo[19] action (a federal district court) and after that the decision of the Supreme Court, both generally adopting and confirming the report of the *promotor fiscal*. In an important case, there will be extracts from notes of the oral arguments of counsel.

Turning through a number of these cases, we found one in which the district court, in finding for a petitioner that a certain tax collected from

18 The *Semanario Judicial de la Federación* is the officially established publication of all decisions of the Mexican Supreme Court. It has gone through six épocas and is in the middle of the seventh. In earlier épocas each volume contained the decisions for three or four months, all paged consecutively. Beginning with the sixth época, there has been a volume per month, with each volume divided into five "parts." The first part covers decisions of the full court; the second covers decisions of the First Chamber; the third, decisions of the Second Chamber; the fourth, decisions of the Third Chamber; and the fifth, decisions of the Fourth Chamber. The pages of each part of each volume are numbered separately. This makes citation pretty complicated, and the court has never worked out a satisfactory short form. In this essay I have invented my own: for the earlier épocas, volume number, epoch number, page number—e.g. 123 SJF5a 2047; beginning with the sixth época, volume number, followed by epoch number, followed by part number, followed by page number—e.g. 76 SJF6a 4:84.

19 Amparo is "'shelter, protection"; the basic action in Mexico and several other countries under which any person in the country can claim judicial protection against invasion by any branch of the government of rights guaranteed to him by the constitution. It thus includes what in the United States would be *habeas corpus, quo warranto*, injunction, test of constitutionality of legislation. In Mexico, among the rights guaranteed by the constitution is the right to have the law correctly applied in any judicial decision; so the amparo action in the Supreme Court also includes what in France and other countries is *cassation*. It works well, and the Mexicans are justly very proud of it.

him was unconstitutional, based its finding on a similar decision by the Supreme Court in an identical case two years earlier.[20] We found another in which counsel quoted from a text written by a colleague; his adversary cited Carleval, Voet, Story, Wheaton, Calvo, "and many others"; and the Supreme Court cited 1.32, tit. 2°, Part 3ª [*Las Siete Partidas*] contemporary Mexican practice manual. (The case, incidentally, involved an action against an estate about some land in another state; all concerned treated the questions of choice of proper forum and choice of proper law as the same—i.e., that the forum, once chosen, would automatically apply forum law, and that statutory provisions about applicable law led necessarily to choice of the proper forum. The court found the proper forum to be the last domicile of the deceased—*actor forum rei sequitur*.) [21]

In another case,[22] involving the right of a householder to continue to receive water from a town well, the *promotor fiscal* cites Justinian's *Institutes*, the *Digest*, and the *Partidas*, while the district court cites only the *Partidas* and the Supreme Court cites only a contemporaneous Executive Order.

In their brief for the petitioner for amparo in a capital case,[23] counsel support their point that criminal laws are not to be applied retroactively by citing the whole chain of legal authority from the *Codigo de Legibus*, 1.7. through the *Leyes de Estilo*, the *Fuero Real*, the *Partidas*, and the *Novisima Recopilación*. They cite a similar chain of laws and half a dozen commentators on the inadmissibility of the testimony of accomplices, and go back to the *Partidas* to support their argument that a witness who contradicts himself is not entitled to be believed! They won their case!

Here then, in 1871 in Mexico, was confirmation of the civil-law system as it has always been perceived—a heavy emphasis on statutes, going as far back as may be pertinent, enlightened by learned commentators, but with only casual reference to a recent Supreme Court decision which a district court judge happened to remember by name and date but not by citation.

Moving on thirty years, to the first hundred civil cases decided by the

20 C. Francisco Diego, 10 Jan. 1871, 1 SJF1a, 88, 90, citing decision in case of Lic. Rodolfo Canton, 12 Nov. 1868.
21 Municipalidad de Maltrata, 7 Feb. 1871, 1 SJF1a 92, 102.
22 Eugenio López, 16 Feb. 1871, 1 SJF1a 130, 135.
23 Pascual Valdés, 1 SJF1a 148, 150.

Mexican Supreme Court in 1900, we find substantial changes in the style and format of decisions. The *promotor fiscal* increasingly exercises the privilege the law gives him of not intervening in cases dealing with purely private rights. The lower-court decisions are no longer always printed in full, but sometimes show up only by being quoted either by the Supreme Court or in petitioner's brief (often, in the latter case, accompanied by counsel's references to it in terms we would find scandalous). The Supreme Court is developing the nonstop sentence as a hallmark of judicial writing.

Licenciado Rodriguez finds that of these first hundred decisions, ninety-seven are decided solely by the application to the facts of the case of a particular statutory provision which the court finds controlling. In all these cases, the court's decision is almost bare of reasoning or interpretation; the language is simply something to the effect that "This case is clearly controlled by Article 754 of the Code of Civil Procedure, which provides . . ."

It is true that the cases tend to be simple ones: land-ownership cases, with a plaintiff suing for possession; *habeas corpus* cases, with a plaintiff either in jail or in the armed services without his consent and, in his opinion, in violation of his constitutional rights; or procedural cases. At any rate, the Supreme Court makes them *sound* simple; it reviews the facts and the proceedings below, briefly, then says, "It is plain that . . ." And the reader wonders how so straightforward a case ever got to the Supreme Court.

Two of these hundred decisions of 1900 are cited by Licenciado Rodriguez as being based on "jurisprudence" of the Supreme Court. In one of these, the *promotor fiscal* observes that a complaint as to the weight given to evidence in the lower courts "cannot according to the jurisprudence of the Supreme Court of Justice be the basis for an amparo proceeding."[24] In the other, the Supreme Court itself pronounces that "the jurisprudence of the courts of the Federation has established that no judicial proceeding can prejudice a third party who has been neither cited nor heard in proper form."[25]

In one case only out of the hundred,[26] (the nonstop sentence made

---

24 José M. de la Torre, 5 SJF4a 777.
25 Maria de la Luz and Rodrigo Trujano, 5 SJF4a 892.
26 Aristides F. Pinto, 5 SJF4a 751, at 762.

reading rapidly extremely difficult) and we may have missed some, did we find a district court citing doctrine: "At this point," says Emilio Reus in his commentaries on the Code of Civil Procedure, "a *litis* exists."

The same district court in the same opinion, at page 770, refers to the showing of two of the complainants that they were neither cited, heard, nor defeated in proceedings in which the petitioner below was put in possession of property adjoining or overlapping theirs; "which was a violation of constitutional guarantees, as the Supreme Court of Justice has laid down in various decisions."

Between 1900 and 1930 we must note the intervention of an important piece of legislation, the new *Ley de Amparo* of October 18, 1919. This law for the first time uses the word "*jurisprudencia*" in referring to decisions of the Supreme Court, and establishes the binding nature for inferior courts of "*jurisprudencia*" laid down by five consonant decisions of the Supreme Court.[27] It is thus natural to expect more citation of jurisprudence as this reform works its way into the Mexican judicial process; and this is in fact what happened.

In studying the first hundred 1930 civil cases, Licenciado Rodriguez finds eighteen of them based on jurisprudence, seventy-one on the application of controlling statutes and eleven on citations of doctrinal writings.

The style and format of decision-writing in 1930 has not changed much from that of 1900. The Ministerio Público (the old *promotor fiscal*) hardly ever intervenes; the lower court's decision appears mostly in the form of quotations in petitioner's brief of those parts of it which he deems most objectionable; the Supreme Court feels the need for somewhat—but not much—more support for its decision than to say "It is clear that . . ."

In the eleven cases out of the hundred in which doctrinal writings are cited, the citations are more specific than they were in 1871; but some of them are elucidating European code provisions different from the Mexican and contribute little to the court's reasoning. Even in the eighteen cases out of the hundred in which the court relies on its own jurisprudence, only in two or three of these does the court actually cite any cases by name. The court feels the pressure to support its decisions; but it usually does so by some such statement as "as this Supreme Court has decided in numerous cases . . ."

---

[27] URBINA, NUEVA LEGISLATIÓN DE AMPARO 46 (16th ed. 1970).

We may note in passing that at this time it was still extremely difficult to find "jurisprudencia" in Mexico. At the end of each volume of the *Semanario Judicial* there was a listing, by alphabetical order of key words, of the headnotes of decisions in that volume; but it does not appear to have occurred to anybody to organize these into one publication anywhere.

By 1968 this had radically changed, and Mexico had various publications in which court or counsel could look for the rules of decision laid down in reported cases. The presiding justice in his annual report had initiated a section in which he referred to the more important rulings handed down during the year. And through the years 1932–1955, the *Semanario* published a series of appendices covering cumulatively all jurisprudence established since 1917. This series culminated with the publication, in 1955, of a three-volume *compilación* covering decisions of the court for the years 1917–1954. In this compilation are listed, alphabetically by key word, the headnotes of rules which had been enunciated in five decisions of the court (thus becoming *jurisprudencia* binding on all lower courts) and citations to those decisions. Under each heading the editors of the *Semanario* also, in a very interesting development, set out the headnotes and the citation of individual cases which lay down "related rules which establish precedent, but not jurisprudence." One notes in passing that, as might be expected, the "jurisprudence" tends to be one or two headnotes on each topic, citing five or more cases enunciating quite elementary rules of law, and that the "related rules" are much more interesting, varied, and useful.

In 1965 the editors of the *Semanario* published another of their appendices covering the years 1917–1965. This one is in five volumes, one for the full court and one for each of the chambers, and follows the format of the 1955 appendix. In his introductory *advertencia*, Mr. Justice José Carlos Estrada says:

> The three volumes which make up the last Appendix are out of print and are the subject of price speculation. . . . Nevertheless, in spite of these and many other almost insuperable difficulties, there is one universally recognized fact: that the diffusion of rules of decision constituting "jurisprudencia" has been considerable and has made an important contribution to the unification of rules of interpretation of the law by the courts of the Republic, to such an extent that it is not uncommon to see, even in the decisions of municipal courts when they are appealable before State courts of first instance, the citation of decisions of our Supreme Court. Something similar is taking place in the Mexican Bar: *more frequently than the authoritative opinions of recog-*

nized authors, one notes in bills of complaint and in briefs a reliance by lawyers on the decisions of the Court. [Emphasis added.] [28]

And in 1965 Licenciado Sergio Torres Eyras published the best and most ambitious compilation yet, in five volumes covering respectively the decisions of the full court and of each of the four chambers for the years 1955–1963.[29] It is interesting to note that his index covers *all* decisions of the respective chambers, and that the ritual series of five decisions to constitute binding *jurisprudencia* are distinguished only by the word "*jurisprudencia*" in capital letters in the citation of each decision. In other words, *precedent* is becoming the more important concept; the formal binding character of *jurisprudencia* is frosting on the cake.

It is not surprising, therefore, that in his analysis of the first hundred civil cases decided by the Mexican Supreme Court, in 1968, Licenciado Rodriguez finds fifty-one in which the court cites its own jurisprudence, forty-two in which the decision is by application of a clearly controlling statute, and only two which contain any citation of doctrinal writings. Moreover, in turning through these cases, one finds that prior cases are no longer referred to only in general terms like "It has been decided in numerous cases by this Supreme Court that . . . " They are now referred to by specific title, citation and more often than not by quotation of the applicable headnote.

We may summarize:

CIVIL DECISIONS OF THE MEXICAN SUPREME COURT BASED ON CITATION OF:			
First 100 cases in	Controlling statute	Doctrinal writings	Court's own "jurisprudencia"
1900	97	1	2
1930	71	11	18
1968	42	2	51

It is hard to know which is the chicken and which is the egg; but it is certainly true that in Mexico judicial precedent is much easier to find than in the past; and that in the decision-reaching process, precedent is now much more used and carries much more weight than doctrinal writings.

28 APÉNDICE, 1917–1965, DE JURISPRUDENCIA DE LA SUPREMA CORTE 7.
29 EYRAS, JURISPRUDENCIA Y TÉSIS SOBRESALIENTES, 1955–1963 (5 vols. Mayo ed. 1965).

CONCLUSION

For a long time—for at least a century everywhere, for many centuries in Britain—judges have been under varying degrees of compulsion to decide each case by applying to it an already-established rule rather than by deciding what to the judge seems to be fair to the parties in the individual case. This already-established rule was found in each system by reference to different "sources of law." In common-law countries, it was found in statutes and judicial "precedent"—the rule of *stare decisis*—and the judge regarded the already-established rule as binding on him almost absolutely. In civil-law countries, it was found in statutes, then in the interpretation of statutes in the writing of recognized commentators, and finally in "jurisprudence." And the difficulty of finding the already established rule often left the judge much more freedom to judge than he really wanted.

Today there are specific developments that make less important the differences in philosophy between the two systems. The controlling development is a response by judges to the pressures of social change around them, and a growing feeling that reaching a decision in each case that achieves a just result in that case is more important than respect for any already-established rule. This throws "stability" and "predictability" overboard.[30] It also in many circumstances throws overboard hard lessons of history. It may, as Justice Black observed in his dissent to *International Shoe*, "make judges the supreme arbiters of the country's law and practices [and thus] alter the form of government our Constitution provides."[31]

Judges may not all be the paragons of wisdom and impartial thought they are supposed to be; but we common-law lawyers like to say that "the glory of the common law is its sensitivity to the facts of the particular case," and it is hard to quarrel with a philosophy that sets "justice in the particular case" as its goal.

---

30 Except to the extent that counsel, on all the facts of the case, may be able to predict a "just result" as clearly as the judge can, and perhaps more clearly than counsel can in the present chaotic state of "precedent." This writer thinks this is a consideration to which not enough weight has been given.

31 International Shoe Co. v. Washington, 326 U.S. 310, 326, 90 L.Ed. 95 (1945).

ABBREVIATIONS

A.C.	Appeal Cases (English Reports)
Ch. civile	Chambre civile (Court of Cassation)
D.	Dalloz
S.	Sirey
U.S.	United States Supreme Court Reports

XIV

A Selective Bibliography*

Charles Szladits
ADJUNCT PROFESSOR OF COMPARATIVE LAW, COLUMBIA UNIVERSITY

This bibliography is a selection of writings on the rôle of judicial decisions and doctrine in the sphere of civil (private) law in France, Germany, Switzerland, Austria, and Italy, with a few items about Belgium, the Netherlands, and Spain. A selection of books and articles in English about foreign and comparative law has been added. In making the selection, certain works were disregarded: the standard treatises on French private law which all deal with the subject (among these the treatises by Ripert & Boulanger, Carbonnier, and Marty & Raynaud are most useful), the numerous German works on philosophy of law and jurisprudence (*Einleitung in die Rechtswissenschaft, allgemeine Rechtslehre*) which usually discuss the problem of judicial practice and of doctrine, and most of the frequently used commentaries. Works dealing primarily with public law or criminal law were (with few exceptions) omitted.

To evaluate this selection, made from an extensive literature, would be beyond the scope of this compilation. It may, however, be useful to indicate which authors were found most helpful and instructive by the compiler. These were, among the French, the writings by Boulanger, and Maury & Perreau; among the Germans, the works by Esser, Larenz, Less, and the more recent works by Canaris, Kriele, and the sociologically oriented Luhmann; among the Swiss, the works by Germann and Meyer-Hayoz; and among the works in English, Dawson's masterly study and Sereni's essay.

* A list of the abbreviations used in this chapter appears on page 344.

FRANCE

Aubry & Rau. *Droit civil français*. 7th ed. Paris, 1964. Vol. I, pp. 55–59.

Bonnecase, J. *La Pensée juridique française de 1804 à l'heure présente*. Bordeaux, 1933. 2 vols.

———. *Précis de pratique judiciaire et extrajudiciaire*. Paris, 1927. 458 pp.

Bonnecase, Julien. *L'École de l'exégèse en droit civil*. 2nd ed. Paris, 1924. 285 pp.

Boulanger, J. *La Méthode depuis le code civil de 1804 au point de vue de l'interprétation judiciaire*. Paris, 1950. Pp. 57–64.

——— *Rôle du juge en cas de silence ou d'insuffisance de la loi*. Paris, 1949. Pp. 61–73.

———. *Notions sur le pouvoir créateur de la jurisprudence civile*. R.T. 1961. Pp. 417–41.

Boulanger, Jean. "Jurisprudence," *Répertoire de droit civil*. Paris, 1953. Vol. 3, pp. 17–23.

Carré de Malberg, Raymond. *Contribution à la théorie générale de l'Etat, Tome I*. Paris, 1920. 837 pp.

Centre National de Recherches de Logique. *Le Fait et le droit: Etudes de logique juridique*. Brussels, 1961. 278 pp. (Comparative)

Chrétien, Maxime. *Les Règles de droit d'origine juridictionnelle*. Lille, 1936. 208 pp.

Dupeyroux, Olivier. "La Jurisprudence, source abusive de droit," in *Mélanges Maury*. Paris, 1960. Vol. 2, pp. 349–77.

Esmein, Adhémar. *La Jurisprudence et la doctrine*. R.T., 1902. Pp. 5–19.

Esmein, Paul. *La Jurisprudence et la loi*. R.T., 1952. Pp. 17–23.

Fragistas, Ch. N. "Les Précédents judiciaires en Europe continentale," in *Mélanges Maury*. Paris, 1960. Vol. 2, pp. 139–72. (Comparative)

Gaudemet, Eugène. *L'Interprétation du Code civil en France depuis 1804*. Bâle-Paris, 1935. 75 pp.

Gény, François. *Méthodes d'interprétation et sources en droit privé positif*. 2nd ed. Paris, 1919. 2 vols.

Hébrand, Pierre. *Du règlement juridictionnel des litiges comportant une virtualité de généralisation; prohibition des arrêts de règlement, et de la motivation par référence à une précédente décision* (Note). R.T., 1955. Pp. 696–99.

Maury, Jacques. "Observations sur la jurisprudence en tant que source du droit," in *Études Ripert (Le droit privé français au milieu du XX siècle)*. Paris, 1950. Vol. 1, pp. 28–50.

Meynial, Ed. "Les Recueils d'arrêts et les arrêtistes," in *Livre du centenaire. Le Code Civil*. Paris, 1904. Vol. 1, pp. 173–204.

Motulsky, Henri. *Principes d'une réalisation méthodique du droit privé*. Paris, 1948. 183 pp.

Perelman, Chaim, ed. Études de logique juridique. Brussels, Vol. I, 1966; Vol. II, 1967. (Contains studies by various authors on "Droit et logique" and "Les lacunes en droit.")

Perreau, E. H. Technique de jurisprudence en droit privé. Paris, 1923. 2 vols.

Portalis, Jean-Etienne-Marie. "Discours préliminaire sur le Projet du Code civil," in Frédéric Portalis, ed. Discours, rapports et travaux inédits sur le Code Civil. Paris, 1844. Pp. 1–62.

Ripert, Georges. Les Forces créatrices du Droit. Paris, 1955.

Sauvel, Tony. "Essai sur la notion de précédent," in Receuil Dalloz, Chronique, p. 93 (1955).

———. "Histoire des jugements motivés," Revue de droit public (1955), 5-53. (Historical)

Sergène, A. "Le Précédent judiciaire au Moyen Age." Revue historique de droit français et étranger (1961), 224–54, 359–70. (Historical)

Waline, Marcel. "Pouvoir normatif de la jurisprudence," in Mélanges G. Scelle (Études en l'honneur de G. Scelle). Paris, 1950. Vol. 2, pp. 613–32.

GERMANY

Arndt, Adolf. "Gesetzesrecht und Richterrecht." NJW, (1963), 1, 273.

Bastian, Hermann. "Der Richter als Gesetzgeber." Dissertation, Mainz, 1955. 166 pp.

Becker, Walter G. "Rechtsvergleichende Notizen zur Auslegung," in Festschrift für Heinrich Lehmann. Berlin-Tübingen, 1956. Vol. 1, pp. 70–96.

Bender, Bernd. "Zur Methode der Rechtsfindung bei der Auslegung und Fortbildung gesetzten Rechts." JZ (1957), 593.

———. "Inhalt und Grenzen des Gebots der verfassungskonformen Gesetzesauslegung." MDR (1959), 441.

Bendix, Ludwig. Zur Psychologie der Urteilstätigkeit des Berufsrichters. Neuwied and Berlin, 1968. 450 pp. New ed. (Soziologische Texte)

Betti, Emilio. Allgemeine Auslegungslehre als Methodik der Geisteswissenschaften. Tübingen, 1967. 771 pp.

———. "Ergänzende Rechtsfortbildung als Aufgabe der richterlichen Gesetzesauslegung," in Festschrift für Leo Raape. Hamburg, 1948. P. 379.

Boehmer, Gustav. Grundlagen der bürgerlichen Rechtsordnung, Vol. II of Praxis der richterlichen Rechtschöpfung. Tübingen, 1952. 231 pp.

Brändl, Franz. Einleitung in Staudingers Kommentar zum Bürgerlichen Gesetzbuch. 11th ed. Berlin, 1957.

Bülow, Oskar. Gesetz und Richteramt. Leipzig, 1885. 48 pp.

Canaris, Claus-Wilhelm. Feststellung von Lüken im Gesetz. Berlin, 1964. 219 pp.

———. *Systemdenken und Systembegriff in der Jurisprudenz.* Berlin, 1969. 169 pp.

Coing, Helmut. *Grundzüge der Rechtsphilosophie.* 2nd ed. Berlin, 1969. 369 pp.

———. *Juristische Auslegungsmethoden und die Lehren der allgemeinen Hermeneutik.* Köln-Opladen, 1959. 56 pp.

Edelmann, Johann. *Die Entwicklung der Interessenjurisprudenz: Eine historisch-kritische Studie über die deutsche Rechtsmethodologie vom 18. Jahrhundert bis zur Gegenwart.* Bad Hamburg-Berlin, 1967. 114 pp.

Ehrlich, Eugen. *Grundlegung der Soziologie des Rechts.* Berlin, 1913.

Engisch, Karl. "Der Begriff der Rechtslücke," in *Festschrift für Wilhelm Sauer.* Berlin, 1949. P. 85.

———. *Die Idee der Konkretisierung in Recht und Rechtswissenschaft unserer Zeit.* Heidelberg, 1953. 294 pp.

———. *Einführung in das juristische Denken.* 3rd ed. Stuttgart, 1964. 256 pp.

———. *Logische Studien zur Gesetzesanwendung.* 3rd ed. Heidelberg, 1963. 126 pp.

Esser, Josef. *Grundsatz und Norm in der richterlichen Fortbildung des Privatrechts.* Tübingen, 1956. 394 pp.

———. "Die Interpretation im Recht," VII *Studium Generale,* p. 372 (1954).

———. "Richterrecht, Gerichtsbrauch und Gewohnheitsrecht," in *Festschrift für Fritz von Hippel.* Tübingen, 1967. Pp. 95–130.

———. *Vorverständnis und Methodenwahl in der Rechtsfindung.* Frankfurt am Main, 1970. 218 pp.

———. *Wertung, Konstruktion und Argument im Zivilurteil.* Karlsruhe, 1965. 28 pp.

Fechner, Erich. *Rechtsphilosophie.* 2nd ed. Tübingen, 1962. 303 pp.

Flume, Werner. "Richter und Recht, Vortrag vor dem 46. Deutschen Juristentag," in *Veröffentlichungen des 46. DJT.* Vol. II, Teil K. Munich and Berlin, 1967.

Hanach, Ernst-Walter. *Der Ausgleich divergierender Entscheidungen in der oberen Gerichtsbarkeit.* Hamburg-Berlin, 1962. 420 pp.

Heck, Philipp. *Gesetzesauslegung und Interessenjurisprudenz.* Tübingen, 1914. 319 pp.

———. *Begriffsbildung und Interessenjurisprudenz.* Tübingen, 1932. 228 pp.

Hedemann, Justus Wilhelm. *Die Flucht in die Generalklausel.* Tübingen, 1933. 76 pp.

Henckel, Wolfram. "Die egränzende Vertragsauslegung." AcP 159, p. 106.

Henkel, Heinrich. *Einführung in die Rechtsphilosophie.* Munich, 1964. 468 pp.

Hilger, Marie Louise. "Überlegungen zum Richterrecht," in *Festschrift für Karl Larenz zum 70. Geburtstag,* Munich, 1973. Pp. 109–23.

Isay, Hermann. *Rechtsnorm und Entscheidung.* Berlin, 1923. 379 pp.

Jellinek, Walter. *Gesetz, Gesetzesanwendung und Zweckmässigkeitserwägung.* Leipzig, 1913. 167 pp.

———. "Richterrecht, Gerichtsbrauch und Gewohnheitsrecht," in *Festschrift für Fritz von Hippel.* Tübingen, 1967. Pp. 95–130.

Kantorowicz, Hermann. *Rechtswissenschaft und Soziologie: Ausgewählte Schriften.* Karlsruhe, 1962. 172 pp. (Contains Der Kampf um die Rechtswissenschaft.)

König, Wilhelm, and Rudolf Reinhardt. *Richter und Rechtsfindung.* Munich, 1957. 46 pp.

Kriele, Martin. *Kriterien der Gerechtigkeit.* Berlin, 1963. 109 pp.

———. *Theorie der Rechtsgewinnung: Entwickelt am Problem der Verfassungsinterpretation.* Berlin, 1966. 334 pp.

Kruse, Heinrich Wilhelm. *Das Richterrecht als Rechtsquelle des innerstaatlichen Rechts.* Tübingen, 1971. 20 pp. (Recht und Staat Heft, 396).

Kübler, Friedrich Karl. "Amt und Stellung des Richters in der Gesellschaft von Morgen." *Deutsche Richter Z.* (1969), 379–85.

———. "Der deutsche Richter und das demokratische Gesetz." AcP 162 p. 104.

Larenz, Karl. *Die Methode der Auslegung der Rechtsgeschäfte.* Leipzig, 1930; reprinted 1966. 106 pp.

———. "Ergänzende Vertragsauslegung und dispositives Recht." NJW (1963), 737.

———. *Methodenlehre der Rechtswissenschaft.* 2nd ed. Berlin, 1969. 507 pp.

———. "Uber das Verhältnis von Interpretation und richterlicher Rechtsfortbildung," in *Festskrift till Olivecrona.* Stockholm, 1964. P. 384.

———. "Uber die Bindungswirkung von Präjudizien," in *Festschrift für Hans Schima.* Vienna, 1969. Pp. 247–64.

———. "Wegweiser zur richterlichen Rechtsschöpfung," in *Festschrift für Artur Nikisch.* Tübingen, 1958. P. 275.

———. *Kennzeichen geglückter richterlichen Rechtsfortbildung.* Karlsruhe, 1965. 14 pp.

Less, Günther. *Von Wesen und Wert des Richterrechts.* Erlangen, 1954. 112 pp.

Lorenz, Werner. "Rechtsvergleichung als Methode zur konkretisierung der allgemeinen Grundsätze des Rechts." JZ (1962), 269.

Luhmann, Niklas. *Legitimation durch Verfahren.* Neuwied and Berlin, 1969.

———. "Funktionale Methode und juristische Entscheidung." *Archiv für öffentl. Recht* 91, p. 1 (1969).

———. *Grundrechte als Institution; ein Beitrag zur politischen Soziologie.* Berlin, 1965. 223 pp.

Merz, Hans. "Auslegung, Lückenfüllung und Normberichtigung." *AcP* 163, p. 305 (1964).

Müller, Friedrich. *Normstruktur und Normativität: Zum Verhältnis von Recht und Wirklichkeit in der juristischen Hermeneutik, entwickelt an Fragen der Verfassungsinterpretation.* Berlin, 1966. 232 pp.

Nawiasky, Hans. *Allgemeine Rechtslehre als System der rechtlichen Grundbegriffe.* 2nd ed. Einsiedeln-Zürich-Köln, 1948. 313 pp.

Nipperdey, Hans-Carl, in Enneccerus-Nipperdey, *Allgemeiner Teil des Bürgerlichen Rechts.* 15th ed. Tübingen, 1959. 2 vols.

Raiser, Ludwig. "Rechtswissenschaft und Rechtspraxis." *NJW* (1964), 1, 201.

Ramm, Thilo. "Auslegung und gesetzesändernde Rechtsfortbildung." *Arbeit und Recht* (1962), 353.

Rasehorn, Theo. "Rechtsfindung und Gerichtspraxis." *NJW* (1972), 81.

Schneider, Hans Peter. *Richterrecht, Gesetzesrecht und Verfassungsrecht.* Frankfurt am Main, 1969. 54 pp.

Schwarz, A. B. "Der Einfluss der Professoren auf die Rechtsentwicklung im Laufe der Jahrhunderte," in *Rechtsgeschichte und Gegenwart.* Karlsruhe, 1960. Pp. 181–205.

Siebert, Wolfgang. *Die Methode der Gesetzesauslegung.* Heidelberg, 1958. 47 pp.

Viehweg, Theodor. *Topik und Jurisprudenz.* 4th ed. Munich, 1969. 77 pp.

Weinkauff, Hermann. *Richtertum und Rechtsfortbildung in Deutschland.* Tübingen, 1952.

Wenzel, Leonhard. "Die Problematik der richterlichen husfüllung von Gesetzeslücken." *JZ* (1960), 713.

Wieacker, Franz. *Gesetz und Richterkunst: Zum Problem der aussergesetzlichen Rechtsordnung.* Karlsruhe, 1958. 22 pp.

———. *Zur rechtstheoretischen Präzisierung des §242 BGB.* Tübingen, 1956. 53 pp.

Wilburg, Walter. *Entwicklung eines beweglichen Systems in Bürgerlichen Recht.* Graz, 1950. 26 pp.

Winter, Gerd. "Tatsachenurteile im Prozess richterlicher Rechtssetzung." 2 *Rechtstheorie*, 171 (1971).

Zajtay, Imre. "Begriff, System und Präjudiz in den kontinentalen Rechten und im Common Law." *AcP* 165, p. 97.

Zippelius, Reinhold. "Problemjurisprudenz und Topik." NJW (1967), 2, 229.

———. Das Wesen des Rechts. 2nd ed. Munich, 1969. 187 pp.

———. Einführung in die juristische Methodenlehre. Munich, 1972. 137 pp.

———. Wertungsprobleme im System der Grundrechte. Munich and Berlin, 1962. 220 pp.

Zweigert, Konrad. "Juristische Interpretation." Studium Generale (1954), 380.

SWITZERLAND

Baumgarten, Arthur. Grundzüge der juristischen Methodenlehre. Bern, 1939. 192 pp.

Burckhardt, Walter. Die Lücken des Gesetzes und Gesetzesauslegung. Bern, 1925. 106 pp.

———. Methode und System des Rechts. Zurich, 1936. 302 pp.

Deschenaux, Henri. "Der Einleitungstitel," in M. Gutzwiller, ed., Schweizerisches Privatrecht. Basel, 1967. Vol. 2, pp. 67–142.

Dubs, Hans. Praxisänderung. Basel, 1949. 183 pp.

Ehrlich, Eugen. "Die 'bewährte Lehre und Überlieferung'." SJZ 16, p. 225 (1919/20).

Friedrich, Hans-Peter. "Die Analogie als Mittel der richterlichen Rechtsfindung." ZSR 71, p. 439 (1952).

Germann, Oskar A. Methodische Grundfragen. Basel, 1946. 160 pp.

———. "Präjudizielle Tragweite höchstinstanzlicher Urteile, insbesondere der Urteile des Schweizerischen Bundesgerichts." ZSR 68, pp. 297–332, 423–56 (1949).

———. Präjudizien als Rechtsquellen. Stockholm-Göteborg-Uppsala, 1960. 52 pp.

———. Probleme und Methoden der Rechtsfindung. Bern, 1965. 418 pp.

———. "Zum Verhältnis zwischen Rechtsquellen und Rechtsfindung," in Festschrift für Hans Lewald. Basel, 1953. P. 485.

Gmür, Max. Die Anwendung des Rechts nach Art. 1. des schweizerischen Zivilgesetzbuches. Bern, 1908. 152 pp.

Gutzwiller, Max. "Zur Lehre von der Natur der Sache," in Freiburger Festgabe zum schweizerischen Juristentag. Fribourg, 1924. P. 282.

Huber, Eugen. "Bewährte Lehre." Politisches Jahrbuch der schweizerischen Eidgenossenschaft 25, p. 3 (1911).

———. Erläuterungen zum Vorentwurf des ZGB. 2nd ed. Bern, 1914. 2 vols.

Huber/Mutzner. 1 System und Geschichte des schweizerischen Privatrechts. Parts 1–3. Basel, 1932–37 (no longer published).

Liver, Peter. "Der Begriff des Rechtsquelle," 91 bis Rechtsquellenprobleme im Schweizerischen Recht, Zschft. des Berner Juristenvereins, (special issue), 1 (1955).

———. Der Wille des Gesetzes. Bern, 1954.

Meyer-Hayoz, Arthur, in Berner Kommentar, Schweizerische Zivilgesetzbuch. Bern, 1962. Vol. 1. Annotations to Art. 1, pp. 78–212.

———. Der Richter als Gesetzgeber. Zurich, 1951. 290 pp.

———. "Privatrechtswissenschaft und Rechtsfortbildung." ZSR 78, p. 89 (1959).

Pasquier, Claude du. Introduction à la théorie générale et la philosophie du droit. 4th ed. Neuchâtel, 1967. 364 pp.

———. Les Lacunes de la loi et la jurisprudence du Tribunal fédéral suisse sur l'art. 1er Code civil suisse. Basel, 1957. 74 pp.

Rechtsquellenprobleme im schweizerischen Recht. Berner Festgabe für den schweizerischen Juristenverein 1955. Bern, 1955. 439 pp.

Simonius, August. "Gesetzesauslegung und wissenschaftliche Tradition," in Festgabe für Paul Speiser. Basel, 1926. P. 83.

———. "Quelques observations sur le rôle de la doctrine dans l'application des dispositions générales du Code des obligations." La Semaine judiciaire, 71, 201 (1949).

Spiro, Karl. Uber den Gerichtsbrauch zum allgemeinen Teil des revidierten Obligationenrechts. Basel, 1948. 358 pp.

Uyterhoeven, Hugo. Richterliche Rechtsfindung und Rechtsvergleichung. Bern, 1959. 97 pp.

AUSTRIA

Ehrenzweig, Armin. System des österreichischen allgemeinen Privatrechts. 6th ed. Vienna, 1925. Vol. 1, §§ 9–19.

Gschnitzer, Franz. "Schaft Gerichtsbrauch Recht?" in Festschrift zur Jahrhundertfeier des österreichischen Obersten Gerichthofes. Vienna, 1950. P. 40.

———. "Rechtsprechung und Lehre im Gegen- und Zusammenspiel." Jur. Blätter, 76, p. 345 (1954).

Klang, Heinrich. "Rechtsprechung und Gesetzgebung." Jur. Blätter, 74, p. 1 (1952).

Merkl, Adolf. "Zum Interpretationsproblem." Grünhuts Zschft. 42, p. 535 (1916).

Pisko, Oskar, in Kommentar zum ABGB, hg. von Klang. 1st ed. Vienna, 1927. Vol. 1, §§ 4 ff.

Schey, Josef. "Gesetzbuch und Richter," in Festschrift ABGB. Vienna, 1911. Vol. 1, p. 499.

Wolff, Karl. *Kommentar zum ABGB*, hg. von Klang. 2nd ed. Vienna, 1948. Vol. 1, p. 85.

———. *Die Gesetzessprache*. Vienna, 1952. 120 pp.

Wurzel, Karl Georg. *Das juristische Denken*. 2nd ed., Vienna-Leipzig, 1924. 104 pp.

ITALY

Betti, Emilio. See under Germany.

Bigiavi, W. "Appunti sul diritto giudiziario," in *Studi urbanati*, Vol. 8 (1933), Vol. 9 (1934).

Calamandrei, P. "La funzione della giurisprudenza." *Rivista trimestriale di diritto e procedura civile* (1955), 252.

Colesanti, V. "Giurisprudenza," in *Novissimo Digesto Italiano*. Turin, 1961. Vol. 7, p. 1,001.

Degni, F. *L'interpretazione della legge*. 2nd ed. Naples, 1909.

Donati, Donato. *Il problema delle lacune dell'ordinamento giuridico*. Milan, 1910. 267 pp.

Ferrar, F. "Potere del legislatore e funzione del giudice," in *Scritti Giuridici*. Milan, 1954. Vol. 1, p. 11.

Gorla, Gino. *L'interpretazione del diritto*. Milan, 1941. 162 pp.

Lombardi, Luigi. *Saggio sul diritto giurisprudenziale*. Milan, 1967. 615 pp.

Messineo, Francesco. *Manuale di diritto civile e commerciale*. 8th ed., Milan, 1952. Vol. 1, p. 93.

Pugliatti, S. "La giurisprudenza come scienza pratica." *Rivista italiana per le scienze giuridiche*, 49 (1950).

Rotondi, M. "Interpretazione della Legge," in *Nuovo Digesto Italiano*. Turin, 1938. Vol. 7, p. 736.

Scialoja, A. "Le fonti e l'interpretazione del diritto commerciale," in *Saggi di vario diritto*. Rome, 1927. Vol. 1, p. 253.

BELGIUM

Bekaert, Henri. *Introduction à l'étude du droit*. 3rd ed. Brussels, 1969. 550 pp. Chapter 2, § 6; Chapters 6–7.

Pescatore, Pierre. *Introduction à la science du droit*. Luxembourg, 1960. 523 pp. (§§ 64–73 deal with Luxembourg and Belgian law.)

NETHERLANDS

Apeldoorn, L. J. van. *Inleiding tot studie van het Nederlandse recht*. 15th ed. Zwolle, 1963. 450 pp. (Pp. 128–43, 325–49)

Bellefroid, J. H. P. *Inleiding tot de rechtswetenschap in Nederland*. 8th ed. Nijmegen, 1953. 218 pp. (Chapter 1, § 4, Chapter 3, § 5)

Drion, J. *Stare decisis. Het gesag van precedenten.* Gravenhage, 1950. 44 pp.

Scholten, P. "Kenmerken van Recht," and "L'interprétation de la loi et la justice," in *Verzamelde Geschriften van Prof. Paul Scholten, Deel I.* Zwolle, 1949. Pp. 1–120, 318–29.

Telders, B. M. "Het B.W. en de rechtspraak van 1838 tot heden, in het bizonder de standaardarresten van den Hoogen Raad (Arrêts de Règlement)," in *Gedenkboek burgerlijk wetboek 1838–1938.* Zwolle, 1938. P. 179.

SPAIN

Clemente de Diego, Felipe. *Fuentes del derecho civil español.* Madrid, 1922. 365 pp.

———. *La Jurisprudencia como fuente del derecho.* Madrid, 1925. 157 pp.

Herzog, Jacques Bernard. *Le Droit jurisprudentiel et le Tribunal Supreme en Espagne.* Toulouse, 1942. 500 pp.

Sabadie, Henri. *Les Sources du droit civil espagnol.* Carcassonne, 1926. 153 pp.

Sanchez Roman, Felipe. *Estudios de derecho civil, Tomo I.* Madrid, 1899.

BOOKS AND ARTICLES IN ENGLISH ON COMPARATIVE LAW OR FOREIGN LAW

Allen, C. K. *Law in the Making.* 7th ed. Oxford, 1966. 649 pp.

Allott, A. N. "The Authority of English Decisions in Colonial Courts," 1 *Journal of African Law,* 23–39 (1957).

———. "Judicial Precedent in Africa Revisited." 12 *Journal of African Law,* 3–31 (1968).

Ancel, Marc. "Case Law in France." 16 *Journal of Comparative Legislation,* 3rd ser., 1–17 (1934).

Baur, Fritz. "The Place of Court Decisions in a Codified Legal System." 4 *Texas Law Forum,* 340–58 (1968).

Beckman, Nils. "Precedents and the Construction of Statutes." 7 *Scandinavian Legal Studies,* 9–24 (1963).

Cappelletti, Mauro, John Henry Merryman, and Joseph M. Perillo. *The Italian Legal System.* Stanford, Calif., 1967.

Chloros, A. G. "Certainty and Function of Precedent in Comparative Law." 9 *Revue Hellénique de Droit International,* 66–79 (1956).

Cohn, E. J. "Precedents in Continental Law." 5 *Cambridge Law Journal,* 366–70 (1935).

Constantinoff, J. "Two Creations of Praetorian Jurisprudence under French Law." 24 *Tulane Law Review,* 302–10 (1950).

Dainow, Joseph. "The Civil Law and the Common Law: Some Points of Comparison." 15 *American Journal of Comparative Law,* 419–35 (1966–67).

―――. "The Method of Legal Development through Judicial Interpretation in Louisiana and Puerto Rico." 22 *Revista Juridica de la Universidad de Puerto Rico*, 108–53 (1952/53).

―――. "Planiol Citations by Louisiana Courts: 1959–1966." 27 *Louisiana Law Review*, 231–67 (1967).

Davidson, C. Y. "Stare Decisis in Louisiana." 7 *Tulane Law Review*, 100–18 (1932).

Dawson, J. P. *The Oracles of the Law*. Ann Arbor, Mich., 1968. 520 pp.

Deák, Francis. "The Place of the 'Case' in the Common Law and the Civil Law." 8 *Tulane Law Review*, 337–57 (1934).

De Santos, Alejandro. "The Philippine Doctrine of Judicial Precedent." 4 *U.M.L. Gazette*, 201–12 (1954).

Dror, Yehezkiel. "Some Recent Developments of the Doctrine of Precedent in Israel," in *Scripta Hierosolymitana*. Jerusalem, 1958. Vol. 5, pp. 228–44.

Ehrlich, Eugen. *Fundamental Principles of the Sociology of Law*. Translated by Walter L. Moll. Cambridge, Mass., 1936. 341 pp.

Elias, T. O. "Colonial Courts and the Doctrine of Judicial Precedent." 18 *Modern Law Review*, 356–70 (1955).

Eyben, W. E. von. "The Attitude towards Judicial Precedent in Danish and Norwegian Courts." *Scandinavian Studies in Law*, 53–86 (1959).

―――. "Judicial Law Making in Scandinavia." 5 *American Journal of Comparative Law*, 112–15 (1956).

Friedmann, Wolfgang. "Limits of Judicial Lawmaking and Prospective Overruling." 29 *Modern Law Review*, 593–607 (1966).

―――. "Stare Decisis at Common Law and under the Civil Code of Quebec." 31 *Canadian Bar Review*, 313–15 (1953).

Fulda, C. H. "Prospective Overruling of Court Decisions in Germany and the United States." 13 *American Journal of Comparative Law*, 438–41 (1964).

Gardiner, J. C. "Comparative Examination of the Doctrine of Judicial Precedent in Scots Law." 50 *Juridical Review*, 119–35 (1938).

―――. "Comparison of the Doctrine of Judicial Precedents in American Law and in Scots Law." 26 *American Bar Association Journal*, 778–80 (1940) and 52 *Juridical Review*, 144–67 (1940).

―――. "Judicial Decisions as a Source of Scots Law." 53 *Juridical Review*, 33–67 (1941).

―――. *Judicial Precedent in Scots Law*. Edinburgh, 1936. 108 pp.

Gény, François. *Method of Interpretation and Sources in Private Positive Law*. Translated by Jaro Mayda (La. St. L. Inst. Baton Rouge, 1963), 624 pp.

Goodhart, A. L. "Precedent in English and Continental Law." 50 *Law Quarterly Review*, 40–65 (1934).

Gray, J. C. "Judicial Precedents: A Short Study in Comparative Jurisprudence." 9 *Harvard Law Review*, 27–41 (1895).

Hahlo, H. R., and Ellison Kahn. *The South African Legal System and Its Background*. Cape Town, 1968. 603 pp. Chapter 7, "Sources of Law—Judicial Precedent"; Chapter 9, "Judicial Lawmaking."

Hippel, Ernst von. "The Role of Natural Law in the Legal Decisions of the German Federal Republic." 4 *Natural Law Forum*, 106–18 (1959).

Ireland, Gordon. "Precedents' Place in Latin Law." 40 *West Virginia Law Quarterly*, 115–34 (1934).

The Jurisprudence of Interests: Selected Writings of M. Rümelin, P. Heck, P. Oertmann, H. Stoll, J. Binder, H. Isay. Translated and edited by M. M. Schock. Cambridge, Mass., 1948. 328 pp.

Kahn, Ellison. "Have Certain English Precedents Binding Force in South Africa?" 82 *South African Law Journal*, 526–38 (1965).

———. "The Rules of Precedent Applied in South African Courts." 84 *South African Law Journal*, 43–55, 175–93, 308–30 (1967).

Kaufman, Arthur, and Winfried Hassemer. "Enacted Law and Judicial Decision in German Jurisprudential Thought." 19 *University of Toronto Law Journal*, 461–86 (1969).

Kawashima, Takeyoshi. "The Concept of Judicial Precedent in Japanese Law," in *Jus Privatum Gentium*. Tübingen, 1969. Vol. 1, pp. 85–101.

Kerr, A. J. "The Courts and the Law." 86 *South African Law Journal*, 179–93 (1969).

Kotzé, J. G. "Judicial Precedent." 34 *South African Law Journal*, 280–315 (1917).

Lambert, Edouard, and M. J. Wassermann. "Case Method in Canada and the Possibilities of Its Adaptation in Civil Law." 39 *Yale Law Journal*, 1–21 (1929).

Lazaro y Mina, Emiliano. "Doctrine of Stare Decisis and the Supreme Court of the Philippine Islands." 16 *Philippine Law Journal*, 404–19 (1937).

Lipstein, Kurt. "The Doctrine of Precedent in Continental Law." 38 *Journal of Comparative Legislation*, 34–44 (1946).

Lobingier, C. S. "Precedent in Past and Present Legal Systems" 44 *Michigan Law Review*, 953–96 (1946).

Loussouarn, Yvon. "The Relative Importance of Legislation, Custom, Doctrine, and Precedent in French Law." 18 *Louisiana Law Review*, 235–70 (1958).

McGregor, A. J. "Judicial Precedent." 63 *South African Law Journal*, 12–24 (1946).

Meijers, E. M. "Case Law and Codified Systems of Private Law," 3rd ser. 33 *Journal of Comparative Legislation*, 8–17 (1951).

Merryman, John Henry. *The Civil Law Tradition.* Stanford, Calif., 1969.

―――."The Italian Style I: Doctrine." 18 *Stanford Law Review,* 39 (1965).

―――. "The Italian Style II: Law." 18 *Stanford Law Review,* 396 (1966).

―――. "The Italian Style III: Interpretation." 18 *Stanford Law Review,* 583 (1966).

Mignault, P. B. "The Authority of Decided Cases." 3 *Canadian Bar Review,* 1–24 (1925).

Neville Brown, L. "The Sources of Spanish Civil Law." 5 *International and Comparative Law Quarterly,* 364–77 (1956).

Planiol, Marcel, and Georges Ripert. *Treatise on the Civil Law.* 12th ed. La. St. L. Inst. transl. Baton Rouge, 1959.

Rheinstein, Max. "Approach to German Law." 34 *Indiana Law Journal,* 546–58 (1959).

―――. Review of Joseph Esser, *Grundsatz und Norm in der richterlichen Fortbildung des Privatrechts: Rechtsvergleichende Beiträge zur Rechtsquellen—und Interpretationslehre.* 24 *University of Chicago Law Review,* 597–606 (1957).

Saxena, Ishwar Chandra. "The Doctrine of Precedent in India: A Study of Some of Its Aspects." 3 *Jaipur Law Journal,* 188–214 (1963).

Schiller, A. A. "A Definition of Jurists' Law," in *Symbolae iuridicae et historicae Martino David dedicatae.* Leiden, 1968. Vol. 1, pp. 181–200.

―――. "The Nature and Significance of Jurists' Law." 47 *Boston University Law Review,* 20–39 (1967).

―――. "Jurists' Law." 58 *Columbia Law Review* 1226–38 (1958).

Schmidt, Folke. *The "Ratio Decidendi": A Comparative Study of a French, a German and an American Supreme Court Decision.* Stockholm, 1965. 38 pp.

Sereni, A. P. "The Code and Case Law," in Bernard Schwartz, *The Code Napoleon and the Common Law World.* New York, 1956. Pp. 55–79.

Silving, Helen. " 'Stare decisis' in the Civil and the Common Law." 35 *Revista Juridica de la Universidad de Puerto Rico,* 196–242 (1966).

Smith, T. B. *The Doctrine of Judicial Precedent in Scots Law.* Edinburgh, 1952. 115 pp.

―――. *Studies Critical and Comparative.* Edinburgh–New York, 1962. 324 pp.

Sperl, Hans. "Case Law and the European Codified System." 19 *Illinois Law Review,* 505–22 (1925).

Stone, Julius. *Recent Trends in English Precedent, with a Comparative Introduction on the Civil Law.* Sydney, 1945. 76 pp. (Also in *The Province and Function of Law.* Sydney, 1946.)

Szladits, Charles. "A Comparison of Hungarian Customary Law with English Case Law." 3rd ser. 19 *Journal of Comparative Legislation,* 165–78 (1937).

———. *Guide to Foreign Legal Materials: French, German, Swiss.* New York, 1959. Pp. 16–42, 136–76, 380–401.

Tate, Albert, Jr. "The Rule-Making Powers of the Courts in Louisiana." 24 *Louisiana Law Review*, 555–70 (1964).

———. "Techniques of Judicial Interpretation in Louisiana." 22 *Louisiana Law Review*, 727–55 (1962).

Tucker, J. H., Jr. "The Code and the Common Law in Louisiana," in Bernard Schwartz, *The Code Napoleon and the Common-Law World*. New York, 1956. Pp. 19–45.

Vanderlinden, J. "Some Reflections on the Law-Making Powers of the French Judiciary." 13 (n.s.) *Juridical Review*, 1–20 (1968).

Van Loon, J. F. G. "The Sources of Law (Netherlands)," in P. Graulich et al., *Guide to Foreign Legal Materials*. Belgium-Luxembourg-Netherlands, Dobbs Ferry, 1968. Chapters 4–6.

Von Mehren, Arthur. "The Judicial Process in the United States and in France: A Comparative Study." 22 *Revista Juridica de la Universidad de Puerto Rico*, 235–65 (1952/53).

———. *The Judicial Process: A Comparative Analysis.* Chapter 16 of *The Civil System: Cases and Materials*. Englewood Cliffs, N.J., 1957. Pp. 821–54.

Wetter, J. G. *The Style of Appellate Judicial Opinions: A Case Study in Comparative Law.* Leyden, 1960. 392 pp.

Williams, Ivy. *The Sources of Law in the Swiss Civil Code.* Oxford, 1923. 199 pp.

Witkon, P. "Some Reflections on Judicial Law-Making." 2 *Israel Law Review*, 475–87 (1967).

ABBREVIATIONS

AcP	Archiv für civilistische Praxis
JZ	Juristenzeitung
MD	Monatschrift für deutsches Recht
NJW	Neue Juristische Wochenschrift
RT	Revue trimestrielle de droit civil
SJZ	Schweizerische Juristenzeitung
ZSR	Zeitschrift für schweizerisches Recht

Index

Vera Bolgár
RESEARCH ASSOCIATE, UNIVERSITY OF MICHIGAN LAW SCHOOL

Bartolus de Saxoferrato, 204
Blackstone, William, 211
Bynkershoek, Cornelis van, 242

Canada:
    Canadian Pacific Railways Co. v. Robinson, 19
    stare decisis in, and comparison with France, 12
    Supreme Court in, 16–20
        influence on legal unification, 20
        methodology in "mixed" interpretation, 16–20
Civil law:
    authorities in, 91ff.
    compared with common law, 315
    current trends in, 316, 317
    doctrinal writings in, 104–106, 314
    French doctrine in, 107–10
    historical aspects of, 316–17
    historical comparison of, 317
    influence of:
        in Israel, 272–73, 275, 293, 294, 296–97, 308, 309
        in Louisiana, 1, 22, 26, 27, 34, 38ff., 186–87
        in Quebec, 1, 211, 215
        in Scotland, 202, 211, 215
        in South Africa, 233, 238–39, 244
    judicial interpretation of, 313
    legal commentaries on, 320–21
    teaching methods in, 315
    tradition in, 43
Common law:
    format of judgments in, 15–16
    influence of:
        in Israel, 274, 275, 277, 297, 301
        in Louisiana, 8, 9, 11, 15–21, 23–24, 25, 27, 30, 36
        in Quebec, 8, 9, 11, 15–21
        in Scotland, 202, 212–13, 218
        in South Africa, 229, 231, 233, 236, 237–38, 240n, 247, 255, 269
    stare decisis in, 12ff
Corpus Juris Civilis. See Roman law
Cour de Cassation. See France

Denial of justice:
    prohibition of, 46, 119, 319
    statutory rules, 313–14, 314n
    See also Germany; Italy
Doctrine, 28, 29, 65, 69ff., 82ff., 104, 106–107, 202ff., 224ff., 311ff.
    See also England; France; Italy
Domat, Jean, 84, 216

England:
    Duchess of Kingston case, 14
    equity in, 277, 297
    Houldsworth v. City of Glasgow Bank, 212–13
    House of Lords in, 12, 13, 212–13, 214, 220, 322
    Orr Ewing's Trs. v. Orr Ewing, 213
    precedent in, 12–13, 255–57
    Privy Council in, 257–69 passim
    stare decisis in, 212–13, 250, 277, 298
Equity, 7, 18, 35, 46, 70, 71. See also England; France; Israel; Louisiana

France:
    administrative law:
        abuse of power, 125–27, 131
        abuse of rights, 125–27
        excès de pouvoir, 131
    application of general principles of law in administrative courts, 120–21, 130
    arrêts de réglement in, 73

bon père de famille, 21
Code Civil:
   art. 4 (prohibition of denial of justice), 46, 119
   art. 5 (prohibition of judicial control), 73, 96
   art. 15 (res judicata), 96
   art. 1382 (civil liability), 122, 124
   gaps in the law, 119–20
   Projet of, 71
Council of State, 120, 131
Cour de Cassation, 101ff., 322 and n
   doctrine in, 85, 104–107
   equity in, 7, 73, 121–24
   fraus omnia corrumpit in, 123, 128
   good morals (bonnes moeurs), 127–30
   ideological influences of:
     on eighteenth-century rationalism, 124
     on Ihering, 85, 104
     on Roman legal concepts, 123, 124
     on socialist concepts, 125
   influence of:
     on Israeli law, 274
     on Louisiana law, 3, 4, 22, 27, 33–34, 40–41, 56–57
     on Quebec law, 2, 3, 6, 7–8, 15
   jurisprudence, 12, 15, 91–95, 97,
     authority of, 97, 103
     formation of, 92–93
     history of, 100
     legislative policy of, 101
     pourvoi en cassation, 93–95
     reports of, 98–100
     revirement de, 104
     theory of, 102
   penal code in, 119, 122
   prerevolutionary system in, 7, 123
   private international law in, 127
   public order (ordre public) in, 127–30
   référé législatif, 7
   sources of law in:
     arrêts de réglement, 73
     doctrine, 104
     equity, 7, 73, 121–24
     general principles of law, 121
     jurisprudence, 12, 15, 91, 97
   supereminent principles, 119ff.
   treatises and monographs, 84–85, 107
Tribunal de Cassation, 7

General principles of law. See France; South Africa
Gény, François, 13, 17, 18, 21, 30, 34, 41, 42, 44–45, 119
Germany:
   abuse of right in, 142
   application of law in, 135
   Basic Law in, 138, 139, 153
   Besitzkonstitut in, 142
   bilateral contract in, 146–47
   chattel mortgage in, 148
   Civil Code (Bürgerliches Gesetzbuch) in, 141–44, 147, 233
   Civil Procedure Code (Zivilprozessordnung) in, 144
   "closed circle" of rights in rem, 143
   culpa in contrahendo in, 150–52
   denial of justice in, 137
   federal courts in, 138–39
   gaps in the law in, 141ff., 149
   jurisprudence constante in, 152–56
   jurisprudence of the courts in, 152–56, 158–61
   legal developments in, 133ff.:
     following legal-ethical principles, 148ff.
     following the demand for legal transactions (Rechtsverkehr), 143ff.
     regarding the "nature of the thing," 145ff.
   protection of personality rights in, 152–53
   Sicherungseigentum (chattel mortgage) in, 143
   sources of law in:
     legislation, 138
     precedent, 156–61
   sociological jurisprudence in, 145
   statutory interpretation in, 134ff.
   theory of knowledge in, 136–37
   transfer of movables (Sicherungsübereignung) in, 142
Groot Placaet-Boeck, 242
Grotius, Hugo, 241

Huber, Ulric, 243

Israel:
   adjudicated rule (precedent) in, 304–305
   basic laws in, 291
   Bergman v. Minister of Finance, 292

Index | 347

Blaliti v. Greek-Catholic Association, 302
Boker v. Anglo Israeli Management and Trust Co., 308n, 309
civil law influence in, 272–73, 297, 307, 308
civil rights in, 292–93
Cohavi v. Beker, 298
Cohen v. Minister of the Defence, 302, 303
compared with America, 283–85
Dr. Bar-Haj v. Steiner, 303
Eisick (Schick) v. Minister of the Interior, 306
English common law influence, 274, 275, 277, 297, 301
equity in, 274, 275, 277, 286, 297
French law influence, 274, 275
history of, 272–73, 282, 296–98
Israeli common law, 299–300
Jewish law, 279–80, 298, 308
judicial interpretation in:
    comparison of statutes, 309
    legislative history, 308
    resort to foreign laws, 309
judicial lawmaking in, 296ff.
judge-made law v. codification in, 280–82, 300–301
jurisprudence constante in, 305n
law and codification in, 280–82, 300–301
legislative policies in, 280, 281, 287, 293–94
matrimonial partnership in, 299–300
matrimonial property law in, 300
the New Version, 286
recent legislation in, 288–92
sources of law in:
    custom, 301
    English common law, 274, 275, 277, 291, 301
    equity, 274, 275, 277, 286, 297
    Jewish law, 280, 298, 308
    Ottoman law, 274, 276
    stare decisis (adjudicated rule), 303, 304–305, 306
    Torah, 279
stare decisis in, 277, 298, 303–306
statutory construction in, 307–308
Supreme Court decisions in, 291, 299–302, 302n, 304
See also Mejelle

Italy:
    Code of Civil Procedure in, 194
    compared with America, 171, 191
    compared with common-law jurisdictions, 163–64, 191, 200
    constitutional change in, 198ff.
    Constitutional Court in, 176, 193, 197
    Council of State in, 193
    Court of Cassation in, 175, 194
    denial of justice in, 177
    doctrine in, 165ff.
    folklore of interpretation in, 167ff.
    folklore v. practice in, 174ff.
    gaps in the law in, 179ff.
    her influence on Latin America, 201n
    judicial *immobilismo* in, 175, 189
    judicial interpretation in:
        Ascarelli thesis (evolutive interpretation), 185ff.
        Betti thesis, 187ff.
        Calamandrei thesis, 187ff.
        comparison with common law jurisdictions, 163–64, 191, 200
        practice of, 172ff.
        statutory interpretation, 178
    law reports in, 175–76
    nulla poena sine lege in, 180
    sources of law in:
        massime and decisions, 169, 175–76, 189, 195
        precedents, 193ff.
        stare decisis, 169–70
    statutory interpretation in, 178
    style of opinion in, 168–69

Jhering, Rudolf von, 124, 150–51
Judicial function, 8–10, 24–26, 45ff., 281ff. See also Judicial interpretation; Judicial technique
Judicial interpretation:
    comparative aspects of, 15–16, 35–36, 45–51
    Cour de Cassation, 97, 101ff., 322n
    differences in psychology, 15
    filling gaps in the law, 123ff., 140ff.
    law-creating functions of, 9–10, 46, 141
    maxims of, 115ff.
    mentioned, 9, 16ff., 134ff.
    methods of, 112–13, 313ff.
    practical rules of, 114ff.
    precedents in, 14, 156

recent trends in, 321–22
sociology of, 117
theory of, 118
through equity, 126, 156
tools of, 114
travaux préliminaires, 17
travaux préparatories, 112, 117, 118
Judicial technique:
in civilian jurisdictions, 43ff., 49ff.
in development of substantive law, 26ff.
filling gaps in the law, 49ff.
"Grand style" v. "Formal style" in, 29ff.
influence of civil law on, 18ff., 27
influence of common law on, 9–10, 19–20, 25–26
mentioned, 16ff., 19, 20, 26ff.
in mixed jurisdictions, 23ff., 35ff.
Jurisprudence, 69ff., 311ff.
See also Judicial interpretation; Judicial technique
Jurisprudence constante. See Germany; Israel; Louisiana; Quebec

Legal theory, 102ff., 133ff.
Ley de Amparo. See Mexico
Lingenthal, Zachariae von, 84, 108
Locré de Roissy, Jean Guillaume, 18, 46–47
Louisiana:
Blanchard v. Ogima, 53, 55
Civil Code in, 4–5, 45–46, 48, 53, 54, 56, 59–63, 71, 73–74, 86
civilian renaissance in, 38ff.
effects, 39–40
future, 64ff.
civilian tradition in, 38–40
Compiled Edition of the Civil Codes of Louisiana, 65
Dickson v. Sandefur, 56
doctrine in, 86–87
Flower v. Griffin, 48
Hilliard v. Shuff, 61
influence of:
French law, 3, 4, 27, 33–34
French doctrine, 22, 40–41, 56–57
the common law, 5, 8, 9, 11, 15, 21, 25–26, 30, 36
Institute of Civil Law Studies, 42
judicial interpretation in, 9, 15–16, 35–36, 49–51
judicial review in, 51–53, 55–58

jurisprudence constante in, 13, 48, 74, 78
Langlois v. Allied Chemical Corporation, 52–53, 60
law faculties in, 87–88
legislation and precedent in, 31–34
Louisiana Blueprint articles, 23
Pringle Associated Mortgage Co. v. Eanes, 14, 57, 81
Projet of 1822, pp. 56, 86
Reymond v. State Department of Highways, 58
role of judiciary in, 23–26, 34–36
role of law schools in, 39–40
sources of law in:
custom, 51, 69–70
doctrine, 56–57, 70, 82–84
equity, 46, 70, 71
jurisprudence, 15–16
legislation, 31–34, 69–70
precedent, 31–34, 75–77
stare decisis, 10–13, 78
strict liability
evolution of principle, 58ff.
compared to French system, 62
Louisiana Law Review, 41
Louisiana State Law Institute, 26, 41, 88
its activities in Code revision, 41, 66, 89
publications of, 89–90

Mejelle, the, 274, 276, 288
Mexico:
actor forum rei sequitur, 324
Code of Civil Procedure in, 325
decisions in, 324–25
"jurisprudencia" as binding precedent in, 320n, 326–28
law reports in, 327
Ley de Amparo in, 326
Ministerio Publico in, 326
promotor fiscal in, 325, 326
Semanario Judicial in, 327
Siete Partidas and early Spanish codes in, 324
Supreme Court in, 324–26, 328
Ministerio Publico. See Mexico
Montesquieu, Charles de Secondat de la Brede, 7

Pandectists. See South Africa
Pothier, Robert, 5, 84, 211, 216, 241, 244–45
Precedent. See *Stare decisis*

Index | 349

Quebec:
  Civil Code in, 2, 4–7, 17, 19
  civil liability in, 21
  coutume jurisprudentielle in, 13
  influence of:
    common law, 8, 9, 11, 15
    French law, 2, 3, 6, 16
  prerevolutionary French system of, 7–8
  judicial interpretation in, 16–20
  jurisprudence constante in, 13–16
  legislation in, 4ff., 6, 10
  stare decisis in, 10, 12
  Supreme Court of Canada, 17–20

Roman-Dutch law. *See* South Africa
Roman law:
  Corpus Juris Civilis, 165, 245
  functions of property, 144–45
  in Middle Ages, 317–18
  in Scotland, 204, 210, 216, 217
  in South Africa, 225–31 passim, 236, 238, 241, 245, 254, 263, 265
  jurisconsults, 164, 316
  mentioned, 121, 164–65, 204, 316, 324
  unjust enrichment under, 124, 128

Scotland:
  Beith Trs. v. Beith, 213–14
  Court of Session in, 203, 209, 212–14, 217
  Donoghue v. Stevenson, 219n
  early law reports and treaties in, 203–11
  Faculty Decisions in, 206, 209
  Glasgow Corp. v. Lord Advocate, 216–17
  history of, 202
  Houldsworth v. City of Glasgow Bank, 212–13
  influence of English law on, 202, 213
  "institutional" writers in, 215ff.
  Jus Feudale in, 204
  Lord Advocate v. Aberdeen University, 217n
  modern law reporting and treatises in, 218
  Orr Ewing's Trs. v. Orr Ewing, 213
  precedent in:
    doctrine, 212ff.
    history, 205ff.
    modern practice, 214, 218–19
  Roman law in, 204, 210, 216, 217
  sources of law in:
    "authority" vs. "principle," 211, 219
    custom, 205, 209, 210
    doctrine, 124ff., 214ff.
    equity, 220
    hierarchy of authorities, 220
    statute, 210
    stare decisis in, and comparison with England, 212–13
  and *Virtue v. Alloa Police Commrs.*, 212
Scottish Universities' Law Institute, 218
Semanario Judicial. See Mexico
Sources of law, 69ff. *See also* Germany; Israel; Italy; Louisiana; Scotland; South Africa
South Africa:
  administration of justice in, 251
  agency (undisclosed principal) in, 235–36
  civil law in, 233, 238–39, 244
  Civil Proceedings Evidence Act of 1965, p. 268
  communis error facit ius, 232
  Company Law Commission, 228
  comparative aspects of, 235, 240
  conflict of laws in, 239
  court system in, 258–61
  Criminal Procedure Act, 259n, 261, 268
  doctrine and comparison with English and French practice, 245, 247–50
  English common law, 225–31, 235, 247
  equity in, 264
  general principles of law in, 236
  Glazer v. Glazer, N.O., 136
  Government of the Republic of South Africa v. Ngubane, 254
  history of, 224ff.
  influence of:
    civil law, 233, 238–39, 244
    English common law, 225–31, 235, 247
    United States law, 247
  John Bell & Co. Ltd. v. Esselen, 260
  legal literature in, 251–54
  Magistrates' Courts Act of 1944, p. 262
  mercantile law in, 237–38
  Oud Vaderlands recht, 241

Pandectists in, 241, 245
precedent:
   in the Appellate Division, 256ff.
   in the Magistrates' courts, 267–68
   in the Provincial courts, 267
   principles of, 258
   rules of, 257
Privy Council in, 257, 259, 261, 269
Roman-Dutch law in, 224–27, 234, 241–45, 254, 261ff.
Roman law in, 225–31 passim, 236, 238, 241, 245, 254, 263, 265
sources of law in:
   doctrine, 247–49, 250
   equity, 264
   legislation: *Groot Placaet-Boeck*, 242
   Observationes Tumultuariae Novae, 242
   legal opinions, 242–43
   legal treatises, 243
   precedents, 242, 254ff., 257
stare decisis in:
   effects of, 258ff.
   historical aspects of, 257–58
   obiter dictum, 263
   statutory recognition of, 261–62
   ratio decidendi, 263–64
statistics on administration of justice in, 251
Supreme Court of South Africa, Appellate Division, 234–37, 256, 260–63, 265–69
Trust Bank van Afrika Bpk. v. Eksteen, 234
trust law in, 232
undisclosed principal in, 235–36
United States law, 247
usus modernus Pandectarum, 245
textbooks and treatises in, 243, 248n, 252–54
Van der Linde v. Calitz, 269
Voet vs. Pothier, 244–45
See also *Groot Placaet-Boeck*
Stare decisis, 10, 12ff., 103, 212–13, 277, 298, 303, 306–307, 311–15
Swiss Civil Code, 103
Swiss Code of Obligations, 233

Torah, the, 279
Toullier, C. B. M., 84, 107

United States:
   Erie R.R. v. Tomkins, 312n
   influence of in Israel, 283, 284–85, 289
   Intern. Shoe Co. v. Washington, 329
   legal commentaries on, 320–21
   Supreme Court in, 50, 80
   Swift v. Tyson, 312n

Voet, Johannes, 209, 216, 241, 243, 244–45

DATE DUE	
MAR 2 7 2002	
MAR 2 7 2002	
GAYLORD	PRINTED IN U.S.A.